S0-ABA-627

Buried inside QuickTime are a host of powerful tools for creating, delivering, and playing digital media. The official QuickTime documentation explains "what" each API function does. But knowing what each function does isn't enough to allow a developer to take full advantage of QuickTime. QuickTime Toolkit fills in the gap—providing plenty of practical examples of "how" to use QuickTime to perform all kinds of useful tasks. More importantly, [this book] goes beyond "how" and into "why"—providing readers with a deeper understanding of QuickTime and how to benefit from using it in their own products.

—Peter Hoddie
cofounder of Kinoma and former QuickTime architect

[The author] manages to present all components of the occasionally difficult QuickTime framework in a clear—even entertaining—fashion. His numerous examples and sample code snippets are clear and well thought out and are great starting points for new projects. QuickTime Toolkit fills some gaps in Apple's official documentation and is an essential book for anyone preparing to dive into the powerful depths of low-level QuickTime programming.

—Jurgen Schaub
founder, BOPJET Media, and QuickTime abuser

When QuickTime application developers get stuck, one of the first places they look for help is example code from the QuickTime column in MacTech. Finally, these well-crafted examples and clear descriptions are available in book form—a must-have for anyone writing applications that import, export, display, or interact with QuickTime movies.

—Matthew Peterson
University of California, Berkeley; the M.I.N.D.
Institute; and author of *Interactive QuickTime*

QuickTime Developer Series

Apple's QuickTime is a way to deliver multimedia—video, sound, styled text, MIDI, Flash, virtual reality, 3D models, sprites, and more—wrapped in a package that will play on Windows or Macintosh computers, on CD-ROM, over the Internet, in a browser window, a PDF document, a PowerPoint presentation, a Word document, or all by itself. The **QuickTime Developer Series**, developed in close cooperation with Apple, is devoted to exploring all of the capabilities of this powerful industry standard. Books in the series are written by experienced developers, including engineers from within the development team at Apple. All of the books feature a practical, hands-on approach and are prepared according to the latest developments in Quick-Time technology.

QuickTime Toolkit, Volume One:
Basic Movie Playback and Media Types
Apple

QuickTime Toolkit, Volume Two:
Advanced Movie Playback and Media Types
Apple

Interactive QuickTime: Authoring Wired Media
Matthew Peterson

QuickTime for the Web:
For Windows and Macintosh, Third Edition
Apple

QuickTime Toolkit

Volume Two: Advanced Movie Playback and Media Types

Apple

ELSEVIER

AMSTERDAM • BOSTON • HEIDELBERG • LONDON
NEW YORK • OXFORD • PARIS • SAN DIEGO
SAN FRANCISCO • SINGAPORE • SYDNEY • TOKYO

Morgan Kaufmann Publishers is an imprint of Elsevier

MORGAN KAUFMANN PUBLISHERS

Senior Editor	Tim Cox
Publishing Services Manager	André Cuello
Project Editor	Anne B. McGee
Project Management	Elisabeth Beller
Editorial Coordinator	Rick Camp
Cover Design	Laurie Anderson
Cover Image/Photo	© Digital Vision/Getty Images
Series Text Design	Rebecca Evans
Composition	Nancy Logan
Illustration	Dartmouth Publishing, Inc.
Copyeditor	Yonie Overton
Proofreader	Jennifer McClain
Indexer	Steve Rath
Interior Printer	The Maple-Vail Book Manufacturing Group
Cover Printer	Phoenix Color Corporation

Morgan Kaufmann Publishers is an imprint of Elsevier.
500 Sansome Street, Suite 400, San Francisco, CA 94111

Library of Congress Cataloguing-in-Publication
Application submitted.

ISBN: 0-12-088402-X

For information on all Morgan Kaufmann publications,
visit our website at *www.mkp.com*.

Printed in the United States of America

04 05 06 07 08   5 4 3 2 1

This book is printed on acid-free paper.

Contents

Preface   **xiii**
Development Platforms   xiii

Acknowledgements   **xiv**

Chapter 1   **F/X**   **1**
Introduction   1
QuickTime Video Effects in Movies   5
Effects Utilities   8
   Creating a Sample Description   8
   Creating an Effect Description   9
   Getting an Effect Type   11
Generators   12
Filters   15
Transitions   18
Effects Parameters   24
   Using the Effects Parameters Dialog Box   25
   Setting the Poster Images   27
   Handling Events in the Effects Parameters Dialog Box   28
   Sending Events to the Effects Parameters Dialog Box   31
Effects Parameter Files   33
Conclusion   35

Chapter 2   **F/X 2**   **37**
Introduction   37
Video Effects and Movie Segments   37
Video Effects and Images   41
   Decompressing Images   41
   Decompressing Image Sequences   43
   Storing the Decompression Data   45
   Setting Up the Effect   47
   Running the Effect   51
   Finishing Up   54

Video Effects and Sprites   55
   Using Effects as Image Overrides   55
   Passing Clicks to an Effects Component   58
Low-Level Video Effects Functions   61
Conclusion   64

Chapter 3   **The Skin Game**   **65**
Introduction   65
Skins   67
Creating Skinned Movies   69
   Searching Media Characteristics   70
   Using the QuickTime XML Importer   71
   Creating Skin Tracks Programmatically   72
Skinned Movie Playback   76
   Setting Up the Application Data   77
   Specifying a Custom Window Shape   83
   Writing a Custom Window Definition Procedure   85
   Handling Dragging on Windows Computers   91
   Shutting Down   95
Conclusion   96

Chapter 4   **Captured**   **97**
Introduction   97
Sequence Grabber Overview   98
   Opening the Sequence Grabbing Components   100
   Configuring Video Channels   101
   Configuring Audio Channels   103
Previewing   105
Channel Settings   109
   Handling Update Events   109
   Displaying the Settings Dialog Boxes   113
Monitor Window Size   116
Recording   118
   Setting the Output File   118
   Setting Channel Output Files   119
   Recording the Captured Data   121
Conclusion   124

Chapter 5   **Broadcast News**   **125**
Introduction   125
QuickTime Streaming   127

QuickTime Broadcasting   128
   Setting Up for Broadcasting   129
   Creating a Presentation   132
Broadcasting   139
   Starting the Broadcast   140
   Controlling the Broadcast   142
Broadcast Settings   143
Monitor Window Control   147
Conclusion   149

Chapter 6   **The Flash**   **151**

Introduction   151
Flash Overview   153
Flash and Video   156
   Converting QuickTime Video into an Image Sequence   157
   Including Flash Data in a QuickTime File   158
Buttons   159
The Flash File Format   163
   Reading Bytes from a Stream   164
   Reading Bits from a Stream   167
   Reading Rectangle Data   169
   Parsing the Header Block   170
   Parsing the Tagged Data Blocks   172
   Importing Flash Files   175
FSCommands   181
Flash Media Handler Functions   184
Conclusion   188

Chapter 7   **The Flash II**   **189**

Introduction   189
Wired Actions Targeted at Flash Tracks   190
Wired Actions in Flash Tracks   195
   Handling the Menu Item   196
   Finding Actions for Button State Transitions   201
   Reading the Button Data   203
   Adjusting Length Tags   208
Conclusion   211

Chapter 8   **Big**   **213**

Introduction   213
The Theory   215

Entering and Exiting Full-Screen Mode   215
Changing the Screen Resolution   216
Scaling the Movie   218
The Practice   220
Initializing the Movie Window Data   221
Handling Events for the Full-Screen Window   229
Exiting Full-Screen Mode   232
Flash Application Messages   234
QuickTime Application Messages   235
Handling Full-Screen Messages   237
Handling Close-Window Messages   237
Presentation Movie User Data   238
Time Base Callback Functions   242
Installing a Time Base Callback Function   244
Handling a Time Base Callback   246
Conclusion   248

Chapter 9   **Event Horizon**   **249**

Introduction   249
Carbon Events Overview   251
Document Windows   255
Specifying Events   255
Installing Event Handlers   256
Handling Window Events   258
Menus   261
Defining Command IDs   262
Adjusting Menus   264
Handling Menu Selections   265
Installing the Application Event Handler   267
Modal Windows   267
Handling Events for the About Box   268
Handling Nondocument Windows   270
Event Loop Timers   274
Tasking Interval Management   276
Adjusting the Classic Event Loop Interval   276
Adjusting the Carbon Event Loop Timer Interval   277
Handling Task-Sooner Notifications   278
The Carbon Movie Control   279
Conclusion   281

Chapter 10   **Virtuosity**   **283**

Introduction 283

The QuickTime VR Manager 286

QuickTime VR Movie Playback 287

    Initializing the QuickTime VR Manager 287

    Getting the QTVR Instance 288

    Controlling View Angles 290

    Drawing on a Panorama 291

    Intercepting QuickTime VR Manager Functions 292

The QuickTime VR File Format 294

    Working with Node Information 294

    Working with a VR World 296

Wired Actions and QuickTime VR 298

    Sending Actions to QuickTime VR Movies 298

    Adding Actions to QuickTime VR Movies 301

    Adding Actions to a Hotspot 301

    Adding Actions to a Node 303

    Updating the Media Property Atom 305

    Saving the Modified Media Data 306

Conclusion 311

Chapter 11   **Trading Places**   **313**

Introduction 313

Alternate Tracks 314

    Getting and Setting a Media's Language 316

    Getting and Setting a Media's Quality 318

    Creating Alternate Groups 319

    Getting and Setting a Movie's Language 320

    Enabling and Disabling Alternate Track Selection 323

    Changing Alternate Tracks with Wired Actions 324

Alternate Movies 325

    Creating Alternate Reference Movies 328

    Specifying an Alternate Movie 329

    Specifying Selection Criteria 331

    Adding a Contained Movie 334

Conclusion 339

Chapter 12   **A Bug's Life**   **341**

Introduction 341

Error-Reporting Functions 342

    Getting the Current Error 343

Getting the Sticky Error   343
Error Notification Functions   346
Mysterious Errors   347
A Framework Bug   348
Fixing the Bug   348
Adding Some More Protections   351
Conclusion   352

Chapter 13   **Loaded**   **353**

Introduction   353
Asynchronous Movie Loading   356
Allowing Asynchronous Movie Loading   356
Checking the Movie Load State   357
Modifying the Application Framework   359
Handling Load State Changes   363
Adjusting Menu Items   366
Movie Drawing-Complete Procedures   367
Drawing on Top of a Movie   369
Installing a Drawing-Complete Procedure   371
Loader Tracks   373
Creating the Sprite Track   374
Adding the Loader Sprite Image   376
Wiring the Loader Sprite   377
QuickTime VR Movie Loading   381
Conclusion   384

Chapter 14   **Human Resources**   **387**

Introduction   387
Development on Windows   391
Creating Resource Files   391
Embedding Resource Files in an Application   393
Adding a Post-link Step   394
Development on Macintosh   395
Setting Up a Droplet   396
Wacking the Resources   399
CodeWarrior Plug-Ins   405
Writing a Post-linker Plug-In   406
Handling Post-link Errors   411
Writing a Settings Panel Plug-In   413
Conclusion   418

Chapter 15   **She's Gotta Have It**   **419**

Introduction 419

Media Sample References 420
    Creating Sample References Indirectly 421
    Creating Sample References Directly 421
    Getting Sample References 423

Slideshow Movies 423
    Handling Dropped Files 424
    Creating the Slideshow Movie 425
    Retrieving the Picture Information 425
    Adding a Sample Reference 426

Movie Tracks 430
    Getting the Current Media Sample 431
    Loading the Child Movie Data into Memory 432
    Creating a "Flattened" Child Movie Media Sample 434
    Replacing a Media Sample 435

Memory-Based Movies 442
    Creating Movies in Memory 442
    Saving Movies from Memory 445

Conclusion 449

Chapter 16   **Modern Times**   **451**

Introduction 451

File Selection 453
    Choosing a File to Open 453
    Choosing a Filename to Save 457
    Showing the Save Changes Dialog Box 458
    Setting the Default Location 460

Movie Storage Functions 462
    Maintaining Movie Storage Identifiers 464
    Opening a Movie 464
    Saving Changes to a Movie 466
    Closing a Movie 466

Conclusion 467

Glossary   **469**

Index   **485**

About the CD   **511**

Preface

This book, *QuickTime Toolkit, Volume Two: Advanced Movie Playback and Media Types*, continues the investigation of QuickTime application programming that we began in Volume One. Here we'll consider a handful of the more advanced media types supported by QuickTime, including video effects, skins, Flash, and QuickTime VR. We'll also see how to capture movies from sound and video input sources, broadcast movies to the Internet or a LAN, play movies full screen, and load movies asynchronously. This book revisits some of the key topics covered in Volume One; in particular, we'll take an important second look at data references and see how they are connected with media sample references. We'll also see how to attach wired actions to Flash and QuickTime VR movies. This book ends by updating the Mac OS X version of our sample application QTShell to support the latest QuickTime and Carbon APIs.

Development Platforms

Once again, I place a premium on developing code that can be deployed on both Macintosh and Windows operating systems. For the most part, this can be achieved fairly easily by paying attention to a few simple rules that we encountered in Volume One (such as writing all atom data in big-endian format). In rare cases, however, this dedication to multiple platforms will require more intricate measures, and we'll bump into one of those cases in the very first chapter. To correctly handle the effects parameters dialog box on Windows, we'll need to write a callback function to handle Windows messages that apply to that dialog box. This callback function is not elaborate; indeed, it's barely a dozen lines of code. The trick, however, is knowing that we need it at all. That's why you need this book.

Another example of this dedication to cross-platform development occurs later in this book. We'll see how to write a plug-in module for the Mac version of the CodeWarrior integrated development environment that allows us to perform the task of adding Macintosh resources to a Window application (called *resource wacking*). Previously, it was necessary to perform at least this step on Windows, using the console-based tool RezWack. With this plug-in at hand, we can now create complete Windows applications on Macintosh computers.

Acknowledgements

These books grew out of a series of articles published over the last four years in *MacTech* magazine. I am indebted to the staff at *MacTech* for giving a sustained voice to QuickTime in their publication; thanks are due to Nick DeMello, Eric Gundrum, Dave Mark, and especially to Jessica Stubblefield and Neil Ticktin.

My colleagues at Apple, particularly in the QuickTime engineering group, have contributed in countless ways to my understanding of QuickTime and her foibles. A number of them have also directly influenced this book, either by reviewing portions of it or by providing sample code or sample content. I wish I could name them individually. I also wish I could thank by name those tireless colleagues in Apple's developer relations and technical publications groups with whom I have worked over the years. You guys rock!

It is a pleasure to thank the team at Morgan Kaufmann who worked so hard to bring these books to print in amazingly short order. Special thanks are due to Elisabeth Beller, Richard Camp, and Tim Cox. I'd also like to thank Yonie Overton, Jennifer McClain, and Nancy Logan for their contributions.

Finally, and not least, I should recognize Nathan and Raisa for their patience and support throughout the time I was writing these articles and books.

F/X

Using Video Effects in Movies

 Introduction

The *QuickTime video effects architecture*, introduced in QuickTime 3, is an extensible system for applying video effects to images or video tracks. An effect applied to one image or track is called a *filter,* and an effect applied to two images or tracks is called a *transition.* QuickTime includes an implementation of the 133 standard transitions defined by the Society of Motion Picture and Television Engineers (SMPTE), as well as some additional effects developed by the QuickTime team. The SMPTE effects include various forms of wipe effects, iris effects, radial effects, and matrix effects. Of all of these, my personal favorite is a wipe effect called the *horizontal barn zigzag,* shown in Figure 1.1.

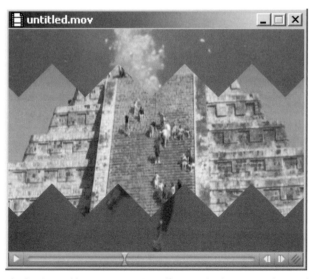

Figure 1.1   The horizontal barn zigzag wipe effect applied to two video tracks.

The additional QuickTime effects include transitions like a simple *explode* (where the first image is exploded outward to reveal the second image) and a *push* (where the first image is pushed aside by the second image). Figures 1.2 and 1.3 show these effects applied to two penguin images. QuickTime also includes a very nice *cross-fade* or *dissolve* transition (which produces a smooth alpha blending from the first image to the second) and a nifty *film noise* filter that makes a video track look like old, faded, dusty, and scratched film. Figure 1.4 shows a frame of a movie with the film noise effect.

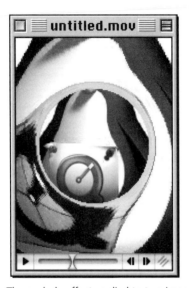

Figure 1.2   The explode effect applied to two images.

Figure 1.3   The push effect applied to two images.

Figure 1.4 The film noise effect applied to a movie frame.

Figure 1.5 The fire effect in a movie.

There are several video effects that operate on no source images or video tracks at all, called effects *generators*. For instance, we can use the *fire* effect to generate a fairly good-looking fire (Figure 1.5), and we can use the *cloud* effect to generate a wind-pushed, moving cloud. With generators, we will usually want to composite the effect onto some other image or video track. Figure 1.6 shows the fire effect composited onto the penguin image. (Ouch, that's gotta hurt!)

The data describing an effect is stored in a video track, and the actual effect itself is generated in real time as the movie is played. These effects use extremely little data to achieve the desired visual output. For instance, a video track that specifies the fire effect is only about 60 bytes in size; when the track is played, QuickTime generates a nonrepeating, dynamic fire image.

Figure 1.6 The fire effect composited onto an image.

Generators, filters, and transitions are implemented in the general Quick-Time architecture as *image decompressor components* (of type decompressor-ComponentType). This means that we can reference a specific effect by providing a four-character code, which is an image decompressor component subtype. Here are a few of the available effects types:

```
enum {
    kWaterRippleCodecType          = FOUR_CHAR_CODE('ripl'),
    kFireCodecType                 = FOUR_CHAR_CODE('fire'),
    kFilmNoiseImageFilterType      = FOUR_CHAR_CODE('fmns'),
    kWipeTransitionType            = FOUR_CHAR_CODE('smpt'),
    kIrisTransitionType            = FOUR_CHAR_CODE('smp2'),
    kRadialTransitionType          = FOUR_CHAR_CODE('smp3'),
    kMatrixTransitionType          = FOUR_CHAR_CODE('smp4'),
    kCrossFadeTransitionType       = FOUR_CHAR_CODE('dslv'),
    kPushTransitionType            = FOUR_CHAR_CODE('push')
};
```

This also means that we can use QuickTime video effects anywhere we might use a decompressor, not only in connection with QuickTime movies. We can just as easily apply a transition between two arbitrary images (perhaps contained in two offscreen graphics worlds). I've seen this capability used in applications that support QuickTime video effects as transitions between QuickTime VR nodes. The default behavior of QuickTime VR is simply to jump from one node to the next. It's much nicer to render some video effect, say, a nice smooth dissolve, when moving from node to node.

Test	
Make Fire Movie...	⌘1
Make Fade-In Movie...	⌘2
Add Film Noise To Movie	⌘3
Add Film Noise to Image	⌘4
Make Effect Movie...	⌘5
Standalone Movie	⌘6
✓ Referenced Movie	⌘7
Add Effect Segment to Movie	⌘8
Make Sprite Effect Movie...	⌘9

Figure 1.7 The Test menu of QTEffects.

In this chapter and the next, we're going to work with QuickTime video effects. We'll see how to create the fire movie shown in Figure 1.5 and how to apply a filter to a video track or image. We'll also see how to display and manage the effects parameters dialog box, which allows the user to select an effect and modify the parameters of that effect. Finally, we'll see how to apply an effect to only part of an existing movie and how to use effects as sources of sprite images.

Our sample application in these two chapters is called QTEffects; its Test menu is shown in Figure 1.7. In this chapter, we'll see how to handle all these menu items except for the fourth (which happens to be grayed out) and the final two. We'll postpone consideration of those three items to the next chapter.

◖ QuickTime Video Effects in Movies

It's quite easy to add a video effect to a QuickTime movie. In the simplest case, where the effect lasts for the entire length of the movie, we just add an effects track to the movie. An *effects track* is a video track (of type Video-MediaType) whose media data is an effect description. An *effect description* is an atom container that indicates which effect to perform and which parameters, if any, to use when rendering the effect. The effect description also indicates which other tracks in the movie are to be used as the input sources for the effect. These are called the *effect source tracks* (or *effect sources*). A transition needs two source tracks; a filter needs one source track; a generator needs no source tracks. Figure 1.8 illustrates the general structure of the fire movie shown in Figure 1.5. And Figure 1.9 illustrates the general structure of a movie that contains a two-source effect (perhaps the zigzag transition shown in Figure 1.1).

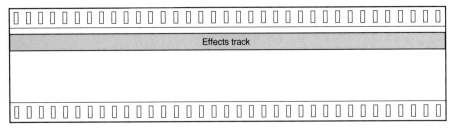

Figure 1.8 The structure of a zero-source effect movie.

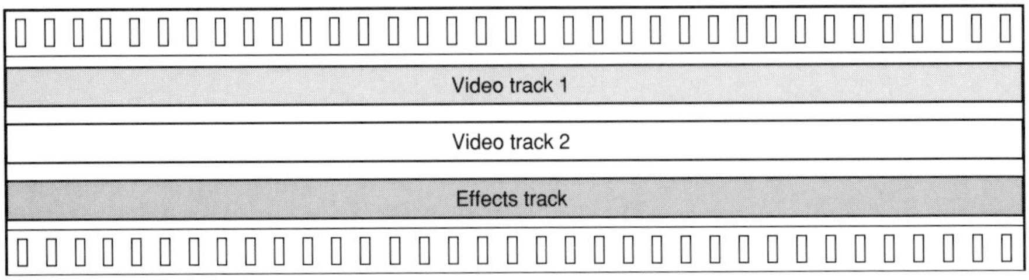

Video track 1

Video track 2

Effects track

Figure 1.9 The structure of a two-source effect movie.

The source tracks for a video effect can be any tracks that have the visual media characteristic, including video tracks, sprite tracks, text tracks, and others. In particular, because an effects track is a video track, it too can be a source track for another effects track. This allows us to *stack* effects so that the output of one effect is used as input for another effect. For example, we could set up a cross-fade transition from one video track to another, and then apply a film noise filter to the resulting images. Keep in mind, however, that some effects can use a significant amount of CPU power so that stacking effects may result in movies that do not play smoothly in real time on slower machines.

As we'll see in greater detail later, we connect an effects track to its source tracks by setting up track references from the effects track to the source tracks. These references tell QuickTime where to get the data for the effects track. We also need to configure the effects track's input map so that the effects track knows how to interpret the data it receives from the source tracks. The source tracks operate as modifier tracks, whose data is not presented directly to the user; rather, their data is used as input for the effects track. This is important, particularly when we want to apply an effect to only part of a source track. You might think that we could just construct an effects track with the appropriate start time and duration, as shown in Figure 1.10. But this won't work, since once we've created a track reference from the effects track to the video track and set the effects track's input map appropriately, the video track will send *all* of its data to the effects track, not just the data in the track segment that overlaps the effects track.

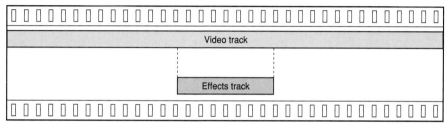

Figure 1.10 A filter applied to part of a video track (wrong).

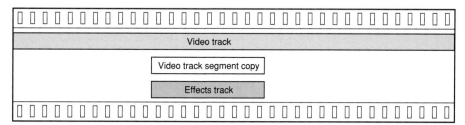

Figure 1.11 A filter applied to part of a video track.

To apply an effect to a part of a track, we can create another track that has the desired start time and duration and that references data in the video track. Then we use this new track segment as the source track for the effect, as shown in Figure 1.11. The new track segment doesn't contain a copy of the media data; instead, it contains references to the media data that already exists in the video track. So we don't increase the size of a movie file very much at all when we add effects to it. All three of the tracks shown in Figure 1.11 are enabled; to prevent the original video track from covering up the effects track, we need to make sure that the effects track has a lower track layer than the video track. We'll see exactly how to do all this in the next chapter, when we discuss applying effects to track segments.

It's worth mentioning that the QuickTime video effects architecture was originally designed to render effects in real time using software effects components (which, as we've seen, are image decompressor components). Recently, QuickTime 5 added support for hardware acceleration of effects rendering. This acceleration is used only when the user's machine has the appropriate hardware installed, and it occurs automatically (without any intervention by the effects movie creator or the playback application).

It's also worth mentioning that a video effect can have more than two sources. QuickTime 5 introduced a three-source effect, the *traveling matte* effect. In this chapter and the next, we'll always work with two or fewer sources, but our code can in fact handle up to three.

▶ Effects Utilities

Before we begin creating effects movies, let's take a brief moment to define a couple of functions that will be useful throughout our effects code.

Creating a Sample Description

When we build an effects track, we need to pass AddMediaSample an image description that provides information about the effect. In the past, we've always created sample descriptions and image descriptions by calling NewHandleClear and then setting the fields of the structure appropriately. When we are working with effects, however, we need to use the function MakeImageDescriptionForEffect, which allocates a handle to an image description and fills in some of its fields; it also attaches an *image description extension* to the end of the image description. This extension indicates that that image description applies to an effect. For most purposes this extension is ignored, but it's necessary when we want to create stacked effects.

MakeImageDescriptionForEffect was introduced in QuickTime 4.0; if we want our code to run also under versions 3.x, we can set the USES_MAKE_ IMAGE_DESC_FOR_EFFECT compiler flag to 0. Listing 1.1 shows our definition of EffectsUtils_MakeSampleDescription, which we'll call quite a few times in QTEffects to create an image description for an effect.

Listing 1.1 Creating a sample description for an effect.

```
ImageDescriptionHandle EffectsUtils_MakeSampleDescription (OSType theEffectType,
                          short theWidth, short theHeight)
{
  ImageDescriptionHandle      mySampleDesc = NULL;

#if USES_MAKE_IMAGE_DESC_FOR_EFFECT
  OSErr                       myErr = noErr;

  // create a new sample description
  myErr = MakeImageDescriptionForEffect(theEffectType, &mySampleDesc);
  if (myErr != noErr)
    return(NULL);
#else
  // create a new sample description
  mySampleDesc = (ImageDescriptionHandle)NewHandleClear(sizeof(ImageDescription));
  if (mySampleDesc == NULL)
    return(NULL);
```

```
  // fill in the fields of the sample description
  (**mySampleDesc).cType = theEffectType;
  (**mySampleDesc).idSize = sizeof(ImageDescription);
  (**mySampleDesc).hRes = 72L << 16;
  (**mySampleDesc).vRes = 72L << 16;
  (**mySampleDesc).frameCount = 1;
  (**mySampleDesc).depth = 0;
  (**mySampleDesc).clutID = -1;
#endif

  (**mySampleDesc).vendor = kAppleManufacturer;
  (**mySampleDesc).temporalQuality = codecNormalQuality;
  (**mySampleDesc).spatialQuality = codecNormalQuality;
  (**mySampleDesc).width = theWidth;
  (**mySampleDesc).height = theHeight;

  return(mySampleDesc);
}
```

Notice that we need to set a few fields of the image description even if we call MakeImageDescriptionForEffect.

Creating an Effect Description

It's also useful to define a utility function to build an effect description. As we've learned, an effect description is an atom container that specifies an effect and its sources. Listing 1.2 shows the definition of the utility EffectsUtils_CreateEffectDescription. The essential step is to add an atom of type kParameterWhatName and ID kParameterWhatID whose data is the four-character code for the desired effect.

Listing 1.2 Creating an effect description.

```
QTAtomContainer EffectsUtils_CreateEffectDescription (OSType theEffectType,
               OSType theSourceName1, OSType theSourceName2, OSType theSourceName3)
{
  QTAtomContainer      myEffectDesc = NULL;
  OSType               myType = EndianU32_NtoB(theEffectType);
  OSErr                myErr = noErr;

  // create a new, empty effect description
  myErr = QTNewAtomContainer(&myEffectDesc);
  if (myErr != noErr)
    goto bail;
```

```
  // create the effect ID atom
  myErr = QTInsertChild(myEffectDesc, kParentAtomIsContainer, kParameterWhatName,
          kParameterWhatID, 0, sizeof(myType), &myType, NULL);
  if (myErr != noErr)
    goto bail;

  // add the first source
  if (theSourceName1 != kSourceNoneName) {
    myType = EndianU32_NtoB(theSourceName1);
    myErr = QTInsertChild(myEffectDesc, kParentAtomIsContainer,
            kEffectSourceName, 1, 0, sizeof(myType), &myType, NULL);
    if (myErr != noErr)
      goto bail;
  }

  // add the second source
  if (theSourceName2 != kSourceNoneName) {
    myType = EndianU32_NtoB(theSourceName2);
    myErr = QTInsertChild(myEffectDesc, kParentAtomIsContainer,
            kEffectSourceName, 2, 0, sizeof(myType), &myType, NULL);
    if (myErr != noErr)
      goto bail;
  }

  // add the third source
  if (theSourceName3 != kSourceNoneName) {
    myType = EndianU32_NtoB(theSourceName3);
    myErr = QTInsertChild(myEffectDesc, kParentAtomIsContainer,
            kEffectSourceName, 3, 0, sizeof(myType), &myType, NULL);
  }

bail:
  return(myEffectDesc);
}
```

EffectsUtils_CreateEffectDescription builds an effect description with up to three *source name atoms* of type kEffectSourceName. The data in these atoms is a *source name* of type OSType. Source names are used to link the source tracks to the effects track. These names are arbitrary, but Apple recommends using names of the form 'src*X*', where *X* is an uppercase letter. In the file EffectsUtilities.h, we define these constants for our source names:

```
#define kSourceOneName              FOUR_CHAR_CODE('srcA')
#define kSourceTwoName              FOUR_CHAR_CODE('srcB')
#define kSourceThreeName            FOUR_CHAR_CODE('srcC')
#define kSourceNoneName             FOUR_CHAR_CODE('srcZ')
```

When we call EffectsUtils_CreateEffectDescription, we'll pass the constant kSourceNoneName for any unused sources.

Getting an Effect Type

Sometimes we might get hold of an effect description and need to know what kind of effect it describes. We can get this information by inspecting the data of the atom of type kParameterWhatName and ID kParameterWhatID that's inside that effect description. The function EffectsUtils_GetTypeFromEffectDescription defined in Listing 1.3 accomplishes this.

Listing 1.3 Getting the type of an effect.

```
OSErr EffectsUtils_GetTypeFromEffectDescription
        (QTAtomContainer theEffectDesc, OSType *theEffectType)
{
  QTAtom        myEffectAtom = 0;
  long          myEffectTypeSize = 0;
  Ptr           myEffectTypePtr = NULL;
  OSErr         myErr = noErr;

  if ((theEffectDesc == NULL) || (theEffectType == NULL))
    return(paramErr);

  myEffectAtom = QTFindChildByIndex(theEffectDesc, kParentAtomIsContainer,
                    kParameterWhatName, kParameterWhatID, NULL);
  if (myEffectAtom != 0) {

    myErr = QTLockContainer(theEffectDesc);
    if (myErr != noErr)
      goto bail;

    myErr = QTGetAtomDataPtr(theEffectDesc, myEffectAtom, &myEffectTypeSize,
            &myEffectTypePtr);
    if (myErr != noErr)
      goto bail;

    if (myEffectTypeSize != sizeof(OSType)) {
      myErr = paramErr;
      goto bail;
    }
```

```
    *theEffectType = *(OSType *)myEffectTypePtr;
    *theEffectType = EndianU32_BtoN(*theEffectType);

    myErr = QTUnlockContainer(theEffectDesc);
  }

bail:
  return(myErr);
}
```

Notice that we call QTLockContainer on the effect description, even though it isn't strictly necessary here. QTGetAtomDataPtr returns a pointer to the actual leaf atom data. We need to call QTLockContainer only when we make calls that might move memory; in this case, we're just reading a few bytes into a local variable, and this operation will not cause any memory movement. The calls to QTLockContainer and QTUnlockContainer are fairly lightweight, so we'll make them anyway.

Generators

Let's begin our hands-on work with QuickTime video effects by building a movie that uses a generator, or zero-source effect. In this case, we'll build the fire movie shown earlier in Figure 1.5. This movie has only one track, which is an effects track that has only one media sample. We'll set the dimensions of the effects track and its duration using some hard-coded values:

```
#define kDefaultTrackWidth          160
#define kDefaultTrackHeight         120
#define kEffectMovieDuration        (10 * kOneSecond)
```

We create the new movie file by calling CreateMovieFile, and then we create a new effects track and media like this:

```
myEffectTrack = NewMovieTrack(myMovie, IntToFixed(kDefaultTrackWidth),
               IntToFixed(kDefaultTrackHeight), kNoVolume);

myEffectMedia = NewTrackMedia(myEffectTrack, VideoMediaType, kOneSecond,
               NULL, 0);
```

Now we are ready to use the utility functions we defined in the previous section. We create the sample description and the effect description:

```
mySampleDesc = EffectsUtils_MakeSampleDescription(kFireCodecType,
                    kDefaultTrackWidth, kDefaultTrackHeight);

myEffectDesc = EffectsUtils_CreateEffectDescription(kFireCodecType,
                    kSourceNoneName, kSourceNoneName, kSourceNoneName);
```

The fire effect takes no sources, so we pass the constant kSourceNoneName for all three source name parameters.

Now we are essentially done; we add the effect description as a media sample using the usual media editing song and dance (BeginMediaEdits, Add-MediaSample, EndMediaEdits, and InsertMediaIntoTrack). The key step is the call to AddMediaSample:

```
myErr = AddMediaSample(myEffectMedia, myEffectDesc, 0,
            GetHandleSize(myEffectDesc), kEffectMovieDuration,
            (SampleDescriptionHandle)mySampleDesc, 1, 0, &mySampleTime);
```

It's really just that easy to create a zero-source effects movie. Listing 1.4 shows the complete definition of QTEffects_MakeFireMovie, which we call in response to the Make Fire Movie menu item.

Listing 1.4   Creating a zero-source effects movie.

```
void QTEffects_MakeFireMovie (void)
{
    FSSpec                    myFile;
    Boolean                   myIsSelected = false;
    Boolean                   myIsReplacing = false;
    StringPtr                 myPrompt =
                                QTUtils_ConvertCToPascalString(kEffectsSaveMoviePrompt);
    StringPtr                 myFileName =
                                QTUtils_ConvertCToPascalString(kEffectsFireMovieFileName);
    Movie                     myMovie = NULL;
    short                     myMovieRefNum = kInvalidFileRefNum;
    short                     myResID = movieInDataForkResID;
    Track                     myEffectTrack = NULL;
    Media                     myEffectMedia = NULL;
    QTAtomContainer           myEffectDesc = NULL;
    ImageDescriptionHandle    mySampleDesc = NULL;
    TimeValue                 mySampleTime = 0;
    long                      myFlags = createMovieFileDeleteCurFile
                                | createMovieFileDontCreateResFile;
    OSType                    myType = FOUR_CHAR_CODE('none');
    OSErr                     myErr = noErr;
```

```
// ask the user for the name of the new movie file
QTFrame_PutFile(myPrompt, myFileName, &myFile, &myIsSelected, &myIsReplacing);
if (!myIsSelected)
  goto bail;                        // deal with user cancelling

// create a movie file for the destination movie
myErr = CreateMovieFile(&myFile, sigMoviePlayer, smSystemScript, myFlags,
          &myMovieRefNum, &myMovie);
if (myErr != noErr)
  goto bail;

// select the "no controller" movie controller
myType = EndianU32_NtoB(myType);
SetUserDataItem(GetMovieUserData(myMovie), &myType, sizeof(myType),
  kUserDataMovieControllerType, 1);

// create the effects track
myEffectTrack = NewMovieTrack(myMovie, IntToFixed(kDefaultTrackWidth),
                IntToFixed(kDefaultTrackHeight), kNoVolume);
if (myEffectTrack == NULL)
  goto bail;

myEffectMedia = NewTrackMedia(myEffectTrack, VideoMediaType, kOneSecond, NULL, 0);
if (myEffectMedia == NULL)
  goto bail;

// create the sample description
mySampleDesc = EffectsUtils_MakeSampleDescription(kFireCodecType,
                kDefaultTrackWidth, kDefaultTrackHeight);
if (mySampleDesc == NULL)
  goto bail;

// create the effect description
myEffectDesc = EffectsUtils_CreateEffectDescription(kFireCodecType,
                kSourceNoneName, kSourceNoneName, kSourceNoneName);
if (myEffectDesc == NULL)
  goto bail;

// add the effect description as a sample to the effects track media
myErr = BeginMediaEdits(myEffectMedia);
if (myErr != noErr)
  goto bail;
```

```
    myErr = AddMediaSample(myEffectMedia, myEffectDesc, 0,
            GetHandleSize(myEffectDesc), kEffectMovieDuration,
            (SampleDescriptionHandle)mySampleDesc, 1, 0, &mySampleTime);
    if (myErr != noErr)
      goto bail;

    myErr = EndMediaEdits(myEffectMedia);
    if (myErr != noErr)
      goto bail;

    myErr = InsertMediaIntoTrack(myEffectTrack, 0, mySampleTime,
            kEffectMovieDuration, fixed1);
    if (myErr != noErr)
      goto bail;

    AddMovieResource(myMovie, myMovieRefNum, &myResID, NULL);

bail:
    if (myMovieRefNum != kInvalidFileRefNum)
      CloseMovieFile(myMovieRefNum);

    if (myMovie != NULL)
      DisposeMovie(myMovie);

    if (myEffectDesc != NULL)
      QTDisposeAtomContainer(myEffectDesc);

    if (mySampleDesc!= NULL)
      DisposeHandle((Handle)mySampleDesc);

    free(myPrompt);
    free(myFileName);

    return;
}
```

With the fire effect, the duration is fairly arbitrary. Any nonzero duration would produce the same visual output.

▶ Filters

It's just about as easy to add a filter to a video track in an existing movie—for instance, to handle the Add Film Noise To Movie menu item. We add an effects track, whose media data consists of an effect description. This time, however, we need to specify a source name in the effect description. We'll call our utility EffectsUtils_CreateEffectDescription like this, passing kSourceOneName as the first source name parameter:

```
myEffectDesc = EffectsUtils_CreateEffectDescription
                    (kFilmNoiseImageFilterType, kSourceOneName,
                     kSourceNoneName, kSourceNoneName);
```

We also need to create an input map for the effects track, which specifies which track is to be used as the effect source. Listing 1.5 shows the code we use to create, configure, and set the input map.

Listing 1.5   Creating an input map for an effects track.

```
// create the input map and add references for the first effects track
myErr = QTNewAtomContainer(&myInputMap);
if (myErr != noErr)
  goto bail;

myErr = EffectsUtils_AddTrackReferenceToInputMap(myInputMap, myTrack, mySrcTrack,
        kSourceOneName);
if (myErr != noErr)
  goto bail;

// add the input map to the effects track
myErr = SetMediaInputMap(myMedia, myInputMap);
```

An input map for an effects track is an atom container that holds one atom of type kTrackModifierInput for each source track that is sending data to the effects track. The ID of each such atom must be set to the reference index returned by AddTrackReference when the track reference between the effects track and that source track is created. Each atom of type kTrackModifierInput must contain at least two child atoms. One of these children is of type kTrackModifierType and specifies the kind of data the target track is going to receive from the source track; in the case of an effects track, the type of the modifier track input is kTrackModifierTypeImage. The second child atom in an input map entry atom specifies the name of the source track and is of type kEffectDataSourceType; the data in this atom is of type OSType. Figure 1.12 shows the structure of the input map we'll use to add the film noise filter to a video track.

Listing 1.6 shows our definition of the EffectsUtils_AddTrackReferenceTo-InputMap function, which we use to add the appropriate children to an existing input map for an effects track.

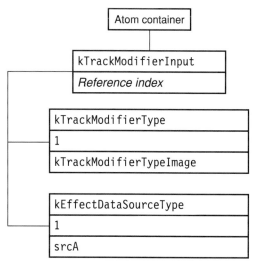

Figure 1.12 The structure of an input map for an effects track.

Listing 1.6 Adding track references to an input map.

```
OSErr EffectsUtils_AddTrackReferenceToInputMap
        (QTAtomContainer theInputMap, Track theTrack, Track theSrcTrack,
        OSType theSrcName)
{
  QTAtom        myInputAtom;
  long          myRefIndex;
  OSType        myType;
  OSErr         myErr = noErr;

  myErr = AddTrackReference(theTrack, theSrcTrack, kTrackReferenceModifier, &myRefIndex);
  if (myErr != noErr)
    goto bail;

  // add a reference atom to the input map
  myErr = QTInsertChild(theInputMap, kParentAtomIsContainer, kTrackModifierInput,
          myRefIndex, 0, 0, NULL, &myInputAtom);
  if (myErr != noErr)
    goto bail;

  // add two child atoms to the parent reference atom
  myType = EndianU32_NtoB(kTrackModifierTypeImage);
  myErr = QTInsertChild(theInputMap, myInputAtom, kTrackModifierType,
            1, 0, sizeof(myType), &myType, NULL);
  if (myErr != noErr)
    goto bail;
```

```
myType = EndianU32_NtoB(theSrcName);
myErr = QTInsertChild(theInputMap, myInputAtom, kEffectDataSourceType,
        1, 0, sizeof(myType), &myType, NULL);

bail:
  return(myErr);
}
```

If `EffectsUtils_AddTrackReferenceToInputMap` seems familiar, that's because we've already bumped into similar functions (for instance, when we worked with sprite image overrides in *QuickTime Toolkit, Volume One,* Chapter 15).

▶ Transitions

Adding a transition to a movie with two video tracks is really no more complicated than adding a filter to a movie with one video track. We pass `kSourceTwoName` as the second source name parameter when calling `Effects-Utils_CreateEffectDescription`, and we call `EffectsUtils_AddTrackReference-ToInputMap` a second time to create a track reference between the effects track and the second source video track. For fun, let's see how to re-create our appearing-penguin movie using QuickTime video effects. We'll also take this opportunity to play a little more with our favorite Image Compression Manager (ICM) functions, `GetMaxCompressionSize` and `CompressImage`.

Given what we've learned so far, all we really need to do is create two video tracks to serve as the source tracks for a cross-fade transition. The first video track is an all-white frame that lasts for the duration of the movie; the second video track is the fully opaque penguin picture, also lasting for the duration of the movie. As always, we'll set the duration of the movie to 10 seconds, this time using the constant `kEffectMovieDuration`. Then we'll add the effects track to the movie, specifying a cross-fade from the first source track to the second.

The two images that we'll use to create our video tracks are stored in our application's resource fork in two 'PICT' resources with these IDs:

```
#define kWhiteRectID                    129
#define kPenguinPictID                  128
```

So we need to read each image and create a video track of the desired length. We'll split our work into two parts. First we'll write a utility, `EffectsUtils_GetPictResourceAsGWorld`, that reads a 'PICT' resource and draws it into an offscreen graphics world. Then we'll write another utility, `EffectsUtils_AddVideoTrackFromGWorld`, that creates a video track from the image in an offscreen graphics world. Once we've got these two utilities, we can create the two video tracks using the code shown in Listing 1.7.

Listing 1.7 Creating two video tracks from two 'PICT' resources.

```
myErr = EffectsUtils_GetPictResourceAsGWorld(kWhiteRectID,
        kPenguinTrackWidth, kPenguinTrackHeight, 0, &myGW1);
if (myErr != noErr)
  goto bail;

myErr = EffectsUtils_GetPictResourceAsGWorld(kPenguinPictID,
        kPenguinTrackWidth, kPenguinTrackHeight, 0, &myGW2);
if (myErr != noErr)
  goto bail;

myErr = EffectsUtils_AddVideoTrackFromGWorld(&myMovie, myGW1, &mySrc1Track, 0,
        kEffectMovieDuration, kPenguinTrackWidth, kPenguinTrackHeight);
if (myErr != noErr)
  goto bail;

myErr = EffectsUtils_AddVideoTrackFromGWorld(&myMovie, myGW2, &mySrc2Track, 0,
        kEffectMovieDuration, kPenguinTrackWidth, kPenguinTrackHeight);
```

To create an offscreen graphics world that holds the image stored in a 'PICT' resource, we get the picture data from the resource (by calling GetPicture), create an offscreen graphics world of the required size (by calling QTNewGWorld), and then draw the picture data into that new graphics world (by calling DrawPicture). Before drawing into our graphics world, however, we need to call LockPixels to lock the offscreen pixel image. Listing 1.8 shows our definition of EffectsUtils_GetPictResourceAsGWorld.

Listing 1.8 Creating a graphics world from a 'PICT' resource.

```
OSErr EffectsUtils_GetPictResourceAsGWorld (short theResID,
        short theWidth, short theHeight, short theDepth, GWorldPtr *theGW)
{
  PicHandle         myHandle = NULL;
  PixMapHandle      myPixMap = NULL;
  CGrafPtr          mySavedPort;
  GDHandle          mySavedDevice;
  Rect              myRect;
  OSErr             myErr = noErr;

  // get the current drawing environment
  GetGWorld(&mySavedPort, &mySavedDevice);
```

```
  // read the specified 'PICT' resource from the application's resource file
  myHandle = GetPicture(theResID);
  if (myHandle == NULL) {
    myErr = ResError();
    if (myErr == noErr)
      myErr = resNotFound;
    goto bail;
  }

  // set the size of the GWorld
  MacSetRect(&myRect, 0, 0, theWidth, theHeight);

  // allocate a new GWorld
  myErr = QTNewGWorld(theGW, theDepth, &myRect, NULL, NULL, kICMTempThenAppMemory);
  if (myErr != noErr)
    goto bail;

  SetGWorld(*theGW, NULL);

  // get a handle to the offscreen pixel image and lock it
  myPixMap = GetGWorldPixMap(*theGW);
  LockPixels(myPixMap);

  EraseRect(&myRect);
  DrawPicture(myHandle, &myRect);

  if (myPixMap != NULL)
    UnlockPixels(myPixMap);

bail:
  // restore the previous port and device
  SetGWorld(mySavedPort, mySavedDevice);

  if (myHandle != NULL)
    ReleaseResource((Handle)myHandle);

  return(myErr);
}
```

Now we want to create a video track in a movie that lasts for a specified duration and whose data is the image contained in an offscreen graphics world. Listing 1.9 shows the complete definition of EffectsUtils_AddVideo-TrackFromGWorld. This function is a tad long since we need to create a new track and add a media sample to it; we also need to call GetMaxCompression-Size and CompressImage to compress the data in the original graphics world to reduce the size of the resulting new movie track. Notice that we return the track identifier to the caller through the theSourceTrack parameter. (For more details on calling GetMaxCompressionSize and CompressImage, see Volume One, Chapter 6.)

Listing 1.9 Creating a video track from a graphics world.

```
OSErr EffectsUtils_AddVideoTrackFromGWorld (Movie *theMovie, GWorldPtr theGW,
        Track *theSourceTrack, long theStartTime, TimeValue theDuration,
        short theWidth, short theHeight)
{
  Media                 myMedia;
  ImageDescriptionHandle mySampleDesc = NULL;
  Rect                  myRect;
  Rect                  myRect2;
  Rect                  myRect3;
  long                  mySize;
  Handle                myData = NULL;
  Ptr                   myDataPtr = NULL;
  GWorldPtr             myGWorld = NULL;
  CGrafPtr              mySavedPort = NULL;
  GDHandle              mySavedGDevice = NULL;
  PicHandle             myHandle = NULL;
  PixMapHandle          mySrcPixMap = NULL;
  PixMapHandle          myDstPixMap = NULL;
  OSErr                 myErr = noErr;

  // get the current port and device
  GetGWorld(&mySavedPort, &mySavedGDevice);

  // create a video track in the movie
  *theSourceTrack = NewMovieTrack(*theMovie, IntToFixed(theWidth),
                    IntToFixed(theHeight), kNoVolume);
  if (theSourceTrack == NULL)
    goto bail;

  myMedia = NewTrackMedia(*theSourceTrack, VideoMediaType, kVideoTrackTimeScale,
            NULL, 0);
  if (myMedia == NULL)
    goto bail;

  // get the rectangle for the movie
  GetMovieBox(*theMovie, &myRect);
```

```
  // begin editing the new track
  myErr = BeginMediaEdits(myMedia);
  if (myErr != noErr)
    goto bail;

  // create a new GWorld; we draw the picture into this GWorld and then compress it
  // (note that we are creating a picture with the maximum bit depth)
  myErr = NewGWorld(&myGWorld, 32, &myRect, NULL, NULL, OL);
  if (myErr != noErr)
    goto bail;

  mySrcPixMap = GetGWorldPixMap(theGW);
  myDstPixMap = GetGWorldPixMap(myGWorld);
  LockPixels(myDstPixMap);

  // create a new image description;
  // CompressImage will fill in the fields of this structure
  mySampleDesc = (ImageDescriptionHandle)NewHandle(4);

  SetGWorld(myGWorld, NULL);
#if TARGET_OS_MAC
  GetPortBounds(theGW, &myRect2);
  GetPortBounds(myGWorld, &myRect3);
#endif
#if TARGET_OS_WIN32
  myRect2 = theGW->portRect;
  myRect3 = myGWorld->portRect;
#endif

  // copy the image from the specified GWorld into the new GWorld
  CopyBits((BitMapPtr)*mySrcPixMap, (BitMapPtr)*myDstPixMap, &myRect2, &myRect3,
    srcCopy, NULL);

  // restore the original port and device
  SetGWorld(mySavedPort, mySavedGDevice);

  myErr = GetMaxCompressionSize(myDstPixMap, &myRect, 0, codecNormalQuality,
          kJPEGCodecType, anyCodec, &mySize);
  if (myErr != noErr)
    goto bail;

  myData = NewHandle(mySize);
  if (myData == NULL)
    goto bail;
```

```
    HLockHi(myData);
#if TARGET_CPU_68K
    myDataPtr = StripAddress(*myData);
#else
    myDataPtr = *myData;
#endif
    myErr = CompressImage(myDstPixMap, &myRect, codecNormalQuality,
            kJPEGCodecType, mySampleDesc, myDataPtr);
    if (myErr != noErr)
      goto bail;

    myErr = AddMediaSample(myMedia, myData, 0, (**mySampleDesc).dataSize,
            theDuration, (SampleDescriptionHandle)mySampleDesc, 1, 0, NULL);
    if (myErr != noErr)
      goto bail;

    myErr = EndMediaEdits(myMedia);
    if (myErr != noErr)
      goto bail;

    myErr = InsertMediaIntoTrack(*theSourceTrack, theStartTime,
            0, GetMediaDuration(myMedia), fixed1);

bail:
    // restore the original port and device
    SetGWorld(mySavedPort, mySavedGDevice);

    if (myData != NULL) {
      HUnlock(myData);
      DisposeHandle(myData);
    }

    if (mySampleDesc != NULL)
      DisposeHandle((Handle)mySampleDesc);

    if (myDstPixMap != NULL)
      UnlockPixels(myDstPixMap);

    if (myGWorld != NULL)
      DisposeGWorld(myGWorld);

    return(myErr);
}
```

See the file `QTEffects.c` for the complete listing of `QTEffects_MakePenguin-Movie`, which we call in response to the Make Fade-In Movie menu item. It's really just a longer version of `QTEffects_MakeFireMovie` (see Listing 1.4) that incorporates the extra code in Listing 1.7.

Before we move on, it's worth reflecting on the fact that the movie created by `QTEffects_MakePenguinMovie` is now the *fourth* version of our penguin movie. We first created an appearing-penguin movie in Volume One, Chapter 6, where we built a video track with 100 frames, each frame having slightly more opacity than the previous. The total size of the movie file was about 470 Kbytes. Also in Volume One, in Chapter 14, we created a second version of the penguin movie, using a sprite image in a key frame with zero opacity and 99 override frames that gradually increased the level of opacity of the sprite image. This version of the penguin movie file was only about 36 Kbytes. In the very next chapter (Chapter 15), we reworked that sprite version using a tween track to change the graphics mode of the penguin sprite image. The total size of that version was about 28 Kbytes. Finally, in this chapter, we've created a movie file that uses the cross-fade transition to blend a totally white frame into the penguin image; this version is only about 10 Kbytes (most of which is occupied by the compressed penguin image).

Notice how varied these movies are. The first version contains a single video track. The second version contains a single sprite track. The third version contains a sprite track and a tween track. This fourth version contains two video tracks (the sources) and an effects track. None of these versions is inherently any better or worse than any of the others (though it's hard not to choke on the beefy size of the first version). Which of them we employ for a specific purpose depends on various factors. For instance, if we want the smallest file size, we would use the effects version; if we want to be able to add wiring to the movie, then a sprite version is preferable.

Effects Parameters

So far, our effect descriptions contain only a single `kParameterWhatName` atom and zero or more `kEffectSourceName` atoms. All of the built-in QuickTime video effects also support *effects parameters*, which specify additional information about the effect. For instance, the fire effect supports four parameters, which indicate the desired spread rate, sputter rate, water rate, and restart rate for the fire. The *sputter rate* (or *decay rate*) specifies how quickly the flames die down as they move upward. Larger values of the decay rate result in very low flames.

We specify a value for an effects parameter by inserting a parameter atom into the effect description. For instance, once we've created an effect description for the fire effect (by calling `EffectsUtils_CreateEffectDescription`), we can add a parameter atom to set the decay rate to 11, like this:

```
myRate = EndianS32_NtoB(11);
myErr = QTInsertChild(myEffectDesc, kParentAtomIsContainer,
        FOUR_CHAR_CODE('decy'), 1, 0, sizeof(myRate), &myRate, NULL);
```

The type of the parameter atom indicates the kind of parameter we are setting, and the data in the parameter atom is the desired value for that parameter.

Not all parameters are optional. With the SMPTE effects, the effect type indicates which of the four general classes of SMPTE effects (wipe, iris, radial, or matrix) the effect belongs to. To select a specific effect from those classes, we need to add a wipe ID parameter atom to the effect description. For instance, to specify the horizontal barn zigzag effect (shown in Figure 1.1), we could execute this code:

```
myWipe = EndianS32_NtoB(kHorizontalBarnZigZagWipe);
myErr = QTInsertChild(myEffectDesc, kParentAtomIsContainer,
        FOUR_CHAR_CODE('wpID'), 1, 0, sizeof(myWipe), &myWipe, NULL);
```

The constant kHorizontalBarnZigZagWipe and constants for the remaining SMPTE effects are defined in the standard header file ImageCodec.h.

Using the Effects Parameters Dialog Box

When we build an effects movie, it would be nice to provide the user with an interactive way to set any of the optional effects parameters. To this end, the QuickTime video effects architecture includes support for displaying and managing the *effects parameters dialog box*, shown in Figure 1.13. (Sometimes this dialog box is also called the *standard parameters dialog box*.) As you can see, this dialog box includes a list of available effects (in this case, just the one-source effects) and some controls allowing the user to modify the parameters associated with the selected effect. It also includes a preview pane holding a poster image that is dynamically updated to reflect the current parameter settings.

QuickTime provides the QTCreateStandardParameterDialog function for displaying the effects parameters dialog box, which is declared essentially like this:

```
OSErr QTCreateStandardParameterDialog (
        QTAtomContainer effectList,
        QTAtomContainer parameters,
        QTParameterDialogOptions dialogOptions,
        QTParameterDialog *createdDialog);
```

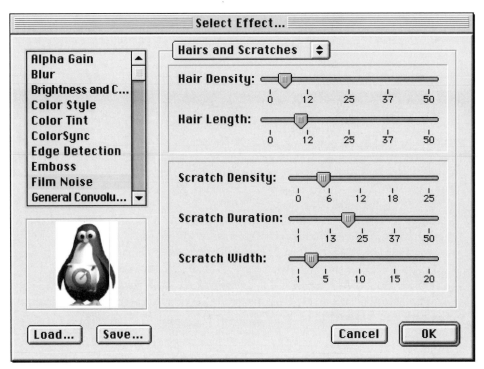

Figure 1.13 The effects parameters dialog box.

The effectList parameter specifies which effects we want to appear in the list on the left side of the dialog box. QuickTime also provides a function that we can use to get a list of all effects that take a certain number of sources:

```
myErr = QTGetEffectsList(&gEffectList, theSpecCount, theSpecCount, 0);
```

The second and third parameters to QTGetEffectsList specify the minimum and maximum number of sources; in this case, we set both of those parameters to the number of sources selected by the user. QTGetEffectsList returns, through its first parameter, an atom container that holds at least two atoms for every available effect that has the requisite number of sources. These two atoms specify the name and type of the effect. The atoms are sorted alphabetically by effect name. (That is, the atom of type kEffectName-Atom with ID 1 is the first name alphabetically; the atom of type kEffect-NameAtom with ID 2 is next; and so forth.)

The second parameter to QTCreateStandardParameterDialog is an atom container in which information will be returned to us when the user finishes selecting an effect and its parameters. We need to allocate that atom container ourselves, like so:

```
myErr = QTNewAtomContainer(&gEffectDesc);

myErr = QTCreateStandardParameterDialog(gEffectList, gEffectDesc, 0,
            &gEffectsDialog);
```

The third parameter specifies some flags (which we set to 0 here), and the fourth parameter is the location of a variable of type QTParameterDialog; if QTCreateStandardParameterDialog completes successfully, it returns in that location an identifier for the effects parameters dialog box. We'll use that identifier in subsequent operations on the dialog box.

Setting the Poster Images

After we call QTCreateStandardParameterDialog, the effects parameters dialog box is not actually displayed on the screen until the dialog box receives an event. (As we'll see shortly, we pass events to the dialog box by calling QTIsStandardParameterDialogEvent.) This delay gives us an opportunity to do any necessary configuration in the dialog box before the user actually sees it. The main thing we want to do is set the poster image or images displayed in the box.

We set a poster image by calling the QTStandardParameterDialogDoAction function, which is declared essentially like this:

```
OSErr QTStandardParameterDialogDoAction (QTParameterDialog createdDialog,
        long action, void *params);
```

The action parameter specifies which action we want to perform on the dialog box. In QTEffects, we will use these three actions:

```
enum {
  pdActionConfirmDialog               = 1,
  pdActionSetPreviewPicture           = 6,
  pdActionModelessCallback            = 12
};
```

To set the preview image, we use the pdActionSetPreviewPicture action; in that case, the params parameter is a pointer to a *parameter dialog box preview record*, declared like this:

```
struct QTParamPreviewRecord {
  long                    sourceID;
  PicHandle               sourcePicture;
};
```

The sourcePicture field contains a picture handle for the preview image, which must not be disposed until the dialog box is dismissed. The sourceID field indicates the index of the image. A filter should have one preview image with this field set to 1, and a transition should have two preview images with this field set to 1 and 2. Listing 1.10 shows how we would set the preview image for a filter.

Listing 1.10 Setting a preview image.

```
if (mySrcTrack != NULL) {
  gPosterA = GetTrackPict(mySrcTrack, GetMoviePosterTime(mySrcTrack));
  if (gPosterA != NULL) {
    QTParamPreviewRecord        myPreviewRecord;

    myPreviewRecord.sourcePicture = gPosterA;
    myPreviewRecord.sourceID = 1;
    myErr = QTStandardParameterDialogDoAction(gEffectsDialog, pdActionSetPreviewPicture,
            &myPreviewRecord);
  }
}
```

QuickTime provides a number of other selectors for customizing the effects parameters dialog box and its operation. For instance, to set a custom title on the dialog box, we can use the pdActionSetDialogTitle action selector, like this:

```
StringPtr myPtr = QTUtils_ConvertCToPascalString(kMyTitle);

myErr = QTStandardParameterDialogDoAction(gEffectsDialog,
          pdActionSetDialogTitle, myPtr); free(myPtr);
```

See Apple's effects documentation for a complete list of the action selectors supported by QTStandardParameterDialogDoAction.

Handling Events in the Effects Parameters Dialog Box

Once we've configured the effects parameters dialog box to our liking, we need to start sending events to it so that it is displayed on the screen and the user can interact with it. We use the QTIsStandardParameterDialogEvent function to send events to that dialog box, like this:

```
myErr = QTIsStandardParameterDialogEvent(theEvent, gEffectsDialog);
```

QTIsStandardParameterDialogEvent determines whether the specified event is meant for the effects parameters dialog box (rather in the same way that IsDialogEvent determines whether an event is meant for a typical dialog box). If the event does apply to that dialog box, it's handled; in any case, QTIsStandardParameterDialogEvent returns a result code to its caller that indicates what action, if any, it took. We need to inspect that result code and react accordingly. Currently, QTIsStandardParameterDialogEvent returns one of four result codes:

1. If codecParameterDialogConfirm is returned, the user has clicked the OK button; in this case, we need to tell QuickTime to fill the effect description we earlier passed to QTCreateStandardParameterDialog with atoms that reflect the user's selections in the dialog box. Then we should close the dialog box and use the information in that effects description.

2. If userCanceledErr is returned, the user has clicked the Cancel button in the dialog box. In this case, we should close the dialog box and perform any necessary cleanup operations.

3. If noErr is returned, the event was completely handled by the effects parameters dialog box code; we should proceed with further event processing.

4. If featureUnsupported is returned, the event was not handled by the effects parameters dialog box code; we should allow the event to be processed by our application normally.

Listing 1.11 shows our definition of the QTEffects_HandleEffectsDialog-Events function, which we use to send events to the effects parameters dialog box and respond appropriately.

Listing 1.11 Handling dialog events.

```
Boolean QTEffects_HandleEffectsDialogEvents
          (EventRecord *theEvent, DialogItemIndex theItemHit)
{
#pragma unused(theItemHit)
    Boolean        isHandled = false;
    OSErr          myErr = noErr;

    // pass the event to the standard effects parameters dialog box handler
    myErr = QTIsStandardParameterDialogEvent(theEvent, gEffectsDialog);

    switch (myErr) {
```

```
case codecParameterDialogConfirm:
case userCanceledErr:
  // the user clicked the OK or Cancel button;
  // dismiss the dialog box and respond accordingly
  gDoneWithDialog = true;

  if (myErr == codecParameterDialogConfirm)
    QTStandardParameterDialogDoAction(gEffectsDialog, pdActionConfirmDialog, NULL);
  QTDismissStandardParameterDialog(gEffectsDialog);
  gEffectsDialog = 0L;
  QTEffects_RespondToDialogSelection(myErr);
  isHandled = true;
  break;

case noErr:
  // the event was completely handled by QTIsStandardParameterDialogEvent
  isHandled = true;
  break;

case featureUnsupported:
  // the event was not handled by QTIsStandardParameterDialogEvent;
  // let the event be processed normally
  isHandled = false;
  break;

default:
  // the event was not handled by QTIsStandardParameterDialogEvent;
  // do not let the event be processed normally
  isHandled = true;
  break;
}

return(isHandled);
}
```

Notice that the code for the codecParameterDialogConfirm result code calls QTStandardParameterDialogDoAction with the pdActionConfirmDialog action parameter; this fills in the effect description with the current values in the dialog box. That code also calls QTDismissStandardParameterDialog to close the dialog box; then it calls the application function QTEffects_RespondToDialogSelection to respond to the user's selection. We won't consider the QTEffects_RespondToDialogSelection function in this chapter, since it pretty much reprises code we've seen earlier in this chapter, to build an effects movie. That function does, however, contain some important cleanup code, shown in Listing 1.12.

Listing 1.12 Cleaning up after the dialog box is closed.

```
gEffectsDialog = 0L;

// we're finished with the effect list and movie posters
if (gEffectList != NULL)
  QTDisposeAtomContainer(gEffectList);

if (gPosterA != NULL)
  KillPicture(gPosterA);

if (gPosterB != NULL)
  KillPicture(gPosterB);
```

Sending Events to the Effects Parameters Dialog Box

Now we know how to send events to the effects parameters dialog box and how to respond to the result codes that are returned to us. But when should we call QTEffects_HandleEffectsDialogEvents in our application code? On Macintosh systems, this is pretty easy, since our basic Macintosh application framework calls the function QTApp_HandleEvent for every event it receives from WaitNextEvent. Our application can inspect the gEffectsDialog global variable to see whether the effects parameters dialog box is currently displayed; if it is, we'll just call QTEffects_HandleEffectsDialogEvents, as shown in Listing 1.13.

Listing 1.13 Looking for events for the effects parameters dialog box.

```
Boolean QTApp_HandleEvent (EventRecord *theEvent)
{
  Boolean          isHandled = false;

  // see if the event is meant for the effects parameters dialog box
  if (gEffectsDialog != 0L)
    isHandled = QTEffects_HandleEffectsDialogEvents(theEvent, 0);
  return(isHandled);
}
```

On Windows, things are a bit trickier here. In our Windows application framework, QTApp_HandleEvent is called only when a movie window is open. So we can't rely on QTApp_HandleEvent to trigger the QTEffects_Handle-EffectsDialogEvents function. Instead, we can use SetModelessDialogCall-backProc to install a callback function to handle Windows messages that apply to the effects parameters dialog box. (This function works equally well with modal dialog boxes, so don't worry about the name.) We'll call SetModelessDialogCallbackProc like this:

```
SetModelessDialogCallbackProc(FrontWindow(),
  (QTModelessCallbackUPP)QTEffects_EffectsDialogCallback);
```

The specified callback procedure, QTEffects_EffectsDialogCallback, is called by QuickTime Media Layer (QTML) when it's handling events in dialog boxes. When our callback function is executed, QTML has already done any control-tracking for controls in the dialog box. If a control has been selected, its ID is passed to us in the theItemHit parameter. Listing 1.14 shows our definition of QTEffects_EffectsDialogCallback.

Listing 1.14 Handling events for the effects parameters dialog box.

```
static void QTEffects_EffectsDialogCallback
          (EventRecord *theEvent, DialogRef theDialog, DialogItemIndex theItemHit)
{
  QTParamDialogEventRecord                    myRecord;

  myRecord.theEvent = theEvent;
  myRecord.whichDialog = theDialog;
  myRecord.itemHit = theItemHit;

  if (gEffectsDialog != 0L) {

    QTStandardParameterDialogDoAction(gEffectsDialog, pdActionModelessCallback,
      &myRecord);

    // see if the event is meant for the effects parameters dialog box
    QTEffects_HandleEffectsDialogEvents(theEvent, theItemHit);
  }
}
```

As you can see, we pass the event to QTEffects_HandleEffectsDialogEvents. (We also pass the index of the item hit, but it's ignored by that function.) We also call QTStandardParameterDialogDoAction, this time with the action pdActionModelessCallback. This is some magic that ensures that QTML properly updates the dialog box and its controls.

One last "gotcha" on Windows: we need to make sure that idle events are sent to the dialog box so that it can run the effect in the preview pane. To accomplish this, we attach a custom window procedure to the dialog box by calling QTMLSetWindowWndProc, like this:

```
QTMLSetWindowWndProc(FrontWindow(), QTEffects_CustomDialogWndProc);
```

QTEffects_CustomDialogWndProc, defined in Listing 1.15, is called whenever the dialog box receives a message.

Listing 1.15 Handling messages for the effects parameters dialog box.

```
LRESULT CALLBACK QTEffects_CustomDialogWndProc
                (HWND theWnd, UINT theMessage, UINT wParam, LONG lParam)
{
  EventRecord                myEvent = {0};

  if (!gDoneWithDialog && (theMessage == 0x7FFF))
    QTEffects_EffectsDialogCallback(&myEvent, GetNativeWindowPort(theWnd), 0);

  return(DefWindowProc(theWnd, theMessage, wParam, lParam));
}
```

QTEffects_CustomDialogWndProc looks for messages of the type 0x7FFF (which is a special message produced by QTML to simulate Macintosh idle events); when it finds one, and if the dialog box is still active, it calls the function QTEffects_EffectsDialogCallback with an event record for an idle event.

Effects Parameter Files

Notice that the effects parameters dialog box in Figure 1.13 contains two buttons, labeled Save and Load. These buttons allow the user to save the effects parameters currently displayed in the dialog box and to reload a saved set of parameters. For various purposes, it might be useful to perform these actions programmatically. For instance, once the user has selected a set of parameters for an effect, we might want to save them into a file, whence we can retrieve them the next time the application is run. The format of these files is publicly defined and is indeed quite easy to read and write.

An *effects parameter file* is a file that specifies an effect and zero or more of its parameters; it may also specify the poster picture that appears in the effects parameters dialog box. An effects parameter file is organized as a series of "classic" atoms. Currently, three kinds of atoms are included in one of these files:

1. An atom of type 'qtfx' (required). The atom data is an atom container that holds information about the effect type and parameters. In other words, the atom data is an effect description.

2. An atom of type 'pnot' (optional). The atom data is organized as a preview resource record (of type PreviewResourceRecord). This atom specifies the type and index of some other atom, which contains the actual poster data. Usually the other atom is of type 'PICT'.

3. An atom of type 'PICT' (optional). The atom data is a picture that's used as the poster image in the effects parameters dialog box.

Other atoms may be included in an effects parameter file; applications that aren't expecting other atoms should be smart enough to skip them. By convention, an effects parameter file has the file extension .qfx; on Macintosh systems, the file type is 'qtfx'.

Currently, QuickTime does not provide any functions for reading or writing effects parameter files, but based on what we've learned hitherto (especially in Volume One, Chapter 8), we can easily write our own. Listing 1.16 shows a simple routine that we can use to open an effects parameter file and read the data of the 'qtfx' atom it contains.

Listing 1.16 Getting an effect description from an effects parameter file.

```
QTAtomContainer EffectsUtils_GetEffectDescFromQFXFile (FSSpec *theFSSpec)
{
    Handle          myEffectDesc = NULL;
    short           myRefNum = 0;
    long            mySize = 0L;
    OSType          myType = 0L;
    long            myAtomHeader[2];
    OSErr           myErr = noErr;

    myErr = FSpOpenDF(theFSSpec, fsRdPerm, &myRefNum);
    if (myErr != noErr)
      goto bail;

    SetFPos(myRefNum, fsFromStart, 0);

    while ((myErr == noErr) && (myEffectDesc == NULL)) {
      // read the atom header at the current file position
      mySize = sizeof(myAtomHeader);
      myErr = FSRead(myRefNum, &mySize, myAtomHeader);
      if (myErr != noErr)
        goto bail;

      mySize = EndianU32_BtoN(myAtomHeader[0]) - sizeof(myAtomHeader);
      myType = EndianU32_BtoN(myAtomHeader[1]);
```

```
    if (myType == FOUR_CHAR_CODE('qtfx')) {
      myEffectDesc = NewHandleClear(mySize);
      if (myEffectDesc == NULL)
        goto bail;

      myErr = FSRead(myRefNum, &mySize, *myEffectDesc);

    } else {
      SetFPos(myRefNum, fsFromMark, mySize);
    }
  }
}

bail:
  return((QTAtomContainer)myEffectDesc);
}
```

The effect description returned by this function can be used anywhere we use an effect description.

▶ Conclusion

In this chapter, we've seen how to create movies that contain QuickTime video effects. We've worked with generators, filters, and transitions, and we've seen how to display and manage the effects parameters dialog box. We've also seen how to read data from an effects parameter file. The Quick-Time video effects architecture provides a rich source of new capabilities that we can tap into with some very simple programming. If you're familiar with Volume One of the *QuickTime Toolkit*, the only really new thing we've encountered in this chapter is building effect descriptions, and even that turns out to be just another exercise in building atom containers.

You already know what's in store for us in the next chapter: we're going to see how to apply effects to images (not just to tracks in movies). We're also going to see how to apply an effect to part of a movie and how to use an effect as the image for a sprite.

F/X 2

Using Video Effects with Movie Segments, Images, and Sprites

Introduction

In Chapter 1, "F/X," we investigated a few of the most basic ways to use the QuickTime video effects architecture, which allows us to apply video effects to tracks in movies and to images. We saw how to work with generators (zero-source effects) and how to apply a filter to a video track and a transition to a pair of video tracks. We also saw how to specify effects parameters and use the effects parameters dialog box to elicit an effect and some effects parameters from the user.

In this chapter, we're going to continue working with QuickTime video effects. We'll see how to apply an effect to part of a movie and how to use an effect as the image for a sprite. We're also going to see how to apply an effect to an image (that is, not to a track in a movie). This will lead us, for the first time, to work directly with image decompressors.

Our sample application once again is QTEffects (the same one as in the first chapter); its Test menu is shown in Figure 2.1. In this chapter, we'll see how to handle the fourth menu item and the final two. Let's begin by seeing how to add an effect to a movie segment.

Video Effects and Movie Segments

The previous chapter showed us that it's fairly simple to add a video effect to an entire track. We just add an effects track that has the same track offset and duration as the source track, and we link the effects track to the source track by creating track references from the effects track to the source track and by setting the input map of the effects track appropriately. The media handler for the source track feeds all of its decompressed frames to the component specified in the effects track, which processes those frames further.

Test

Make Fire Movie...	⌘1
Make Fade-In Movie...	⌘2
Add Film Noise To Movie	⌘3
Add Film Noise to Image	⌘4
Make Effect Movie...	⌘5
Standalone Movie	⌘6
✓ Referenced Movie	⌘7
Add Effect to Movie Segment	⌘8
Make Sprite Effect Movie...	⌘9

Figure 2.1   The Test menu of QTEffects.

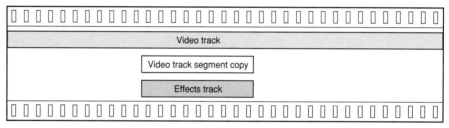

Figure 2.2   A filter applied to part of a video track.

To apply a video effect to only *part* of a source track requires a bit more work. As we saw briefly in the previous chapter, we can do this by creating a copy of the track segment to which we want to apply the effect; the effect then uses the track segment copy as its source, as shown in Figure 2.2.

When we want to add a two-source effect to part of a movie, the ideas are fundamentally the same. Suppose we've got a movie with two video tracks that overlap for some part of the movie (as shown in Figure 2.3). We want to apply a transition during the time the two tracks overlap; to do this, we can make copies of the appropriate track segments and use them as sources for the effects track, as seen in Figure 2.4.

Given what we learned in the previous chapter, all we really need to learn now is how to create a new track that holds only part of the data of an existing track. But in fact, we already know how to do that. In Volume One, Chapter 9, when we were discussing data references, we saw how to use the InsertTrackSegment function to copy media data from one track to another. We can use that function here to create the video track segment copy, as shown in Listing 2.1. Notice that we also call CopyTrackSettings to copy the source track matrix, clipping region, graphics mode, and other properties into the destination track.

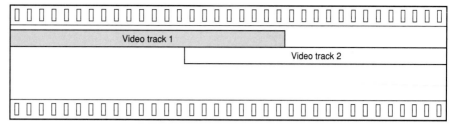

Figure 2.3 Two overlapping video tracks.

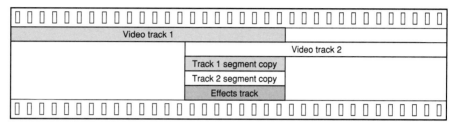

Figure 2.4 A transition applied to parts of two video tracks.

Listing 2.1 Creating a copy of a video track segment.

```
mySrcTrack1 = NewMovieTrack(theMovie, myWidth, myHeight, kNoVolume);
if (mySrcTrack1 == NULL)
  return(paramErr);

mySrcMedia1 = NewTrackMedia(mySrcTrack1, VideoMediaType, myTimeScale, NULL, 0);
if (mySrcMedia1 == NULL)
  return(paramErr);

#if COPY_MOVIE_MEDIA
myErr = BeginMediaEdits(mySrcMedia1);
if (myErr != noErr)
  return(myErr);
#endif
myErr = CopyTrackSettings(myVidTrack1, mySrcTrack1);
myErr = InsertTrackSegment(myVidTrack1, mySrcTrack1, theStartTime, theDuration,
          theStartTime);
if (myErr != noErr)
  return(myErr);

#if COPY_MOVIE_MEDIA
EndMediaEdits(mySrcMedia1);
#endif
```

The value of the compiler flag COPY_MOVIE_MEDIA determines whether the new track segment contains a copy of the media data in the original video track or the new track segment contains only references to that media data. In QTEffects, we set the value of that flag to 0, to minimize the resulting file size.

To make sure that the original video track is hidden behind the new effects track for the duration of the effect, we need to set the track layer of the effects track to be lower than the track layer of the video track. Toward the beginning of QTEffects_AddEffectToMovieSegment, we call the Effects-Utils_GetFrontmostTrackLayer function to retrieve the lowest layer of any video track in the movie, like this:

```
myLayer = EffectsUtils_GetFrontmostTrackLayer(theMovie, VideoMediaType);
```

Once we've created the effects track, we then set its layer like this:

```
SetTrackLayer(myEffectTrack, myLayer - 1);
```

Listing 2.2 shows our definition of EffectsUtils_GetFrontmostTrackLayer.

Listing 2.2 Finding the lowest layer of a track of a certain kind.

```
short EffectsUtils_GetFrontmostTrackLayer (Movie theMovie, OSType theTrackType)
{
    short       myLayer = 0;
    short       myIndex = 1;
    Track       myTrack = NULL;

    // get the layer number of the first track of the specified kind;
    // if no track of that kind exists in the movie, return 0
    myTrack = GetMovieIndTrackType(theMovie, 1, theTrackType,
                movieTrackMediaType | movieTrackEnabledOnly);
    if (myTrack == NULL)
      return(myLayer);

    myLayer = GetTrackLayer(myTrack);

    // see if any of the remaining tracks have lower layer numbers
    while (myTrack != NULL) {
      if (myLayer > GetTrackLayer(myTrack))
        myLayer = GetTrackLayer(myTrack);
      myIndex++;
      myTrack = GetMovieIndTrackType(theMovie, myIndex, theTrackType,
                movieTrackMediaType | movieTrackEnabledOnly);
    }

    return(myLayer);
}
```

See the file `QTEffects.c` for the complete definition of the `QTEffects_Add-EffectToMovieSegment` function, which is called in response to the Add Effect to Movie Segment menu item.

Video Effects and Images

Up to now, we've considered QuickTime video effects only as applied to movies. It's also possible to apply effects to still images. For instance, Figure 2.5 shows a still image that's had the *emboss* effect applied to it. Figure 2.6 shows the same image, with the X-ray version of the *color tint* effect.

In this section, we'll see how to apply a filter to an image. We won't actually learn how to apply a transition to a pair of images, but we'll write our code in such a way that it will be easy for the motivated reader to extend it to do so.

Decompressing Images

When we apply an effect to a track in a movie, the data describing the effect is stored in the movie itself (in an effects track, of course), and the effect is rendered automatically by QuickTime when the movie is played. Our job, as we've seen, is simply to create the effects track and link it to its source tracks. QuickTime takes care of the nitty-gritty details of retrieving the effect description, interpreting the effects track input map, and applying the effect to the source tracks over time.

Figure 2.5 An image with the emboss effect.

Figure 2.6 An image with the X-ray color tint effect.

When we want to apply an effect to an image, however, we're more or less on our own. Our application is going to have to keep track of the relevant effects data (that is, the effect description and the image description, along with the source data) and render the effect by making the appropriate API calls. Since QuickTime effects are implemented as image decompressor components, we need to open an image decompressor and apply it to the source data (the original image). We've previously worked with image compressors to compress single images and sequences of images. (See Volume One, Chapter 13.) Now it's time to tackle the other end of the compression/decompression process.

Let's begin by seeing how to decompress a single image. Remember that we can compress an image by calling the Image Compression Manager (ICM) functions `GetMaxCompressionSize` and `CompressImage`. `GetMaxCompressionSize` tells us the maximum size of the buffer we'll need to hold a compressed image, and `CompressImage` actually compresses the image. The source data is stored as a pixel map, and the compressed data is written into a buffer. To decompress an image, we can call `DecompressImage`, which takes a buffer of data and expands it into a pixel map. `DecompressImage` is declared essentially like this:

```
OSErr DecompressImage (Ptr data, ImageDescriptionHandle desc,
        PixMapHandle dst, const Rect *srcRect,
        const Rect *dstRect, short mode, RgnHandle mask);
```

The `data` parameter points to the compressed data that we want to decompress, and the `dst` parameter is a handle to a pixel map into which the data will be decompressed. The `desc` parameter is a handle to an image description, which specifies (among other things) the format of the compressed data and the bounds of the image. The `srcRect` parameter specifies which part of the image rectangle we want to decompress. This rectangle must lie within the rectangle whose upper-left corner is (0, 0) and whose lower-right corner is ((**desc).width, (**desc).height). To specify the entire source rectangle, we can pass the value `NULL` for the `srcRect` parameter.

The `dstRect` parameter specifies the rectangle into which the image is to be decompressed. Typically, we'll decompress into the entire destination pixel map, so we would pass the value (**dst).bounds. The `mode` parameter indicates the desired transfer mode, which is often `srcCopy`. Finally, the `mask` parameter is a handle to a region that specifies a drawing mask (or clipping region) for the destination pixel map; only pixels that lie within the mask are drawn into the destination pixel map. To draw into the entire pixel map, set this parameter to `NULL`.

Here's a typical call to `DecompressImage`:

```
myErr = DecompressImage(myData, myDesc, myPixMap, NULL,
        (**myPixMap).bounds, srcCopy, NULL);
```

If this call completes successfully, then we could use `myPixMap` anywhere we would use a pixel map; for instance, we could copy it into a window by calling the `CopyBits` function.

For greater control of decompression operations, we can use the `FDecompressImage` function. `FDecompressImage` takes all the parameters of the `DecompressImage` function, plus a handful of additional parameters that allow us to translate or scale the image during decompression, select a particular image quality, specify a progress function that displays a progress dialog box during lengthy decompressions, and so forth.

It turns out, however, that neither `DecompressImage` nor `FDecompressImage` allows us to handle QuickTime video effects. Their main limitation is that they provide no easy way to specify an effect's source or sources. To do that, we need to use ICM functions that decompress an image sequence.

Decompressing Image Sequences

In Volume One, Chapter 13, we compressed a sequence of images using the three standard image compression dialog component functions `SCCompressSequenceBegin`, `SCCompressSequenceFrame`, and `SCCompressSequenceEnd`. The ICM also provides the more general functions `CompressSequenceBegin`, `CompressSequenceFrame`, and `CDSequenceEnd` for initiating and managing a compression sequence. To decompress a sequence of images, we'll use Decompress-SequenceBeginS, DecompressSequenceFrameWhen, and CDSequenceEnd. (Notice that CDSequenceEnd can be used to end both an image compression sequence and an image decompression sequence.)

To begin a decompression sequence, we call DecompressSequenceBeginS, which is declared essentially like this:

```
OSErr DecompressSequenceBeginS (ImageSequence *seqID,
        ImageDescriptionHandle desc, Ptr data, long dataSize,
        CGrafPtr port, GDHandle gdh, const Rect *srcRect,
        MatrixRecordPtr matrix, short mode, RgnHandle mask,
        CodecFlags flags, CodecQ accuracy,
        DecompressorComponent codec);
```

Some of the parameters here are identical to the parameters of Decompress Image. As with DecompressImage, we pass in a buffer of data, a source rectangle, a transfer mode, and a drawing mask. As with FDecompressImage, we pass in a transformation matrix and a quality setting (in the accuracy parameter). The port and gdh parameters specify the graphics port and graphics device into which the decompressed data will be written. (We shall decompress our data into an offscreen graphics world, in which case we can set gdh to NULL.) The codec parameter specifies the image decompressor component that we want to be used for the decompression sequence; since the image description already indicates the relevant codec, we'll pass NULL in this parameter. Finally, the flags parameter is used to specify any special memory-allocation requirements for the decompressor component; we'll pass 0 to indicate no special requirements here.

DecompressSequenceBeginS uses the image data passed in the data parameter and the other information to preflight the decompression sequence. An instance of the specified decompressor component is opened and initialized, and any additional buffers are allocated. If DecompressSequenceBeginS completes successfully, it returns in the seqID parameter a *sequence identifier*, which we'll use in subsequent calls to manage the decompression sequence. A sequence identifier is of type ImageSequence, which is declared like this:

```
typedef long            ImageSequence;
```

Once we've set up a decompression sequence, we can decompress individual frames of the image sequence by calling DecompressSequenceFrameWhen. We pass in the sequence identifier, the data to be decompressed, and some information about the frame's time location in the sequence. For most filters (one-source effects), the notion of time is not really relevant. But for transitions, the effects components do need to know where in the complete image sequence a particular frame lies. So we need to attach some timing information to the image sequence. We'll do this by creating a time base.

Storing the Decompression Data

Let's see how we can tie all this into our sample application, QTEffects. As you know, the shell application upon which we've built QTEffects is able to open image files in a window, using a graphics importer to draw the image whenever necessary—namely, whenever the image window receives an update event (on Macintosh) or a WM_PAINT message (on Windows). By default, the graphics importer is configured (by a call to GraphicsImportSet-GWorld) to draw directly into the image window. To support adding a filter to an image, we need to set the graphics importer to draw into an offscreen graphics world, which we then use as the source for the effect. When we call DecompressSequenceBeginS, we'll set the image window as the drawing destination. So the original image is first drawn into an offscreen graphics world and then "decompressed" (using an effects component) into the onscreen image window.

Each image window opened by QTEffects therefore needs to have some additional data associated with it. As usual, we store such additional window-specific data in an application data record, a handle to which is stored in the fAppData field of the window data record. Here's how we'll declare the ApplicationDataRecord structure for QTEffects:

```
typedef struct ApplicationDataRecord {
    OSType                      fEffectType;
    ImageDescriptionHandle      fSampleDescription;
    ImageSequence               fEffectSequenceID;
    QTAtomContainer             fEffectDescription;
    TimeBase                    fTimeBase;
    GWorldPtr                   fGW;
    ImageDescriptionHandle      fGWDesc;
} ApplicationDataRecord, *ApplicationDataPtr, **ApplicationDataHdl;
```

The fEffectType field specifies the type of filter we want to apply to the image; in QTEffects, this is always kFilmNoiseImageFilterType. The fSample-Description field is a sample description for the effect, and the fEffect-Description field is an effect description for the effect. The fEffectSequenceID field holds the sequence identifier returned by DecompressSequenceBeginS. The fGW field holds a pointer to the offscreen graphics world that serves as the effect source, and the fGWDesc field is a handle to a second image description, which describes the image in the offscreen graphics world. Finally, the fTime-Base field specifies the time base that we'll use for timing information. Once again, this field is largely nugatory for filters, but I've included it to make it easier to extend this code to support transitions.

When we open a new image window, we'll execute this line of code to create the application data record:

```
(**theWindowObject).fAppData = QTEffects_InitWindowData(theWindowObject);
```

The QTEffects_InitWindowData function is defined in Listing 2.3.

Listing 2.3 Initializing the data for an image window.

```
Handle QTEffects_InitWindowData (WindowObject theWindowObject)
{
  ApplicationDataHdl    myAppData = NULL;

  // if we already have some window data, dump it
  myAppData = (ApplicationDataHdl)QTFrame_GetAppDataFromWindowObject(theWindowObject);

  if (myAppData != NULL)
    QTEffects_DumpWindowData(theWindowObject);

  // allocate and initialize our application data
  myAppData = (ApplicationDataHdl)NewHandleClear(sizeof(ApplicationDataRecord));

  return((Handle)myAppData);
}
```

As you can see, we clear out any existing data attached to the window (by calling QTEffects_DumpWindowData, discussed later) and then call NewHandle-Clear to allocate a new block of memory to hold an application data record. When the user selects the Add Film Noise To Image menu item, we call the QTEffects_AddFilmNoiseToImage function, defined in Listing 2.4.

Listing 2.4 Filling in the application data record.

```
void QTEffects_AddFilmNoiseToImage (WindowObject theWindowObject)
{
  ApplicationDataHdl        myAppData = NULL;
  GraphicsImportComponent   myImporter = NULL;
  Rect                      myRect;

  if (theWindowObject == NULL)
    return;
```

```
myAppData = (ApplicationDataHdl)(**theWindowObject).fAppData;
if (myAppData == NULL)
    return;

myImporter = (**theWindowObject).fGraphicsImporter;
if (myImporter == NULL)
    return;

GraphicsImportGetBoundsRect(myImporter, &myRect);

// set up the initial state
(**myAppData).fSampleDescription = EffectsUtils_MakeSampleDescription(kImageEffectType,
                                myRect.right - myRect.left,
                                myRect.bottom - myRect.top);
(**myAppData).fEffectDescription = EffectsUtils_CreateEffectDescription
                                (kImageEffectType, kSourceOneName,
                                kSourceNoneName, kSourceNoneName);
(**myAppData).fEffectType          = kImageEffectType;
(**myAppData).fEffectSequenceID    = 0L;
(**myAppData).fTimeBase            = NULL;

QTEffects_SetUpEffectSequence(theWindowObject);
}
```

QTEffects_AddFilmNoiseToImage creates the sample description and the effect description, using utility functions defined in the file EffectsUtilities.c. It also sets the effect type to the film noise effect, using the constant kImageEffectType (which is defined as kFilmNoiseImageFilterType in the file QTEffects.h). Finally, QTEffects_AddFilmNoiseToImage calls the function QTEffects_SetUpEffectSequence to complete the effects setup process.

Setting Up the Effect

So far we've managed to allocate the storage we need to maintain the information about our decompression sequence and to create the sample description and the effect description for the film noise effect. We can go ahead and call DecompressSequenceBeginS, like this:

```
myErr = DecompressSequenceBeginS(
        &(**myAppData).fEffectSequenceID,
        (**myAppData).fSampleDescription,
        *(**myAppData).fEffectDescription,
        GetHandleSize((**myAppData).fEffectDescription),
```

```
(CGrafPtr)QTFrame_GetPortFromWindowReference(
  (**theWindowObject).fWindow),
NULL, NULL, NULL, ditherCopy, NULL, 0,
codecNormalQuality, NULL);
```

The first parameter is the location in which a sequence identifier will be returned to us. The next two parameters specify the sample description and effect description, which we created earlier in the QTEffects_AddFilmNoise-ToImage function. Notice that the effect description is the buffer of data that is "decompressed" to render the effect. That's right: the effects component takes as its input data the effect description. The image data to which the effect is applied is specified as the *source* of the effect. (We'll see how to do that in a moment.) We tell the effects component to draw the rendered effect into the onscreen image window specified by this expression:

```
(CGrafPtr)QTFrame_GetPortFromWindowReference((**theWindowObject).fWindow)
```

Now we need to allocate the offscreen graphics world into which the graphics importer will draw the image and from which the effects component will take its source data. We can do so like this:

```
GraphicsImportGetBoundsRect(myImporter, &myRect);
HLock((Handle)myAppData);

myErr = QTNewGWorld(&(**myAppData).fGW, 32, &myRect, NULL, NULL,
         kICMTempThenAppMemory);
```

The kICMTempThenAppMemory flag tells QuickTime to try to allocate the off-screen graphics world from any available memory that's not assigned to any running process; if there isn't enough of that memory, QuickTime allocates the graphics world from the application's heap. (This flag is useful mainly on Mac OS 9, where applications have heaps of a fixed size.)

Once we've successfully allocated the offscreen graphics world, we want to draw the original image into it. We can accomplish this with two easy graphics importer calls:

```
GraphicsImportSetGWorld(myImporter, (**myAppData).fGW, NULL);
GraphicsImportDraw(myImporter);
```

Next, we need to set the image in this offscreen graphics world to be the source data for the image sequence. We'll use the CDSequenceNewDataSource function to create a new data source and the CDSequenceSetSourceData function to install that source as the image sequence source. CDSequenceNewDataSource takes the sequence identifier and an image description for the source and returns a value of type ImageSequenceDataSource:

```
myErr = CDSequenceNewDataSource((**myAppData).fEffectSequenceID, &mySrc,
        kSourceOneName, 1, (Handle)(**myAppData).fGWDesc, NULL, 0);
```

We can create the image description contained in `(**myAppData).fGWDesc` by calling the `MakeImageDescriptionForPixMap` function. Once we've got the new source identifier, we'll call `CDSequenceSetSourceData`:

```
CDSequenceSetSourceData(mySrc, GetPixBaseAddr(mySrcPixMap),
    (**(**myAppData).fGWDesc).dataSize);
```

We're almost done setting up the decompression sequence. All that remains is to create a time base and attach it to the decompression sequence.

```
(**myAppData).fTimeBase = NewTimeBase();

SetTimeBaseRate((**myAppData).fTimeBase, 0);
myErr = CDSequenceSetTimeBase((**myAppData).fEffectSequenceID,
        (**myAppData).fTimeBase);
```

Notice that we set the time base rate to 0, since the effect is going to be run outside of a QuickTime movie. We can't count on QuickTime to run the effect for us, so we're going to have to call `DecompressSequenceFrameWhen` ourselves. Before we get to that, however, let's take a look at the complete definition of `QTEffects_SetUpEffectSequence` (Listing 2.5).

Listing 2.5   Setting up the effect decompression sequence.

```
static OSErr QTEffects_SetUpEffectSequence (WindowObject theWindowObject)
{
    ApplicationDataHdl          myAppData = NULL;
    ImageSequenceDataSource     mySrc = 0;
    PixMapHandle                mySrcPixMap = NULL;
    GraphicsImportComponent     myImporter = NULL;
    Rect                        myRect;
    OSErr                       myErr = paramErr;

    myAppData = (ApplicationDataHdl)QTFrame_GetAppDataFromWindowObject(theWindowObject);

    if (myAppData == NULL)
        goto bail;

    // if an effect sequence is already set up, end it
    if ((**myAppData).fEffectSequenceID != 0L) {
        CDSequenceEnd((**myAppData).fEffectSequenceID);
        (**myAppData).fEffectSequenceID = 0L;
    }
```

```
// if there is a time base already set up, dispose of it
if ((**myAppData).fTimeBase != NULL) {
  DisposeTimeBase((**myAppData).fTimeBase);
  (**myAppData).fTimeBase = NULL;
}

// make an effects sequence
HLock((Handle)(**myAppData).fEffectDescription);

// prepare the decompression sequence for playback
myErr = DecompressSequenceBeginS(
          &(**myAppData).fEffectSequenceID,
          (**myAppData).fSampleDescription,
          *(**myAppData).fEffectDescription,
          GetHandleSize((**myAppData).fEffectDescription),
          (CGrafPtr)QTFrame_GetPortFromWindowReference((**theWindowObject).fWindow),
          NULL,
          NULL,
          NULL,
          ditherCopy,
          NULL,
          0,
          codecNormalQuality,
          NULL);

HUnlock((Handle)(**myAppData).fEffectDescription);
if (myErr != noErr)
  goto bail;

// create the offscreen GWorld holding the original image data
myImporter = (**theWindowObject).fGraphicsImporter;
if (myImporter == NULL)
  goto bail;

// set the size of the GWorld
GraphicsImportGetBoundsRect(myImporter, &myRect);

HLock((Handle)myAppData);

// allocate a new GWorld
myErr = QTNewGWorld(&(**myAppData).fGW, 32, &myRect, NULL, NULL, kICMTempThenAppMemory);
if (myErr != noErr)
  goto bail;

// lock the pixmap
LockPixels(GetGWorldPixMap((**myAppData).fGW));
```

```
GraphicsImportSetGWorld(myImporter, (**myAppData).fGW, NULL);
GraphicsImportDraw(myImporter);

// get the pixel maps for the GWorlds
mySrcPixMap = GetGWorldPixMap((**myAppData).fGW);
if (mySrcPixMap == NULL)
  goto bail;

// make the effect source
if ((**myAppData).fGW == NULL)
  goto bail;

myErr = MakeImageDescriptionForPixMap(mySrcPixMap, &(**myAppData).fGWDesc);
if (myErr != noErr)
  goto bail;

myErr = CDSequenceNewDataSource((**myAppData).fEffectSequenceID, &mySrc,
          kSourceOneName, 1, (Handle)(**myAppData).fGWDesc, NULL, 0);
if (myErr != noErr)
  goto bail;

CDSequenceSetSourceData(mySrc, GetPixBaseAddr(mySrcPixMap),
  (**(**myAppData).fGWDesc).dataSize);

// create a new time base and associate it with the decompression sequence
(**myAppData).fTimeBase = NewTimeBase();
myErr = GetMoviesError();
if (myErr != noErr)
  goto bail;

SetTimeBaseRate((**myAppData).fTimeBase, 0);
myErr = CDSequenceSetTimeBase((**myAppData).fEffectSequenceID, (**myAppData).fTimeBase);
bail:
  HUnlock((Handle)myAppData);

  return(myErr);
}
```

Running the Effect

The only important step that remains is for us to call DecompressSequence-
FrameWhen to draw the image, with the film noise effect, into the onscreen
image window. For most filters, applying an effect is a one-shot deal. That is
to say, we really need to call DecompressSequenceFrameWhen only once to get

the full visual effect (ignoring of course any redrawing that is required to handle update events and paint messages). But the film noise effect is an oddball here, since the hairs and scratches applied to the image change over time. The film noise effect isn't a transition, but it is sensitive to the passage of time. So we want to call DecompressSequenceFrameWhen repeatedly. Our standard way to do that is to add some code to the QTApp_Idle function; Listing 2.6 shows the lines we'll add to our idle-time handler.

Listing 2.6 Tasking the effect decompression sequence.

```
if ((**myWindowObject).fGraphicsImporter != NULL) {
  ApplicationDataHdl                    myAppData;

  myAppData = (ApplicationDataHdl)(**myWindowObject).fAppData;
  if (myAppData != NULL)
    if ((**myAppData).fEffectSequenceID != 0L)
      QTEffects_RunEffect(myWindowObject, 0);
}
```

If myWindowObject picks out an image window that has an active effect, then we call the function QTEffects_RunEffect to run the effect.

QTEffects_RunEffect is fairly simple; indeed, it consists largely of a call to DecompressSequenceFrameWhen. The only complication is that we need to specify a time value when we call DecompressSequenceFrameWhen, passing in an *ICM frame time record* (of type ICMFrameTimeRecord). The ICM frame time record is declared like this:

```
struct ICMFrameTimeRecord {
    wide            value;
    long            scale;
    void            *base;
    long            duration;
    Fixed           rate;
    long            recordSize;
    long            frameNumber;
    long            flags;
    wide            virtualStartTime;
    long            virtualDuration;
};
```

For rendering a filter, most of these fields can be set to 0 (except for recordSize, which should of course be sizeof(ICMFrameTimeRecord)). The QTEffects_RunEffect function, shown in Listing 2.7, sets them to values that are appropriate when running a transition.

Listing 2.7 Running the effect decompression sequence.

```
OSErr QTEffects_RunEffect (WindowObject theWindowObject, TimeValue theTime)
{
   ApplicationDataHdl        myAppData = NULL;
   ICMFrameTimeRecord        myFrameTime;
   OSErr                     myErr = paramErr;

   myAppData = (ApplicationDataHdl)QTFrame_GetAppDataFromWindowObject(theWindowObject);
   if (myAppData == NULL)
      goto bail;

   if (((**myAppData).fEffectDescription == NULL) ||
         ((**myAppData).fEffectSequenceID == OL))
      goto bail;

   // set the time base time to the step of the sequence to be rendered
   SetTimeBaseValue((**myAppData).fTimeBase, theTime, gNumberOfSteps);

   myFrameTime.value.hi                = 0;
   myFrameTime.value.lo                = theTime;
   myFrameTime.scale                   = gNumberOfSteps;
   myFrameTime.base                    = 0;
   myFrameTime.duration                = gNumberOfSteps;
   myFrameTime.rate                    = 0;
   myFrameTime.recordSize              = sizeof(myFrameTime);
   myFrameTime.frameNumber             = 1;
   myFrameTime.flags                   = icmFrameTimeHasVirtualStartTimeAndDuration;
   myFrameTime.virtualStartTime.l      = 0;
   myFrameTime.virtualStartTime.hi     = 0;
   myFrameTime.virtualDuration         = gNumberOfSteps;

   HLock((Handle)(**myAppData).fEffectDescription);

   myErr = DecompressSequenceFrameWhen((**myAppData).fEffectSequenceID,
            *((Handle)(**myAppData).fEffectDescription),
            GetHandleSize((Handle)(**myAppData).fEffectDescription),
            0, NULL, NULL, &myFrameTime);

   HUnlock((Handle)(**myAppData).fEffectDescription);

bail:
   return(myErr);
}
```

Notice that we passed NULL as the fifth parameter to DecompressSequence-FrameWhen. If, instead, we were to pass a pointer to a variable of type Codec-Flags (which is an unsigned short integer), then DecompressSequenceFrameWhen would return in that location a set of *decompression status flags* that give us information about the just completed decompression operation. As of Quick-Time 6.0, these flags are defined:

```
enum {
    codecFlagOutUpdateOnNextIdle          = (1L << 9),
    codecFlagOutUpdateOnDataSourceChange  = (1L << 10),
    codecFlagSequenceSensitive            = (1L << 11),
    codecFlagOutUpdateOnTimeChange        = (1L << 12),
    codecFlagImageBufferNotSourceImage    = (1L << 13),
    codecFlagUsedNewImageBuffer           = (1L << 14),
    codecFlagUsedImageBuffer              = (1L << 15)
};
```

We can inspect the codecFlagOutUpdateOnTimeChange flag (which is, alas, currently undocumented) to see whether we should render the effect repeatedly, as time changes. If that flag is clear, then we need to call Decompress-SequenceFrameWhen again only when the source image changes. I'll leave it as an exercise for the reader to modify QTEffects to avoid calling Decompress-SequenceFrameWhen unnecessarily.

Finishing Up

So we've completed the work required to apply a video effect to an image. When the user closes the image window, we need to call CDSequenceEnd to end the decompression sequence and then dispose of any additional memory we allocated to run the sequence. Listing 2.8 shows our definition of QTEffects_DumpWindowData, which handles all this cleanup.

Listing 2.8 Disposing of the application data.

```
void QTEffects_DumpWindowData (WindowObject theWindowObject)
{
    ApplicationDataHdl      myAppData = NULL;

    myAppData = (ApplicationDataHdl)QTFrame_GetAppDataFromWindowObject(theWindowObject);
    if (myAppData != NULL) {
        if ((**myAppData).fGWDesc != NULL)
            DisposeHandle((Handle)(**myAppData).fGWDesc);

        if ((**myAppData).fGW != NULL)
            DisposeGWorld((**myAppData).fGW);
```

```
    if ((**myAppData).fSampleDescription != NULL)
      DisposeHandle((Handle)(**myAppData).fSampleDescription);

    if ((**myAppData).fEffectDescription != NULL)
      QTDisposeAtomContainer((**myAppData).fEffectDescription);

    if ((**myAppData).fEffectSequenceID != 0L)
      CDSequenceEnd((**myAppData).fEffectSequenceID);

    if ((**myAppData).fTimeBase != NULL)
      DisposeTimeBase((**myAppData).fTimeBase);

    DisposeHandle((Handle)myAppData);
    (**theWindowObject).fAppData = NULL;
  }
}
```

⬤ Video Effects and Sprites

Let's continue our investigation of the QuickTime video effects architecture by learning how to use a video effect as a sprite image. In Volume One, Chapter 15, we saw how to use a video track as a sprite image override, so that the sprite uses the frames in the video track as the source for its images. It's just as easy to use an effect as the source for a sprite's images, and this opens up the door to some truly impressive QuickTime movies. Figure 2.7 shows a simple example, where the image of a sprite is provided by the fire effect.

Figure 2.8 shows another simple example, where the image of a sprite is provided by the *ripple* effect. The ripple effect makes it appear that the penguin is submerged in a pool of water that gently undulates. (This is rather difficult to see from a single screenshot, however.) In this section, we'll see how to create a sprite movie that uses an effect to supply the images for one of the sprites in the movie. We'll also see how to pass user actions to an effects component, to take advantage of any special capabilities of that component.

Using Effects as Image Overrides

In the movie shown in Figure 2.8, the sprite track contains two sprites: our standard penguin sprite and a sprite whose bounding box fills the entire movie rectangle. We use the ripple effect as an image override for the second sprite so that the entire movie, including the penguin, appears to be under water.

Figure 2.7 A sprite image overridden by the fire effect.

Figure 2.8 A sprite image overridden by the ripple effect.

When the user selects the Make Sprite Effect Movie menu item, QT-Effects calls the `QTEffects_MakeSpriteEffectMovie` function. We won't consider this function in detail, as it's virtually identical to functions we've considered in the past (for instance, see `QTSprites_CreateSpritesMovie` in Volume One, Chapter 14). The important step in `QTEffects_MakeSpriteEffect-`

Movie consists of a single line of code, which we use to add the appropriate samples to the sprite media:

```
QTEffects_AddPenguinMovieSamplesToMedia(myMedia);
```

Recall that a sprite track consists of one or more key frame samples, which contain the images for the sprites in the track and which also specify the initial properties of those sprites. (Sprite tracks can also contain override samples to animate the sprite by specifying changes to the sprite properties; our current sprite movie does not contain any override samples.) The image data for the penguin sprite is stored in an atom of type kSpriteImage-DataAtomType in the key frame sample and consists of an image description followed immediately by the sprite image data. We specify the penguin image data in our standard way, by calling the utility function Sprite-Utils_AddPICTImageToKeyFrameSample. The image data for the ripple sprite is also stored in an atom of type kSpriteImageDataAtomType; in this case, however, the atom data consists of an image description followed immediately by the effect description for the desired effect. To add the image data for the ripple sprite, we call the function QTEffects_AddRippleEffectAsSpriteImage, defined in Listing 2.9.

Listing 2.9 Adding an effect as a sprite image.

```
void QTEffects_AddRippleEffectAsSpriteImage
       (QTAtomContainer theKeySample, QTAtomID theImageID)
{
  ImageDescriptionHandle      mySampleDesc = NULL;
  QTAtomContainer             myEffectDesc = NULL;
  OSType                      myType = kWaterRippleCodecType;
  OSErr                       myErr = noErr;

  // create a sample description
  mySampleDesc = EffectsUtils_MakeSampleDescription(myType,
              kPenguinTrackWidth, kPenguinTrackHeight);
  if (mySampleDesc == NULL)
    goto bail;

  // create an effect description
  myEffectDesc = EffectsUtils_CreateEffectDescription(myType,
              kSourceNoneName, kSourceNoneName, kSourceNoneName);
  if (myEffectDesc == NULL)
    goto bail;
```

```
SpriteUtils_AddCompressedImageToKeyFrameSample(theKeySample, mySampleDesc,
    GetHandleSize(myEffectDesc), *myEffectDesc, theImageID, NULL, NULL);

bail:
  if (mySampleDesc != NULL)
    DisposeHandle((Handle)mySampleDesc);

  if (myEffectDesc != NULL)
    QTDisposeAtomContainer(myEffectDesc);

  return;
}
```

This is straightforward: create a sample description for the ripple effect, create an effect description with no sources, and then call Sprite-Utils_AddCompressedImageToKeyFrameSample to add the sample description and the effect description as the ripple sprite's image data.

For this movie to work properly, the ripple sprite must be situated in front of the penguin sprite, since the ripple effect is applied only to the movie area that lies underneath the ripple sprite. We can accomplish this, of course, by appropriately setting the sprite layer. In QTEffects, we'll set the penguin sprite's layer to 0 and the ripple sprite's layer to –1 when we create the sprite key frame sample (in QTEffects_AddPenguinMovieSamplesToMedia, considered shortly).

Passing Clicks to an Effects Component

The ripple effect component has a very cool feature: if the user clicks on a sprite whose image is supplied by the ripple effect, then additional concentric ripples are drawn to simulate a stone's having been dropped in the water at the point of the mouse click. Figure 2.9 shows a few frames of the penguin movie immediately after the user has clicked the mouse button.

Remember that the user's clicks on the ripple sprite are intercepted by the movie controller and passed to the sprite media handler for processing. We can instruct the sprite media handler to send them to the ripple effect component by adding some wiring to the sprite, like this:

```
WiredUtils_AddQTEventAndActionAtoms(mySpriteData, kParentAtomIsContainer,
    kQTEventMouseClick, kActionSpritePassMouseToCodec, NULL);
```

The kActionSpritePassMouseToCodec action tells the sprite media handler to pass the current location of the cursor to whatever component is drawing the sprite's image. Not all components can do anything useful with that information; in fact, the ripple component is currently the only effects component that accepts mouse locations.

Figure 2.9   New ripples from a user click.

Listing 2.10 shows the complete definition of QTEffects_AddPenguinMovie-SamplesToMedia.

Listing 2.10   Adding samples to the ripple penguin sprite track.

```
static void QTEffects_AddPenguinMovieSamplesToMedia (Media theMedia)
{
  QTAtomContainer      mySample = NULL;
  QTAtomContainer      mySpriteData = NULL;
  RGBColor             myKeyColor;
  Point                myLocation;
  short                isVisible, myIndex, myLayer;
  OSErr                myErr = noErr;

  // create a new, empty key frame sample
  myErr = QTNewAtomContainer(&mySample);
  if (myErr != noErr)
    goto bail;

  myKeyColor.red = myKeyColor.green = myKeyColor.blue = 0xffff;         // white

  // add images to the key frame sample
  SpriteUtils_AddPICTImageToKeyFrameSample(mySample, kPenguinPictID, &myKeyColor,
    1, NULL, NULL);
  QTEffects_AddRippleEffectAsSpriteImage(mySample, 2);
```

```
myErr = QTNewAtomContainer(&mySpriteData);
if (myErr != noErr)
  goto bail;

// the penguin sprite
myLocation.h        = 0;
myLocation.v        = 0;
isVisible           = true;
myIndex             = 1;
myLayer             = 0;

SpriteUtils_SetSpriteData(mySpriteData, &myLocation, &isVisible, &myLayer,
  &myIndex, NULL, NULL, NULL);
SpriteUtils_AddSpriteToSample(mySample, mySpriteData, 1);

QTDisposeAtomContainer(mySpriteData);

myErr = QTNewAtomContainer(&mySpriteData);
if (myErr != noErr)
  goto bail;

// the ripple sprite
myLocation.h        = 0;
myLocation.v        = 0;
isVisible           = true;
myIndex             = 2;
myLayer             = -1;

SpriteUtils_SetSpriteData(mySpriteData, &myLocation, &isVisible, &myLayer,
  &myIndex, NULL, NULL, NULL);
WiredUtils_AddQTEventAndActionAtoms(mySpriteData, kParentAtomIsContainer,
  kQTEventMouseClick, kActionSpritePassMouseToCodec, NULL);
SpriteUtils_AddSpriteToSample(mySample, mySpriteData, 2);

SpriteUtils_AddSpriteSampleToMedia(theMedia, mySample, kSpriteMediaFrameDurationPenguin,
  true, NULL);

bail:
  if (mySample != NULL)
    QTDisposeAtomContainer(mySample);

  if (mySpriteData != NULL)
    QTDisposeAtomContainer(mySpriteData);
}
```

For fun, you might try changing kQTEventMouseClick into kQTEventMouse-Moved. In that case, the additional concentric ripples will occur every time you move the cursor when it's over the movie rectangle. Surf's up!

Low-Level Video Effects Functions

Before we leave the topic of video effects, it's worth mentioning that Quick-Time provides a set of low-level APIs that we can use in certain cases where we need greater control over the standard effects parameters dialog box. These low-level calls begin with the prefix "ImageCodec" instead of "QT"; so, for instance, we can call ImageCodecIsStandardParameterDialogEvent in places we previously called QTIsStandardParameterDialogEvent.

The parameter lists for these two functions are identical except that the low-level function adds a parameter for a component instance. This allows us to restrict the operation to a specific effects component. For example, consider the standard effects parameters dialog box, shown once again in Figure 2.10. As you can see, all the one-source effects are listed in the upper-left

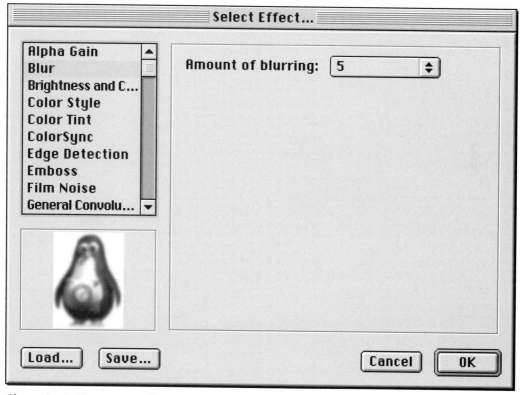

Figure 2.10   The standard effects parameters dialog box.

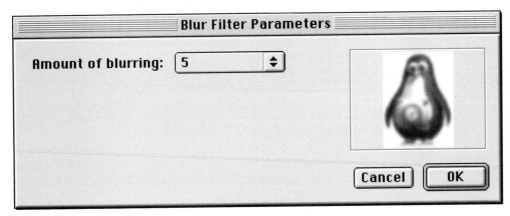

Figure 2.11 An effects parameters dialog box for a single effect.

corner of the dialog box. For certain purposes, we might want to display only the parameters that are relevant to a single effect. In that case, a dialog box like the one shown in Figure 2.11 is preferable.

We can display the dialog box shown in Figure 2.11 by calling the Image-CodecCreateStandardParameterDialog function, whose first parameter is a component instance for the desired effects component. Listing 2.11 shows some code that we might use to do this.

Listing 2.11 Showing the parameters dialog box for a specific effect.

```
ComponentDescription        myCD;
Component                   myComponent = NULL;
ComponentInstance           myInstance = NULL;
QTAtomContainer             myParamDesc = NULL;
QTParameterDialog           myEffectsDialog = OL;

// set up a component description
myCD.componentType          = decompressorComponentType;
myCD.componentSubType       = kBlurImageFilterType;
myCD.componentManufacturer  = 0;
myCD.componentFlags         = 0;
myCD.componentFlagsMask      = 0;

// find the required component
myComponent = FindNextComponent(myComponent, &myCD);
if (myComponent == NULL)
  return(paramErr);
```

```
// open the component
myInstance = OpenComponent(myComponent);

// get the list of parameters for the effect
myErr = ImageCodecGetParameterList(myInstance, &myParamDesc);

// display the dialog box
myErr = ImageCodecCreateStandardParameterDialog(myInstance,
        myParamDesc, myEffectDesc, 0, NULL, 0, &myEffectsDialog);
```

The low-level APIs are also useful if we want to embed the effects parameter dialog items into a custom dialog box, as illustrated in Figure 2.12. To do this, we need to call ImageCodecCreateStandardParameterDialog, as in Listing 2.11, passing a pointer to an existing dialog box as the fifth parameter and the dialog item index of a user item as the sixth parameter. The user item is replaced by the controls from the standard parameters dialog box.

In general, you should use either the low-level interfaces or the high-level interfaces, but not both. So if we call ImageCodecCreateStandardParameter-Dialog to display the effects parameters dialog box or to embed some effects parameter controls into a custom dialog box, then we should also call ImageCodecStandardParameterDialogDoAction to process events in the dialog box and ImageCodecDismissStandardParameterDialog to close the dialog box.

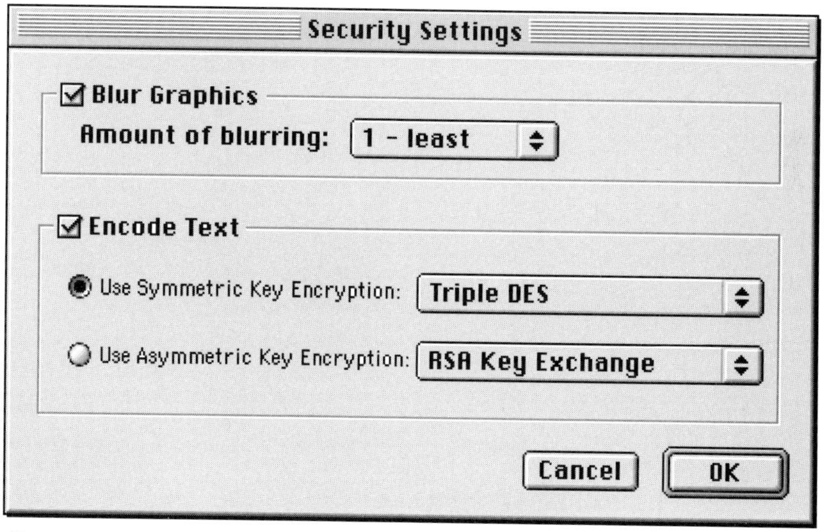

Figure 2.12 Effects parameter dialog items embedded in a custom dialog box.

Certain high-level functions, however, can safely be intermixed with the low-level functions. A good example is QTGetEffectsList, for which there is no low-level equivalent.

▶ Conclusion

The QuickTime video effects architecture provides an extremely powerful set of tools for adding video effects to movies and images. We can use it to access over 100 different generators, filters, and transitions. In this chapter and the opening one, we've seen how to add effects to movies, images, and sprite tracks. We've also seen how to display the effects parameters dialog box to allow the user to fine-tune an effect. And we've briefly touched on the low-level effects functions that QuickTime provides.

The Skin Game
Working with QuickTime Skins

▶ Introduction

QuickTime 5 introduced support for displaying movies inside of arbitrarily shaped windows. These windows are called *skinned movie windows,* and the custom shape of one of those windows is called its *skin.* Up to now, our sample applications have always displayed QuickTime movies inside a standard document window, which occupies a rectangular area on the screen. Even QuickTime Player, which uses a snazzy brushed-metal window frame with rounded edges, always shows a movie inside a rectangular pane inside the frame. Skins give us a way to break out of this rectangular mold. For instance, Figure 3.1 shows a QuickTime movie with a skin that's shaped like the QuickTime logo.

This movie contains two video tracks, one for the grainy, grayscale video showing in the center of the logo, and one for the logo image itself. (The second video track contains a single sample that extends for the entire duration of the first track.) The user can start and stop the movie by pressing the spacebar or by clicking the visible portion of the grayscale video. And the user can move the window around on the screen by clicking anywhere on the blue logo and dragging.

Figure 3.2 shows another possibility. Here is our penguin sprite movie once again, but this time as a skinned movie. It's still got a tween track that changes the sprite's graphics mode from total transparency to total opacity. But now I've set the looping mode to palindrome looping so that the penguin fades in and out as the movie plays.

Figure 3.3 shows yet another skinned movie window. Most of what you see here, including all the buttons and draggable handles, is provided by a Flash track. The grayscale image is once again a frame of a video track, which we can start, stop, pause, and play in slow motion using the tools palette on the right side of the movie window.

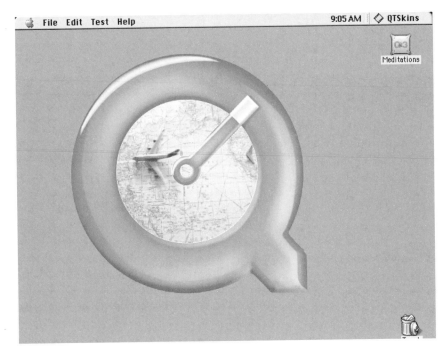

Figure 3.1 A QuickTime movie with a skin.

Figure 3.2 Another QuickTime movie with a skin.

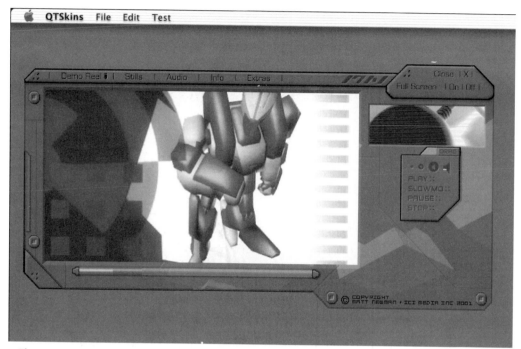

Figure 3.3 Yet another QuickTime movie with a skin.

Add Skin Track...   ⌘1

Figure 3.4 The Test menu of QTSkins.

In this chapter, we're going to learn how to create skinned movies. More important, we're also going to learn how to open a skinned movie file and display the movie to the user in a window of the appropriate shape. Our sample application in this chapter is called QTSkins. The Test menu of QTSkins is shown in Figure 3.4; as you can see, it has only one menu item, which allows us to add a skin track to a movie.

▶ **Skins**

Perhaps the best way to think of QuickTime skins is like this: a skinned movie is just a QuickTime movie with a custom window shape. A skin provides a way of selecting some portion of an existing movie and having that portion be all that's displayed to the user when the movie is opened. Skinned movies don't have title bars or window frames, and they don't display a controller bar. As a result, if we want the user to be able to interact with the movie, we'll need to supply our own controls. We can use wired sprite tracks or Flash tracks for this, or perhaps even wired text tracks.

The data that defines the custom window shape is contained in the skinned movie file itself. This fact has some very important consequences. For one thing, it means that we can select on a per-movie basis whether a movie is displayed in a normal document window or in a custom-shaped skinned window. We're not modifying the general appearance of the playback application (which is perhaps the typical use of the term "skins"). Rather, we're modifying the specific appearance of what's being played back. In a nutshell, we're changing the movie, not the movie player. Previously, the movie data represented some content that plays back inside a document window or pane, usually under the supervision of a movie controller and controller bar. Now the movie data can represent the content *and* the window *and* the controller. For the first time, really, the movie author has complete control over the user's playback experience.

So what kind of data do we use to construct a skinned movie? The first thing we need is some way of specifying which portion of the movie rectangle we want to appear as the content region of the skinned movie window. The *content region* of a window is the portion of the window in which an application displays the contents of a document; in our case, it's where the movie data and any movie controls are displayed. We specify the skinned movie's content region by providing a 1-bit (that is, black and white) mask that's the same size as the movie rectangle. If a pixel in the mask is black, then the corresponding pixel in the movie rectangle is displayed; otherwise, the corresponding pixel is not displayed. Let's call this mask the *content region mask*. Figure 3.5 shows the content region mask for the skinned movie shown in Figure 3.1.

Figure 3.5   A content region mask.

Figure 3.6 A drag region mask.

We typically also need some way to move the skinned movie window around on the screen. Usually, of course, we move a window by grabbing its title bar or window frame and then dragging. But because skinned movie windows don't have title bars or frames, we need to explicitly indicate the portion of the skinned movie window that the user can grab and drag. We do this by specifying a second mask, the *drag region mask*. (This is also a 1-bit mask.) A user can click anywhere in this region and drag the window around. Figure 3.6 shows the drag region mask for the skinned movie shown in Figure 3.1.

You'll notice that the drag region mask is entirely contained within the content region mask so that the user can grab only in some visible portion of the movie window. In addition, the drag region mask should exclude any areas of the movie rectangle that you want to be interactive. It won't do any good, for instance, to have a skinned movie's drag region overlap any wired sprites, since a click in that area will be interpreted as the beginning of a drag operation.

So we need three ingredients to create a skinned movie. We need the movie data itself. We need a content region mask to indicate the portion of the movie rectangle that is displayed to the user. And, we need a drag region mask to indicate the portion of the movie rectangle that can be grabbed.

Creating Skinned Movies

The typical way to create a skinned movie is to add a *skin track* to an existing movie. The skin track contains data that specifies the content region and the drag region of the movie window. In this section, we'll investigate two different ways to add a skin track to a movie. First, though, we'll take a brief moment to learn about media characteristics. This will help us see that skin data can in fact be contained in other kinds of tracks as well.

Searching Media Characteristics

Let's begin by considering a utility function we'll call several times in our application, QTSkin_IsSkinnedMovie (defined in Listing 3.1). This function returns a Boolean value that indicates whether the specified movie contains skin data.

Listing 3.1 Determining whether a movie is a skinned movie.

```
Boolean QTSkin_IsSkinnedMovie (Movie theMovie)
{
   return(GetMovieIndTrackType(theMovie, 1, SkinMediaType, movieTrackCharacteristic)
        != NULL);
}
```

We've worked with GetMovieIndTrackType a handful of times previously, but only using the movieTrackMediaType flag as the last parameter, to search for a track of a given index that has a specific media type. Here, you'll notice, we use the movieTrackCharacteristic flag instead, which tells Get-MovieIndTrackType to search for a track of a given index that has a specific media characteristic. A *media characteristic* is a feature that can be shared by two or more track types, such as the ability to draw data. Originally, in QuickTime version 2.0, there were two supported media characteristics, indicating whether the track has video or audio data in it:

```
enum {
   VisualMediaCharacteristic            = FOUR_CHAR_CODE('eyes'),
   AudioMediaCharacteristic             = FOUR_CHAR_CODE('ears')
};
```

Any track that displays visible data to the user has the VisualMediaCharacteristic media characteristic; some examples are video tracks, sprite tracks, text tracks, MPEG tracks, and timecode tracks. Similarly, any track that plays audible data to the user has the AudioMediaCharacteristic media characteristic; some examples are sound tracks and music tracks. QuickTime has subsequently added a few other searchable media characteristics, including kCharacteristicProvidesActions for tracks that contain wired actions.

In Listing 3.1, we were looking to see whether any track in the movie contains skin data. Skin tracks contain skin data, so they have this characteristic. But other kinds of tracks may very well contain skin data, and so they too would have this characteristic. (If we are interested in knowing whether a specific track has a given characteristic, we can call the MediaHasCharacteristic function.) By searching for the skin media characteristic instead of the skin media type, we allow our application to work with any movie tracks that contain skin data. Right now, as far as I know, there are no track types with that characteristic aside from skin tracks, but we are equipped to deal with them when they come along.

Using the QuickTime XML Importer

By far the easiest way to create a movie with a skin track is to use a Quick-Time XML importer, introduced in QuickTime 5. *XML* (for *Extensible Markup Language*) is a textual description of a document that contains structured information. It's similar in flavor to HTML, but differs significantly in that XML does not have a predefined set of markup tags. Rather, XML is more of a metalanguage for describing structured information. A *QuickTime XML importer* is a movie importer that knows how to parse certain kinds of XML files. QuickTime provides an importer that knows how to parse XML files that contain tags describing a skinned movie. Listing 3.2 shows the file used to construct the skinned movie shown in Figure 3.1. As you can see, this XML file specifies three other files, which contain the original movie data, a mask for the content region of the window, and a mask for the drag region of the window.

Listing 3.2 An XML file that specifies a skinned movie.

```
<?xml version="1.0"?>
<?quicktime type="application/x-qtskin"?>
<skin>
  <movie src="QTLogo.mov"/>
  <contentregion src="contentmask.pct"/>
  <dragregion src="dragmask.pct"/>
</skin>
```

If we open this file using QuickTime Player or any other skin-savvy application, we'll see the skinned movie shown in Figure 3.1. The application probably calls `NewMovieFromFile` or `NewMovieFromDataRef` to open the XML file. QuickTime will see that the file doesn't contain a movie atom and then go looking for a suitable movie importer. (See Volume One, Chapter 5, for a more in-depth discussion of how this works.) In the present case, Quick-Time will invoke the XML importer to import the movie data and return a movie to the calling application. Some importers, including the QuickTime XML importer, seem to ignore the `newMovieActive` flag passed to `NewMovie-FromFile`. So we'll add the following line of code to the `QTFrame_OpenMovieIn-Window` function, after we call `NewMovieFromFile`:

```
SetMovieActive(myMovie, true);
```

We can create a self-contained skinned movie file by calling `FlattenMovie-Data` on the open skinned movie. Our sample applications make this call when the user selects the Save As menu item. The self-contained movie file is easier to move around and to transport from machine to machine. It's also preferable for Web-based movie delivery.

Creating Skin Tracks Programmatically

Using the XML importer is fine and dandy, but we'd also like to be able to create skinned movies directly, using the QuickTime APIs. Once again, we'll do this by adding a skin track to an existing movie. We've already created many kinds of tracks in QuickTime movies, so we've got the drill down. You'll recall that it goes basically like this:

1. Create a new track and media (`NewMovieTrack` and `NewTrackMedia`).
2. Create a new sample description (`NewHandle`).
3. Start a media editing session (`BeginMediaEdits`).
4. Add media data to the new media (`AddMediaSample`).
5. End the media editing session (`EndMediaEdits`).
6. Insert the new media data into the track (`InsertMediaIntoTrack`).

It turns out, however, that we need to use a slightly different method for constructing a skin track. When we build (for instance) a video track or a sprite track, we need to know the exact structure of the media sample data, and we need to fill out a sample description that describes that data (its size, its compression type, and so forth). Moreover, when we call `AddMediaSample`, we need to specify the duration of the media sample. But with skin media data, the notion of duration doesn't really apply. After all, we're just specifying a couple of masks for a window shape, not any time-based data.

To simplify the handling of media data that isn't time based, QuickTime 5 introduced *public media information*, which can be any data associated with a media that does not need to be pegged to a specific time in a track. Currently, to my knowledge, only the skin media handler supports public media information (to maintain the content and drag region masks).

QuickTime 5 includes two new functions for working with public media information, `MediaSetPublicInfo` and `MediaGetPublicInfo`. `MediaSetPublicInfo` is declared essentially like this:

```
ComponentResult MediaSetPublicInfo(MediaHandler mh,
    OSType infoSelector, void *infoDataPtr, Size dataSize);
```

The mh parameter specifies the media handler we're giving the information to; in the present case, it's the skin media handler. The infoSelector parameter specifies the kind of public information we're setting. The skin media handler currently understands two selectors, 'skcr' (for the content region mask) and 'skdr' (for the drag region mask). The parameters info-DataPtr and dataSize specify the memory location and size of the public media information data. With the skin media handler, however, dataSize should be 0 and infoDataPtr should be a picture handle (of type PicHandle). For instance, here's how we'll set the content region mask:

```
myErr = MediaSetPublicInfo(myHandler, FOUR_CHAR_CODE('skcr'),
        (void *)myContentPic, 0);
```

Our work really boils down to this: have the user select two pictures, one for the content region mask and another for the drag region mask; then create a new track and media (of type SkinMediaType), call MediaSetPublicInfo for each of the pictures selected by the user, and finish up by calling InsertMedia-IntoTrack. Once we've got the two picture handles, the six-step sequence listed above reduces to this:

1. Create a new track and media (NewMovieTrack and NewTrackMedia).

2. Add media data to the new media (MediaSetPublicInfo).

3. Insert the new media data into the track (InsertMediaIntoTrack).

Let's consider, then, how to get the two picture handles. Ideally, we'd like to allow the user to work with any kind of image file that QuickTime can open (just like the XML importer does). MediaSetPublicInfo expects the data we pass it to be a PicHandle, so we need to convert the image data in a file selected by the user into a PicHandle. Happily, there is a graphics importer function, GraphicsImportGetAsPicture, that does precisely this. Listing 3.3 defines the QTSkin_GetPicHandleFromFile function, which we use (in Listing 3.4) to prompt the user for the two images we need. (For more information about graphics importers, see Volume One, Chapter 4.)

Listing 3.3 Getting a picture handle from an image file.

```
PicHandle QTSkin_GetPicHandleFromFile (void)
{
    OSType                    myTypeList = kQTFileTypeQuickTimeImage;
    short                     myNumTypes = 1;
    FSSpec                    myPictSpec;
    QTFrameFileFilterUPP      myFilterUPP = NULL;
    GraphicsImportComponent   myImporter = NULL;
    PicHandle                 myPicture = NULL;
    OSErr                     myErr = noErr;
```

```
#if TARGET_OS_MAC
  myNumTypes = 0;
#endif

  // have the user select an image file
  myFilterUPP = QTFrame_GetFileFilterUPP((ProcPtr)QTSkin_FileFilterFunction);
  myErr = QTFrame_GetOneFileWithPreview(myNumTypes, (QTFrameTypeListPtr)&myTypeList,
          &myPictSpec, myFilterUPP);
  if (myErr != noErr)
    goto bail;

  // get a graphics importer for the image file
  myErr = GetGraphicsImporterForFile(&myPictSpec, &myImporter);
  if (myErr != noErr)
    goto bail;

  // convert the image into a PicHandle
  myErr = GraphicsImportGetAsPicture(myImporter, &myPicture);

bail:
  if (myFilterUPP != NULL)
    DisposeNavObjectFilterUPP(myFilterUPP);

  if (myImporter != NULL)
    CloseComponent(myImporter);

  return(myPicture);
}
```

We are finally ready to put this all together. When the user selects the Add Skin Track menu item, we execute the QTSkin_AddSkinTrack function defined in Listing 3.4.

Listing 3.4 Adding a skin track to a movie.

```
OSErr QTSkin_AddSkinTrack (Movie theMovie)
{
  Track           myTrack = NULL;        // the movie track
  Media           myMedia = NULL;        // the movie track's media
  Rect            myRect;
  MediaHandler    myHandler = NULL;
  PicHandle       myContentPic = NULL;
  PicHandle       myDragPic = NULL;
  OSErr           myErr = paramErr;
```

```
if (theMovie == NULL)
    goto bail;

// elicit the two pictures from the user
myContentPic = QTSkin_GetPicHandleFromFile();
if (myContentPic == NULL)
    goto bail;

myDragPic = QTSkin_GetPicHandleFromFile();
if (myDragPic == NULL)
    goto bail;

// get the movie's dimensions
GetMovieBox(theMovie, &myRect);
MacOffsetRect(&myRect, -myRect.left, -myRect.top);

// create the skin track and media
myTrack = NewMovieTrack(theMovie,
            FixRatio(myRect.right, 1), FixRatio(myRect.bottom, 1), kNoVolume);
if (myTrack == NULL)
    goto bail;

myMedia = NewTrackMedia(myTrack, SkinMediaType, GetMovieTimeScale(theMovie), NULL, 0);
if (myMedia == NULL)
    goto bail;

myHandler = GetMediaHandler(myMedia);
if (myHandler == NULL)
    goto bail;

// add the skin content picture as public media information
myErr = MediaSetPublicInfo(myHandler, FOUR_CHAR_CODE('skcr'),
        (void *)myContentPic, 0);
if (myErr != noErr)
    goto bail;

// add the skin drag picture as public media information
myErr = MediaSetPublicInfo(myHandler, FOUR_CHAR_CODE('skdr'),
        (void *)myDragPic, 0);
if (myErr != noErr)
    goto bail;

// add the media to the track
myErr = InsertMediaIntoTrack(myTrack, 0, 0, GetMediaDuration(myMedia), fixed1);
```

```
bail:
  if (myContentPic != NULL)
    KillPicture(myContentPic);

  if (myDragPic != NULL)
    KillPicture(myDragPic);

  return(myErr);
}
```

As you can see, using MediaSetPublicInfo greatly simplifies the process of creating a skin track. We don't have to create a sample description, and we don't need to call BeginMediaEdits or AddMediaSample or EndMediaEdits. The skin media handler takes care of all the details of storing the content and drag region masks in the skin media.

Skinned Movie Playback

So now we know how to build a skinned movie, using either the QuickTime XML importer or our own application code. As mentioned earlier, we also want our application to be able to open and play back skinned movies. This turns out to be significantly more complicated, however, since we need to be able to assign a custom window shape to a movie window and window shapes are handled by the application, not by QuickTime. So, we're going to have to get acquainted with some of the low-level, window-handling capabilities of our host operating systems if we want to be able to open and manipulate skinned movies.

On Macintosh operating systems, we assign a custom shape to a movie window by writing a custom *window definition procedure*. Under Carbon, the code for a custom window definition procedure is contained in the application itself, not in a code resource of type 'WDEF' (as in the pre-Carbon Mac world). Once we've defined our custom procedure, we can call the Create-CustomWindow function to create a skinned movie window. Whenever the Window Manager needs to draw our custom window or handle clicks in it, it calls our custom window definition procedure.

On Windows operating systems, it's even easier to assign a custom shape to a window: we can call the SetWindowRgn function when opening the movie window to assign an arbitrary region as the window shape. We'll also add a little code to our basic movie window procedure QTFrame_MovieWndProc to handle skinned window dragging.

Before we can do any of this, however, we need to get hold of the skin data that determines the window's appearance and drag behavior. That is, we need to read the content and drag region masks out of the skinned movie file. As you might guess, we'll use `GetMediaPublicInfo` to get the picture data stored in the skin track. Then we'll need to convert that picture into a region, which we'll pass to the operating system window handlers.

Setting Up the Application Data

For each skinned movie file we open, we need to maintain some application-specific data. In particular, we need a place to keep track of the various regions describing the geometry of the skinned movie window. In the file `ComApplication.h`, we'll declare the `ApplicationDataRecord` data structure like this:

```
typedef struct ApplicationDataRecord {
  RgnHandle           fContentRegion;           // content region of window
  RgnHandle           fDragRegion;              // drag region of window
  RgnHandle           fStructRegion;            // structure region of window
#if TARGET_OS_WIN32
  HRGN                fWinHRGN;                 // window region
#endif
} ApplicationDataRecord, *ApplicationDataPtr, **ApplicationDataHdl;
```

The `fContentRegion` and `fDragRegion` fields hold handles to the content region and the drag region of the window, which we retrieve from the skin track as we're opening a skinned movie. The `fStructRegion` field holds the structure region of the skinned window. A window's *structure region* is the entire screen area occupied by the window, including the window's content region and its window frame. For skinned movies, the structure region is usually identical to its content region. The `fWinHRGN` field holds the window content region as an object of type `HRGN`. This is the object we'll pass to Set-WindowRgn when we set the window's shape on Windows.

Recall that the data stored in a skin track is of type `PicHandle`. We can retrieve that data by calling `GetMediaPublicInfo`, passing it a selector for the type of information we want. For instance, to retrieve the content region mask from a skin track, we can execute this code:

```
myPicture = (PicHandle)NewHandle(0);
myErr = MediaGetPublicInfo(myHandler, FOUR_CHAR_CODE('skcr'), myPicture,
        NULL);
```

If `GetMediaPublicInfo` completes successfully, `myPicture` will contain a handle to the picture data. We then need to convert this picture data into a region, since that's the kind of data we'll need to work with in our custom window definition procedure. We make this conversion by calling the application function `QTSkin_ConvertPictureToRegion`:

```
myErr = QTSkin_ConvertPictureToRegion(myPicture,
          &(**myAppData).fContentRegion);
```

QTSkin_ConvertPictureToRegion creates a region that contains every non-white pixel in the specified picture. The key step is using QuickDraw's Bit-mapToRegion function to convert a bitmap or a pixel map into a region. So we need to create a pixel map from our picture data. But this is very easy: we simply create a new offscreen graphics world and draw the picture data into it. We can then use the GetGWorldPixMap function to get the pixel map associated with that graphics world. Listing 3.5 shows our definition of QTSkin_ConvertPictureToRegion.

Listing 3.5 Converting a picture into a region.

```
OSErr QTSkin_ConvertPictureToRegion (PicHandle thePicture, RgnHandle *theRegionPtr)
{
    Rect            myRect;
    GWorldPtr       myGWorld = NULL;
    PixMapHandle    myPixMap = NULL;
    CGrafPtr        mySavedPort = NULL;
    GDHandle        mySavedDevice = NULL;
    RgnHandle       myRegion = NULL;
    OSErr           myErr = noErr;

    if ((thePicture == NULL) || (theRegionPtr == NULL))
      return(paramErr);

    // get the current graphics port and device
    GetGWorld(&mySavedPort, &mySavedDevice);

    // get the bounding box of the picture
    myRect = (**thePicture).picFrame;
    myRect.bottom = EndianS16_BtoN(myRect.bottom);
    myRect.right = EndianS16_BtoN(myRect.right);

    // create a new GWorld and draw the picture into it
    myErr = QTNewGWorld(&myGWorld, k1MonochromePixelFormat, &myRect, NULL, NULL,
            kICMTempThenAppMemory);
    if (myGWorld == NULL)
      goto bail;

    SetGWorld(myGWorld, NULL);

    myPixMap = GetGWorldPixMap(myGWorld);
    if (myPixMap == NULL)
      goto bail;
```

```
  LockPixels(myPixMap);
  HLock((Handle)myPixMap);

  EraseRect(&myRect);
  DrawPicture(thePicture, &myRect);

  // create a new region and convert the pixmap into a region
  myRegion = NewRgn();
  myErr = MemError();
  if (myErr != noErr)
    goto bail;

  myErr = BitMapToRegion(myRegion, (BitMap *)*myPixMap);

bail:
  if (myErr != noErr) {
    if (myRegion != NULL) {
      DisposeRgn(myRegion);
      myRegion = NULL;
    }
  }

  if (myGWorld != NULL)
    DisposeGWorld(myGWorld);

  // restore the original graphics port and device
  SetGWorld(mySavedPort, mySavedDevice);

  *theRegionPtr = myRegion;

  return(myErr);
}
```

For our Windows applications, we need to take one further step and convert the Macintosh region (of type RgnHandle) into a Windows region (of type HRGN). The QuickTime Media Layer provides a function that will do this for us:

```
(**myAppData).fWinHRGN = MacRegionToNativeRegion
                    ((**myAppData).fContentRegion);
```

All of this start-up code will go into the function QTSkin_InitWindowData, which is called by QTApp_SetupWindowObject to perform any application-specific initialization of the movie window and its associated data. QTApp_SetupWindowObject contains this code to handle skinned movies:

```
if (QTSkin_IsSkinnedMovie(myMovie)) {
  // hide the controller bar
  MCSetVisible(myMC, false);

  // detach the controller
  MCSetControllerAttached(myMC, false);

  // initialize the window data for a skinned movie
  (**theWindowObject).fAppData =
        (Handle)QTSkin_InitWindowData(theWindowObject);
}
```

When QTApp_SetupWindowObject is called, the skinned movie window has already been created, but it has not yet been displayed to the user. On Windows, we used our standard function QTFrame_CreateMovieWindow to create the movie window. So at this point, on Windows, we can already call Set-WindowRgn to set the shape of the skinned movie window:

```
if ((**myAppData).fWinHRGN != NULL) {
  RECT       myRect;
  int        myResult;

  GetRgnBox((**myAppData).fWinHRGN, &myRect);

  OffsetRgn((**myAppData).fWinHRGN,
    -myRect.left + GetSystemMetrics(SM_CXFRAME),
    -myRect.top + GetSystemMetrics(SM_CYCAPTION) +
              GetSystemMetrics(SM_CYFRAME));
  myResult = SetWindowRgn((**theWindowObject).fWindow,
              (**myAppData).fWinHRGN, true);
}
```

SetWindowRgn sets the visible region of a window; it expects the origin of the window region we pass it to be relative to the upper-left corner of the window, not relative to the client area of the window. So we need to offset the stored window region (**myAppData).fWinHRGN horizontally by the width of the window frame and vertically by the height of the window frame and the height of the title bar (or caption). Figure 3.7 shows the penguin window with these offsets.

As far as Windows is concerned, the window frame and window controls still exist—they just are not visible on the screen. The window is a full-fledged MDI child window, just like any of our other (nonskinned) movie windows. The only difference is that the skinned movie window has a special visible region.

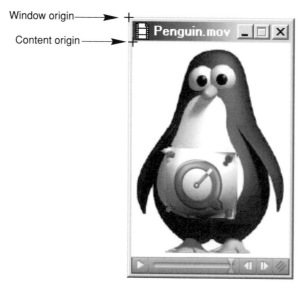

Window origin

Content origin

Figure 3.7 The client region offsets.

Listing 3.6 shows the full version of our skinned movie window initialization code.

Listing 3.6 Initializing the application data for a skinned movie.

```
ApplicationDataHdl QTSkin_InitWindowData (WindowObject theWindowObject)
{
  ApplicationDataHdl      myAppData = NULL;
  Track                   myTrack = NULL;
  MediaHandler            myHandler = NULL;
  PicHandle               myPicture = NULL;
  MatrixRecord            myMatrix;
  OSErr                   myErr = noErr;

  // if we already have some window data, dump it
  myAppData = (ApplicationDataHdl)QTFrame_GetAppDataFromWindowObject(theWindowObject);
  if (myAppData != NULL)
    QTSkin_DumpWindowData(theWindowObject);      // see Listing 3.14

  myAppData = (ApplicationDataHdl)NewHandleClear(sizeof(ApplicationDataRecord));
  if (myAppData != NULL) {
```

```
        myTrack = GetMovieIndTrackType((**theWindowObject).fMovie, 1, SkinMediaType,
                movieTrackCharacteristic);
    if (myTrack != NULL) {
      myHandler = GetMediaHandler(GetTrackMedia(myTrack));
      if (myHandler != NULL) {

          // get the current movie matrix
          GetMovieMatrix((**theWindowObject).fMovie, &myMatrix);

          myPicture = (PicHandle)NewHandle(0);
          if (myPicture == NULL)
            goto bail;

          // get the content region picture
          myErr = MediaGetPublicInfo(myHandler, FOUR_CHAR_CODE('skcr'), myPicture, NULL);
          if (myErr != noErr)
            goto bail;

          // convert it to a region
          myErr = QTSkin_ConvertPictureToRegion(myPicture, &(**myAppData).fContentRegion);
          if (myErr != noErr)
            goto bail;

          // scale that region so the window scales with the movie
          myErr = TransformRgn(&myMatrix, (**myAppData).fContentRegion);
          if (myErr != noErr)
            goto bail;

#if TARGET_OS_WIN32
          (**myAppData).fWinHRGN = MacRegionToNativeRegion((**myAppData).fContentRegion);
          if ((**myAppData).fWinHRGN != NULL) {
            RECT        myRect;
            int         myResult;

            GetRgnBox((**myAppData).fWinHRGN, &myRect);
            // the coordinates of a window region are relative to the upper-left corner
            // of the window (not to the client area of the window)
            OffsetRgn((**myAppData).fWinHRGN,
              -myRect.left + GetSystemMetrics(SM_CXFRAME),
              -myRect.top + GetSystemMetrics(SM_CYCAPTION) + GetSystemMetrics(SM_CYFRAME));
            myResult = SetWindowRgn((**theWindowObject).fWindow,
              (**myAppData).fWinHRGN, true);
```

```
          if (myResult == 0) {
            // SetWindowRgn failed
            DeleteObject((**myAppData).fWinHRGN);
            (**myAppData).fWinHRGN = NULL;
            goto bail;
          }
        }
      }
#endif

      // repeat with drag region picture
      myErr = MediaGetPublicInfo(myHandler, FOUR_CHAR_CODE('skdr'), myPicture, NULL);
      if (myErr != noErr)
        goto bail;

      // convert it to a region
      myErr = QTSkin_ConvertPictureToRegion(myPicture, &(**myAppData).fDragRegion);
      if (myErr != noErr)
        goto bail;

      // scale that region so the window scales with the movie
      myErr = TransformRgn(&myMatrix, (**myAppData).fDragRegion);
      if (myErr != noErr)
        goto bail;

      // copy the content region into the structure region
      (**myAppData).fStructRegion = NewRgn();
      MacCopyRgn((**myAppData).fContentRegion, (**myAppData).fStructRegion);
    }
  }
}

bail:
  if (myPicture != NULL)
    DisposeHandle((Handle)myPicture);

  return(myAppData);
}
```

Specifying a Custom Window Shape

As we've seen, it's child's play on Windows operating systems to specify a custom window shape: just pass the shape (as an HRGN) to SetWindowRgn. On the Mac, it's quite a bit more complicated. We need to write a custom window definition procedure and attach it to any skinned movies that the user opens. In our framework function QTFrame_OpenMovieInWindow, we'll add a few Mac-specific lines before the existing call to QTFrame_CreateMovieWindow:

```
#if TARGET_OS_MAC
  // create a new window to display the movie in
  if (QTSkin_IsSkinnedMovie(myMovie))
    myWindow = QTSkin_CreateSkinsWindow();
  else
#endif
    myWindow = QTFrame_CreateMovieWindow();
```

On Macintosh computers, QTFrame_CreateMovieWindow calls the Window Manager function NewCWindow to create a standard document window. For skinned windows, we need to call CreateCustomWindow, as shown in Listing 3.7.

Listing 3.7 Opening a window with a custom shape.

```
WindowReference QTSkin_CreateSkinsWindow (void)
{
  WindowPtr                myWindow = NULL;
  WindowReference          myWindowRef = NULL;
  Rect                     myRect = {10, 60, 200, 200};

  // call CreateCustomWindow to create a window using our custom window defproc
  CreateCustomWindow(&gDefSpec, kDocumentWindowClass, kWindowNoAttributes,
    &myRect, &myWindow);
  if (myWindow != NULL) {
    // get the "window reference" for this window
    myWindowRef = QTFrame_GetWindowReferenceFromWindow(myWindow);

    // create a new window object associated with the new window
    QTFrame_CreateWindowObject(myWindowRef);
  }

  return(myWindowRef);
}
```

This call to CreateCustomWindow asks for a document window with no special attributes. (The rectangle parameter is arbitrary, since we'll change the window size later.) The window definition procedure to be used to handle the custom window is specified by the &gDefSpec parameter, which is a pointer to a *window definition specification*, declared like this:

```
struct WindowDefSpec {
  WindowDefType              defType;
  union {
    WindowDefUPP             defProc;
    Void                     *classRef;
    Short                    procID;
  } u;
};
```

The `defType` field specifies which member of the union u we want to use. In the present case, we want to use the `defProc` member, so we set `defType` to `kWindowDefProcPtr`. And we'll set the `defProc` member to a universal procedure pointer for our custom window definition procedure. We initialize the `gDefSpec` global variable in the application start-up code for QTSkins by calling the `QTSkin_Init` function defined in Listing 3.8.

Listing 3.8 Setting up a window definition specification.

```
void QTSkin_Init (void)
{
  // set up the window definition specification structure
  gDefSpec.defType = kWindowDefProcPtr;
  gDefSpec.u.defProc = NewWindowDefUPP(QTSkin_SkinWindowDef);
}
```

Writing a Custom Window Definition Procedure

On Macintosh operating systems, the appearance and behavior of our skinned movie windows are determined by `QTSkin_SkinWindowDef`, our custom window definition procedure. `QTSkin_SkinWindowDef` is declared like this:

```
static PASCAL_RTN long QTSkin_SkinWindowDef
  (short theVarCode, WindowRef theWindow, short theMessage, long theParam);
```

Here, `theMessage` is a *window definition message* that indicates which task the window definition procedure is to perform. These are the common window definition messages:

```
enum {
    kWindowMsgDraw                          = 0,
    kWindowMsgHitTest                       = 1,
    kWindowMsgCalculateShape                = 2,
    kWindowMsgInitialize                    = 3,
    kWindowMsgCleanUp                       = 4,
    kWindowMsgDrawGrowOutline               = 5,
    kWindowMsgDrawGrowBox                   = 6,
    kWindowMsgGetFeatures                   = 7,
    kWindowMsgGetRegion                     = 8,
    kWindowMsgDragHilite                    = 9,
    kWindowMsgModified                      = 10,
    kWindowMsgDrawInCurrentPort             = 11,
    kWindowMsgSetupProxyDragImage           = 12,
    kWindowMsgStateChanged                  = 13,
    kWindowMsgMeasureTitle                  = 14,
    kWindowMsgGetGrowImageRegion            = 19
};
```

We can ignore most of these messages in our procedure. For instance, our skinned movie windows don't have grow boxes, so we can ignore the kWindowMsgDrawGrowOutline and kWindowMsgDrawGrowBox messages. In fact, we'll need to handle only three of these messages: kWindowMsgHitTest, kWindowMsgGetFeatures, and kWindowMsgGetRegion.

When we receive the kWindowMsgGetFeatures message, we need to return (through theParam) a value that indicates the capabilities of our custom window definition procedure. Really all our custom procedure can do is return information about various window regions. So we'll set the features information like this:

```
case kWindowMsgGetFeatures:
  if (theParam != 0L)
    *(OptionBits *)theParam = kWindowCanGetWindowRegion | kWindowIsOpaque;
  return(1);
```

The meaning of the return value of our custom window definition procedure varies, depending on the message the procedure is handling. In this case, the documentation tells us to return 1.

When we receive the kWindowMsgHitTest message, we need to return one of these values, indicating the region of the movie (if any) that was clicked:

```
enum {
  wNoHit                          = 0,
  wInContent                      = 1,
  wInDrag                         = 2,
  wInGrow                         = 3,
  wInGoAway                       = 4,
  wInZoomIn                       = 5,
  wInZoomOut                      = 6,
  wInCollapseBox                  = 9,
  wInProxyIcon                    = 10
};
```

With this message, theParam contains the coordinates of the mouse click, which we can extract like this:

```
myPoint.v = HiWord(theParam);
myPoint.h = LoWord(theParam);
```

This point is in global screen coordinates. Our regions, however, are stored with the upper-left corner set to (0, 0). So we need to map myPoint into the window's local coordinate system, as follows:

```
GetPort(&myPort);
SetPortWindowPort(theWindow);

myLocal = myPoint;
GlobalToLocal(&myLocal);

MacSetPort(myPort);
```

The GlobalToLocal function maps the specified point into the coordinate system of the current graphics port, so we need to make sure that our custom window is the current graphics port (taking care to save and restore the previous current port).

Now that we've got a point local to the skinned movie window, we can use the PtInRgn function to do the required hit testing:

```
if (PtInRgn(myLocal, (**myAppData).fDragRegion))
  return(wInDrag);

if (PtInRgn(myLocal, (**myAppData).fContentRegion))
  return(wInContent);

return(wNoHit);
```

We first look to see whether the specified point is in the drag region. If not, we look to see whether it's in the content region. If the point is in neither region, we indicate that no hit occurred.

When we receive the kWindowMsgGetRegion message, theParam is a pointer to a structure of type GetWindowRegionRec:

```
struct GetWindowRegionRec {
  RgnHandle                     winRgn;
  WindowRegionCode              regionCode;
};
```

The regionCode field indicates which region we are supposed to return (through the winRgn field). Our skinned movie windows have only three interesting regions, the content region, the drag region, and the structure region (which is typically identical to the content region). So we'll respond to only three values for the regionCode field: kWindowContentRgn, kWindowDrag-Rgn, and kWindowStructureRgn.

The region whose handle we return in the winRgn field is supposed to be specified in global screen coordinates. Our stored regions, however, are specified in coordinates local to the client region of the movie window. So we need to offset those regions before we return them from our window definition procedure. First, then, we need to figure out the global coordinates of the top-left corner of the window, like this:

```
GetPort(&myPort);
SetPortWindowPort(theWindow);

GetPortBounds(GetWindowPort(theWindow), &myPortBounds);

myTopLeft.h = myPortBounds.left;
myTopLeft.v = myPortBounds.top;
LocalToGlobal(&myTopLeft);

MacSetPort(myPort);
```

Then we need to offset any of the regions we pass back. For instance, we'll pass back the window's drag region like this:

```
MacCopyRgn((**myAppData).fDragRegion, myRgnRec->winRgn);
MacOffsetRgn(myRgnRec->winRgn, myTopLeft.h, myTopLeft.v);
```

Listing 3.9 shows our complete window definition procedure for skinned movie windows.

Listing 3.9 Handling skinned movie window messages.

```
static PASCAL_RTN long QTSkin_SkinWindowDef
  (short theVarCode, WindowRef theWindow, short theMessage, long theParam)
{
#pragma unused(theVarCode)

  switch (theMessage) {

    case kWindowMsgInitialize:
    case kWindowMsgCleanUp:
    case kWindowMsgDrawGrowOutline:
    case kWindowMsgDrawGrowBox:
    case kWindowMsgDraw:
      // nothing here
      break;

    case kWindowMsgHitTest: {
      ApplicationDataHdl     myAppData = NULL;
      Point                  myPoint;
      Point                  myLocal;
      GrafPtr                myPort;

      myAppData = (ApplicationDataHdl)QTFrame_GetAppDataFromWindow
                     (QTFrame_GetWindowReferenceFromWindow(theWindow));
      if (myAppData == NULL)
        return(wNoHit);

      // on entry, theParam contains the mouse location in global screen coordinates
      myPoint.v = HiWord(theParam);
      myPoint.h = LoWord(theParam);

      // the content and drag regions are offset relative to the window origin
      GetPort(&myPort);
      SetPortWindowPort(theWindow);

      myLocal = myPoint;
      GlobalToLocal(&myLocal);

      MacSetPort(myPort);

      // look first to see if the mouse event is in the drag region;
      // it takes precedence over the content region
      if (PtInRgn(myLocal, (**myAppData).fDragRegion))
        return(wInDrag);
```

```
      if (PtInRgn(myLocal, (**myAppData).fContentRegion))
        return(wInContent);

      return(wNoHit);
    }

    case kWindowMsgGetFeatures:
      if (theParam != 0L)
        *(OptionBits *)theParam = kWindowCanGetWindowRegion | kWindowIsOpaque;
      return(1);

    case kWindowMsgGetRegion: {
      GetWindowRegionRec      *myRgnRec = (GetWindowRegionRec *)theParam;
      ApplicationDataHdl      myAppData = NULL;
      GrafPtr                 myPort;
      Rect                    myPortBounds;
      Point                   myTopLeft;

      myAppData = (ApplicationDataHdl)QTFrame_GetAppDataFromWindow
                      (QTFrame_GetWindowReferenceFromWindow(theWindow));
      if (myAppData == NULL)
        break;

      // get the top-left corner of the window, in global coordinates
      GetPort(&myPort);
      SetPortWindowPort(theWindow);

#if TARGET_API_MAC_CARBON
      GetPortBounds(GetWindowPort(theWindow), &myPortBounds);
#else
      myPortBounds = theWindow->portRect;
#endif
      myTopLeft.h = myPortBounds.left;
      myTopLeft.v = myPortBounds.top;
      LocalToGlobal(&myTopLeft);

      MacSetPort(myPort);

      switch (myRgnRec->regionCode) {
        case kWindowTitleBarRgn:
        case kWindowCloseBoxRgn:
          break;

        case kWindowDragRgn:
          MacCopyRgn((**myAppData).fDragRegion, myRgnRec->winRgn);
          MacOffsetRgn(myRgnRec->winRgn, myTopLeft.h, myTopLeft.v);
          break;
```

```
      case kWindowContentRgn:
        MacCopyRgn((**myAppData).fContentRegion, myRgnRec->winRgn);
        MacOffsetRgn(myRgnRec->winRgn, myTopLeft.h, myTopLeft.v);
        break;

      case kWindowStructureRgn:
        MacCopyRgn((**myAppData).fStructRegion, myRgnRec->winRgn);
        MacOffsetRgn(myRgnRec->winRgn, myTopLeft.h, myTopLeft.v);
        break;

      default:
        break;
    }

    return(noErr);
    }

  default:
    break;
  }

  return(0L);
}
```

Handling Dragging on Windows Computers

Earlier we saw how to assign a custom window shape to a movie on Windows operating systems, by calling SetWindowRgn. We still need to see how to handle window dragging on Windows. Let's begin by reviewing briefly how our window procedure for movie windows processes the messages it receives. Listing 3.10 shows a snippet from QTFrame_MovieWndProc. First of all, it fills out an MSG structure and translates the Windows message into a Macintosh event by calling WinEventToMacEvent. Then it passes the Mac event to the application function QTApp_HandleEvent. Then, if QTApp_HandleEvent did not handle the event, QTFrame_MovieWndProc passes the Mac event to MCIsPlayerEvent.

Listing 3.10 Sending Windows messages to the movie controller.

```
MSG         myMsg = {0};
LONG        myPoints = GetMessagePos();

myMsg.hwnd = theWnd;
myMsg.message = theMessage;
myMsg.wParam = wParam;
```

```
myMsg.lParam = lParam;
myMsg.time = GetMessageTime();
myMsg.pt.x = LOWORD(myPoints);
myMsg.pt.y = HIWORD(myPoints);

// translate a Windows event to a Mac event
WinEventToMacEvent(&myMsg, &myMacEvent);

// let the application-specific code have a chance to intercept the event
myIsHandled = QTApp_HandleEvent(&myMacEvent);

// pass the Mac event to the movie controller
if (!myIsHandled)
  if (myMC != NULL)
    if (!IsIconic(theWnd))
      myIsHandled = MCIsPlayerEvent(myMC, (EventRecord *)&myMacEvent);
```

With skinned windows, the drag regions and the content regions virtually always overlap, so we need to prevent the movie controller from getting any mouse clicks that are in the drag region (since it would likely interpret them as clicks in the content region). We can do this quite easily by having QTApp_HandleEvent look to see whether the event it's passed is a mouse click in the drag region and, if it is, return true. Listing 3.11 shows the QTSkins version of QTApp_HandleEvent. Note that this code is conditionalized for Windows applications only, since on Macintosh the window definition procedure is responsible for finding clicks in the drag region.

Listing 3.11 Looking for drag region clicks (Windows).

```
Boolean QTApp_HandleEvent (EventRecord *theEvent)
{
#if TARGET_OS_MAC
#pragma unused(theEvent)
#endif

  Boolean            myIsHandled = false;

#if TARGET_OS_WIN32
  ApplicationDataHdl myAppData = (ApplicationDataHdl)QTFrame_GetAppDataFromFrontWindow();
  Point              myPoint;

  if (theEvent == NULL)
    goto bail;
```

```
    if (theEvent->what == mouseDown) {
      myPoint = theEvent->where;
      GlobalToLocal(&myPoint);

      if (myAppData != NULL)
        if (PtInRgn(myPoint, (**myAppData).fDragRegion))
          myIsHandled = true;
    }
#endif

bail:
  return(myIsHandled);
}
```

So far, then, we've managed to prevent the movie controller associated with a movie window from getting clicks in the window's drag region. Now we need to actually handle those clicks. On Windows, we can look for messages of type WM_LBUTTONDOWN and see if they are in the drag region. If they are, we want to trick the default window procedure into thinking that the clicks are on the title bar so that the default window procedure will handle the dragging for us. We can do this by sending a message of type WM_NCLBUTTONDOWN to the default window procedure, like this:

```
SendMessage(theWnd, WM_NCLBUTTONDOWN, (WPARAM)HTCAPTION, MAKELPARAM(5, 5));
```

The WM_NCLBUTTONDOWN message reports a button-down event in a nonclient area of a window. The first parameter indicates which part of the window is directly under the cursor hotspot at the time of the click. In our case, we want to say that the click occurred in the title bar (indicated by the HTCAPTION constant). The second parameter indicates the location of the cursor hotspot, in coordinates that are relative to the upper-left corner of the screen. As best I can tell, the default window procedure ignores that parameter when the first parameter is set to HTCAPTION. So we'll pass an arbitrary value of (5, 5). Our complete left-button click handling is shown in Listing 3.12.

Listing 3.12 Handling drag region clicks (Windows).

```
case WM_LBUTTONDOWN:
  // handle potential clicks in window drag region;
  // if we get one, map it into a click on the title bar
  if (QTSkin_IsSkinnedMovie(myMovie))
    if (QTSkin_IsDragClick(myWindowObject, lParam)) {
      SendMessage(theWnd, WM_NCLBUTTONDOWN, (WPARAM)HTCAPTION, MAKELPARAM(5, 5));
      myIsHandled = true;
    }
```

```
  // do any application-specific mouse-button handling,
  // but only if the message hasn't already been handled
  if (!myIsHandled)
    QTApp_HandleContentClick(theWnd, &myMacEvent);

  break;
```

The only thing left to consider is the definition of QTSkin_IsDragClick, which we call in Listing 3.12 to determine whether the specified point is in the drag region of the skinned movie window. Here we have several possibilities. We saw above that our version of QTApp_HandleEvent returns true if the specified event is a mouse-down event in the window's drag region. So we could just use that function. Alternatively, we can convert the Mac-style drag region (saved in our application data record) to a Windows region (of type HRGN) and call the Windows function PtInRegion to see whether the specified point is in that region. That's the strategy we'll use here; Listing 3.13 shows our definition of QTSkin_IsDragClick.

Listing 3.13 Finding drag region clicks (Windows).

```
#if TARGET_OS_WIN32
Boolean QTSkin_IsDragClick (WindowObject theWindowObject, LONG lParam)
{
  WindowObject        myWindowObject = NULL;
  ApplicationDataHdl  myAppData = NULL;
  HRGN                myRegion = NULL;
  POINT               myPoint;
  Boolean             isDragClick = false;

  myAppData = (ApplicationDataHdl)QTFrame_GetAppDataFromWindowObject(theWindowObject);
  if (myAppData != NULL) {
    myPoint.x = LOWORD(lParam);
    myPoint.y = HIWORD(lParam);

    myRegion = MacRegionToNativeRegion((**myAppData).fDragRegion);
    if (PtInRegion(myRegion, myPoint.x, myPoint.y))
      isDragClick = true;

    DeleteObject(myRegion);
  }

  return(isDragClick);
}
#endif
```

The lParam parameter that was passed to WM_LBUTTONDOWN (which we also pass to QTSkin_IsDragClick) specifies a point in coordinates that are local to the client area of the window. As a result, we don't need to offset the drag region in Listing 3.13. So now we've completely handled a click in the drag region of a skinned movie window on Windows.

Shutting Down

When the user closes a skinned movie window, we need to deallocate any memory used for displaying the movie in a skin. In particular, we need to dispose of the window regions that we're storing in the application data record. Listing 3.14 shows the definition of QTSkin_DumpWindowData, which is called by QTApp_RemoveWindowObject.

Listing 3.14 Cleaning up when a skinned window is closed.

```
void QTSkin_DumpWindowData (WindowObject theWindowObject)
{
   ApplicationDataHdl                  myAppData = NULL;

   myAppData = (ApplicationDataHdl)QTFrame_GetAppDataFromWindowObject(theWindowObject);
   if (myAppData != NULL) {
     if ((**myAppData).fContentRegion != NULL)
       DisposeRgn((**myAppData).fContentRegion);

     if ((**myAppData).fDragRegion != NULL)
       DisposeRgn((**myAppData).fDragRegion);

     if ((**myAppData).fStructRegion != NULL)
       DisposeRgn((**myAppData).fStructRegion);

     DisposeHandle((Handle)myAppData);
     (**theWindowObject).fAppData = NULL;
   }
}
```

You'll notice that we didn't do anything to free up the memory addressed by (**myAppData).fWinHRGN. The documentation for the SetWindowRgn function indicates that the operating system owns the region we pass it; this means that we don't need to call DeleteObject on that region.

When our application shuts down, we need to deallocate the universal procedure pointer contained inside of the gDefSpec structure. Listing 3.15 shows how we do this.

Listing 3.15 Cleaning up at application shutdown.

```
void QTSkin_Stop (void)
{
  // dispose of the window procedure UPP
  if (gDefSpec.u.defProc != NULL)
    DisposeWindowDefUPP(gDefSpec.u.defProc);
}
```

▶ Conclusion

If you've made it this far, you deserve a pat on the back. We've had our usual dose of new QuickTime APIs, but we've also had a big gulp of low-level window management. On the Macintosh, we had to write a custom window definition procedure in order for our application to handle skinned movie windows. And on Windows, we had to tinker with our application's event handling to support skinned movie window dragging. But it's certainly worth the effort, precisely because skinned movies are such great stuff. As we've noted, the movie author now has virtually complete control over the appearance and behavior of movie windows. The movie interface has become part of the movie content. The medium is now part of the message.

Captured

Using the Sequence Grabber to Capture Video and Sound

▶ Introduction

From its inception, QuickTime has included the ability to capture video and sound data from devices attached to a computer. These devices include camcorders, laserdisk players, televisions, and videocassette recorders. We can capture sound alone using an internal or external microphone, or by attaching a CD player or other sound-only device to the computer.

On the Macintosh models available in the early days of QuickTime, special add-on hardware (usually in the form of a NuBus or PCI card) was required to digitize an analog stream from an external device. Some models, beginning with the Power Macintosh 6100AV, included built-in audiovisual hardware that allowed the user to connect external devices to RCA-type or S-video connectors. Nowadays, all Macintosh computers (and many Windows computers) support FireWire connections, which allow a pure digital stream of audiovisual data to be sent to the computer from camcorders and other devices.

At the lowest level, QuickTime interacts with video and sound hardware using software modules called *video digitizer components* (or just *video digitizers*) and *sound input device drivers*. A video digitizer component digitizes the video data stream, if necessary, and often provides additional services such as resizing the video, clipping out portions of the video, and converting colors in the video. A sound input device driver manages communications between applications and the sound input hardware.

Normally, however, we don't work with video digitizers or sound input device drivers directly. Instead, we'll work with a *sequence grabber component*, a part of QuickTime that provides a set of high-level APIs for capturing video and sound data. Since there is virtually always just one available sequence grabber component, we'll usually talk about *the* sequence grabber. The sequence grabber insulates us from having to know about any of the low-level details of video digitizers and sound input device drivers, and it provides some additional capabilities. We can use the sequence grabber to display video in a window, capture individual frames of video as pictures, and capture sequences of video frames as QuickTime movies. The sequence grabber can also capture sound data and synchronize the video and sound streams when displaying them in a window or capturing them to a movie file.

In this chapter, we're going to see how to use the sequence grabber to capture video and sound data. We'll develop an application, called QTCapture, which can capture video and sound from any available devices. The Test menu of QTCapture (on Windows, for a change) is shown in Figure 4.1. The first two menu items display dialog boxes that allow us to configure the video and sound capture settings. For instance, we can set the video or sound source (the device from which we want to capture data) and the desired compression to be applied to the captured data. The third and fourth menu items allow us to specify whether we want to capture video, sound, or both. Using the Split Track Files menu item, we can specify that the captured video and sound data be written to different files. (By default, the sequence grabber writes the video and sound data into the same output file.) The next block of menu items allows us to select the size of the *monitor window*, the window in which the incoming video stream is displayed.

Figure 4.2 shows QTCapture's monitor window at its default size. We use the last menu item to begin recording data to a file; in QTCapture, the recording stops when the user clicks the mouse button. We'll begin by taking a look at the sequence grabber and where it fits into the QuickTime architecture. Then we'll see how to monitor the captured data, adjust the capture settings, and write the captured data into a file.

Sequence Grabber Overview

The sequence grabber is the part of QuickTime that can be used to monitor video and sound sources, capture images and sequences of images, and synchronize captured sound and video. The sequence grabber provides two main services to applications: previewing and recording. To *preview* a data source is to display the captured data in a window on the screen (if it's visual data) or to play back the captured data through the sound output hardware (if it's audio data). To *record* a data source is to write the captured data into one or more files on disk.

In QuickTime version 2.5, the sequence grabber gained the ability to capture text data, using text digitizer components. A *text digitizer component* captures text data from external sources, such as the closed-captioned data

Test		
Video Settings...	Ctrl+1
Sound Settings...	Ctrl+2
✔ Record Video	Ctrl+3
✔ Record Sound	Ctrl+4
Split Track Files	Ctrl+5
Quarter Size	Ctrl+6
✔ Half Size	Ctrl+7
Full Size	Ctrl+8
Record	Ctrl+R

Figure 4.1 The Test menu of QTCapture.

Figure 4.2 The monitor window of QTCapture.

embedded in some television broadcasts. The process of capturing text is entirely analogous to the process of capturing video or sound, and it would be easy to extend our sample application QTCapture to also capture text data and record it into a text track in a QuickTime movie. Because very few computers are equipped to capture text data, however, we won't consider the sequence grabber's text capturing abilities further.

A sequence grabber component does not communicate directly with either a video digitizer or a sound input device driver. Instead, it communicates with one or more *sequence grabber channel components*. The sequence grabber channel components, in turn, communicate with the video digitizer components and sound input device drivers. Channel components send control information to them and receive digitized data from them; the digitized data is then passed to other parts of QuickTime for previewing or recording.

A sequence grabber component is also responsible for displaying any dialog boxes required to elicit capture settings from the user, such as the video

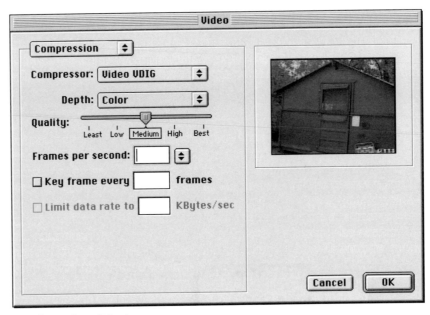

Figure 4.3 The video settings dialog box.

settings dialog box shown in Figure 4.3. To do this, a sequence grabber component calls a *sequence grabber panel component*. A panel component then communicates with a channel component or the digitizer component to get and set the capture settings.

Opening the Sequence Grabbing Components

In practice, our applications need to work directly with only three components: a sequence grabber component and two sequence grabber channel components. QTCapture permits only one preview or record operation at a time, so it uses some global variables to keep track of these three components:

```
SeqGrabComponent       gSeqGrabber = NULL;
SGChannel              gVideoChannel = 0;
SGChannel              gSoundChannel = 0;
```

We'll open an instance of a sequence grabber component by calling the OpenDefaultComponent function, like this:

```
gSeqGrabber = OpenDefaultComponent(SeqGrabComponentType, 0);
```

We then need to initialize this component by calling the SGInitialize function:

```
myErr = SGInitialize(gSeqGrabber);
```

SGInitialize allocates any additional memory the sequence grabber may need and performs other necessary setup for subsequent previewing and recording.

Since we are going to be previewing video data, we need to tell the sequence grabber where to draw the previewed data. We do this by calling the SGSetGWorld function. With QTCapture, our monitor window is simply a dialog box, which we open like this:

```
gMonitor = GetNewDialog(kMonitorDLOGID, NULL, (WindowPtr)-1L);
```

If we successfully open this dialog box and initialize the sequence grabber, we can then set the sequence grabber's graphics world by calling SGSet-GWorld:

```
myErr = SGSetGWorld(gSeqGrabber, GetDialogPort(gMonitor), NULL);
```

It's even easier to open the two sequence grabber channel components we need; we just call SGNewChannel, passing in the media type of the data to be captured:

```
SGNewChannel(gSeqGrabber, VideoMediaType, &gVideoChannel);
SGNewChannel(gSeqGrabber, SoundMediaType, &gSoundChannel);
```

Our actual code, of course, checks the result codes returned by SGNewChannel.

Configuring Video Channels

Before we can begin previewing or recording from these channels, we need to do some preliminary configuration of the channels and of our application. The first thing we want to do is set the *channel usage flags* of the video channel. These flags tell the channel component what operations we're going to want it to perform. Currently, these channel usage flags are defined (in the file QuickTimeComponents.h):

```
enum {
  seqGrabRecord                        = 1,
  seqGrabPreview                       = 2,
  seqGrabPlayDuringRecord              = 4
};
```

The seqGrabRecord and seqGrabPreview flags tell a sequence grabber channel component that its channel will be used for recording and previewing, respectively. The seqGrabPlayDuringRecord flag indicates that we are going to want to preview the captured data while we are recording it. The previewed video may get choppier if we enable this flag (since we're devoting some processor time to recording), but at least it will continue playing.

In QTCapture, we want to enable all of these flags for the video channel. So we'll call SGSetChannelUsage like this:

```
myErr = SGSetChannelUsage(gVideoChannel,
            seqGrabPreview | seqGrabRecord | seqGrabPlayDuringRecord);
```

We also want to set the initial size of our monitor window to its default size, which is half the size of the video digitizer's *active source rectangle* (the portion of the digitizer's source rectangle that actually contains video data). We call the SGGetSrcVideoBounds function to get the size of the active source rectangle and then we resize our monitor window to half that size, using the code in Listing 4.1. (We'll see the complete definition of QTCap_Init later, in Listing 4.3.)

Listing 4.1 Setting the initial size of the monitor window.

```
short        myWidth;
short        myHeight;

myErr = SGGetSrcVideoBounds(gVideoChannel, &gActiveVideoRect);
if (myErr == noErr) {
  myWidth = (gActiveVideoRect.right – gActiveVideoRect.left) / 2;
  myHeight = (gActiveVideoRect.bottom – gActiveVideoRect.top) / 2;
  SizeWindow(GetDialogWindow(gMonitor), myWidth, myHeight, false);
}
```

The final thing we need to do is tell the channel component the size of the *display boundary rectangle,* which is the rectangle in which the previewed video data is to be displayed. We can do this by retrieving the current size of the monitor window's content region and then passing that size to the sequence grabber channel component by calling SGSetChannelBounds, like so:

```
GetPortBounds(GetDialogPort(gMonitor), &myRect);
myErr = SGSetChannelBounds(gVideoChannel, &myRect);
```

If any of this configuring should fail, then we won't be able to capture or preview data from the video source. In that case, we want to close down the video channel and set the global variable gVideoChannel to NULL, indicating that we don't have an open video channel:

```
if (myErr != noErr) {
  SGDisposeChannel(gSeqGrabber, gVideoChannel);
  gVideoChannel = NULL;
}
```

Configuring Audio Channels

Our audio channel is somewhat easier to configure. First, we want to set the channel usage, like this:

```
myErr = SGSetChannelUsage(gSoundChannel, seqGrabPreview | seqGrabRecord);
```

You'll notice that we did not set the seqGrabPlayDuringRecord flag. This makes good sense, since we don't want the channel's sound data to be played while it's being recorded. On the other hand, we do want the sound to be played while it's being previewed. Even in that case, however, we want to make sure that the volume of the sound played back is low enough to avoid any feedback that might arise if the sound input hardware (usually, the microphone) happens to be too near the speakers. So we'll call SGSet-ChannelVolume to set the sound channel volume to a fairly low setting:

```
myErr = SGSetChannelVolume(gSoundChannel, 0x0010);
```

One other thing we want to do is add some sample rates to the Rate pop-up menu in the sound settings dialog box. By default, the only rates that appear in that menu are those that the underlying sound hardware indicates it can handle natively. On most modern Macintosh computers, for instance, only the 44.1 kHz rate appears (as seen in Figure 4.4), and on slightly older models only the 44.1 kHz and 22.050 kHz rates appear. The sequence grabber provides the SGSetAdditionalSoundRates function, which we can use to add some more rates to that menu. Listing 4.2 shows the code we use to add another five common sound sample rates to the Rate pop-up menu. The expanded menu is shown in Figure 4.5.

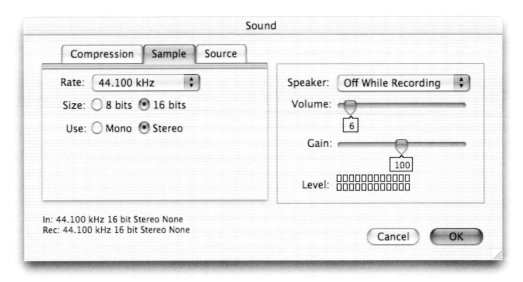

Figure 4.4 The default Rate pop-up menu.

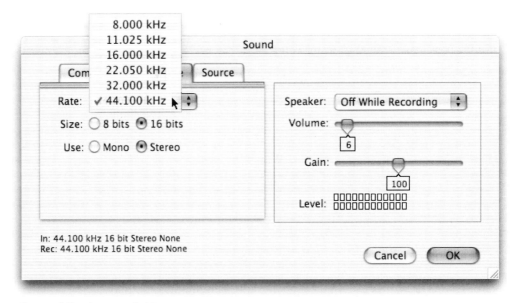

Figure 4.5 The expanded Rate pop-up menu.

Listing 4.2   Adding sample rates to the sound settings dialog box.

```
Handle          myRates = NULL;

myRates = NewHandleClear(5 * sizeof(Fixed));
if (myRates != NULL) {
  *((long *)(*myRates) + 0) = Long2Fix(8000);
  *((long *)(*myRates) + 1) = Long2Fix(11025);
  *((long *)(*myRates) + 2) = Long2Fix(16000);
  *((long *)(*myRates) + 3) = Long2Fix(22050);
  *((long *)(*myRates) + 4) = Long2Fix(32000);
  SGSetAdditionalSoundRates(gSoundChannel, myRates);

  DisposeHandle(myRates);
}
```

Once again, if any of this configuring should fail, we want to close down the sound channel and set the global variable gSoundChannel to NULL:

```
if (myErr != noErr) {
  SGDisposeChannel(gSeqGrabber, gSoundChannel);
  gSoundChannel = NULL;
}
```

▶ Previewing

Let's reflect on what we've accomplished so far. We've opened an instance of the sequence grabber component. We've also opened two sequence grabber channels—one for video and one for sound—and we've configured both of those channels. We've also opened our monitor window and resized it to its default size. We haven't yet displayed the monitor window, however, so let's do that now:

```
MacShowWindow(GetDialogWindow(gMonitor));
```

All that remains, then, is to start the previewing. We can do that with a single call:

```
myErr = SGStartPreview(gSeqGrabber);
```

We also need to make sure that the sequence grabber gets some processor time periodically. We do that by calling SGIdle fairly often. In QTCapture, we'll insert these lines of code into the application function QTApp_Idle:

```
   if (gSeqGrabber != NULL)
     SGIdle(gSeqGrabber);
```

And we're done! The application will display the captured video in the monitor window and play the captured sound through the computer's speakers. Listing 4.3 shows the complete definition of the QTCap_Init function, which performs all the necessary setup and then starts the preview rolling.

Listing 4.3 Initializing and starting the sequence grabber.

```
ComponentResult QTCap_Init (void)
{
  ComponentResult                 myErr = noErr;

  // open the sequence grabber component
  gSeqGrabber = OpenDefaultComponent(SeqGrabComponentType, 0);
  if (gSeqGrabber == NULL) {
    myErr = cantOpenHandler;
    goto bail;
  }

  // open the monitor window
  gMonitor = GetNewDialog(kMonitorDLOGID, NULL, (WindowPtr)-1L);
  if (gMonitor == NULL) {
    myErr = memFullErr;
    goto bail;
  }

  SetPortDialogPort(gMonitor);
  MacMoveWindow(GetDialogWindow(gMonitor), 10, 30 + GetMBarHeight(), 0);

  // initialize the sequence grabber
  myErr = SGInitialize(gSeqGrabber);
  if (myErr == noErr) {
    // configure the sequence grabber component
    myErr = SGSetGWorld(gSeqGrabber, GetDialogPort(gMonitor), NULL);
    if (myErr != noErr)
      goto bail;

    // create a video channel
    myErr = SGNewChannel(gSeqGrabber, VideoMediaType, &gVideoChannel);
    if ((gVideoChannel != NULL) && (myErr == noErr)) {
      short      myWidth;
      short      myHeight;
      Rect       myRect;
```

```
  myErr = SGGetSrcVideoBounds(gVideoChannel, &gActiveVideoRect);
  if (myErr == noErr) {
    myWidth = (gActiveVideoRect.right - gActiveVideoRect.left) / 2;
    myHeight = (gActiveVideoRect.bottom - gActiveVideoRect.top) / 2;
    SizeWindow(GetDialogWindow(gMonitor), myWidth, myHeight, false);
  }

  myErr = SGSetChannelUsage(gVideoChannel,
            seqGrabPreview | seqGrabRecord | seqGrabPlayDuringRecord);
  if (myErr == noErr) {
    GetPortBounds(GetDialogPort(gMonitor), &myRect);
    myErr = SGSetChannelBounds(gVideoChannel, &myRect);
  }

  // if an error occurred while configuring video channel, dispose of it
  if (myErr != noErr) {
    SGDisposeChannel(gSeqGrabber, gVideoChannel);
    gVideoChannel = NULL;
  }
}

// create a sound channel
myErr = SGNewChannel(gSeqGrabber, SoundMediaType, &gSoundChannel);
if ((gSoundChannel != NULL) && (myErr == noErr)) {
  Handle        myRates = NULL;

  myErr = SGSetChannelUsage(gSoundChannel, seqGrabPreview | seqGrabRecord);
  if (myErr == noErr) {
    // set the volume low to prevent feedback when we start the preview
    myErr = SGSetChannelVolume(gSoundChannel, 0x0010);
  }

  // add some sample rates to the sound settings dialog box Rate pop-up menu
  myRates = NewHandleClear(5 * sizeof(Fixed));
  if (myRates != NULL) {
    *((long *)(*myRates) + 0) = Long2Fix(8000);
    *((long *)(*myRates) + 1) = Long2Fix(11025);
    *((long *)(*myRates) + 2) = Long2Fix(16000);
    *((long *)(*myRates) + 3) = Long2Fix(22050);
    *((long *)(*myRates) + 4) = Long2Fix(32000);
    SGSetAdditionalSoundRates(gSoundChannel, myRates);

    DisposeHandle(myRates);
  }
```

```
      // if an error occurred while configuring sound channel, dispose of it
      if (myErr != noErr) {
        SGDisposeChannel(gSeqGrabber, gSoundChannel);
        gSoundChannel = NULL;
      }
    }
  }

  // display the monitor window
  MacShowWindow(GetDialogWindow(gMonitor));

  // start previewing
  if (myErr == noErr)
    myErr = SGStartPreview(gSeqGrabber);

bail:
  // if an error occurred, clean up
  if (myErr != noErr)
    QTCap_Stop();

  return(myErr);
}
```

We call `QTCap_Init` when QTCapture starts up, so that the monitor window appears immediately at application launch time. Our menu-adjusting function `QTApp_AdjustMenus` contains these lines, which disable the Close menu item in the File menu if the monitor window is the frontmost window:

```
if (QTFrame_GetFrontAppWindow() == QTFrame_GetWindowReferenceFromWindow
                                 (GetDialogWindow(gMonitor)))
    QTFrame_SetMenuItemState(myMenu, IDM_FILECLOSE, kDisableMenuItem);
```

So the monitor window will remain open for as long as QTCapture is running. When QTCapture quits, we close the monitor window and shut down our sequence grabber components by calling the `QTCap_Stop` function (defined in Listing 4.4).

Listing 4.4 Shutting down the sequence grabber.

```
void QTCap_Stop (void)
{
  if (gSeqGrabber != NULL) {
    SGStop(gSeqGrabber);
    CloseComponent(gSeqGrabber);
```

```
    gSeqGrabber = NULL;
  }

  if (gMonitor != NULL) {
    DisposeDialog(gMonitor);
    gMonitor = NULL;
  }
}
```

You'll notice that we didn't explicitly close the sequence grabber channel component instances gVideoChannel or gSoundChannel. The sequence grabber does that automatically for us when we call CloseComponent on the sequence grabber component instance we opened.

Channel Settings

QTCapture includes menu items for displaying dialog boxes that allow the user to configure the settings of the video and sound channels. We've already seen the sound settings dialog box (in Figures 4.4 and 4.5) and the video settings dialog box (in Figure 4.3); Figure 4.6 shows another pane of the video settings dialog box. In both cases, we display the settings dialog box by calling the SGSettingsDialog function, passing in our instances of the sequence grabber component and the appropriate channel component. There are, however, a few extra details that we need to consider when we call SGSettingsDialog.

Handling Update Events

As you can see, the settings dialog boxes are movable modal dialog boxes. This means that, on Macintosh computers, we'll also need to specify a modal dialog filter function to handle idle events and to pass update events to windows located behind the settings dialog box. If we didn't do this, and if the user were to move the settings dialog box on top of another QTCapture window and then move it away, that window would not get redrawn. (On Windows computers, paint messages are sent directly to the affected window, so we don't need a modal dialog filter function.)

We've already developed a basic modal dialog filter function that is able to redraw any movie or image windows that our application has open. (See, for instance, Volume One, Chapter 13.) In the present case, we also want to redraw the monitor window itself, in case it gets covered up and then uncovered by a settings dialog box. The sequence grabber provides the SGUpdate function, which instructs the sequence grabber to refresh its display. In

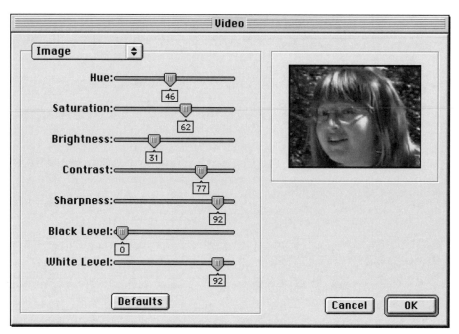

Figure 4.6 The video settings dialog box.

theory, we could use SGUpdate here to redraw the monitor window, except for one small problem: *QuickTime steals our sequence grabber component instance while the video settings dialog is displayed.* Look again at Figure 4.6 and notice that the right-hand side of the dialog box contains a pane in which the previewed video data is displayed. The input for that pane is provided by our very own sequence grabber component, gSeqGrabber. So we can call SGUpdate until the cows come home and our monitor window will never get refreshed.

There is a simple workaround to this theft. We can take a snapshot of the monitor window just before we call SGSettingsDialog to display a settings dialog box and then redraw the monitor window using that snapshot whenever necessary. Listing 4.5 shows our function QTCap_GetChannelSettings, which we'll call to display a video or sound settings dialog box. As you can see, we call SGGrabPict to get a picture that contains the current image in the monitor window. Then we call SGSettingsDialog and later clean up by disposing of the grabbed picture.

Listing 4.5 Displaying a settings dialog box.

```
static ComponentResult QTCap_GetChannelSettings (SGChannel theChannel)
{
  SGModalFilterUPP        myFilterUPP = NULL;
  ComponentResult         myErr = noErr;

  // get rid of any existing monitor picture
  if (gMonitorPICT != NULL) {
    KillPicture(gMonitorPICT);
    gMonitorPICT = NULL;
  }

  // get the picture currently in the monitor window
  SGGrabPict(gSeqGrabber, &gMonitorPICT, NULL, 0, grabPictOffScreen);

  // display the settings dialog box
#if TARGET_OS_MAC
  myFilterUPP = NewSGModalFilterUPP(QTCap_SGModalFilterProc);
#endif

  myErr = SGSettingsDialog(gSeqGrabber, theChannel, 0, NULL, OL, myFilterUPP,
            (long)gMonitor);
#if TARGET_OS_MAC
  DisposeSGModalFilterUPP(myFilterUPP);
#endif

  // get rid of the monitor picture
  if (gMonitorPICT != NULL) {
    KillPicture(gMonitorPICT);
    gMonitorPICT = NULL;
  }

  return(myErr);
}
```

Strictly speaking, we need to call SGGrabPict only when we're about to
display the video settings dialog box. But the code for redrawing the uncovered monitor window is in fact much simpler if we grab the picture in the
monitor window in both cases (that is, for both the video and sound settings
dialog boxes).

Listing 4.6 shows our complete sequence grabber modal dialog filter function. It's pretty much identical to the modal dialog filter functions we've
encountered in Volume One, except that it contains code to determine

whether the window to be updated is the monitor window gMonitor. If it is, we get the size of the monitor window and draw the saved snapshot into that window by calling DrawPicture. As you can see, QTCap_SGModalFilterProc assumes that the theRefCon parameter is a pointer to the monitor dialog box. If you look back at Listing 4.5, you'll see that indeed we pass gMonitor as the last parameter to SGSettingsDialog.

Listing 4.6 Handling events.

```
#if TARGET_OS_MAC
static PASCAL_RTN Boolean QTCap_SGModalFilterProc
  (DialogPtr theDialog, const EventRecord *theEvent, short *theItemHit, long theRefCon)
{
  Boolean             myEventHandled = false;
  WindowPtr           myWindow = NULL;
  RgnHandle           myWindowRgn = NULL;
  GrafPtr             mySavedPort;
  Rect                myRect;
  DialogPtr           myMonitor = (DialogPtr)theRefCon;

  switch (theEvent->what) {
    case updateEvt:
      // find out which window needs to be updated
      myWindow = (WindowPtr)theEvent->message;
      if (myWindow == GetDialogWindow(myMonitor)) {
        // update the monitor window, using the stored picture
        GetPort(&mySavedPort);
        MacSetPort(GetWindowPort(myWindow));

#if TARGET_API_MAC_CARBON
        GetPortBounds(GetDialogPort(myMonitor), &myRect);
#else
        myRect = myWindow->portRect;
#endif

        // draw the saved monitor picture into the monitor window
        if (gMonitorPICT != NULL)
          DrawPicture(gMonitorPICT, &myRect);

        // clear the update region
        BeginUpdate(myWindow);
        EndUpdate(myWindow);
```

```
      MacSetPort(mySavedPort);
      myEventHandled = true;
    } else if ((myWindow != NULL) && (myWindow != GetDialogWindow(theDialog))) {
      // update the specified window, if it's behind the modal dialog box
      QTFrame_HandleEvent((EventRecord *)theEvent);
      myEventHandled = false;
    }
    break;

  case nullEvent:
    // do idle-time processing for all open windows in our window list
    if (gAppInForeground)
      QTFrame_IdleMovieWindows();

    myEventHandled = false;
    break;

  default:
    myEventHandled = false;
    break;
  }

  // let the OS's standard filter proc handle the event, if it hasn't already been handled
  if (gHasNewDialogCalls && (myEventHandled == false))
    myEventHandled = StdFilterProc(theDialog, (EventRecord *)theEvent, theItemHit);

  return(myEventHandled);
}
#endif
```

Displaying the Settings Dialog Boxes

Now we've got the necessary tools we need to display the sound and video settings dialog boxes. Listing 4.7 shows the definition of the QTCap_GetSound-Settings function. Pretty simple, eh?

Listing 4.7   Displaying the sound settings dialog box.

```
void QTCap_GetSoundSettings (void)
{
  QTCap_GetChannelSettings(gSoundChannel);
}
```

For the video settings dialog box, however, we need to do a little more work. The principal complication is that some of the user's selections may cause the video digitizer's active source rectangle to change. Indeed, the user can even change the video digitizer itself by selecting a new video input source. So we need to pay attention to any size changes that may occur and then recalculate and reset the size of the monitor window accordingly.

Before we call QTCap_GetChannelSettings on the video channel, we want to pause the preview operation. We can do that by calling SGPause:

```
SGPause(gSeqGrabber, true);
```

At this point, we can call QTCap_GetChannelSettings, passing in the video channel component instance:

```
myErr = QTCap_GetChannelSettings(gVideoChannel);
if (myErr != noErr)
    goto bail;
```

If QTCap_GetChannelSettings returns successfully, we'll retrieve the new video boundary rectangle:

```
SGGetSrcVideoBounds(gVideoChannel, &myNewActiveVideoRect);
```

The *video source boundary rectangle* defines the size of the source video image being captured by the video channel. The active source rectangle is usually a part of the video source boundary rectangle.

Now we need to adjust the size of the monitor window if the active source rectangle has changed size (that is, if myNewActiveVideoRect differs from gActiveVideoRect). Listing 4.8 shows the code we execute in that case.

Listing 4.8 Adjusting the size of the monitor window.

```
if (!MacEqualRect(&gActiveVideoRect, &myNewActiveVideoRect))
{
    short          myDivisor = 1;                    // assume gFullSize

    if (gQuarterSize)
      myDivisor = 4;
    else if (gHalfSize)
      myDivisor = 2;

    myWidth = (myNewActiveVideoRect.right - myNewActiveVideoRect.left) / myDivisor;
    myHeight = (myNewActiveVideoRect.bottom - myNewActiveVideoRect.top) / myDivisor;
```

```
gActiveVideoRect = myNewActiveVideoRect;
SizeWindow(GetDialogWindow(gMonitor), myWidth, myHeight, false);

GetPortBounds(GetDialogPort(gMonitor), &myRect);
SGSetChannelBounds(gVideoChannel, &myRect);
}
```

Note that we resize the monitor window and then reset the display boundary rectangle. Listing 4.9 shows our complete definition of QTCap_GetVideoSettings.

Listing 4.9   Displaying the video settings dialog box.

```
void QTCap_GetVideoSettings (void)
{
  Rect                    myNewActiveVideoRect;
  short                   myWidth, myHeight;
  GrafPtr                 mySavedPort;
  SGModalFilter           myFilterUPP = NULL;
  Rect                    myRect;
  ComponentResult         myErr = noErr;

  // get our current state
  GetPort(&mySavedPort);

  // pause previewing
  SGPause(gSeqGrabber, true);

  // display the video settings dialog box
  myErr = QTCap_GetChannelSettings(gVideoChannel);
  if (myErr != noErr)
    goto bail;

  // retrieve the user's choices
  SGGetSrcVideoBounds(gVideoChannel, &myNewActiveVideoRect);

  // set up our port
  SetPortDialogPort(gMonitor);

  // has our active rectangle changed?
  // if so, it's because our video standard changed (e.g., NTSC to PAL)
  // and we need to adjust our monitor window
  if (!MacEqualRect(&gActiveVideoRect, &myNewActiveVideoRect)) {
    short          myDivisor = 1;               // assume gFullSize
```

```
    if (gQuarterSize)
      myDivisor = 4;
    else if (gHalfSize)
      myDivisor = 2;

    myWidth = (myNewActiveVideoRect.right - myNewActiveVideoRect.left) / myDivisor;
    myHeight = (myNewActiveVideoRect.bottom - myNewActiveVideoRect.top) / myDivisor;

    gActiveVideoRect = myNewActiveVideoRect;
    SizeWindow(GetDialogWindow(gMonitor), myWidth, myHeight, false);

    GetPortBounds(GetDialogPort(gMonitor), &myRect);
    SGSetChannelBounds(gVideoChannel, &myRect);
  }
bail:
  MacSetPort(mySavedPort);

#if !TARGET_OS_MAC
  SGSetChannelBounds(gVideoChannel, &(gMonitor->portRect));
#endif

  // restart previewing
  SGPause(gSeqGrabber, false);
}
```

As you can see, on Windows we call SGSetChannelBounds to reset the channel bounds rectangle to the size of the monitor window. This is necessary to get the previewing to start up again after the dialog box is dismissed.

▶ Monitor Window Size

While we're on the subject of resizing the monitor window to fit the active source rectangle, let's see how QTCapture handles the three menu items that adjust the size of the monitor window. The application function QTApp_HandleMenu contains the lines of code shown in Listing 4.10.

Listing 4.10 Handling the size-related menu items.

```
case IDM_QUARTER_SIZE:
  QTCap_ResizeMonitorWindow(4);
  myIsHandled = true;
  break;
```

```
case IDM_HALF_SIZE:
  QTCap_ResizeMonitorWindow(2);
  myIsHandled = true;
  break;

case IDM_FULL_SIZE:
  QTCap_ResizeMonitorWindow(1);
  myIsHandled = true;
  break;
```

In all three cases, we call the function QTCap_ResizeMonitorWindow, passing in the appropriate divisor. QTCap_ResizeMonitorWindow is defined in Listing 4.11; it should be fairly clear, given the similar code we just encountered in Listing 4.9.

Listing 4.11   Resizing the monitor window.

```
void QTCap_ResizeMonitorWindow (short theDivisor)
{
  Rect                 myRect;
  short                myWidth, myHeight;
  GrafPtr              mySavedPort;
  ComponentResult      myErr = noErr;

  // calculate the new width and height
  myWidth = (gActiveVideoRect.right - gActiveVideoRect.left) / theDivisor;
  myHeight = (gActiveVideoRect.bottom - gActiveVideoRect.top) / theDivisor;

  gQuarterSize = (theDivisor == 4);
  gHalfSize = (theDivisor == 2);
  gFullSize = (theDivisor == 1);

  // resize the monitor window
  GetPort(&mySavedPort);
  SetPortDialogPort(gMonitor);

  SGPause(gSeqGrabber, true);

  SizeWindow(GetDialogWindow(gMonitor), myWidth, myHeight, false);

  GetPortBounds(GetDialogPort(gMonitor), &myRect);
  SGSetChannelBounds(gVideoChannel, &myRect);

  MacSetPort(mySavedPort);
  SGPause(gSeqGrabber, false);
}
```

We resize the monitor window to its new height and width by calling Size-Window. We also reset the video channel's display boundary rectangle (the rectangle in which the previewed data is displayed) by calling SGSetChannel-Bounds. Because the display boundary rectangle completely fills the content area of the monitor window, we are able to keep the geometry calculations fairly simple. In a more typical case, where the preview occupies only part of a window, we'd need to do some more complicated calculations.

▶ Recording

Finally, it's time to see how to use the sequence grabber to record captured video and sound data into a movie file. This is actually a fairly simple task, as the sequence grabber provides the SGStartRecord and SGStop functions that we can use to start and stop recording. First, however, we need to tell the sequence grabber where to put the captured data.

Setting the Output File

The first thing we want to do is have the user select a file to hold the captured data. We'll use our framework function QTFrame_PutFile and then call DeleteMovieFile if the selected file already exists and the user tells us to overwrite that existing file, as shown in Listing 4.12.

Listing 4.12 Eliciting an output file from the user.

```
QTFrame_PutFile(myPrompt, myFileName, &myFile, &myIsSelected, &myIsReplacing);
myErr = myIsSelected ? noErr : userCanceledErr;
if (myErr != noErr)
  goto bail;

// delete any existing movie file, if the user so instructs
if (myIsReplacing)
  DeleteMovieFile(&myFile);
```

Next we'll call the SGSetDataOutput function to set the selected file as the output file for the recorded data. The sequence grabber stores the data in the file as a QuickTime movie, complete with the requisite movie metadata (that is, the movie atom) and the captured sound and video tracks.

```
myErr = SGSetDataOutput(gSeqGrabber, &myFile, seqGrabToDisk);
```

The third parameter to SGSetDataOutput is a set of flags that control various aspects of the recording operation. Currently, these flags are available:

```
enum {
  seqGrabToDisk                              = 1,
  seqGrabToMemory                            = 2,
  seqGrabDontUseTempMemory                   = 4,
  seqGrabAppendToFile                        = 8,
  seqGrabDontAddMovieResource                = 16,
  seqGrabDontMakeMovie                       = 32,
  seqGrabPreExtendFile                       = 64,
  seqGrabDataProcIsInterruptSafe             = 128,
  seqGrabDataProcDoesOverlappingReads        = 256
};
```

The first two flags, seqGrabToDisk and seqGrabToMemory, are mutually exclusive. The seqGrabToDisk flag tells the sequence grabber to write the captured data to the output file as the data is captured; the seqGrabToMemory flag tells the sequence grabber first to record the data into memory and then to write it into the output file only when the recording operation is complete. Using the seqGrabToMemory flag can result in better performance (that is, fewer dropped frames), but it limits the amount of recorded data to the memory available to our application. (It's worth noting that this technique for avoiding dropped frames is far less necessary nowadays, as hard disks are significantly faster than in the early days of QuickTime.) As you can see from the preceding, QTCapture specifies the seqGrabToDisk flag. The remaining flags are for more specialized capture operations, and we won't consider them further.

Setting Channel Output Files

By default, each open channel writes its data into the file specified by the SGSetDataOutput function. It's possible, however, to configure the sequence grabber to record different channels into different files. To do this, we need to create a new *sequence grabber output* and attach that output to a particular channel. We create a new channel output by calling the SGNewOutput function, and we attach that output to a channel by calling the SGSetChannelOutput function.

When we call SGNewOutput, we need to specify the output file by passing in a data reference to the destination file; this is unlike SGSetDataOutput, where we passed a pointer to a file specification record. (See Volume One, Chapter 9, for a discussion of data references.) In QTCapture, we prompt the user for a channel output file by calling QTFrame_PutFile, so we need to create an alias data reference for that file:

```
myErr = QTNewAlias(&myFile, &myAliasHandle, true);
```

And then we can call SGNewOutput and SGSetChannelOutput, like this:

```
SGNewOutput(gSeqGrabber, (Handle)myAliasHandle, rAliasType, seqGrabToDisk,
    &myOutput);
SGSetChannelOutput(gSeqGrabber, theChannel, myOutput);
```

Notice that SGNewOutput also takes a parameter that specifies the desired recording options; in this case, we'll pass the same flag, seqGrabToDisk, that we earlier passed to SGSetDataOutput.

QTCapture maintains a global variable, gSplitTracks, that indicates whether the user wants to capture video and sound data into different files. Before we begin recording, we inspect that variable and, if necessary, prompt the user to select the channel output files. Listing 4.13 shows the code that does this.

Listing 4.13 Eliciting channel output files from the user.

```
if ((gSoundChannel != NULL) && gRecordSound &&
  (gVideoChannel != NULL) && gRecordVideo && gSplitTracks) {
  myErr = QTCap_SetTrackFile(gVideoChannel, kVideoSavePrompt, kVideoSaveMovieFileName);
  if (myErr != noErr)
    goto bail;

  myErr = QTCap_SetTrackFile(gSoundChannel, kSoundSavePrompt, kSoundSaveMovieFileName);
  if (myErr != noErr)
    goto bail;
}
```

As you can see, we call the function QTCap_SetTrackFile, defined in Listing 4.14, to do most of the work. QTCap_SetTrackFile just assembles the pieces we've encountered so far in this section.

Listing 4.14 Setting a channel output file.

```
static ComponentResult QTCap_SetTrackFile
        (SGChannel theChannel, char *thePrompt, char *theDefaultName)

{
  FSSpec              myFile;
  Boolean             myIsSelected = false;
  Boolean             myIsReplacing = false;
  StringPtr           myPrompt = QTUtils_ConvertCToPascalString(thePrompt);
  StringPtr           myFileName = QTUtils_ConvertCToPascalString(theDefaultName);
  SGOutput            myOutput;
  AliasHandle         myAliasHandle = NULL;
  OSErr               myErr = noErr;
```

```
// prompt the user for new filename
QTFrame_PutFile(myPrompt, myFileName, &myFile, &myIsSelected, &myIsReplacing);
myErr = myIsSelected ? noErr : userCanceledErr;
if (myErr != noErr)
    goto bail;

myErr = QTNewAlias(&myFile, &myAliasHandle, true);
if (myErr != noErr)
    goto bail;

// create an output from this file
myErr = SGNewOutput(gSeqGrabber, (Handle)myAliasHandle, rAliasType, seqGrabToDisk,
        &myOutput);
if (myErr != noErr)
    goto bail;

// associate this output with the specified channel
myErr = SGSetChannelOutput(gSeqGrabber, theChannel, myOutput);

bail:
    free(myPrompt);
    free(myFileName);

    if (myAliasHandle != NULL)
        DisposeHandle((Handle)myAliasHandle);

    return(myErr);
}
```

Keep in mind that we now have *three* files floating around. We have the main output file (set by a call to SGSetDataOutput); this file contains the movie atom, which in turn contains two track atoms. These track atoms contain references to the two channel output files (set by calls to SGSetChannelOutput). The channel output files are media files; they cannot be opened by QuickTime-savvy applications directly. Instead, they are opened only indirectly, whenever the main output file is opened.

Recording the Captured Data

So we've set the main output file and, if desired, the channel output files. It's time to start recording some captured data into those files. As indicated earlier, we do this by calling SGStartRecord:

```
myErr = SGStartRecord(gSeqGrabber);
```

Once we've called `SGStartRecord`, the sequence grabber will capture sound and video data into the specified output file or files until we tell it to stop (by calling `SGStop`). We need to give some processor time to the sequence grabber, just as we did during previewing, by calling `SGIdle`. In QTCapture, we're going to use a fairly cheesy strategy of just recording until the user clicks the mouse button:

```
while (!Button() && (myErr == noErr))
  myErr = SGIdle(gSeqGrabber);

SGStop(gSeqGrabber);
```

This strategy has the benefit of simplicity and also of providing maximum processing time to the sequence grabber, but it's certainly not appropriate for a real-life capture application. The tasks of providing a better user interface for starting and stopping the recording process and of rewriting the code to use the call to `SGIdle` in our idle-event handler `QTApp_Idle` are left as exercises to the reader.

Listing 4.15 shows our complete recording function, `QTCap_Record`.

Listing 4.15 Recording captured data into a file.

```
void QTCap_Record (void)
{
  FSSpec            myFile;
  Boolean           myIsSelected = false;
  Boolean           myIsReplacing = false;
  StringPtr         myPrompt = QTUtils_ConvertCToPascalString(kCapSavePrompt);
  StringPtr         myFileName = QTUtils_ConvertCToPascalString(kCapSaveMovieFileName);
  long              myFlags = createMovieFileDontOpenFile |
                              createMovieFileDontCreateMovie |
                              createMovieFileDontCreateResFile;
  ComponentResult   myErr = noErr;

  // stop everything while the dialogs are up
  SGStop(gSeqGrabber);

  // prompt the user for new filename
  QTFrame_PutFile(myPrompt, myFileName, &myFile, &myIsSelected, &myIsReplacing);
  myErr = myIsSelected ? noErr : userCanceledErr;
  if (myErr != noErr)
    goto bail;

  // delete any existing movie file, if the user so instructs
  if (myIsReplacing)
    DeleteMovieFile(&myFile);
```

```
  myErr = SGSetDataOutput(gSeqGrabber, &myFile, seqGrabToDisk);
  if (myErr != noErr)
    goto bail;

  // ask for separate video and sound track files, if requested
  if ((gSoundChannel != NULL) && gRecordSound &&
      (gVideoChannel != NULL) && gRecordVideo && gSplitTracks) {
    myErr = QTCap_SetTrackFile(gVideoChannel, kVideoSavePrompt, kVideoSaveMovieFileName);
    if (myErr != noErr)
      goto bail;

    myErr = QTCap_SetTrackFile(gSoundChannel, kSoundSavePrompt, kSoundSaveMovieFileName);
    if (myErr != noErr)
      goto bail;
  }

  // if not recording sound or video, then disable those channels
  if ((gSoundChannel != NULL) && !gRecordSound)
    SGSetChannelUsage(gSoundChannel, 0);

  if ((gVideoChannel != NULL) && !gRecordVideo)
    SGSetChannelUsage(gVideoChannel, 0);

  // attempt to recover the preview area obscured by dialogs
#if TARGET_OS_WIN32
  UpdatePort(gMonitor);
#endif
  SGUpdate(gSeqGrabber, 0);

  // create a movie file for the destination movie
  myErr = CreateMovieFile(&myFile, sigMoviePlayer, smSystemScript, myFlags, NULL, NULL);
  if (myErr != noErr)
    goto bail;

  FlushEvents(mDownMask + mUpMask, 0);

  // record until the user clicks the mouse button
  myErr = SGStartRecord(gSeqGrabber);
  if (myErr != noErr)
    goto bail;

  while (!Button() && (myErr == noErr))
    myErr = SGIdle(gSeqGrabber);

  if (!((myErr == dskFulErr) || (myErr != eofErr)))
    goto bail;
```

```
  // stop the recording that's currently happening
  myErr = SGStop(gSeqGrabber);
  SGStartPreview(gSeqGrabber);

bail:
  free(myPrompt);
  free(myFileName);

  if (myErr == noErr)
    return;

  SGPause(gSeqGrabber, false);
  SGStartPreview(gSeqGrabber);
}
```

Notice that once we're done recording, we restart the previewing process by calling SGStartPreview.

▶ Conclusion

In this chapter, we've learned how to use the sequence grabber and sequence grabber channel components to preview and capture video and sound data from a camera or other audiovisual device attached to our computer. We've seen how to display the settings dialog boxes that permit the user to configure the various channels, and we've also seen how to set the sound and video channels to capture into different output files. And we did all of this without knowing very much at all about the various components that do all the low-level work. That's part of the beauty of the sequence grabber: it gives us a simple, high-level interface to a set of fairly complex operations.

Saving this captured data in a file is great stuff, of course, but there are certainly other things we might want to do with it. For instance, we might want to send it out it over a network, so that people located remotely can watch and listen to our data. In the next chapter, we'll see how QuickTime can help us do that.

Broadcast News
Broadcasting Movies over a Network

 Introduction

The key technology introduced in QuickTime 4 was support for receiving and displaying real-time streamed data. That is to say, QuickTime-savvy applications like QuickTime Player or our own QTShell-based sample applications can receive video, audio, and other kinds of data streamed across the Internet. Real-time streaming, unlike the progressive downloading of movie files that had been available since QuickTime 3, can handle live data and does not require downloading potentially huge files onto the user's computer; this permits QuickTime playback applications to support uses such as video-on-demand and rebroadcast streaming.

The real-time streaming provided by QuickTime 4 was a client-side technology only; it did not provide any means to serve up, or transmit, data streams. At that time, special software was required to create the streams of data that could be sent out over a network and then received and played back by QuickTime-savvy applications. As we'll see, the protocols used in transmitting the data from the server to the client conform to Internet Engineering Task Force (IETF) standards, but implementing those protocols in a transmitter application required intimate knowledge of a handful of IETF specifications, and a good bit of programming.

QuickTime 5 introduced a set of broadcasting APIs that allow us to create transmitter applications. For example, we can take the audiovisual data from a camcorder attached to a computer and broadcast that data to other computers on a network. Together, the transmitter technologies provided by QuickTime 5 and the receiver technologies provided by QuickTime 4 give us the complete set of tools we need to send audiovisual streams from one computer and view them on another. The good news is that we need to know virtually nothing about the applicable IETF specifications to do all this; the really good news is that the amount of code we need to write to create a broadcasting application is surprisingly small. Indeed, we'll be able to write this application using fewer than a dozen of these new broadcasting functions.

In this chapter, we're going to see how to use these new APIs to build a sample application that broadcasts live data to other computers. Let's call this application QTBroadcast. When it starts up, QTBroadcast automatically opens a *monitor window*, shown in Figure 5.1; this is modeled on the monitor window we created in the previous chapter, but now contains a button to start and stop the broadcasting. The Test menu of QTBroadcast is shown in Figure 5.2; as you can see, it contains items that allow the user to select a session description protocol (SDP) file (which we'll encounter later) and to configure the broadcasting settings.

We'll begin by surveying the various streaming capabilities provided by QuickTime, and we'll take a brief look at the protocols that underlie those capabilities. Then we'll consider the code we need to add to our basic application shell to allow it to broadcast live data streams. Note that QuickTime's broadcasting APIs are currently available only on Macintosh operating systems (Mac OS 8, 9, and X).

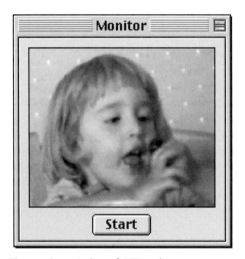

Figure 5.1 The monitor window of QTBroadcast.

Figure 5.2 The Test menu of QTBroadcast.

▶ QuickTime Streaming

Streaming is the process whereby one computer (the *transmitter*) chops up a file or sequence of bytes into discrete chunks (called *packets*) and sends them across a network to another computer (the *receiver* or *client*). The client's job is to reassemble the packets and do the right thing with them. The series of packets is a *stream*. For present purposes, we are interested only in streams of audiovisual data that can be reassembled and played back as a QuickTime movie.

It's important to keep in mind that QuickTime has supported a kind of streaming, called *HTTP streaming* or *progressive downloading*, ever since QuickTime 3 was released in 1998. QuickTime's HTTP streaming allows the QuickTime browser plug-in to begin playing a movie embedded in a Web page before the entire movie has downloaded to the local computer. HTTP streaming is essentially a file transfer protocol, in the sense that the entire movie is downloaded to the user's computer. One key advantage of Quick-Time's HTTP streaming is that a user can begin interacting with Web-based content before the entire movie arrives on the user's computer. As we saw in Volume One, the movie file embedded on the Web page is a standard QuickTime movie file saved in Fast Start format (where the movie atom is among the first atoms in the movie file).

QuickTime 4 introduced a different kind of streaming, called *real-time streaming*. With real-time streaming, packets are sent out over the network in real time (so that, for instance, a 10-minute movie would take 10 minutes to transfer over a network). When packets are received by the client application (for instance, by QuickTime Player), they are reassembled into a Quick-Time movie and played for the user. In general, packets are discarded as soon as they have been played, so no file is ever created on the user's local storage devices.

QuickTime's real-time streaming uses an open IETF streaming protocol known as the *Realtime Transport Protocol* (RTP) to send the packets of video and audio data. For control information, such as establishing a connection between the client and server or telling the server to jump to a new time in a video-on-demand movie, QuickTime uses a different protocol known as the *Realtime Streaming Protocol* (RTSP). RTSP uses the TCP/IP transport layer, while RTP uses the lower-level UDP/IP transport layer.

Because RTP uses UDP/IP, it does not guarantee delivery of packets. So it's possible for some packets to get lost in transit and never arrive at the client computer. This packet loss can result in some degradation of the video and sound when the movie is played back on the client computer. If you need guaranteed delivery of packets, you should use HTTP streaming, which uses TCP/IP to ensure that all transmitted packets are in fact received (by retransmitting any lost packets).

QuickTime supports streaming of video, audio, and text data in any of the formats that can be played locally by QuickTime, including AVI, Sorenson, QDesign, MP3, and MIDI. It cannot currently stream movies that contain sprite tracks or that incorporate features that depend on track references, such as QuickTime video effects, chapter lists, and some tweening effects. To handle these sorts of movies, either you can use HTTP streaming or you can create movies that store some data locally and combine that data with data received via RTP streaming. You can even create movies some of whose tracks are delivered via HTTP streaming and some via RTP streaming.

The files that reside on the streaming server are standard QuickTime movie files, with one important addition: each track in the movie that is to be streamed across the network must be accompanied by a *hint track*. The hint track contains information that tells the server software how to packetize the corresponding streamed track. In other words, the hint track is a sort of blueprint for creating streams of data. Without the hint track, the server software would have to know a great deal about the particular audio or video format contained in the streamed track so that it could know how best to chop the data up into packets (for instance, possibly duplicating some of the packets to protect against losing important frames of video). The hint track insulates the server software from having to know anything about the actual video or audio data it's serving.

This is especially important because it allows streaming servers to run on operating systems that don't run the QuickTime client software. Moreover, Apple has released the source code for the QuickTime Streaming Server under the Apple Public Source License, which conforms to the Open Source community guidelines. Versions of QTSS currently run under Windows and various flavors of UNIX, including Linux.

▶ QuickTime Broadcasting

The broadcasting APIs introduced in QuickTime 5 allow us to create broadcasting applications (or, more simply, broadcasters). A *broadcaster* is an application that takes data from a source other than a hinted movie, compresses that data (if necessary), packetizes that data into streams, and then sends the streams out over a network. In the simplest case, the streams are targeted at a single specific client on the network. This type of serving is called *unicasting*. It's also possible to target a set of streams at more than one client on the network, using a special reserved address; this type of serving is called *multicasting*.

The QuickTime broadcasting APIs support both unicasting and multicasting. Some routers, however, are not configured to allow multicast streams. In this case, we still need to use a streaming server (such as QTSS). We can transmit the streams to a machine running QTSS, which then unicasts distinct streams to any number of remote clients.

The broadcasting APIs can be divided into two general categories, which we'll call the *sourcer APIs* and the *presentation APIs*. We'll use the sourcer APIs to select and configure a source for the broadcast data. (A *sourcer component*, or *sourcer*, is a component that can read data from a specific kind of source.) Currently, QuickTime supports broadcasting data from any of these kinds of sources:

- Data captured using a sequence grabber component from audiovisual devices
- Movie files stored locally on the transmitter
- Precompressed media data that is not stored in a movie file

This last kind of source allows us to broadcast virtually any kind of media data; we simply need to pass the appropriate data, a sample description for that data, and (optionally) a time stamp and duration. Keep in mind, however, that the client receiving the broadcast needs to have a media handler for that kind of data. Also, some kinds of data (for instance, sprite media data or Flash media data) do not respond well to packet loss and hence are currently not good candidates for broadcast streaming.

We use the presentation APIs to present (or broadcast) the data provided by a sourcer. A *presentation* is a collection of one or more streams of data, which can consist of packets of audio, video, text, or other data. You might think of a presentation as the streaming equivalent of a movie and the streams within the presentation as the streaming equivalent of a movie's tracks. The client application receives the presentation and reassembles it into a movie, which it plays back in exactly the same way it plays a local movie.

The sourcer and presentation APIs are a marvel of simplicity. As I mentioned earlier, we will be able to develop a broadcasting application using fewer than a dozen broadcasting functions. In fact, for the moment we won't need to use any of the sourcer functions at all, since we'll rely on Quick-Time's default behavior of using the sequence grabber as the source for the broadcast data. So let's get started writing some code.

Setting Up for Broadcasting

Before we can begin broadcasting live audio and video data captured from an audiovisual device attached to our computer, we need to initialize our application for broadcasting and then create a presentation. As we've seen, a presentation is analogous to a movie: it consists of one or more streams of data targeted at one or more remote computers. In QTBroadcast, we shall allow at most one active presentation at a time, and the data being broadcast will be displayed locally in the monitor window (see Figure 5.1 again), which also contains a button that can be used to start and pause the broadcast. To keep track of the presentation and the monitor window, we'll use these global variables:

```
QTSPresentation          gPresentation = kQTSInvalidPresentation;
QTSNotificationUPP        gNotificationUPP = NULL;
DialogPtr                 gMonitor = NULL;
UserItemUPP               gMonitorUserItemProcUPP = NULL;
Boolean                   gBroadcasting = false;
```

The gPresentation global variable is an identifier for the single presentation supported by QTBroadcast; as you can see, it's of type QTSPresentation and is initialized to the value kQTSInvalidPresentation. Associated with the presentation is a *presentation notification procedure*, which we identify using the gNotificationUPP global variable. Our notification procedure is called on specific events involving the presentation, such as when a presentation is first created and when a connection to the client machine occurs.

We use the gMonitor and gMonitorUserItemProcUPP global variables to keep track of the monitor window and the user item in that window (where we draw the video data that's being broadcast). Finally, we'll use the gBroadcasting global variable to keep track of whether we're currently broadcasting data or not.

When QTBroadcast starts up, it calls the QTBC_Init function, shown in Listing 5.1, to create the monitor window and to allocate the universal procedure pointers gNotificationUPP and gMonitorUserItemProcUPP.

Listing 5.1 Initializing for broadcasting.

```
OSErr QTBC_Init (void)
{
  OSErr          myErr = noErr;

  // allocate global storage
  gNotificationUPP = (QTSNotificationUPP)NewQTSNotificationUPP(QTBC_NotificationProc);
  if (gNotificationUPP == NULL) {
    myErr = paramErr;
    goto bail;
  }

  gMonitorUserItemProcUPP = NewUserItemUPP(QTBC_UserItemProcedure);
  if (gMonitorUserItemProcUPP == NULL) {
    myErr = paramErr;
    goto bail;
  }
```

```
  // open the monitor window
  gMonitor = QTBC_CreateMonitorWindow();
  if (gMonitor == NULL) {
    myErr = memFullErr;
    goto bail;
  }

bail:
  // if an error occurred, clean up
  if (myErr != noErr)
    QTBC_Stop();

  return(myErr);
}
```

QTBC_Init calls NewQTSNotificationUPP and NewUserItemUPP to create the two UPPs, and it calls the application function QTBC_CreateMonitorWindow to create and display the monitor window. We'll consider QTBC_CreateMonitor-Window in depth a bit later (Listing 5.9); for the moment, it's sufficient to know that it calls GetNewDialog to create a dialog window from information in the application's resources.

If any error occurs in QTBC_Init, we don't want to continue. In that case, we'll call the QTBC_Stop function, which is defined in Listing 5.2. QTBC_Stop simply deallocates the two UPPs created by QTBC_Init and disposes of the monitor window.

Listing 5.2 Shutting down broadcasting.

```
void QTBC_Stop (void)
{
  // deallocate any global storage
  if (gNotificationUPP != NULL) {
    DisposeQTSNotificationUPP(gNotificationUPP);
    gNotificationUPP = NULL;
  }
  if (gMonitorUserItemProcUPP != NULL) {
    DisposeUserItemUPP(gMonitorUserItemProcUPP);
    gMonitorUserItemProcUPP = NULL;
  }

  // close the monitor window
  if (gMonitor != NULL)
    DisposeDialog(gMonitor);
}
```

We also call QTBC_Stop just before QTBroadcast terminates; at that time, we will also call the QTBC_StopBroadcasting function, which calls QTSDisposePresentation to dispose of the presentation gPresentation. (QTBC_StopBroadcasting is shown later, in Listing 5.7.) It's important to dispose of the UPPs and the monitor window only *after* we dispose of the presentation itself; accordingly, our application-specific shutdown routine, QTApp_Stop, contains these two lines of code:

```
QTBC_StopBroadcasting();
QTBC_Stop();
```

Creating a Presentation

If QTBC_Init completes successfully, the monitor window is displayed on the screen, but it contains no image and the Start button is inactive (as shown in Figure 5.3). Before we can begin broadcasting data, we need to create a presentation. We do this by calling the QTSNewPresentation function, like this:

```
myErr = QTSNewPresentation(myPresParamsPtr, &gPresentation);
```

The second parameter is the address of our global variable gPresentation; if QTSNewPresentation completes successfully, it returns an identifier for the new presentation in that variable. The first parameter is the address of a *new presentation parameters structure*, which is declared like this:

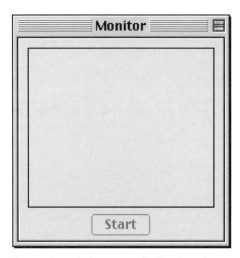

Figure 5.3 The monitor window on application launch.

```
struct QTSNewPresentationParams {
    OSType                  dataType;
    const void *            data;
    UInt32                  dataLength;
    QTSEditListHandle       editList;
    SInt32                  flags;
    TimeScale               timeScale;
    QTSMediaParams *        mediaParams;
    QTSNotificationUPP      notificationProc;
    void *                  notificationRefCon;
};
```

Before we can call QTSNewPresentation, we need to allocate a new presentation parameters structure and fill in most of its fields. We allocate this structure by calling NewPtrClear:

```
myPresParamsPtr = (QTSNewPresentationParams *)
    NewPtrClear(sizeof(QTSNewPresentationParams));
```

The first three fields of the new presentation parameters structure contain information about some of the network settings to be used by the presentation, such as the destination IP address for the broadcast and the ports to use for the data streams. The IETF has defined a standard format for this information, called the *session description protocol* (*SDP*). An SDP file (that is, a file that conforms to the SDP) is used by clients and servers for initiating a network connection and transfer of multimedia streams between a server and its clients. This file describes the types and formats of the media to be transferred, the transport protocols, and the addresses to which the media are to be streamed. Here's a sample SDP file:

```
v=0
c=IN IP4 224.2.1.2/15/1
m=audio 1000 RTP/AVP 12
m=video 2000 RTP/AVP 101
a=rtpmap:101 H263-1998
```

The line beginning with v= specifies the protocol version, which currently is 0. The line beginning with c= specifies the connection information, which consists of a network type and address type (here, IN IP4 for IP version 4 addressing on the Internet), the destination address (here, 224.2.1.2, which is an address reserved for multicasting), a time-to-live value (here, 15), and the number of contiguous multicast addresses (here, 1). The lines beginning with m= indicate which transport protocols and ports to use for specific media types. In the SDP file just shown, the audio data is to be sent via RTP to port 1000, and the video data is to be sent via RTP to port 2000. Finally, the line beginning with a= specifies media attributes. In this case, the rtpmap attribute provides information about dynamic payload binding.

In our sample application QTBroadcast, the user selects an SDP file using the first menu item in the Test menu (namely, Select SDP File). In response to the menu item, we call the QTBC_SetupPresentation function, which in turn uses our standard framework function QTFrame_GetOneFileWithPreview to have the user select an SDP file. QTFrame_GetOneFileWithPreview returns a file system specification for that file. We can then fill in the relevant fields of the new presentation parameters structure like this:

```
myPresParamsPtr->dataType = kQTSFileDataType;
myPresParamsPtr->data = &myFSSpec;
myPresParamsPtr->dataLength = sizeof(myFSSpec);
```

QuickTime also supports SDP information stored in memory (in which case the dataType field should be set to kQTSSDPDataType). In QTBroadcast, we'll restrict our attention to SDP files only.

The editList field of the new presentation parameters structure is a handle to a QTSEditList structure, which holds information about edits for stored streams. For live broadcasting, we can ignore that field.

The flags field of the new presentation parameters structure contains information for the presentation we are about to create. Currently, the following flags are defined:

```
enum {
  kQTSAutoModeFlag                    = 0x00000001,
  kQTSDontShowStatusFlag              = 0x00000008,
  kQTSSendMediaFlag                   = 0x00010000,
  kQTSReceiveMediaFlag                = 0x00020000
};
```

The kQTSAutoModeFlag flag indicates that the presentation should be automatically configured to its default settings; most important, this means that the default sourcer is to be used, which is the sequence grabber. The kQTSDontShowStatusFlag flag indicates that we do not want QuickTime to create a streaming status handler for the presentation; if we request a status handler, it displays connection and status information in the monitor window (that is, in the window associated with the sequence grabber). For instance, when we first create a presentation, QuickTime attempts to connect to the specified target or targets and displays the status message shown in Figure 5.4.

When the presentation is ready and the requisite network connections have been established, we'll see the message shown in Figure 5.5. (Keep in

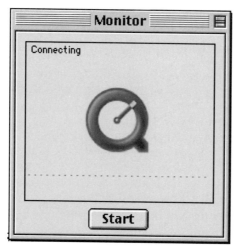

Figure 5.4 The status message while connecting.

Figure 5.5 The status message when ready.

mind that these status messages appear on the transmitter only; the broadcasting client also displays some status information while establishing a connection to the transmitter, which we'll encounter later.)

The remaining two flags, `kQTSSendMediaFlag` and `kQTSReceiveMediaFlag`, indicate whether we want to send or receive data with the presentation we're creating. In QTBroadcast, we set our flags like this:

```
myPresParamsPtr->flags = kQTSAutoModeFlag |
                    kQTSDontShowStatusFlag | kQTSSendMediaFlag;
```

The `timeScale` field of the new presentation parameters structure is currently unused (as far as I can determine); in QTBroadcast, we set that field to 0.

The `mediaParams` field holds a pointer to a *media parameters structure*, of type `QTSMediaParams`:

```
struct QTSMediaParams {
    QTSVideoParams              v;
    QTSAudioParams              a;
};
```

As you can see, this structure contains a *video parameters structure* and an *audio parameters structure* (of types `QTSVideoParams` and `QTSAudioParams`, respectively); these structures contain information about the video and audio media data being previewed locally—that is, the data being displayed in the monitor window and the sound played through the computer's speakers. In QTBroadcast we want to leave the audio settings at their default values, but we want to configure the video settings so that the preview draws in the correct location in the monitor window. We begin by allocating a new media parameters structure:

```
myMediaParamsPtr = (QTSMediaParams *)NewPtrClear(sizeof(QTSMediaParams));
myPresParamsPtr->mediaParams = myMediaParamsPtr;
```

At this point we want to call the `QTSInitializeMediaParams` function, which initializes the media parameters structure to its default values:

```
myErr = QTSInitializeMediaParams(myMediaParamsPtr);
```

Now let's configure the video previewing. The video parameters structure looks like this:

```
struct QTSVideoParams {
    Fixed                       width;
    Fixed                       height;
    MatrixRecord                matrix;
    CGrafPtr                    gWorld;
    GDHandle                    gdHandle;
    RgnHandle                   clip;
    short                       graphicsMode;
    RGBColor                    opColor;
};
```

Notice (in Figure 5.1, once again) that the preview images are drawn in the user item rectangle, which is 176 pixels wide and 144 pixels high and is offset from the window origin by 10 pixels vertically and horizontally. So we'll use these lines of code to place the images in the proper location:

```
myPresParamsPtr->mediaParams->v.width = Long2Fix(176);
myPresParamsPtr->mediaParams->v.height = Long2Fix(144);

TranslateMatrix(&(myPresParamsPtr->mediaParams->v.matrix),
        Long2Fix(10), Long2Fix(10));
```

And we'll set the port and graphics device like this:

```
myPresParamsPtr->mediaParams->v.gWorld = GetDialogPort(gMonitor);
myPresParamsPtr->mediaParams->v.gdHandle = NULL;
```

Finally, the notificationProc and notificationRefCon fields of the new presentation parameters structure specify the notification procedure and a reference constant that is passed to the notification procedure.

```
myPresParamsPtr->notificationProc = gNotificationUPP;
myPresParamsPtr->notificationRefCon = 0L;
```

At long last, we are ready to call QTSNewPresentation and QTSPresPreview:

```
myErr = QTSNewPresentation(myPresParamsPtr, &gPresentation);
myErr = QTSPresPreview(gPresentation, kQTSAllStreams, NULL,
        kQTSNormalForwardRate, 0);
```

Listing 5.3 gives the complete definition for QTBC_SetupPresentation.

Listing 5.3 Setting up a presentation.

```
OSErr QTBC_SetupPresentation (void)
{
    QTSNewPresentationParams      *myPresParamsPtr = NULL;
    QTSMediaParams                *myMediaParamsPtr = NULL;
    FSSpec                         myFSSpec;
    OSType                         myTypeList[] = {kQTFileTypeText};
    short                          myNumTypes = 1;
    QTFrameFileFilterUPP           myFileFilterUPP = NULL;
    OSErr                          myErr = noErr;

#if TARGET_OS_MAC
    myNumTypes = 0;
#endif
```

```
// create a new presentation parameters structure
myPresParamsPtr = (QTSNewPresentationParams *)
  NewPtrClear(sizeof(QTSNewPresentationParams));
if (myPresParamsPtr == NULL) {
  myErr = MemError();
  goto bail;
}

// create a new media parameters structure
myMediaParamsPtr = (QTSMediaParams *)NewPtrClear(sizeof(QTSMediaParams));
if (myMediaParamsPtr == NULL) {
  myErr = MemError();
  goto bail;
}

// initialize the media parameters to default values
myErr = QTSInitializeMediaParams(myMediaParamsPtr);
if (myErr != noErr)
  goto bail;

// elicit an SDP file from the user
myFileFilterUPP = QTFrame_GetFileFilterUPP((ProcPtr)QTFrame_FilterFiles);
myErr = QTFrame_GetOneFileWithPreview(myNumTypes, (QTFrameTypeListPtr)myTypeList,
         &myFSSpec, myFileFilterUPP);
if (myErr != noErr)
  goto bail;

// start broadcasting from an SDP file
myPresParamsPtr->dataType = kQTSFileDataType;
myPresParamsPtr->data = &myFSSpec;
myPresParamsPtr->dataLength = sizeof(myFSSpec);

// set the presentation flags: use Sequence Grabber, don't display blue Q movie,
// and send data
myPresParamsPtr->flags = kQTSAutoModeFlag | kQTSDontShowStatusFlag | kQTSSendMediaFlag;

myPresParamsPtr->timeScale = 0;
myPresParamsPtr->mediaParams = myMediaParamsPtr;

// fill these in to get status notifications
myPresParamsPtr->notificationProc = gNotificationUPP;
myPresParamsPtr->notificationRefCon = 0L;

// define the display size and the default transmission size
myPresParamsPtr->mediaParams->v.width = Long2Fix(176);
myPresParamsPtr->mediaParams->v.height = Long2Fix(144);
```

```
TranslateMatrix(&(myPresParamsPtr->mediaParams->v.matrix), Long2Fix(10), Long2Fix(10));

// set the window that Sequence Grabber will draw into
myPresParamsPtr->mediaParams->v.gWorld = GetDialogPort(gMonitor);
myPresParamsPtr->mediaParams->v.gdHandle = NULL;

// create a new presentation
myErr = QTSNewPresentation(myPresParamsPtr, &gPresentation);
if (myErr != noErr)
    goto bail;

myErr = QTSPresPreview(gPresentation, kQTSAllStreams, NULL, kQTSNormalForwardRate, 0);
bail:
    if (myPresParamsPtr != NULL)
        DisposePtr((Ptr)myPresParamsPtr);

    if (myMediaParamsPtr != NULL)
        DisposePtr((Ptr)myMediaParamsPtr);

    if (myFileFilterUPP != NULL)
        DisposeNavObjectFilterUPP(myFileFilterUPP);

    return(myErr);
}
```

Notice that we dispose of the new presentation parameters structure (myPresParamsPtr) and the media parameters structure (myMediaParamsPtr) before returning from QTBC_SetupPresentation. QTSNewPresentation copies all the information we pass it, including any blocks of memory referenced in the new presentation parameters structure. If we had allocated any other information (for instance, a clip region), we should dispose of that memory too.

▶ Broadcasting

Now we've created a presentation and requested that the video data that is to be broadcast be previewed in the monitor window. In order for the previewing and subsequent broadcasting to proceed, we need to grant Quick-Time some time to process the presentation. We do this by calling the QTSPresIdle function periodically. As usual, we'll add some code to our application's QTApp_Idle function, which is called whenever we receive a null event:

```
if (gPresentation != kQTSInvalidPresentation)
    QTSPresIdle(gPresentation, NULL);
```

This just says: if we have an active presentation, grant it some processor time.

Starting the Broadcast

So far, however, no broadcasting is happening. In QTBroadcast, we wait until the user clicks the Start button in the monitor window to begin broadcasting. When the user clicks that button, QTBroadcast calls the QTBC_Start-Broadcasting function, defined in Listing 5.4. (Later we'll take a look at the code that handles those button clicks.)

Listing 5.4 Starting broadcasting.

```
OSErr QTBC_StartBroadcasting (void)
{
    // stop the preview
    QTSPresPreview(gPresentation, kQTSAllStreams, NULL, kQTSStoppedRate, 0);

    return(QTSPresPreroll(gPresentation, kQTSAllStreams, 0, (Fixed)kQTSNormalForwardRate,
            0L));
}
```

QTBC_StartBroadcasting first calls QTSPresPreview with a rate of kQTS-StoppedRate to stop previewing the data; then it calls QTSPresPreroll, which readies the media for broadcasting and performs any necessary handshaking between the transmitter (that is, the broadcasting computer) and the client computer or computers. (As you've probably guessed, prerolling a presentation with QTSPresPreroll is analogous to prerolling a movie with Preroll-Movie.)

QTSPresPreroll returns fairly quickly, as some of its operations involve establishing network connections and hence should occur asynchronously. We get informed of the success of the prerolling in our presentation notification procedure, by receiving a notification message of type kQTSPrerollAck-Notification. Once we receive this acknowledgement, we can then begin actually broadcasting data by calling the QTSPresStart function. Listing 5.5 shows our complete presentation notification procedure.

Listing 5.5 Handling notification messages.

```
static PASCAL_RTN ComponentResult QTBC_NotificationProc (ComponentResult theErr,
    OSType theNotificationType, void *theNotificationParams, void *theRefCon)
{
#pragma unused(theErr, theNotificationParams, theRefCon)
    QTSPresentation         myPresentation = kQTSInvalidPresentation;
    ComponentResult         myErr = noErr;

    switch (theNotificationType) {

        case kQTSNewPresentationNotification:
            // when we get this notification, the presentation has been created
            // and is sent to us in theNotificationParams;
            // if we needed it, we could retrieve it as follows:
            myPresentation = (QTSPresentation)theNotificationParams;
            break;

        case kQTSPrerollAckNotification:
            myErr = QTSPresStart(gPresentation, kQTSAllStreams, 0L);
            break;

        case kQTSStartAckNotification:
        case kQTSStopAckNotification:
            break;

        default:
            break;
    }

    return(myErr);
}
```

As you can see, we ignore most of the notification messages. We handle the kQTSPrerollAckNotification message to start broadcasting once the prerolling is complete. We also handle the kQTSNewPresentationNotification message, which is sent whenever a new presentation is created; in this case, the identifier for the new presentation is passed in the theNotification-Params parameter. (We don't actually do anything with that identifier; this code is provided to illustrate how to retrieve it if you need it.)

Finally, we're off and running. We've created a presentation, prerolled it, and (hopefully) received a notification that the prerolling was successful—in which case we've called QTSPresStart to start broadcasting data. Now it's up to the client to start receiving the data we're transmitting. This can happen

Figure 5.6 A client status message.

in one of several ways. The easiest way is to provide the client with a copy of the SDP file that we used to initiate the broadcast session. If the user opens this file with a QuickTime-savvy application, then QuickTime's *SDP importer* is called to convert the SDP data into a movie. When the application opens that movie, QuickTime connects to the server, requests that it start sending it data, and then receives the data into a local buffer; while this buffering is happening, the user will see a connection status display like the one shown in Figure 5.6.

The user can then save the movie into a new file; in this case, the new file is a QuickTime movie file that contains a streaming track; the media data for this track is just the text data in the original SDP file. Subsequently opening the movie file is pretty much identical to opening the SDP file.

Controlling the Broadcast

So we now see how to start broadcasting from a transmitter and how to receive the broadcast stream on a client. If we want to pause the broadcasting, we can call the QTBC_PauseBroadcasting function defined in Listing 5.6. This function calls QTSPresStop to stop the presentation and then QTSPresPreview with a rate of kQTSNormalForwardRate to resume previewing in the monitor window.

Listing 5.6 Pausing broadcasting.

```
OSErr QTBC_PauseBroadcasting (void)
{
  OSErr        myErr = noErr;
```

```
  myErr = QTSPresStop(gPresentation, kQTSAllStreams, OL);
  if (myErr != noErr)
    goto bail;

  // restart the preview
  myErr = QTSPresPreview(gPresentation, kQTSAllStreams, NULL, kQTSNormalForwardRate, 0);

bail:
  return(myErr);
}
```

After pausing a broadcast by calling QTBC_PauseBroadcasting, we could later resume the broadcast by calling QTBC_StartBroadcasting once again. If we want to stop broadcasting for good (perhaps because the application is shutting down), we can call the QTBC_StopBroadcasting function defined in Listing 5.7. This function calls QTSPresStop to stop broadcasting and then QTSDisposePresentation to dispose of the presentation. Notice that we also set the global variable gPresentation to kQTSInvalidPresentation, so that QTSPresIdle is no longer called in QTApp_Idle.

Listing 5.7   Stopping broadcasting.

```
OSErr QTBC_StopBroadcasting (void)
{
  OSErr        myErr = noErr;

  if (gPresentation != kQTSInvalidPresentation) {
    myErr = QTSPresStop(gPresentation, kQTSAllStreams, OL);

    if (myErr != noErr)
      myErr = QTSDisposePresentation(gPresentation, OL);

    gPresentation = kQTSInvalidPresentation;
  }

  return(myErr);
}
```

⦿ Broadcast Settings

Once we've created a new presentation based on an existing SDP file, we want to allow the user to view and configure the presentation's settings. QTBroadcast provides the Configure Settings menu item in its Test menu;

when the user selects this item and a presentation is under way, QTBroadcast displays the Transmission Settings dialog box shown in Figure 5.7. This dialog box shows the source, compression algorithm, and packetizer currently being used for the audio and video streams; it also displays the current data rate for each stream. Notice that there is no way for the user to modify any of these settings, since the broadcast has already begun.

If a presentation is not under way, then when the user selects the Configure Settings menu item, QTBroadcast displays the Transmission Settings dialog box shown in Figure 5.8. As you can see, the dialog box now contains some buttons that allow the user to modify various broadcast settings. For instance, if the user clicks the Source button associated with the video stream, the dialog box shown in Figure 5.9 appears. And if the user clicks the Packetizer button associated with the video stream, the dialog box shown in Figure 5.10 appears.

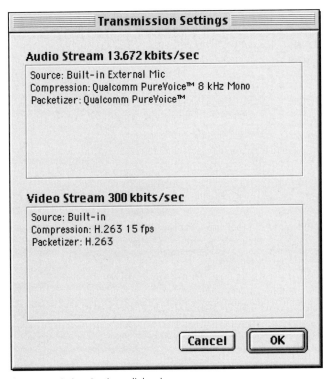

Figure 5.7 The Transmission Settings dialog box.

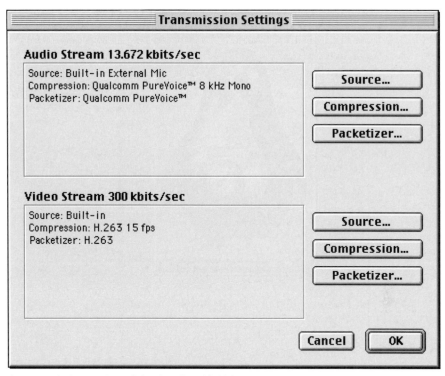

Figure 5.8 The Transmission Settings dialog box (modifiable).

It's actually quite simple to display all these dialog boxes; indeed, we need to call only a single function, QTSPresSettingsDialog, as shown in Listing 5.8 (which lists the code we execute in response to the Configure Settings menu item).

Listing 5.8 Handling the Configure Settings menu item.

```
case IDM_GET_SETTINGS:
  if (gPresentation != kQTSInvalidPresentation)
    myErr = QTSPresSettingsDialog(gPresentation, kQTSAllStreams, 0, NULL, 0L);

  if (myErr != noErr)
    QTFrame_Beep();
  myIsHandled = true;
  break;
```

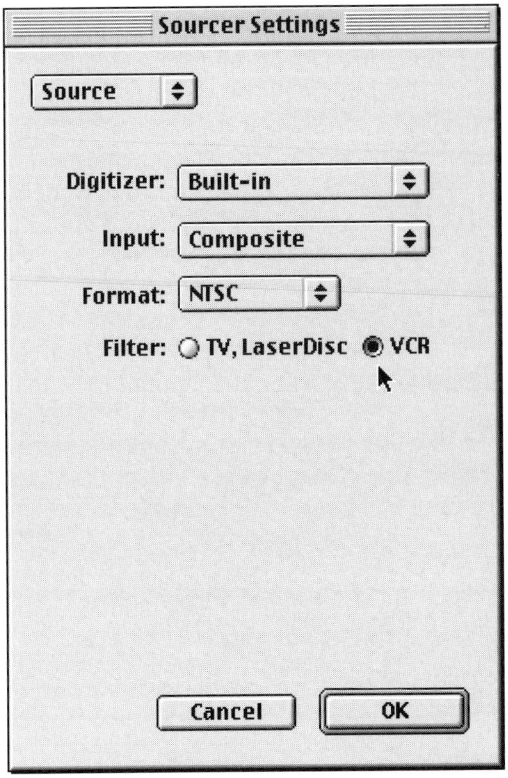

Figure 5.9 The video stream Sourcer Settings dialog box.

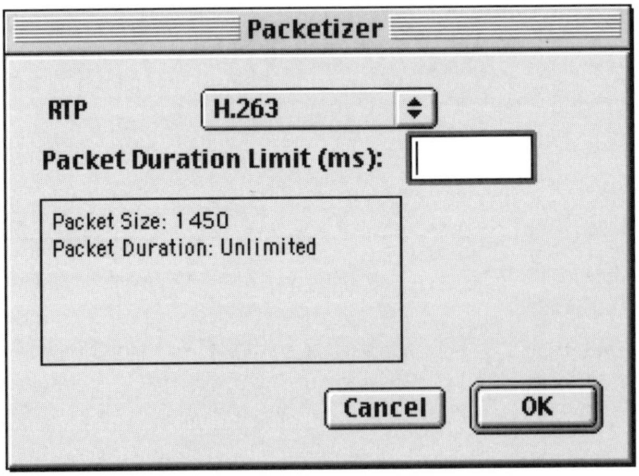

Figure 5.10 The video stream Packetizer dialog box.

◉ Monitor Window Control

We're just about finished learning how to use QuickTime to broadcast data across a network. We've encountered all the basic functions we need to create and preroll presentations, start and stop previewing, and actually start sending streams of data to a remote client. Let's finish off quickly by taking a look at the code we use to create and manage the monitor window.

We create a single monitor window at application launch time by calling the QTBC_CreateMonitorWindow function, defined in Listing 5.9. This function calls GetNewDialog to open a dialog box whose attributes and items are defined by a 'DLOG' resource of ID kMonitorDLOGID.

Listing 5.9 Creating the monitor window.

```
DialogPtr QTBC_CreateMonitorWindow (void)
{
  DialogPtr       myDialog = NULL;

  myDialog = GetNewDialog(kMonitorDLOGID, NULL, (WindowPtr)-1L);
  if (myDialog != NULL) {
    short         myItemKind;
    Handle        myItemHandle = NULL;
    Rect          myItemRect;

    MacSetPort(GetDialogPort(myDialog));

    // set the user item drawing procedure
    GetDialogItem(myDialog, kMonitorUserItemID, &myItemKind, &myItemHandle, &myItemRect);
    SetDialogItem(myDialog, kMonitorUserItemID, myItemKind,
        (Handle)gMonitorUserItemProcUPP, &myItemRect);

    MacShowWindow(GetDialogWindow(myDialog));
    QTBC_UserItemProcedure(myDialog, kMonitorUserItemID);
  }

  return(myDialog);
}
```

QTBC_CreateMonitorWindow also sets the user item procedure for the user item in the monitor window to be the function QTBC_UserItemProcedure, defined in Listing 5.10. This user item procedure draws a frame around the user item and also sets the state of the Start/Pause button; if no presentation is active, we want to disable the button so that it cannot be pressed.

Listing 5.10 Drawing the user item in the monitor window.

```
PASCAL_RTN void QTBC_UserItemProcedure (DialogPtr theDialog, short theItem)
{
    short           myItemKind;
    Handle          myItemHandle = NULL;
    Rect            myItemRect;
    GrafPtr         mySavedPort;
    OSErr           myErr = noErr;

    GetPort(&mySavedPort);
    MacSetPort(GetDialogPort(theDialog));

    if (theItem != kMonitorUserItemID)
        goto bail;

    // draw a frame around the user item rectangle
    GetDialogItem(theDialog, kMonitorUserItemID, &myItemKind, &myItemHandle, &myItemRect);
    InsetRect(&myItemRect, -1, -1);
    MacFrameRect(&myItemRect);

    // enable the Start/Stop button in the monitor window
    GetDialogItem(theDialog, kMonitorButtonID, &myItemKind, &myItemHandle, &myItemRect);
    if (myItemHandle != NULL) {
        if (gPresentation == kQTSInvalidPresentation)
            HiliteControl((ControlHandle)myItemHandle, 255);
        else
            HiliteControl((ControlHandle)myItemHandle, 0);
    }

bail:
    MacSetPort(mySavedPort);
}
```

We handle clicks on the button in the QTBC_HandleMonitorWindowEvents function (Listing 5.11), which is called by QTApp_HandleEvent for any events targeted at a dialog box.

Listing 5.11 Handling events in the monitor window.

```
void QTBC_HandleMonitorWindowEvents (DialogPtr theDialog, DialogItemIndex theItemHit)
{
  short           myItemKind;
  Handle          myItemHandle = NULL;
  Rect            myItemRect;

  if ((theDialog == gMonitor) && (theItemHit == kMonitorButtonID)) {

    GetDialogItem(theDialog, kMonitorButtonID, &myItemKind, &myItemHandle, &myItemRect);
    if (gBroadcasting) {
      QTBC_PauseBroadcasting();
      SetControlTitle((ControlHandle)myItemHandle, "\pStart");
    } else {
      QTBC_StartBroadcasting();
      SetControlTitle((ControlHandle)myItemHandle, "\pPause");
    }

    gBroadcasting = !gBroadcasting;
  }
}
```

▶ Conclusion

The broadcasting support introduced in QuickTime 5 allows us to write applications that transmit data captured or stored on a local server to a client (or set of clients) located remotely on a network. It's important to remember that the streams of media data transmitted by QuickTime's broadcasting components conform to the IETF protocols (principally, RTP and RTSP) and hence can be received by any standards-compliant client application. As we've seen, QuickTime 4 provided support for receiving those kinds of streams. So we can use QuickTime APIs to develop both the transmitter and the receiver.

The Flash

Using Macromedia Flash with QuickTime

▶ Introduction

Macromedia Flash is a multimedia development environment from Macromedia, Inc., for creating and delivering interactive vector-based graphics, animations, and sounds both locally and over the Internet. Because of its low bandwidth requirements and fast rendering capabilities, it has become especially popular for Web-based content delivery. Indeed, Macromedia claims that almost 97% of all online users currently are able to view Flash content using the Flash Web browser plug-in. In addition, users can view Flash movie files locally using the stand-alone Flash Player application. Flash content can even be viewed on some set-top boxes and handheld devices.

In QuickTime 4, Apple introduced the *Flash media handler*, which provides support for including Flash content inside of QuickTime movies. As a result, any QuickTime-savvy application can open and display Flash movie files. The Flash movie data is converted into a *Flash track*, which can then be played by itself or combined with other kinds of tracks. For instance, we can construct a QuickTime movie in which Flash graphic elements (such as buttons and menus) serve to control other tracks in the movie. Figure 6.1 illustrates this possibility. This movie contains three tracks: a video track, a sound track, and a Flash track. The three buttons and the text "Flash and QuickTime" are part of the Flash track, which has a lower layer number than the video track and hence is positioned in front of the video track. The text has no interactive behaviors; the three buttons are configured (from top to bottom) to start the video and sound tracks playing, go to the beginning of the movie, and stop the video and sound tracks. The pointing-hand cursor is displayed automatically by the Flash media handler when the cursor is moved over any of the three buttons.

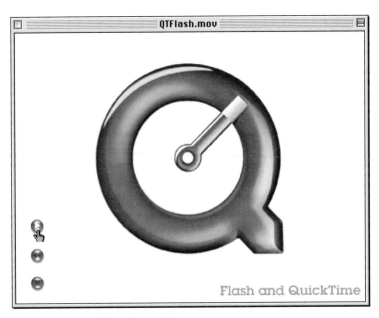

Figure 6.1 A Flash track controlling video and sound tracks.

QuickTime 4 also added the ability to attach wired actions to elements in a Flash movie, thereby supplementing the native Flash interactivity. The Flash track in the movie in Figure 6.1 is able to control the play state and time of the video and sound tracks by virtue of some clever movie authoring, wherein the video track and the Flash track have the same number of frames and the same playback speed (so that jumping to a frame in the Flash track, using Flash scripting, automatically jumps to the corresponding frame in the video track). For nonlinear media types, like QuickTime VR or sprites, we'll need to use wired actions to be able to control our QuickTime movies using Flash buttons and menus.

In this chapter and the next, we're going to investigate a number of ways to work with QuickTime and Flash. We'll see how to import Flash content into QuickTime movies and how to extract Flash tracks from QuickTime movies. Importing Flash content into QuickTime is actually pretty straightforward, but there are a few places we can enhance the work done by QuickTime's Flash movie importer. We'll also see how to combine QuickTime video with Flash, how to handle some of the application-specific actions that can be included in a Flash movie, and how to work directly with the Flash media handler APIs. Finally, we'll see how to attach wired actions

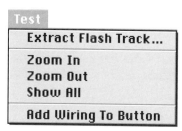

Figure 6.2 The Test menu of QTFlash.

to elements in a Flash track and how to send wired actions from non-Flash tracks to Flash tracks. Those tasks involving wired actions will require us to learn a fair bit about the structure of Flash files and, indeed, will lead us into some of the most intricate code we've encountered so far in this book. The payoff is that we'll be able to use any of the hundred or more QuickTime wired actions inside of a Flash track, in addition to the more limited assortment of native Flash actions.

Our sample application for these two chapters is called QTFlash; its Test menu is shown in Figure 6.2. The first menu item allows us to extract a Flash track from a QuickTime movie (which is essentially the reverse operation of importing a Flash movie file into a QuickTime movie). The middle group of menu items allows us to adjust the magnification of a Flash track. The Zoom In menu item, for instance, doubles the magnification of the image so that the rectangle in the center of the image that is half the width and height of the movie window is expanded to exactly fill the movie window. The last menu item allows us to attach some wired actions to a button in a Flash track. In this chapter, we'll see how to implement all these items but the last, which we'll reserve for extended treatment in the next chapter.

Flash Overview

Macromedia's Flash multimedia development environment is a tightly integrated set of tools for creating and displaying vector-based graphics and animations that are interactive. Flash grew out of a drawing program, written largely by Jonathan Gay, that allowed the user to create graphics and other objects that interact with the user and with one another. Flash provides this capability with a vengeance: in a Flash movie, pressing a button might cause some object to move around inside a window. Or, typing some numbers into a text field might change the size of a graphic element. Or, moving the cursor over an image might load a Web page into the user's browser or start a sound playing. Or, clicking and dragging a slider thumb might adjust the balance of that sound.

If all this sounds familiar, it's because we encountered these kinds of capabilities when we discussed QuickTime's wired sprites in Volume One. What we're working with, in the cases of both QuickTime and Flash, are graphic elements that are associated with actions initiated by user and system events. The events that trigger the actions are quite similar in the two cases; they include mouse-enter events, mouse-exit events, button-click events, and the like. And the actions triggered by those events also overlap to some degree. In both cases, we can jump to specific times in the movie, open URLs, play sounds, adjust video and sound characteristics, and so forth.

Where Flash differs from QuickTime is that Flash was developed from the ground up with Web-based delivery in mind. This focus affects both the basic drawing model and the data storage format. Flash supports bitmapped graphics (for instance, JPEG images), but it was primarily designed to use vector-based images, which typically have a smaller file size than bitmapped graphics and which are also scalable without loss of quality. Moreover, the Flash file format was designed so that Flash movies are streamable over network connections. The Flash playback mechanism was designed to be self-contained—that is, to have minimal reliance on services provided by the host operating system. For instance, much of the text you see in a Flash movie is rendered by the playback application from outline data contained in the Flash file and does not depend on any particular fonts being installed on the user's computer.

Let's take a look, then, at the various pieces of the Flash architecture. We can create some Flash content using an application called Macromedia Flash. This application provides numerous tools for drawing vector shapes and for importing bitmapped graphics and sounds. These items are collected into a library, and instances of those objects can be placed on a stage at certain points in a timeline. Figure 6.3 shows the main window of a Flash document, which includes the stage and the timeline.

We can animate items on the stage by changing their sizes and locations over time. Flash supports several kinds of tweening: *motion tweening* (which is essentially the kind of position tweening we encountered with QuickTime sprites) and *shape tweening* (which is a kind of morphing of one shape into another). We can also attach executable code to frames in the timeline or to buttons in the Flash movie; this code is written in a variant of JavaScript called *ActionScript*.

The data in a Flash document is saved on disk in a *Flash document file* (or *Flash project file*), whose filename extension is usually .fla. When we're ready to publish our work, we typically create a *Flash movie file* (or *Flash file*), whose filename extension is usually .swf. The Flash movie file is a highly optimized version of the data in the Flash project file. This optimization compacts the data and removes any unnecessary elements. For example,

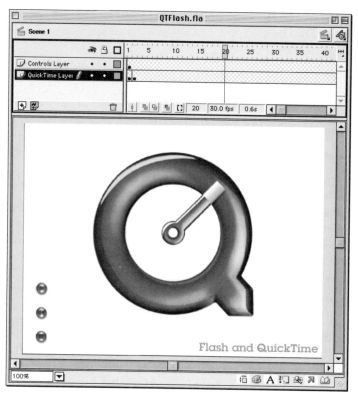

Figure 6.3 A Macromedia Flash document window.

a Flash project file may include a complete outline font, but the Flash movie file contains the outline data for only those characters in the font that are actually displayed in some frame in the movie. As a result, a Flash movie file cannot typically be edited in any useful manner. It's designed solely for playback (unlike QuickTime movie files, which are designed both for playback and for data interchange).

On the playback side of the ledger, we have several possibilities open to us. We can embed the Flash movie file in a Web page, which is then viewable by anyone who has the Flash browser plug-in installed. Or, we can open the Flash movie file from a local disk using an application called *Flash Player* (on Windows, *FlashPla.exe*). Or, as you've probably guessed, we can open the Flash movie file using any QuickTime-savvy application (for instance, QuickTime Player or our own QTShell-based sample applications). Figure 6.4 illustrates the authoring and playback possibilities.

The Flash movie file data is converted into a QuickTime movie by the Flash movie importer. The imported data is written into a Flash track (of type FlashMediaType) and is processed at playback time by the Flash media

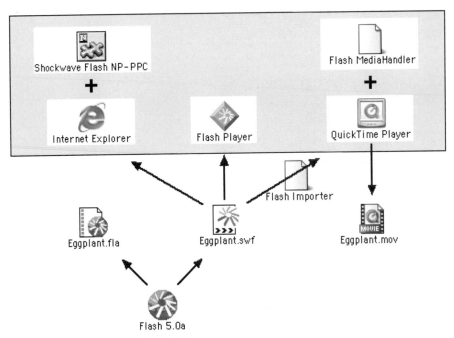

Figure 6.4 The Flash authoring and playback architecture.

handler. If we save the movie, we can create a QuickTime movie file that contains the Flash track.

Not everything in a Flash movie is attached to the main timeline. Flash supports objects with independent timelines, called *movieclips*. An animation in a movieclip may continue running even if the main timeline is stopped. A Flash movieclip is, therefore, analogous to a QuickTime child movie (which can have a time base that's independent of the time base of its parent). Later we'll see that a movieclip is contained in a Flash file in a block of data of type stagDefineSprite; as a result, movieclips are sometimes called *sprites*. This is potentially confusing terminology, at least for us QuickTime programmers. Just keep in mind that a Flash sprite is not at all akin to a Quick-Time sprite; rather, it's a movieclip, which is most like a QuickTime child movie.

▶ Flash and Video

Macromedia Flash provides a powerful array of services, indeed, and each new version of Flash ups the ante by supporting at least one important new feature. Flash version 5 added support for rendering text formatted with

HTML markup tags inside of Flash movies and for exchanging XML-formatted data with remote servers. Flash version 6—dubbed *Flash MX*—added (among other things) the ability to include small video clips inside of a Flash movie. If our projects require us to combine Flash content and video, we can migrate to Flash MX. In that case, however, we must leave Quick-Time behind, for the current Flash media handler supports Flash files that conform to version 5 and earlier.

If we want to stick with versions of Flash that QuickTime can handle and if we want to combine Flash and video, there are two general approaches we can follow. First, we can convert a video clip into a series of individual images, which can be displayed by Flash Player (or any other Flash-savvy application) as bitmapped images. Second, we can build a QuickTime movie that contains a Flash track and other kinds of tracks, including video and sound tracks; the Flash track can contain buttons and other interactive elements, which might control the operations of the other tracks (as we saw in Figure 6.1). Let's investigate each of these approaches briefly.

Converting QuickTime Video into an Image Sequence

There are several commercial products that can convert a QuickTime video movie file into a Flash file. One such product is called Flix and is developed and distributed by Wildform, Inc. Essentially, Flix renders each video frame of the QuickTime movie and writes it into a Flash file as a JPEG image; the sequence of images is drawn at a preset rate to simulate the original video clip. Flix also converts any sound tracks in the movie into streaming sounds in the Flash file. Figure 6.5 shows the video settings panel of the Flix conversion window.

The main advantage with this approach to combining video and Flash content is that the resulting file is a bona fide Flash movie file, which can be opened by the Flash Player application or embedded in a Web page and streamed to the user's computer, where it is handled by the Flash Web browser plug-in. The main disadvantage is that both image quality and playback frame rate must be sacrificed to keep the resulting Flash file size reasonable. The QuickTime movie being compressed in Figure 6.5 is a 20-fps, 480-by-360-pixel movie compressed with Sorenson 2 encoding; the output Flash file contains a 12-fps, 320-by-240-pixel JPEG-encoded stream of images. Moreover, this is really the best-case scenario for Flix, using the settings suitable for a DSL or cable-modem connection. A Flash file suitable for streaming across a 56-Kbps modem is noticeably choppier and of poorer image quality than a QuickTime movie compressed for the same speed.

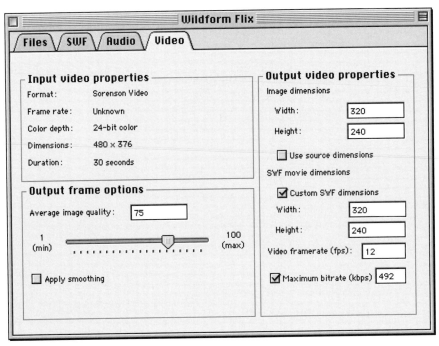

Figure 6.5 The Flix video settings panel.

Including Flash Data in a QuickTime File

To combine Flash content with QuickTime video while retaining high quality and high frame rates for the video, we need to pursue a different strategy: we need to build a QuickTime movie that contains one or more video tracks, a Flash track, and perhaps other kinds of tracks too. The Flash track might add graphic overlays on the video; it might also contain buttons or other interactive elements that control the other tracks in the movie. (We saw both these things in the movie shown in Figure 6.1 earlier.) The Flash track can control the other tracks using either its native Flash scripting (ActionScript) or QuickTime wired actions.

The easiest way to merge Flash and QuickTime in this way is to import the QuickTime movie into a layer in the Macromedia Flash authoring tool. (See Figure 6.3 once again.) The frame rate of the Flash movie should be set to match that of the imported QuickTime movie, and there should be one frame in the Flash timeline for each frame in the QuickTime movie. This allows us to move to specific frames in the QuickTime movie by jumping to the corresponding frame in the Flash track. We can then create Flash elements (buttons, menus, and so forth) in other layers and script them to control the QuickTime video. For instance, we can set this chunk of ActionScript to be executed whenever the user clicks and releases the top button:

```
on (release) {
  play();
}
```

The `play` command starts the Flash track playing, which sets the entire QuickTime movie playing.

Similarly, we can set this chunk of ActionScript to be executed when the user clicks and releases the middle button:

```
on (release) {
  gotoAndStop(1);
}
```

The `gotoAndStop` function jumps to the specified frame number and then pauses playback.

When we are ready to output a file, we must export the data as a QuickTime movie file. The Flash content is written into a Flash track, and the QuickTime data is preserved in its original form. Note that the scripting used on the buttons must be compatible with version 5 of the Flash file format. The most recently released version of QuickTime supports Flash files only up to version 5. (Later we'll see how we can dynamically determine the Flash file format versions supported by QuickTime's Flash media handler.) Any scripting that relies on the more advanced features in Flash MX will not be recognized by the current Flash media handler.

It's important to understand that a Flash track cannot directly control other tracks in a QuickTime movie using only the native Flash scripting capabilities. The middle button in our sample movie manages to rewind the entire QuickTime movie only indirectly, by telling the Flash track to go to its first frame. This prompts the movie controller to jump to the first frame in the Flash track, which—by dint of our clever authoring—corresponds to the first frame in the video track. This scheme would not work with nonlinear QuickTime media types, such as QuickTime VR movies or many sprite movies. To control those sorts of movies using Flash tracks, we need to attach QuickTime wired actions to items in the Flash track. Most often, we'll want to attach wired actions to Flash buttons. So let's take a look at how buttons operate.

▶ Buttons

Buttons are the primary interactive elements in a Flash movie. They respond to mouse events (that is, mouse movements and mouse button clicks) and can trigger one or more actions in response to those events. Every button has three distinct states, called the *up state,* the *over state,* and the *down state.* A button is in the up state (or *idle state*) when the cursor is not within the bounds of the button image. (This is the default state of a button.) A button is in the over state when the cursor is within the bounds of the button image. A button is in the down state when the mouse button is down and the cursor is within the bounds of the button image.

Each state of a button can have an image associated with it. Figure 6.6 shows the images associated with a typical button. The left-hand image is the up state image, where the cursor is outside of the button. The middle image is the over state image; notice that the cursor changes and the round part of the button image reverses its colors. The right-hand image is the down state image; once again, the round part of the image changes to reflect the different state.

Some button states can share an image. Figure 6.7 shows a Flash movie that contains a single button (which, when pressed, plays a penguin screech). In this case, the up state and the over state use the same image. When the mouse button is pressed and the cursor is within the button image, the down state appears (Figure 6.8).

Figure 6.6 The state images for a Flash button.

Figure 6.7 The up and over state images of a Flash button.

Figure 6.8 The down state image of a Flash button.

Flash supports two kinds of buttons. A *push button* (like those shown in Figures 6.6–6.8) is what we usually think of as a button: if you press the mouse button, hold it down, and move the cursor outside of the button image, the button remains in its down state. The button is said to *capture* the mouse. By contrast, a *menu button* is a button that does not capture the mouse; if you click a menu button, hold the mouse button down, and then drag outside of the menu button, the button returns to its up state.

Actions are associated with *button state transitions*, that is, the change from one button state to another. To delineate the possible button state transitions, we need to pay attention to changes in the cursor location and the mouse button state. The cursor can be either outside or inside the button image, and the mouse button can be either up or down. This gives us four possible combinations of cursor location and mouse button state and, hence, eight possible transitions where either the location or mouse button state changes (but not both at the same time).

The transition from mouse button up to mouse button down when the cursor is outside a button is not particularly useful and is ignored by Flash when processing button events. On the other hand, the transition from mouse button down to mouse button up when the cursor is outside a button is, in fact, useful if the mouse button was originally pressed inside the button. So there are seven possible button transitions for a button that allows moving the cursor in or out of a button while the button is down (that is, for a push button). There are six possible button transitions for a menu button. Four of these thirteen total transitions are shared by push buttons and menu buttons, so there are actually only nine total button transitions.

All buttons have these four button state transitions:

1. Mouse button up, cursor enters the button. This is a button *roll-over*.
2. Mouse button up, cursor leaves the button. This is a button *roll-out*.
3. Cursor inside button, mouse button changes from up to down. This is a button *press*.
4. Cursor inside button, mouse button changes from down to up. This is a button *release*.

A push button can have these three additional button state transitions:

1. Mouse button down, cursor enters the button. This is a button *drag-over*.
2. Mouse button down, cursor leaves the button. This is a button *drag-out*.
3. Cursor outside button, mouse button changes from down to up. This is a button *outside release*.

A menu button can have these two additional button state transitions:

1. Mouse button down, cursor enters the button. This is a button *drag-over*.
2. Mouse button down, cursor leaves the button. This is a button *drag-out*.

It might seem like these two additional menu button state transitions are identical with two of the additional push button state transitions, but in fact they result in different visual behaviors. When the cursor is dragged outside of a menu button while the mouse button is down, the button immediately returns to the idle state; by contrast, when the cursor is dragged outside of a push button while the mouse button is down, the button changes from the down to the over state. Accordingly, Flash considers these transitions to be different.

We'll need some way to refer to these nine button state transitions in our code. The file FlashParser.h enumerates a set of constants that specify bit positions in a 16-bit conditions value stored with the button data in a Flash file. (The high-order seven bits are currently reserved.)

```
enum {
    bsIdleToOverUp          = 0,    // roll-over
    bsOverUpToIdle,                 // roll-out
    bsOverUpToOverDown,             // press
    bsOverDownToOverUp,             // release
```

```
// these transitions apply only when tracking "push" buttons
bsOverDownToOutDown,                        // drag-out
bsOutDownToOverDown,                        // drag-over
bsOutDownToIdle,                            // outside release

// these transitions apply only when tracking "menu" buttons
bsIdleToOverDown,                           // drag-over
bsOverDownToIdle                            // drag-out
};
```

We'll define another set of constants that we can use as masks to read those bits:

```
#define kIdleToOverUp           (1L << bsIdleToOverUp)
#define kOverUpToIdle           (1L << bsOverUpToIdle)
#define kOverUpToOverDown       (1L << bsOverUpToOverDown)
#define kOverDownToOverUp       (1L << bsOverDownToOverUp)

#define kOverDownToOutDown      (1L << bsOverDownToOutDown)
#define kOutDownToOverDown      (1L << bsOutDownToOverDown)
#define kOutDownToIdle          (1L << bsOutDownToIdle)

#define kIdleToOverDown         (1L << bsIdleToOverDown)
#define kOverDownToIdle         (1L << bsOverDownToIdle)
```

We'll also use these constants as event types when we build wired actions for Flash tracks. For example, we can build an event atom that triggers on a mouse-down event with this line of code:

```
myErr = QTInsertChild(*theActions, kParentAtomIsContainer, kQTEventType,
        kOverUpToOverDown, 1, 0, NULL, &myEventAtom);
```

But we're getting ahead of ourselves here. Right now we need to delve into the structure of Flash files.

The Flash File Format

A Macromedia Flash file (or SWF) is a stream of bytes that is organized as a header block followed by a series of tagged data blocks, as shown in Figure 6.9.

The *header block* contains general information about the Flash file, such as its size, the dimensions of the Flash movie, and the number of frames in the movie. The *tagged data blocks* define the items that appear in the Flash movie (that is, the buttons, shapes, and sounds) and indicate where and

Header block   Tagged data blocks

Figure 6.9 The format of a Flash file.

when those items are to be drawn or played and possibly also animated. To work with Flash data inside of QuickTime movies, we need to understand this structure in a fair bit of detail. We'll begin by defining some functions that will allow us to read chunks of data from the stream of bytes that comprises a Flash file. Then we'll learn how to parse the header block and the tagged data blocks.

Reading Bytes from a Stream

As mentioned previously, a Flash file is a stream of bytes that is divided into a series of blocks. Except for the header block, each block begins with some data that indicates what kind of block it is (that's the *tag*) and how large it is. A Flash file is, therefore, not unlike a QuickTime file, which consists of a series of atoms, each of which begins with a length and a type. (See Volume One, Chapter 8, for more details on the atom-based structure of QuickTime files.) A tagged data block can contain other tagged data blocks, but for present purposes we will not need to look inside of any hierarchical blocks. So we can accomplish what we need to do by reading the file, byte by byte or sometimes even bit by bit, from beginning to end.

Let's begin by defining some functions that allow us to read chunks of information of various sizes from a stream of data. For instance, we'll define a function GetByte that returns the next 8-bit chunk of the stream and another function GetWord that returns the next 16-bit chunk of the stream. Throughout our stream-parsing code, we'll use these basic data types:

```
typedef unsigned char    U8, *P_U8, **PP_U8;
typedef signed char      S8, *P_S8, **PP_S8;
typedef unsigned short   U16, *P_U16, **PP_U16;
typedef signed short     S16, *P_S16, **PP_S16;
typedef unsigned long    U32, *P_U32, **PP_U32;
typedef signed long      S32, *P_S32, **PP_S32;
typedef signed long      SCOORD, *P_SCOORD;
```

The SCOORD data type represents a coordinate; indeed, a point (of type SPOINT) is simply a pair of coordinates, declared like this:

```
typedef struct SPOINT {
  SCOORD        x;
  SCOORD        y;
} SPOINT, *P_SPOINT;
```

And a rectangle (of type SRECT) is a quadruple of coordinates:

```
typedef struct SRECT {
  SCOORD        xmin;
  SCOORD        xmax;
  SCOORD        ymin;
  SCOORD        ymax;
} SRECT, *P_SRECT;
```

A rectangle occupies 16 bytes of memory; we'll soon see, however, that Flash utilizes a bit-packing scheme that can compress a rectangle to 8 bytes when it is written to a Flash file.

As we're reading through the stream of data, we need to keep track of the current position in the stream, as well as information about the start position and the length of the current tagged data block. For this, we'll use the FlashParserStruct data type, defined like this:

```
typedef struct FlashParserStruct {
  Handle      m_theData;

  // pointer to file contents buffer
  U8          *m_fileBuf;

  // file state information
  U32         m_filePos;
  U32         m_fileSize;
  U32         m_fileStart;
  U16         m_fileVersion;

  S32         m_frameHeight;
  S32         m_frameWidth;
  U32         m_frameRate;
  U32         m_frameCount;

  // bit handling
  S32         m_bitPos;
  U32         m_bitBuf;

  // tag parsing information
  U32         m_tagStart;
  U32         m_tagEnd;
  U32         m_tagLen;
} FlashParserStruct, *FlashParserPtr, **FlashParserHandle;
```

The m_theData field is a handle to the data stream itself, and m_fileBuf is a pointer to the first byte in the data stream. The m_filePos field is the offset of the next byte we need to read from the beginning of the data stream. Each time we read a byte from the data stream, we need to update m_filePos. We'll describe the remaining fields of the FlashParserStruct structure a bit later.

To extract a 1-byte, 2-byte, or 4-byte chunk from the data stream, we can use the functions GetByte, GetWord, and GetDWord defined in Listing 6.1.

Listing 6.1 Reading bytes from a Flash data stream.

```
U8 GetByte (void)
{
  return(gFlashParserData.m_fileBuf[gFlashParserData.m_filePos++]);
}

U16 GetWord (void)
{
  U8 *s = gFlashParserData.m_fileBuf + gFlashParserData.m_filePos;

  gFlashParserData.m_filePos += 2;
  return((U16)s[0] | ((U16)s[1] << 8));
}

U32 GetDWord (void)
{
  U8 *s = gFlashParserData.m_fileBuf + gFlashParserData.m_filePos;

  gFlashParserData.m_filePos += 4;
  return((U32)s[0] | ((U32)s[1] << 8) | ((U32)s[2] << 16) | ((U32)s[3] << 24));
}
```

You'll notice that multibyte data in a Flash file is stored in little-endian format. GetWord and GetDWord read each byte individually and reconstruct a native-endian value by doing the appropriate bit shifting and logical adding.

Some data in a Flash file is stored as a C string (a sequence of bytes followed by a NULL byte). We can use the GetAString function defined in Listing 6.2 to read a string from the current file position. (GetAString is called GetString in the source code from which our parser is derived, but the Macintosh APIs already include a function called GetString; hence the renaming.)

Listing 6.2   Reading a string from a Flash data stream.

```
char *GetAString (void)
{
  // point to the string
  char *myString = (char *)&gFlashParserData.m_fileBuf[gFlashParserData.m_filePos];

  // skip over the string
  while (GetByte())
    ;

  return(myString);
}
```

GetAString returns a pointer to the first character in the string, which is simply the location of the byte at the current file position. We need to advance the file position past the string and the terminating NULL byte, however, so that subsequent reads don't return characters in the string. That's what the while loop accomplishes. Note that GetAString does not return a copy of the string in the data stream, so we wouldn't want to call free on the pointer that it returns.

Reading Bits from a Stream

Some information in a Flash file is contained in sub-byte chunks—that is, in individual bits or in bit fields. The FlashParserStruct structure contains two fields, m_bitPos and m_bitBuf, that are used for reading one or more bits at a time. Listing 6.3 defines the function GetBits, which we can use to read a specified number of bits from the input stream.

Listing 6.3   Reading bits from a Flash data stream.

```
U32 GetBits (S32 n)
{
  U32     v = 0;

  for (;;) {
    S32     s = n - gFlashParserData.m_bitPos;
    if (s > 0) {
      // consume the entire buffer
      v |= gFlashParserData.m_bitBuf << s;
      n -= gFlashParserData.m_bitPos;
```

```
    // get the next buffer
    gFlashParserData.m_bitBuf = GetByte();
    gFlashParserData.m_bitPos = 8;
  } else {
    // consume a portion of the buffer and mask off the consumed bits
    v |= gFlashParserData.m_bitBuf >> -s;
    gFlashParserData.m_bitPos -= n;
    gFlashParserData.m_bitBuf &= 0xff >> (8 - gFlashParserData.m_bitPos);
    return(v);
  }
 }
}
```

Occasionally, we'll want to read a chunk of bits as a signed value; for that, we can use the GetSBits function defined in Listing 6.4.

Listing 6.4 Reading bits as a signed quantity.

```
S32 GetSBits (S32 n)
{
  // get the number as an unsigned value
  S32 v = (S32)GetBits(n);

  // if the number is negative, extend the sign
  if (v & (1L << (n - 1)))
    v |= -1L << n;

  return(v);
}
```

Before we call either GetBits or GetSBits to read some bits from the data stream, we need to initialize the m_bitPos and m_bitBuf fields of our parser data structure. For that, we use the InitBits function defined in Listing 6.5.

Listing 6.5 Initializing the bit data fields.

```
void InitBits (void)
{
  gFlashParserData.m_bitPos = 0;
  gFlashParserData.m_bitBuf = 0;
}
```

Reading Rectangle Data

A Flash data stream contains a number of chunks of data that are structured into points, matrices, colors, and other data types. For present purposes, we need to be able to read only one structured data type, a rectangle. We saw earlier that an SRECT structure contains four coordinates, each of which occupies 4 bytes. When a rectangle is written into a Flash data stream, the information in those 16 bytes is packed into a series of bit fields, primarily to save space in the data stream. The first five bits of the packed data indicate how many bits each of the four coordinates occupies. Then each coordinate follows those initial five bits, occupying the specified number of bits. The entire packed structure is expanded to the nearest byte boundary by appending bits whose value is zero.

We can use the GetRect function defined in Listing 6.6 to read a rectangle from a Flash data stream. As you can see, GetRect uses the InitBits, GetBits, and GetSBits functions just defined.

Listing 6.6 Reading a rectangle from a Flash data stream.

```
void GetRect (SRECT *r)
{
  int       nBits;

  InitBits();

  nBits = (int)GetBits(5);
  r->xmin = GetSBits(nBits);
  r->xmax = GetSBits(nBits);
  r->ymin = GetSBits(nBits);
  r->ymax = GetSBits(nBits);
}
```

Most often, each coordinate of a rectangle is packed into 14 bits. This means that the rectangle data can be stored in 61 bits (that is, 4 times 14, plus the 5-bit length specifier); expanding the chunk to the nearest byte boundary gives a total of 64 bits, or 8 bytes. So a rectangle can usually be compressed into half its original size using this simple bit-packing scheme.

Let's look at a real-life example of this. A particular rectangle might be encoded as 0x7000096000006400. The first five bits of this quantity are 01110, or 14. The next 14 bits are all zeros. The next 14 bits are 01001011000000, which is 0x12C0, or 4800. The third chunk of 14 bits is once again all zeros. The final chunk of 14 bits is 00110010000000, which is 0x0C80, or 3200. So the upper-left corner of this rectangle is (0, 0) and the lower-right corner is (4800, 3200).

Perhaps you are thinking that that's an awfully large rectangle. It turns out that coordinates in Flash movie files are specified in units of twentieths of a pixel (affectionately known as *twips*). So in pixels, this rectangle would be 240 by 160, which is not so big after all.

Parsing the Header Block

We now have sufficient tools to parse a Flash data stream. As you know, a Flash file begins with a header block, which is almost always 20 bytes in length. The first four bytes contain a file signature and a version byte. The next four bytes contain the size of the entire Flash file, in bytes. Following the file length field is a packed rectangle that indicates the dimensions of the Flash movie. As we've seen, this field is almost always eight bytes long. The last four bytes are a two-byte frame rate (interpreted as a Fixed data type, with one byte for the integer part and one byte for the fractional part) and a two-byte frame count. Figure 6.10 shows a typical header block in hexadecimal format, with byte values or decimal values underneath.

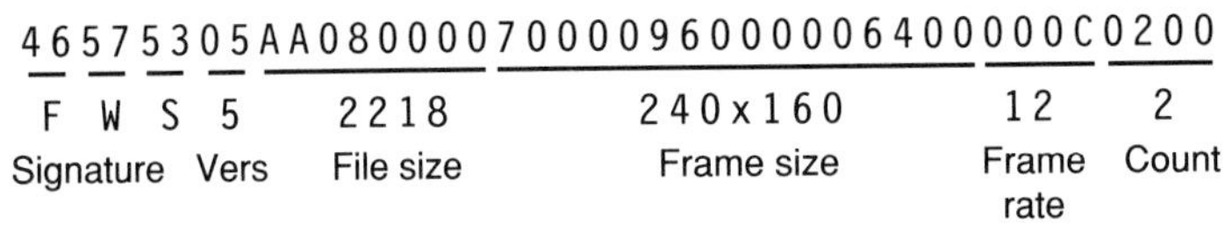

```
46 57 53 05 AA 08 00 00 70 00 09 60 00 00 64 00 00 0C 02 00
 F  W  S  5    22 18       240 x 160        12     2
Signature Vers  File size     Frame size   Frame  Count
                                            rate
```

Figure 6.10 A header block.

You'll notice that the header block of a Flash file contains very little information about the Flash movie. It tells us the frame size, frame rate, and frame count, but not much more than that. In particular, it doesn't give us any information about some important playback characteristics, such as whether the movie should start playing all frames automatically or whether the movie should loop back to the beginning when it reaches the end. In a QuickTime file, this kind of metadata is contained in the movie user data and is available to a playback application when the movie file is opened. If we want to know whether a Flash movie is an autoplay movie, we need to do a bit of work, as we'll see later.

Listing 6.7 shows some code that we can use to parse the header block of a Flash file; it assumes that myMediaData is a handle to the Flash file data that's been read into memory. (Some error handling has been removed from this code in the interests of saving space.)

Listing 6.7 Reading the header block in a Flash data stream.

```
InitParser();
gFlashParserData.m_theData = myMediaData;
HLock(myMediaData);
```

```
gFlashParserData.m_fileBuf = (U8 *)*myMediaData;

// read the file header
myByte = GetByte();                              // should be 'F'
myByte = GetByte();                              // should be 'W'
myByte = GetByte();                              // should be 'S'

myByte = GetByte();
gFlashParserData.m_fileVersion = (U16)myByte;

// get the file size
gFlashParserData.m_fileSize = GetDWord();

// get the file dimensions
GetRect(&myRect);
gFlashParserData.m_frameWidth = (S32)(ceil((float)(myRect.xmax - myRect.xmin) /
            (float)kTwipsPerPixel));
gFlashParserData.m_frameHeight = (S32)(ceil((float)(myRect.ymax - myRect.ymin) /
            (float)kTwipsPerPixel));

// get the frame rate and count
gFlashParserData.m_frameRate = GetWord() >> 8;
gFlashParserData.m_frameCount = GetWord();

gFlashParserData.m_fileStart = gFlashParserData.m_filePos;
```

Once we've run this code, the m_filePos field of the gFlashParserData
structure points at the first byte in the first tagged data block, and some of
the other fields in that structure contain information about the Flash file.

For certain purposes, we might want to skip over the header block and just
set the m_filePos field to the first byte in the first tagged data block. We can
use the function SkipHeaderBlock, defined in Listing 6.8, for this purpose.

Listing 6.8 Skipping over the header block in a Flash data stream.

```
void SkipHeaderBlock (void)
{
  SRECT          myRect;

  gFlashParserData.m_filePos = 8;                // skip signature and file size
  GetRect(&myRect);                              // skip frame size
  gFlashParserData.m_filePos += 4;               // skip rate and count

  gFlashParserData.m_fileStart = gFlashParserData.m_filePos;
}
```

Parsing the Tagged Data Blocks

A tagged data block consists of some data preceded by a *tag header*. A tag header begins with a 2-byte field, whose high-order 10 bits contain a *tag ID* and whose low-order 6 bits specify the length of the data (Figure 6.11). If the amount of data in the tagged data block exceeds 62 bytes, then the 6-bit length field of the tag header contains the value 0x3f (that is, 63), and the 2-byte field is followed immediately by a 4-byte field that contains the length of the data (Figure 6.12).

In short, the tag header occupies 2 bytes if the data in the block is 62 bytes or less, and 6 bytes otherwise. Listing 6.9 shows the definition of the GetTag function, which we'll use to read the tag ID and tag length from a tag header. When GetTag returns, the m_filePos field points to the first byte in the data of the tagged data block. In addition, the fields m_tagStart, m_tagEnd, and m_tagLen contain the starting location, ending location, and length of the tagged data block. We'll use those fields to move from block to block in the data stream.

Listing 6.9 Reading a tag.

```
U16 GetTag (void)
{
  U16      myCode;
  U32      myLength;

  // save the start of the tag
  gFlashParserData.m_tagStart = gFlashParserData.m_filePos;

  // get the combined code and length of the tag
  myCode = GetWord();

  // the length is encoded in the low-order six bits of the tag
  myLength = myCode & 0x3f;

  // remove the length from the code
  myCode = myCode >> 6;

  // determine if another long word must be read to get the length
  if (myLength == 0x3f)
    myLength = (U32)GetDWord();

  // determine the end position of the tag
  gFlashParserData.m_tagEnd = gFlashParserData.m_filePos + (U32)myLength;
  gFlashParserData.m_tagLen = (U32)myLength;

  return(myCode);
}
```

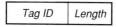

Figure 6.11 A short tag header.

Tag ID	0x3f	Length

Figure 6.12 A long tag header.

The tag ID returned by GetTag indicates the kind of data contained in the tagged data block. Here are a dozen or so tag IDs:

```
enum {
    stagEnd                    = 0,
    stagShowFrame              = 1,
    stagDefineShape            = 2,
    stagFreeCharacter          = 3,
    stagPlaceObject            = 4,
    stagRemoveObject           = 5,
    stagDefineBits             = 6,
    stagDefineButton           = 7,
    stagJPEGTables             = 8,
    stagSetBackgroundColor     = 9,
    stagDefineFont             = 10,
    stagDefineText             = 11,
    stagDoAction               = 12,
    stagDefineFontInfo         = 13
}
```

The first tag in a Flash file is usually stagSetBackgroundColor, and its associated data is a 3-byte value that contains the red, green, and blue components of the color. On the other end of the file, the last two tags in a file are often stagShowFrame and stagEnd. The stagShowFrame tag indicates the end of a frame; the playback application should render any characters that have been defined and placed into the movie rectangle. In addition, the movie is paused for the duration of a single frame. The stagEnd tag marks the end of a Flash file and must always be the last tag in the file.

The stagDoAction tag is of particular interest. Its associated data is an *action list*, a list of actions that are executed during the processing of a stag-ShowFrame tag. An action list can also be attached to a button, in which case the actions are executed during a specified button transition. Here's a sampling of Flash actions:

```
enum {
    sactionNone                     = 0x00,
    sactionGotoFrame                = 0x81,
    sactionGetURL                   = 0x83,
    sactionNextFrame                = 0x04,
    sactionPrevFrame                = 0x05,
    sactionPlay                     = 0x06,
    sactionStop                     = 0x07,
    sactionToggleQuality            = 0x08,
    sactionStopSounds               = 0x09,
    sactionWaitForFrame             = 0x8A,
    sactionSetTarget                = 0x8B,
    sactionGotoLabel                = 0x8C,
    sactionWiredActions             = 0xAA
};
```

As you can see, actions can be used to move from frame to frame, start and stop the Flash movie, stop sounds from playing, open a Flash movie at a specific URL, and so forth. Note the action sactionWiredActions (that is, 0xAA); this is provided specifically to allow us to embed QuickTime wired actions in a Flash movie. We'll investigate this capability more fully in the next chapter.

Let's see how we can traverse the tagged data blocks in a Flash file. Listing 6.10 illustrates a very simple case, in which all we want to do is count the top-level tags in a Flash file.

Listing 6.10 Counting the tags in a Flash file.

```
U32 CountTags (Handle theStream)
{
    U32         myNumTags = 0;
    BOOL        isAtEnd = false;
    U16         myCode;
    U32         myTagEnd;

    if ((theStream == NULL) || (*theStream == NULL))
        goto bail;

    InitParser();
    gFlashParserData.m_theData = theStream;
    gFlashParserData.m_fileBuf = (U8 *)*theStream;

    // set the position to the start position
    SkipHeaderBlock();
```

```
    // loop through each tag
    while (!isAtEnd) {
      // get the current tag and tag-end position
      myCode = GetTag();
      myTagEnd = gFlashParserData.m_tagEnd;

      if (myCode == stagEnd)
        isAtEnd = true;

      myNumTags++;

      // increment past the tag
      gFlashParserData.m_filePos = myTagEnd;
    }

bail:
  return(myNumTags);
}
```

CountTags consists mainly of a while loop, which is exited only when the last tagged data block in the file (which must be of type stagEnd) is found.

Importing Flash Files

Let's use this parsing ability to help us overcome some of the limitations of the Flash movie importer. If we open a Flash file by calling NewMovieFromFile (or one of its sister functions, such as NewMovieFromDataRef), QuickTime will automatically invoke the Flash movie importer to convert the Flash movie into a QuickTime movie. It does this by creating a Flash track whose media data is simply the data in the original Flash file. However, the current Flash movie importer has a few annoying quirks. For one thing, it assumes that all Flash movies should automatically start playing immediately once they are opened. This is indeed the default behavior for Flash movies, but it's possible for the Flash movie author to override that behavior by inserting an sactionStop action before the first stagShowFrame tag.

It's actually quite easy to work around this limitation. Our sample application QTFlash includes the code shown in Listing 6.11 in the function QTFlash_InitWindowData, which is called after a Flash movie is imported but before the new movie window is displayed on the screen.

Listing 6.11 Setting the autoplay characteristic.

```
if ((GetMovieTrackCount(myMovie) == 1) && ((**myAppData).fNumFlashTracks == 1)) {
  myErr = QTFlash_IsAutoPlayMovie(myMovie, &myLong);
  if (myErr == noErr) {
    myBoolean = (Boolean)myLong;
    SetUserDataItem(GetMovieUserData(myMovie), &myBoolean, sizeof(myBoolean),
                    FOUR_CHAR_CODE('play'), 1);
  }
}
```

As you can see, the central step here is the call to QTFlash_IsAutoPlay-Movie, which tells us whether the imported Flash movie should begin to play immediately or stop once the first frame has been rendered. The definition of QTFlash_IsAutoPlayMovie (Listing 6.12) is fairly trivial. It just calls another function, QTFlash_GetFileCharacteristic, with a selector that indicates the kind of metadata it wants retrieved from the file.

Listing 6.12 Determining whether a Flash file is autoplay.

```
OSErr QTFlash_IsAutoPlayMovie (Movie theMovie, UInt32 *isAutoPlay)
{
  return(QTFlash_GetFileCharacteristic(theMovie, isAutoPlay, kFlashIsAutoPlayFile));
}
```

Listing 6.13 shows the complete definition of QTFlash_GetFileCharacteristic. As you can see, we use a while loop similar to the one in Listing 6.10 to traverse the tagged data blocks in the Flash data stream. In this case, however, we can stop once we've found the first stagShowFrame tag.

Listing 6.13 Reading metadata from a Flash data stream.

```
static OSErr QTFlash_GetFileCharacteristic (Movie theMovie, UInt32 *theHasIt,
            UInt32 theCharacteristic)
{
  Track                   myTrack = NULL;
  Media                   myMedia = NULL;
  long                    mySize = 0L;
  Handle                  myMediaData = NULL;
  SampleDescriptionHandle myDesc = NULL;
  Boolean                 myIsAutoPlay = true;
  Boolean                 myIsFullScreen = false;
  Boolean                 myAtEnd = false;
  U8                      myByte;
```

```
   U8                         myAction;
   U16                        myCode, myLength;
   U32                        myTagEnd;
   S32                        myPos;
   SRECT                      myRect;
   OSErr                      myErr = paramErr;

   if ((theMovie == NULL) || (theHasIt == NULL))
      goto bail;

   // get the Flash data stream from the Flash track
   myTrack = GetMovieIndTrackType(theMovie, 1, FlashMediaType, movieTrackMediaType);
   if (myTrack == NULL)
      goto bail;

   myMedia = GetTrackMedia(myTrack);
   if (myMedia == NULL)
      goto bail;

   myMediaData = NewHandle(0);
   if (myMediaData == NULL)
      goto bail;

   myDesc = (SampleDescriptionHandle)NewHandleClear(sizeof(SampleDescription));
   if (myDesc == NULL)
      goto bail;

#if ONLY_ONE_MEDIA_SAMPLE
   // in theory, there should be only one media sample in the Flash track;
   // report an error if we get more than one
   if (GetMediaSampleCount(myMedia) != 1) {
      myErr = invalidMedia;
      goto bail;
   }
#endif

   myErr = GetMediaSample(myMedia, myMediaData, 0, &mySize, (TimeValue)0, NULL, NULL,
            myDesc, NULL, 1, NULL, NULL);
   if (myErr != noErr)
      goto bail;

   // parse the Flash header and file info
   InitParser();
   gFlashParserData.m_theData = myMediaData;
   HLock(myMediaData);
```

```
gFlashParserData.m_fileBuf = (U8 *)*myMediaData;

// verify the file header
myByte = GetByte();
if (myByte != 'F') {
  myErr = invalidMedia;
  goto bail;
}

myByte = GetByte();
if (myByte != 'W') {
  myErr = invalidMedia;
  goto bail;
}

myByte = GetByte();
if (myByte != 'S') {
  myErr = invalidMedia;
  goto bail;
}

myByte = GetByte();
gFlashParserData.m_fileVersion = (U16)myByte;

// get the file size
gFlashParserData.m_fileSize = GetDWord();

// get the file dimensions
GetRect(&myRect);
gFlashParserData.m_frameWidth =
      (S32)(ceil((float)(myRect.xmax - myRect.xmin) / (float)kTwipsPerPixel));
gFlashParserData.m_frameHeight =
      (S32)(ceil((float)(myRect.ymax - myRect.ymin) / (float)kTwipsPerPixel));

// get the frame rate and count
gFlashParserData.m_frameRate = GetWord() >> 8;
gFlashParserData.m_frameCount = GetWord();

gFlashParserData.m_fileStart = gFlashParserData.m_filePos;

// look for the specified characteristic

// initialize the end-of-frame flag
myAtEnd = false;
```

```
// loop through each tagged data block, looking for stagDoAction and stagShowFrame tags;
// we do NOT want to search any stagDefineSprite blocks
while (!myAtEnd) {
  // get the current tag and tag-end position
  myCode = GetTag();
  myTagEnd = gFlashParserData.m_tagEnd;

  switch (myCode) {
    case stagDoAction:
      for (;;) {
        // get the action code
        myAction = GetByte();

        if (myAction == sactionNone)
          // end of this list of actions
          break;

        myLength = 0;
        if (myAction & sactionHasLength)
          myLength = GetWord();

        myPos = gFlashParserData.m_filePos + myLength;

        if (myAction == sactionStop) {
          // we found an sactionStop action that occurs before the first
          // stagShowFrame tag; we can stop looking
          myIsAutoPlay = false;
          myAtEnd = true;
        }

        if (myAction == sactionGetURL) {
          // look for a URL of the form "FSCommand:fullscreen" with argument
          // "true"
          char *myURL = GetAString();
          char *myArg = GetAString();

          // this could be better implemented; should be case-insensitive
          if (strcmp(myURL, "FSCommand:fullscreen") == 0)
            if (strcmp(myArg, "true") == 0)
              myIsFullScreen = true;
        }

        gFlashParserData.m_filePos = myPos;
      }
      break;
```

```
          case stagShowFrame:
            // we found the first stagShowFrame tag on the main timeline; we can stop
            // looking
            myAtEnd = true;
            break;

          case stagEnd:
            // we reached the end of the file
            myAtEnd = true;
            break;

          default:
            break;
      }

      // increment past the tag
      gFlashParserData.m_filePos = myTagEnd;
   }

bail:
   if (myErr == noErr) {
      switch (theCharacteristic) {
         case kFlashIsAutoPlayFile:
            *theHasIt = myIsAutoPlay;
            break;

         case kFlashIsPlayFullScreen:
            *theHasIt = myIsFullScreen;
            break;

         case kFlashIsLoopingFile:
            myErr = unimpErr;                   // not yet implemented
            break;

         default:
            myErr = paramErr;                   // unknown selector
            break;
      }
   }

   return(myErr);
}
```

▶ FSCommands

You'll notice that Listing 6.13 figures out whether a Flash file should be played full-screen by looking for an action of type `sactionGetURL` whose data specifies the target URL `FSCommand:fullscreen` and the target window `true`. To understand what's going on here, it's useful to remember that Flash was originally designed primarily for Web-based content delivery and, hence, needed to operate within a Web browser; the Flash movie sometimes also needed to communicate with that browser. The FSCommand mechanism was originally used for sending commands from Flash movies to a browser-based scripting engine, such as JavaScript or VBScript. I'm guessing, then, that "FSCommand" stands for something like "Flash-to-script command" and that the `sactionGetURL` action was chosen as the storage vehicle for FSCommands because it already provided a way to send text data to a Web browser. (This might not be true, but it makes a pretty good story all the same; another reasonable guess is that the "FS" stands for "Future Splash," the original name of Flash.)

Macromedia has expanded the range of FSCommands by defining five commands that can be targeted at Flash playback applications, including the Flash Player application itself, stand-alone Flash projectors, and of course any QuickTime-savvy application (since they can open and display Flash files). In this case, the string that follows the prefix `FSCommand:` is the *command,* and the target window string is the *argument.* The application-targeted commands are

- `fullscreen`. The argument must be either `true` or `false`. If the argument is `true`, the movie should be played full-screen. If the argument is `false`, the movie should be played in normal window mode (that is, in a window whose original content area has the size specified in the file header block).

- `allowscale`. The argument must be either `true` or `false`. If the argument is `true`, the Flash movie should be scaled to exactly fit the movie window content area if the window is resized. If the argument is `false`, the size of the Flash movie should remain unchanged even if the window is resized. This setting is useful if the movie contains bitmaps that may look pixilated or if playback performance unduly suffers when the window is resized too large. The default value for the `allowscale` property is `true`.

- `showmenu`. The argument must be either `true` or `false`. If the argument is `true`, then a fully enabled contextual menu is displayed when the user right-clicks (on Windows) or option-clicks (on Macintosh) in a Flash movie. (Figure 6.13 shows the Windows version of this contextual menu.) If the argument is `false`, only the About Macromedia Flash Player 5 menu item is enabled. The default value for the `showmenu` property is `true`.

Keep in mind that this contextual menu is provided by the playback application. Flash Player supports it, but QuickTime Player currently does not.

Figure 6.13 The Flash Player contextual menu.

I'll leave it as an exercise for the reader to add a menu like this to QTFlash. (I'll give you a little help, though; shortly we'll see how to handle the zooming menu items.)

- exec. The argument must be a pathname (either full or relative to the location of the Flash playback application) of an external application. That application is launched. Note that no options or filenames are passed to the application. If you need specific options or files to be opened, you can pass the pathname of a batch file (on Windows) or an AppleScript file (on Macintosh).

- quit. The playback application should terminate. This command has no arguments.

When the Flash media handler encounters any of these FSCommands, it sends the movie controller a movie controller action of type mcActionDo-Script. The parameter passed to the application's movie controller action filter function is the address of a structure of type QTDoScriptRecord, which is declared like this:

```
struct QTDoScriptRecord {
  long        scriptTypeFlags;
  char *      command;
  char *      arguments;
};
```

The scriptTypeFlags field indicates the type of script. For FSCommands, this field is set to kScriptIsUnknownType. The command field contains the command (for example, fullscreen), and the arguments field contains the single argument (for example, true).

If we want our applications to handle these FSCommands, we can add a new case statement to our movie controller action filter function, like this:

```
case mcActionDoScript:
    isHandled = QTFlash_DoFSCommand(theMC, (QTDoScriptPtr)theParams,
                    myWindowObject);
    break;
```

The QTFlash sample application contains the definition of QTFlash_DoFS-Command shown in Listing 6.14. As you can see, we handle only the quit command. It wouldn't be too hard to handle the fullscreen command, as QuickTime provides the pair of functions BeginFullScreen and EndFullScreen that allow us to enter and exit full-screen mode. We're a bit short on space, however, so I'll leave implementing the fullscreen command and the other three FSCommands as an exercise for the enterprising reader.

Listing 6.14 Handling FSCommands targeted at an application.

```
Boolean QTFlash_DoFSCommand (MovieController theMC, QTDoScriptPtr theScriptPtr,
        WindowObject theWindowObject)
{
  Boolean           isHandled = false;

  // make sure the parameters are all non-NULL
  if ((theMC == NULL) || (theScriptPtr == NULL) || (theWindowObject == NULL))
    goto bail;

  // we handle scripts only of type kScriptIsUnknownType
  if (theScriptPtr->scriptTypeFlags != kScriptIsUnknownType)
    goto bail;

  // look for quit commands
  if (strcmp(theScriptPtr->command, "quit") == 0) {
    // quit the application
    QTFrame_QuitFramework();
    isHandled = true;
  }

bail:
  return(isHandled);
}
```

There is nothing magical about these five application-targeted FSCommands. We could easily construct a Flash movie whose interface elements issue FSCommands of our own devising. The Flash media handler will happily pass them along to our movie controller action filter function, where we can intercept and process them. This allows us, for instance, to use a Flash movie as the primary user interface for an application (which, incidentally, looks exactly the same on both Mac and Windows).

Flash Media Handler Functions

The Flash media handler supports a dozen or so functions that allow us to programmatically manipulate a Flash track and get information about a Flash track or about the Flash media handler itself. For example, if we are interested in determining which Flash file format versions are supported by the Flash media handler, we can call the FlashMediaGetSupportedSwfVersion function, like this:

```
myErr = FlashMediaGetSupportedSwfVersion(myHandler, &myChar);
```

If this call succeeds, then myChar will contain a byte that indicates the highest version number of Flash movie files supported by the Flash media handler. Here, of course, myHandler is a reference to the Flash media handler, which we can get like this:

```
myTrack = GetMovieIndTrackType(myMovie, 1, FlashMediaType,
        movieTrackMediaType):
myHandler = GetMediaHandler(GetTrackMedia(myTrack));
```

We can use the FlashMediaSetZoom function to support the Zoom In, Zoom Out, and Show All menu items provided by QTFlash. The Zoom In menu item doubles the current magnification of the Flash movie window, while the Zoom Out menu item halves the current magnification. The Show All menu item returns the window to its original magnification. FlashMediaSetZoom takes as a parameter an integer that indicates a relative magnification factor. To my knowledge, the precise meaning of this factor is not currently documented anywhere; a little experimentation, however, reveals that this factor is the percentage of the current window height and width that is to be scaled up or down to fill the window. For instance, to double the magnification, so that the central part of the image that occupies half the current window width and height fills the window after zooming, we would pass a factor of 50. To halve the magnification we would pass a factor of 200. The special factor 0 returns the Flash movie to its original magnification. Listing 6.15 shows the code in our menu-handling function QTApp_HandleMenu that supports the zooming menu items.

Listing 6.15   Handling the zoom menu items.

```
case IDM_ZOOM_IN:
  FlashMediaSetZoom(myHandler, 50);
  myIsHandled = true;
  break;

case IDM_ZOOM_OUT:
  FlashMediaSetZoom(myHandler, 200);
  myIsHandled = true;
  break;

case IDM_SHOW_ALL:
  FlashMediaSetZoom(myHandler, 0);
  myIsHandled = true;
  break;
```

When a Flash track is zoomed in, we can call the FlashMediaSetPan function to move the image around inside the movie window. For instance, we can move down to the right a small amount with this code:

```
FlashMediaSetPan(myHandler, 10, 10);
```

Once again the parameters here are percentages. The first parameter tells the media handler to move right by a distance that is 10% of the window's current width. And the second parameter tells the media handler to move down by a distance that is 10% of the window's current height.

The Flash media handler supplies a handful of additional functions, including FlashMediaGetDisplayedFrameNumber and FlashMediaSetFlashVariable. Look in the file Movies.h (a standard header file provided by Quick-Time) for a complete list.

We've already seen (in Listing 6.13) that we can also use standard media-related functions like GetMediaSampleCount and GetMediaSample on Flash tracks. Listing 6.16 gives another example of using these functions, this time to extract a Flash track into a Flash movie file. We call QTFlash_ExtractFlash-MovieFromTrack in response to the Extract Flash Track menu item in the Test menu.

Listing 6.16 Extracting a Flash track from a movie.

```
OSErr QTFlash_ExtractFlashMovieFromTrack (Movie theMovie, long theIndex)
{
  Track                   myTrack = NULL;
  Media                   myMedia = NULL;
  long                    mySize = 0L;
  Handle                  myMediaData = NULL;
  SampleDescriptionHandle myDesc = NULL;
  FSSpec                  myFSSpec;
  Boolean                 myIsSelected = false;
  Boolean                 myIsReplacing = false;
  StringPtr               myPrompt = QTUtils_ConvertCToPascalString(kSaveFlashPrompt);
  StringPtr               myFileName = NULL;
  char                    *myTrackName = NULL;
  char                    *myString = NULL;
  short                   myLength;
  OSErr                   myErr = noErr;

  myTrack = GetMovieIndTrackType(theMovie, theIndex, FlashMediaType, movieTrackMediaType);
  if (myTrack == NULL)
    goto bail;

  myMedia = GetTrackMedia(myTrack);
  if (myMedia == NULL)
    goto bail;

  myMediaData = NewHandle(0);
  if (myMediaData == NULL)
    goto bail;

  myDesc = (SampleDescriptionHandle)NewHandleClear(sizeof(SampleDescription));
  if (myDesc == NULL)
    goto bail;
#if ONLY_ONE_MEDIA_SAMPLE
  // in theory, there should be only one media sample in the Flash track;
  // report an error if we get more than one
  if (GetMediaSampleCount(myMedia) != 1) {
    QTFrame_Beep();
    goto bail;
  }
#endif
```

```
    myErr = GetMediaSample(myMedia, myMediaData, 0, &mySize, (TimeValue)0, NULL, NULL,
            myDesc, NULL, 1, NULL, NULL);
    if (myErr != noErr)
      goto bail;

    // get the name of the track; we'll use this as the suggested filename
    myTrackName = QTUtils_GetTrackName(myTrack);
    if (myTrackName == NULL)
      // if no existing name, synthesize a track name
      myTrackName = QTUtils_MakeTrackNameByType(myTrack);

    // suggest the track name + .swf as the filename
    myLength = strlen(myTrackName) + strlen(kFlashFileExtension) + 1;
    myString = malloc(myLength);
    memcpy(myString, myTrackName, strlen(myTrackName));
    memcpy(myString + strlen(myTrackName), kFlashFileExtension,
        strlen(kFlashFileExtension));
    myString[myLength - 1] = '\0';

    myFileName = QTUtils_ConvertCToPascalString(myString);

    // get a file from the user
    myErr = QTFrame_PutFile(myPrompt, myFileName, &myFSSpec, &myIsSelected, &myIsReplacing);
    if (myIsSelected) {
      // delete any existing file of that name
      if (myIsReplacing) {
        myErr = FSpDelete(&myFSSpec);
        if (myErr != noErr)
          goto bail;
      }

      // write the Flash media data into a file
      myErr = QTFlash_WriteHandleToFile(myMediaData, &myFSSpec);
    }

bail:
  if (myMediaData != NULL)
    DisposeHandle(myMediaData);

  if (myDesc != NULL)
    DisposeHandle((Handle)myDesc);
```

```
    free(myTrackName);
    free(myString);
    free(myPrompt);
    free(myFileName);

    return(myErr);
}
```

Conclusion

It's sometimes tempting to think of a full-featured interactive graphics and animation package like Macromedia Flash as a competitor to QuickTime, but of course quite the opposite is true. Flash and QuickTime can be combined in ways that enhance the capabilities of each package. Flash brings to the table a sophisticated vector-based drawing engine that's coupled with basic mouse and keyboard interactivity and with an object-oriented scripting capability. QuickTime adds a tight integration with dozens and dozens of popular media types, ranging from video and sound to text and sprites and virtual reality. In addition, it includes a mature wiring capability that vastly surpasses the interactive repertoire of Flash. Together, Flash and QuickTime provide a very powerful content delivery tool.

In this chapter, we've investigated a number of ways to work with Flash data, either alone or in combination with QuickTime movies. We've built the foundation of a parser that can read through Flash files and extract information about the various objects and commands in the file. We've seen how to work with the Flash media handler APIs and how to handle application-specific commands emitted by a Flash movie. Still, some of the best is yet to come. In the next chapter, we'll finally see how to use wired actions with Flash tracks.

The Flash II

Using Wired Actions with Flash Tracks

Introduction

In the previous chapter, we were introduced to Macromedia's Flash multimedia development environment and saw some ways to work with Flash content inside of QuickTime applications. We learned that QuickTime 4 and later versions provide a Flash movie importer and a Flash media handler that allow us to import and display Flash movies as Flash tracks in Quick-Time movies. We developed a simple parser that allows us to read through a Flash file to get some useful information about the Flash movie contained in the file, such as whether it's an autoplay movie and whether the movie should be played full-screen. Finally, we got a taste for working with the public APIs provided by the Flash media handler.

In this chapter, we're going to see how to work with wired actions and Flash tracks. There are two general sorts of capabilities we want to explore here. First, we want to see how to embed wired actions in a Flash track so that (for instance) clicking a button in the Flash track sends one or more wired actions to some other track in the QuickTime movie. Recall that QuickTime provides well over a hundred different wired actions, which can be targeted variously at sprite tracks, individual sprites within sprite tracks, QuickTime VR tracks, hotspots within QuickTime VR tracks, text tracks, the QuickTime movie itself, and indeed external movies and objects within those external movies. So it's potentially very useful to know how to trigger those actions with the interactive behaviors of the Flash track. Indeed, this ability is a necessity for the kind of Flash and QuickTime integration that is all the rage nowadays: using a Flash track and its panoply of interactive elements (buttons, menus, sliders, text boxes, and so forth) to control the operation of a QuickTime movie. Figure 7.1 shows a simple example of using buttons in a Flash track to control the pan, tilt, and zoom parameters of a QuickTime VR movie.

Figure 7.1 A Flash track controlling a QuickTime VR movie.

The second way of using wired actions with Flash tracks is essentially the reverse of the first: instead of sending wired actions from a Flash track to some other kind of track, we might want to send wired actions from other tracks to a Flash track. For instance, user actions in a QuickTime VR node (say, rolling the mouse over a hotspot) might trigger a wired action that tells a Flash track to create a new movieclip. In a simple case, the movieclip might be a rectangle with some text in it whose bottom-right corner is anchored at the current mouse location. This would give a nice *pop-up label* (or *help tag*) capability to the QuickTime VR movie, as illustrated in Figure 7.2.

In this chapter, we're going to investigate these two techniques—embedding wired actions in Flash tracks and sending wired actions to Flash tracks. Our sample application, once again, is called QTFlash, and its Test menu is shown in Figure 7.3. In the previous chapter, we saw how to handle all of these menu items but the last one, which we'll focus on here.

Wired Actions Targeted at Flash Tracks

Let's begin by taking a look at the QuickTime wired actions that can be targeted at a Flash track. When the Flash media handler was first introduced, in QuickTime 4, five new wired actions were added:

Figure 7.2 A pop-up label provided by a Flash track.

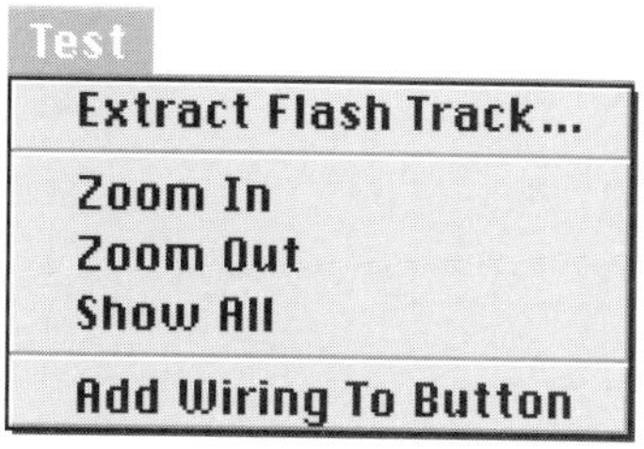

Figure 7.3 The Test menu of QTFlash.

```
enum {
    kActionFlashTrackSetPan             = 10240,
    kActionFlashTrackSetZoom            = 10241,
    kActionFlashTrackSetZoomRe          = 10242,
    kActionFlashTrackGotoFrameNumber    = 10243,
    kActionFlashTrackGotoFrameLabel     = 10244
};
```

The first three actions allow us to zoom in on a Flash track and to pan around inside a zoomed Flash track. The `kActionFlashTrackSetZoom` action takes one parameter, which specifies the percentage of the current movie window to zoom. This parameter is identical to the parameter passed to the

FlashMediaSetZoom function (which we discussed in the previous chapter): to double the magnification, we pass a factor of 50. To halve the magnification, we pass a factor of 200. If, instead of zooming in on the center of the Flash track, we want to zoom in on some other portion of the Flash track, we can use the kActionFlashTrackSetZoomRect action. This action needs four parameters, which are (in order) the left, top, right, and bottom of the rectangle to zoom. Once we're zoomed in on some portion of the Flash track, we can use the kActionFlashTrackSetPan action to pan it horizontally and vertically. This action takes two parameters, which (just as with the FlashMediaSetPan function) specify the percentages of the movie window width and height to pan.

The final two original Flash track wired actions set the current movie time to correspond to a particular frame in the Flash track (that is, to go to that frame in the Flash track). The kActionFlashTrackGotoFrameNumber action jumps to the movie time that corresponds to the Flash track frame number specified in the single parameter atom in the action atom. The kActionFlash-TrackGotoFrameLabel action jumps to the movie time that corresponds to the Flash track frame whose frame label is specified in the single parameter atom; in this case, the parameter atom contains a C string.

QuickTime 5 introduced an updated Flash media handler (capable of handling Flash files up to version 4) along with two new wired actions:

```
enum {
    kActionFlashTrackSetFlashVariable        = 10245,
    kActionFlashTrackDoButtonActions         = 10246
};
```

QuickTime 5 also added one new wired action operand:

```
enum {
    kOperandFlashTrackVariable               = 9216
};
```

We can use the kActionFlashTrackDoButtonActions action to execute the actions associated with a particular state transition for a button in a Flash track. This action takes three parameters, which specify the path to the button, the button ID, and the desired button state transition. We know how to specify a button state transition, using constants like kOverDownToOverUp, which we encountered in the previous chapter. The button ID is simply the *character ID* stored in the button data in the Flash file. The tricky part here is the *button path*. Objects in a Flash file are arranged in a hierarchical structure, beginning with the root object, which is driven by the main timeline. The root object can also contain movieclips, which (as we've seen) are essentially Flash movies embedded within Flash movies. Movieclips can be embedded within movieclips, to an arbitrarily deep level.

To refer to an object in a Flash file, we must provide a *path* to that object. The button path specified as the first parameter to the `kActionFlashTrackDoButtonActions` action must be an absolute path beginning with the root object and containing the names of any movieclips within which the button is embedded. In the simplest case, we can pass an empty path (that is, the string `""`) to refer to the root object. If a button is contained in the movieclip whose name is `"buttonClip"`, we could pass the path `"/buttonClip"`. If the buttonClip movieclip contained yet another movieclip named `"yellow"`, we could target a button in that second movieclip using the path `"/buttonClip/yellow"`.

We can use the `kActionFlashTrackSetFlashVariable` wired action to set the value of a *Flash variable* in a Flash track, and we can use the `kOperandFlashTrackVariable` operand to get the value of a Flash variable. A Flash variable consists of two parts: a name and a value. The name is a string, and the value can be either a string or a number. To specify a variable, we need to provide its name and the path to the object to which it is attached. (A variable can be attached to any object, including the root object.) The `kActionFlashTrackSetFlashVariable` action requires four parameter atoms: (1) the path to the object to which the variable is attached, (2) the variable name, (3) the new variable value, and (4) a Boolean value that indicates whether to change the focus to the object attached to the variable.

Getting and setting Flash variables using wired actions is a simple and efficient way to establish interactions between Flash tracks and other Quick-Time tracks that can be wired (currently, sprite, text, and QuickTime VR tracks). For instance, the hotspot in Figure 7.2 can be wired to trigger a `kActionFlashTrackSetFlashVariable` action that sets some variable to a particular value; an ActionScript in the Flash track can then periodically test that variable to see which text box to pop up.

Here's a particularly nice trick with Flash variables: when we create a text box in a Flash movie, we can configure it as a *dynamic text box*, which displays text that can change dynamically (without the user having to type into the text box). A dynamic text box is automatically associated with a variable, which we specify in the Text Options panel (shown in Figure 7.4). As you can see, the topmost pop-up menu sets the text box to be dynamic, and the name of the variable associated with the text box is set to `"textVar1"`.

Now here's the fun part: we can get and set the text displayed in the text box by getting and setting the value of the variable `textVar1`. Listing 7.1 shows a simple function that builds an atom container with an event atom that changes the text to "Caffe Macs" on a hotspot roll-over.

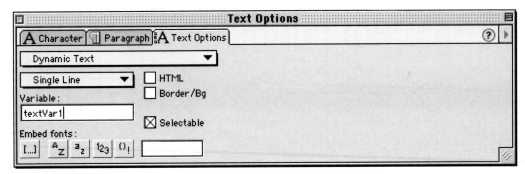

Figure 7.4 The Text Options panel for a dynamic text box.

Listing 7.1 Setting Flash text with a hotspot rollover.

```
OSErr QTFlash_CreateVarAction (QTAtomContainer *theActions)
{
    QTAtom          myActionAtom = 0;
    char            myPath[] = "";
    char            myVarName[] = "textVar1";
    char            myVarValue[] = "Caffe Macs";
    Boolean         myFocus = false;
    OSErr           myErr = noErr;

    myErr = QTNewAtomContainer(theActions);
    if (myErr != noErr)
        goto bail;

    myErr = WiredUtils_AddQTEventAndActionAtoms(*theActions, kParentAtomIsContainer,
                kQTEventMouseEnter, kActionFlashTrackSetFlashVariable, &myActionAtom);
    if (myErr != noErr)
        goto bail;

    myErr = WiredUtils_AddTrackTargetAtom(*theActions, myActionAtom,
                kTargetTrackType, (void *)FlashMediaType, 1);
    if (myErr != noErr)
        goto bail;

    myErr = WiredUtils_AddActionParameterAtom(*theActions, myActionAtom,
                1, strlen(myPath) + 1, myPath, NULL);
    if (myErr != noErr)
        goto bail;
```

```
myErr = WiredUtils_AddActionParameterAtom(*theActions, myActionAtom,
          2, strlen(myVarName) + 1, myVarName, NULL);
if (myErr != noErr)
  goto bail;

myErr = WiredUtils_AddActionParameterAtom(*theActions, myActionAtom,
          3, strlen(myVarValue) + 1, myVarValue, NULL);
if (myErr != noErr)
  goto bail;

myErr = WiredUtils_AddActionParameterAtom(*theActions, myActionAtom,
          4, sizeof(myFocus), &myFocus, NULL);

bail:
  return(myErr);
}
```

QTFlash_CreateVarAction uses a few of the wired action utility functions we developed in Volume One to set the event and action types, to set the target track (namely, to the first Flash track in the movie), and to set the four action parameters. It returns an atom container that can be inserted into the appropriate track. We don't yet know how to wire QuickTime VR movies, however, so you'll have to wait a bit to test this code out—or else attach it to a sprite or text object (which we have learned to wire).

Wired Actions in Flash Tracks

Let's turn now to our second main task: learning how to insert wired actions into a Flash track. The basic idea is quite simple; we can add QuickTime wired actions to a Flash data stream (that is, the data in a Flash track or a Flash file) by adding an action of type sactionWiredActions to an action list in that stream. Recall that actions can be found in two locations in a Flash file: in the action list associated with a button state transition, and in the action list associated with a tagged data block of type stagDoAction. Let's call these *button actions* and *frame actions*, respectively. A button action list is executed immediately when the specified state transition occurs. A frame action is executed immediately after the specified frame is rendered. For button actions and frame actions alike, we add a wired action by adding an action of type sactionWiredActions to the associated action list. The data in that action is simply an atom container that holds the appropriate event, action, target, and parameter atoms.

It turns out, however, that this simple recipe is a tad complicated to actually implement. We need to parse through the Flash data stream to find the button or frame that we want to wire, and then we need to parse through the button data or frame data to find the associated action list. Finally, we need to insert a new action into the list and then update all the relevant offsets and block sizes stored in the data stream. No one of these tasks is very complicated by itself, but accomplishing them all will occupy us for a while. For the moment, we'll focus on adding some wired actions to a button in a Flash track. The source code for QTFlash also shows how to add wired actions to a frame.

Handling the Menu Item

Let's begin at the highest level. When the user selects the Add Wiring To Button menu item, QTFlash calls the QTFlash_AddWiredActionsToFlashMovie function, passing in the identifier for the movie in the frontmost movie window. This function starts off by calling GetMovieIndTrackType to get the first Flash track in the movie, and then it calls GetTrackMedia to retrieve the media for that track. Our current goal is to get the media data, which is the Flash data stream. We do this by calling GetMediaSample. Before we can call GetMediaSample, however, we need to find the media time at which the Flash track begins, like this:

```
myTrackOffset = GetTrackOffset(myTrack);
myMediaTime = TrackTimeToMediaTime(myTrackOffset, myTrack);
```

So we can get the Flash data stored in the Flash track like this:

```
myErr = GetMediaSample(myMedia, mySample, 0, NULL, myMediaTime, NULL,
        &mySampleDuration, (SampleDescriptionHandle)myFlashDesc,
        NULL, 1, NULL, &mySampleFlags);
```

If we happen to know the character ID of the button that we want to wire, we can then call the application function QTFlash_SetWiredActionsTo-Button to attach an existing wired atom container (myActions) to that button:

```
myErr = QTFlash_SetWiredActionsToButton(mySample, myButtonID, myActions);
```

QTFlash, however, assumes that we want to attach the wired actions to the first button in the Flash track, so we'll call the LocateFirstButton function to find the ID of that button. LocateFirstButton is defined in Listing 7.2.

Listing 7.2 Finding the first Flash button in a data stream.

```
OSErr LocateFirstButton (Handle theStream, long *theButtonID)
{
  if ((theStream == NULL) || (theButtonID == NULL))
    return(paramErr);

  *theButtonID = 0;

  InitParser();

  gFlashParserData.m_theData = theStream;

  gFlashParserData.m_fileBuf = (U8 *)*theStream;

  SkipHeaderBlock();

  gFlashParserData.m_fileStart = gFlashParserData.m_filePos;

  ParseTags(false, theButtonID);

  return(noErr);
}
```

There's nothing very intricate about LocateFirstButton; it simply initializes our Flash parser and then traverses the data stream looking for a tagged
data block of type stagDefineButton2. (Flash also supports buttons of type
stagDefineButton, but they respond only to mouse clicks and cannot be configured to trigger actions on any of the other state transitions.) The main
work here is accomplished by the ParseTags function, defined in Listing 7.3.

Listing 7.3 Walking the data stream for a button.

```
void ParseTags (Boolean isSprite, long *theButtonID)
{
  BOOL       isAtEnd;
  U16        myCode;
  U32        myTagEnd;

  if (isSprite) {
    U32 myTagId = (U32)GetWord();
    U32 myFrameCount = (U32)GetWord();
  } else {
    // set the position to the start position
    gFlashParserData.m_filePos = gFlashParserData.m_fileStart;
  }
```

```
    // initialize the end of frame flag
    isAtEnd = false;

    // loop through each tagged data block
    while (!isAtEnd) {
      // get the current tag and tag-end position
      myCode = GetTag();
      myTagEnd = gFlashParserData.m_tagEnd;

      switch (myCode) {
        case stagEnd:
          // we reached the end of the file
          isAtEnd = true;
          break;

        case stagDefineButton2:
          *theButtonID = (U32)GetWord();
          isAtEnd = true;
          break;

        case stagDefineSprite:
          ParseTags(true, theButtonID);
          break;

        default:
          break;
      }

      // increment past the tag
      gFlashParserData.m_filePos = myTagEnd;
    }
}
```

Once we've called `QTFlash_SetWiredActionsToButton`, we want to replace the original media sample in the Flash track with our updated media sample. This is code we've seen before, so we don't need to investigate it in detail. Listing 7.4 shows our complete definition of `QTFlash_AddWiredActions-ToFlashMovie`.

Listing 7.4 Adding wired actions to a Flash track.

```
void QTFlash_AddWiredActionsToFlashMovie (Movie theMovie)
{
  Track                    myTrack = NULL;
  Media                    myMedia = NULL;
```

```
TimeValue               myTrackOffset;
TimeValue               myMediaTime;
TimeValue               mySampleDuration;
TimeValue               mySelectionDuration;
TimeValue               myNewMediaTime;
FlashDescriptionHandle  myFlashDesc = NULL;
Handle                  mySample = NULL;
short                   mySampleFlags;
Fixed                   myTrackEditRate;
QTAtomContainer         myActions = NULL;
long                    myButtonID = 0L;
OSErr                   myErr = noErr;

if (theMovie == NULL)
  return;

// get the first Flash track from the movie
myTrack = GetMovieIndTrackType(theMovie, 1, FlashMediaType, movieTrackMediaType);
if (myTrack == NULL)
  goto bail;

// get first media sample in the Flash track
myMedia = GetTrackMedia(myTrack);
if (myMedia == NULL)
  goto bail;

myTrackOffset = GetTrackOffset(myTrack);
myMediaTime = TrackTimeToMediaTime(myTrackOffset, myTrack);

// allocate some storage to hold the sample description for the Flash track
myFlashDesc = (FlashDescriptionHandle)NewHandle(4);
if (myFlashDesc == NULL)
  goto bail;

mySample = NewHandle(0);
if (mySample == NULL)
  goto bail;

myErr = GetMediaSample(myMedia, mySample, 0, NULL, myMediaTime, NULL, &mySampleDuration,
          (SampleDescriptionHandle)myFlashDesc, NULL, 1, NULL, &mySampleFlags);
if (myErr != noErr)
  goto bail;
```

```
// add button actions; find the first button
myErr = LocateFirstButton(mySample, &myButtonID);
if ((myErr != noErr) || (myButtonID == 0))
  goto bail;

// create an action container for button actions
myErr = QTFlash_CreateButtonActionContainer(&myActions);
if (myErr != noErr)
  goto bail;

// add button actions to sample
myErr = QTFlash_SetWiredActionsToButton(mySample, myButtonID, myActions);
if (myErr != noErr)
  goto bail;

// replace sample in media
myTrackEditRate = GetTrackEditRate(myTrack, myTrackOffset);
if (GetMoviesError() != noErr)
  goto bail;

GetTrackNextInterestingTime(myTrack, nextTimeMediaSample | nextTimeEdgeOK,
  myTrackOffset, fixed1, NULL, &mySelectionDuration);
if (GetMoviesError() != noErr)
  goto bail;

myErr = DeleteTrackSegment(myTrack, myTrackOffset, mySelectionDuration);
if (myErr != noErr)
  goto bail;

myErr = BeginMediaEdits(myMedia);
if (myErr != noErr)
  goto bail;

myErr = AddMediaSample(myMedia,
          mySample,
          0,
          GetHandleSize(mySample),
          mySampleDuration,
          (SampleDescriptionHandle)myFlashDesc,
          1,
          mySampleFlags,
          &myNewMediaTime);
if (myErr != noErr)
  goto bail;
```

```
  myErr = EndMediaEdits(myMedia);
  if (myErr != noErr)
    goto bail;

  // add the media to the track
  myErr = InsertMediaIntoTrack(myTrack, myTrackOffset, myNewMediaTime,
          mySelectionDuration, myTrackEditRate);

bail:
  if (myActions != NULL)
    (void)QTDisposeAtomContainer(myActions);

  if (mySample != NULL)
    DisposeHandle(mySample);

  if (myFlashDesc != NULL)
    DisposeHandle((Handle)myFlashDesc);
}
```

So our work will be finished once we've defined the function
QTFlash_SetWiredActionsToButton.

Finding Actions for Button State Transitions

As we'll see in greater detail later, the button actions contained in a data
block of type stagDefineButton2 are grouped into lists according to the button state transitions that trigger them. However, a wired atom container
(such as the one created in QTFlash by a call to QTFlash_CreateButtonAction-
Container) might contain several event atoms. The event IDs of these atoms
can be any of the nine button state transition constants we encountered in
the previous chapter:

```
#define kIdleToOverUp        (1L << bsIdleToOverUp)
#define kOverUpToIdle        (1L << bsOverUpToIdle)
#define kOverUpToOverDown    (1L << bsOverUpToOverDown)
#define kOverDownToOverUp    (1L << bsOverDownToOverUp)

#define kOverDownToOutDown   (1L << bsOverDownToOutDown)
#define kOutDownToOverDown   (1L << bsOutDownToOverDown)
#define kOutDownToIdle       (1L << bsOutDownToIdle)

#define kIdleToOverDown      (1L << bsIdleToOverDown)
#define kOverDownToIdle      (1L << bsOverDownToIdle)
```

For each of these nine button state transitions, we need to extract from the wired atom container the event atoms of that type and then add the extracted atoms into the action list for the specified button. This is precisely what QTFlash_SetWiredActionsToButton accomplishes, as you can see in Listing 7.5.

Listing 7.5 Finding actions by event type.

```
static OSErr QTFlash_SetWiredActionsToButton
                (Handle theSample, long theButtonID, QTAtomContainer theActions)
{
  short              myIndex;
  QTAtomContainer    myActionContainer;
  QTAtom             myEventAtom = 0;
  QTAtomID           myEventID;
  OSErr              myErr;

  myErr = QTNewAtomContainer(&myActionContainer);
  if (myErr != noErr)
    goto bail;

  for (myIndex = 0; myIndex < (sizeof(gFlashConditions) / sizeof(long)); myIndex++) {
    myEventID = gFlashConditions[myIndex];

    myEventAtom = QTFindChildByID(theActions, kParentAtomIsContainer,
                    kQTEventType, myEventID, NULL);
    if (myEventAtom != 0) {

      myErr = QTFlash_CopyChildren(theActions, myEventAtom, myActionContainer,
                kParentAtomIsContainer);
      if (myErr != noErr)
        goto bail;

      QTFlash_SetWiredActionToButton(theSample, theButtonID,
        myEventID, myActionContainer);

      myErr = QTRemoveChildren(myActionContainer, kParentAtomIsContainer);
      if (myErr != noErr)
        goto bail;
    } else {
      QTFlash_SetWiredActionToButton(theSample, theButtonID, myEventID, NULL);
    }
  }
}
```

```
    myErr = QTDisposeAtomContainer(myActionContainer);

bail:
    return(myErr);
}
```

We won't dissect this function in detail. Essentially, it looks into the atom container theActions for actions to be triggered by the nine distinct button state transitions. For any button state transitions that have actions, it extracts the appropriate event and action atoms into a new atom container and calls QTFlash_SetWiredActionToButton. Note that, if theActions does not contain an action for a specific button transition state, then QTFlash_SetWiredActionsTo-Button calls QTFlash_SetWiredActionToButton with the last parameter set to NULL; this is a signal to QTFlash_SetWiredActionToButton to remove any wired actions of that kind from the target Flash data stream.

Reading the Button Data

QTFlash_SetWiredActionToButton is the real workhorse here. Its job is to parse the data associated with a specific button and to add an action of type sactionWiredActions that is to be triggered by a specific button state transition. So, to understand QTFlash_SetWiredActionToButton, we need to understand the format of the data in a tagged data block of type stagDefine-Button2. Figure 7.5 shows how the data in that block is arranged.

The tagged data block begins with a tag header, of course, whose tag ID is stagDefineButton2. Immediately following the tag header, we find a 16-bit character ID and an 8-bit menu flag (which determines whether the button operates as a push button or a menu button). Then we encounter a 16-bit integer that is the offset from the current location in the data stream to the first *button action condition*. Each button action condition specifies one or more actions that are to be executed on a specific button state transition. Between the offset word and the button action conditions are one or more *button records*, which specify the images to be used for each of the three button states. For present purposes, we don't need to know the structure of these button records, since we'll just be skipping over them (using the offset word) when we process the tagged data block.

QTFlash_SetWiredActionToButton is passed four pieces of information, which are the Flash track media sample (that is, the Flash data stream), the character ID of a button, an event ID (that is, a button state transition constant), and an atom container of wired actions for that button and button state transition. First, we want to tell our parser what data to use:

```
gFlashParserData.m_theData = theSample;
```

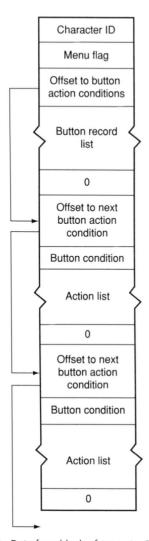

Character ID
Menu flag
Offset to button action conditions
Button record list
0
Offset to next button action condition
Button condition
Action list
0
Offset to next button action condition
Button condition
Action list
0

Figure 7.5 Data for a block of type stagDefineButton2.

Then we want to find the byte offset in that data stream of the beginning of the tagged data block that holds the information about the specified button. We'll call another QTFlash function to get that offset:

```
myOffset = GetOffsetForButton(theButtonID);
```

GetOffsetForButton is easy enough to write; once again, it uses the parsing code we developed in the previous chapter (Listing 7.6).

Listing 7.6 Finding a button in a Flash data stream.

```
U32 GetOffsetForButton (long theButtonID)
{
  BOOL       isAtEnd = false;
  U16        myCode;
  U32        myTagEnd;
  U32        myTagID;

  gFlashParserData.m_fileBuf = (U8 *)*gFlashParserData.m_theData;

  // set the position to the start position
  SkipHeaderBlock();

  // loop through each tagged data block

  while (!isAtEnd) {
    // get the current tag and tag-end position
    myCode = GetTag();
    myTagEnd = gFlashParserData.m_tagEnd;

    switch (myCode) {
      case stagEnd:
        // we have reached the end of the file
        isAtEnd = true;
        break;

      case stagDefineButton2:
        myTagID = (U32)GetWord();
        if (myTagID == theButtonID)
          return(gFlashParserData.m_tagStart);
        break;

      default:
        break;
    }

    // increment past the tag
    gFlashParserData.m_filePos = myTagEnd;
  }

  return(0);
}
```

Once we've determined the starting position of the button data block, we need to pass that information to our parser and then read past the tag header:

```
gFlashParserData.m_fileBuf = (U8 *)*theSample;
gFlashParserData.m_filePos = myOffset;
(void)GetTag();
```

At this point, gFlashParserData.m_filePos points to the first byte in the button data. Let's skip over the character ID and the menu flag to position our data pointer at the offset field. We'll need to remember the location of this field for later, so we'll store it in the variable myOffsetLocation.

```
gFlashParserData.m_filePos += sizeof(U16);        // step over character ID
gFlashParserData.m_filePos += sizeof(U8);         // step over menu flag

myOffsetLocation = gFlashParserData.m_filePos;
myButtonRecordLength = 0;
myActionCount = 0;
```

We also want to retrieve the value in the offset field so that we know how far ahead in the data stream to jump to reach the first button action condition:

```
myOffset = (U32)GetWord();
```

Now let's reposition the data pointer to point to the first button action condition:

```
gFlashParserData.m_filePos += myOffset - sizeof(U16);
```

Notice that we jump ahead by myOffset but then back up 16 bits; this is because the call to GetWord advances the pointer 16 bits, but myOffset is the offset from the beginning of the offset field.

For simplicity, let's assume that the existing button data does not contain a button action condition for the specified state transition that already contains a wired action. This means that we can just insert a new button action condition at the head of the existing list of button action conditions. (The code to handle the general case is fairly complicated but not terribly enlightening, but don't fret; the source code for QTFlash contains the full definition of QTFlash_SetWiredActionToButton.) So we're going to move the existing list of button action conditions down in the data stream to make room for our new condition. Let's get a few sizes:

```
myActionHandleSize = GetHandleSize((Handle)theAction);
myMoveAmount = myDataHandleSize - myStartActionOffset;
myIncreaseAmount = sizeof(U16) + sizeof(U16) + sizeof(U8) + sizeof(U16) +
                   myActionHandleSize + sizeof(U8);
myDataHandleSize += myIncreaseAmount;
```

Now we need to resize the handle that holds the Flash data stream and move all the existing button action conditions down:

```
SetHandleSize(theSample, myDataHandleSize);
myErr = MemError();
if (myErr != noErr)
  goto bail;

BlockMove(*theSample + myStartActionOffset, *theSample +
    myStartActionOffset + myIncreaseAmount, myMoveAmount);
```

At this point, we want to construct a new button action condition. Let's set myPtr to the first byte of the new button action condition:

```
myPtr = *theSample + myStartActionOffset;
```

A button action condition begins with a 16-bit offset to the next action condition. If, on entry to QTFlash_SetWiredActionToButton, we determined that there were no actions in the button data (which is possible but not very useful), then we'd set that offset to 0; otherwise, we'll set that offset to the length of the new button action condition:

```
if (myActionCount > 0) {
  INSERT_U16_AT_LOC(myIncreaseAmount, myPtr);
} else {
  *(U16 *)myPtr = 0;
  myPtr += sizeof(U16);
}
```

The macro INSERT_U16_AT_LOC inserts the specified 16-bit value at the specified location, making sure that that value is written in little-endian form; INSERT_U16_AT_LOC is defined like this:

```
#define INSERT_U16_AT_LOC(val,loc)                        \
            *(U8 *)loc++ = (val & 0xff);                  \
            *(U8 *)loc++ = ((val >> 8) & 0xff)
```

We continue writing data into our new button action condition. Next we patch in the condition:

```
INSERT_U16_AT_LOC(theCondition, myPtr);
```

And then we patch in the action type (namely, sactionWiredActions) and the length of the action data (which is of course the length of the atom container):

```
*(U8 *)myPtr = sactionWiredActions;
myPtr += sizeof(U8);
INSERT_U16_AT_LOC(myActionHandleSize, myPtr);
```

We're finally ready to insert the atom container that holds the wired actions. Each button action condition must end with an 8-bit field whose value is 0, so we'll write that too:

```
BlockMove(*theAction, myPtr, myActionHandleSize);
*(myPtr + myActionHandleSize) = 0;
```

To finish this off, if the original offset to the button action conditions was 0 (that is, if originally there were no actions in the button data), we need to patch in the original offset:

```
if (myActionCount == 0) {
  myPtr = *theSample + myOffsetLocation;
  INSERT_U16_AT_LOC(myButtonRecordLength, myPtr);
}
```

Adjusting Length Tags

We are almost finished attaching a QuickTime wired action to a Flash button. We've spliced a new button action condition into the button's data block, and we've updated (if necessary) the offset to the list of button action conditions. So the actual data in the button's tagged data block is now complete and correct. There remain, however, two length fields that we need to reset: the data length field in the tag header, and the file length field in the file header. We need to add myIncreaseAmount (the length of the new button action condition that we added) to each of the values currently in those fields. We do that by calling the application function SetNewHeaderAndTag-Length, like so:

```
SetNewHeaderAndTagLength(myIncreaseAmount, myIncreaseAmount);
```

Listing 7.7 shows our definition of SetNewHeaderAndTagLength. On the whole this function is straightforward; the only real complication arises from the fact that a tagged data block header can occupy 2 or 6 bytes, depending on the size of the data in the block.

Listing 7.7 Adjusting the file and tag lengths.

```
void SetNewHeaderAndTagLength (U32 theFileDifference, U32 theTagDifference)
{
    U8          *s;
    U16         myCode, myNewCode;
    U32         myLength, myFileLength;
    long        myHandleSize;
    Boolean     myIsLongTag = false;
    OSErr       myErr = noErr;

    // point at the first byte of the 4-byte file-length field in the header block;
    // it's at offset 4 in the header block
    s = (U8 *)*gFlashParserData.m_theData + 4;

    // read the current file length
    myFileLength = (U32)s[0] | ((U32)s[1] << 8) | ((U32)s[2] << 16) | ((U32)s[3] << 24);

    // increment the file length
    myFileLength += theFileDifference;
    s[0] = (myFileLength & 0xFF);
    s[1] = ((myFileLength >> 8) & 0xff);
    s[2] = ((myFileLength >> 16) & 0xff);
    s[3] = ((myFileLength >> 24) & 0xff);

    // point at the first byte of the current tag
    s = (U8 *)*gFlashParserData.m_theData + gFlashParserData.m_tagStart;

    // get the combined code and length of the tag
    myCode = (U16)s[0] | ((U16)s[1] << 8);

    // the length is encoded in the tag
    myLength = myCode & 0x3f;

    // remove the length from the code
    myCode = myCode >> 6;

    // determine whether another long word must be read to get the length
    if (myLength == 0x3f) {
        s += sizeof(U16);
```

```
      myLength = (U32)s[0] | ((U32)s[1] << 8) | ((U32)s[2] << 16) | ((U32)s[3] << 24);
      myIsLongTag = true;
    }

    myLength += theTagDifference;

    if (myLength >= 0x3f) {
      myNewCode = (myCode << 6) | 0x3f;

      if (!myIsLongTag) {                    // need more space
        myHandleSize = GetHandleSize(gFlashParserData.m_theData);

        myHandleSize += sizeof(long);

        SetHandleSize (gFlashParserData.m_theData, myHandleSize);
        myErr = MemError();
        if (myErr != noErr)
          goto bail;

        // now shift the data up
        BlockMove(*gFlashParserData.m_theData + gFlashParserData.m_tagStart,
                  *gFlashParserData.m_theData + gFlashParserData.m_tagStart + sizeof(long),
                  (myHandleSize - sizeof(long)) − gFlashParserData.m_tagStart);

        myFileLength += sizeof(long);
      }

      s = (U8 *)*gFlashParserData.m_theData + 4;
      s[0] = (myFileLength & 0xff);
      s[1] = ((myFileLength >> 8) & 0xff);
      s[2] = ((myFileLength >> 16) & 0xff);
      s[3] = ((myFileLength >> 24) & 0xff);

      s = (U8 *)*gFlashParserData.m_theData + gFlashParserData.m_tagStart;

      s[0] = (myNewCode & 0xff);
      s[1] = ((myNewCode >> 8) & 0xff);

      s += sizeof(U16);
      s[0] = (myLength & 0xff);
      s[1] = ((myLength >> 8) & 0xff);
      s[2] = ((myLength >> 16) & 0xff);
      s[3] = ((myLength >> 24) & 0xff);

    } else {
      myNewCode = (U16)(myCode << 6) | (U16)(myLength & 0x3f);
```

```
if (myIsLongTag) {
  myHandleSize = GetHandleSize(gFlashParserData.m_theData);
  myHandleSize -= sizeof(long);

  // shift the data down
  BlockMove(*gFlashParserData.m_theData + gFlashParserData.m_tagStart + sizeof(long),
            *gFlashParserData.m_theData + gFlashParserData.m_tagStart,
            (myHandleSize - sizeof(long)) - gFlashParserData.m_tagStart);

  SetHandleSize(gFlashParserData.m_theData, myHandleSize);
  myErr = MemError();
  if (myErr != noErr)
    goto bail;

  myFileLength -= sizeof(long);
}

s = (U8 *)*gFlashParserData.m_theData + 4;
s[0] = (myFileLength & 0xff);
s[1] = ((myFileLength >> 8) & 0xff);
s[2] = ((myFileLength >> 16) & 0xff);
s[3] = ((myFileLength >> 24) & 0xff);

s = (U8 *)*gFlashParserData.m_theData + gFlashParserData.m_tagStart;

s[0] = (myNewCode & 0xff);
s[1] = ((myNewCode >> 8) & 0xff);

}

bail:
  return;
}
```

▶ Conclusion

In this chapter, we've investigated some ways to use QuickTime's wired actions in conjunction with Flash tracks. We've seen that QuickTime provides a handful of actions that we can send to Flash tracks, along with a single operand that we can use to get information from a Flash track. Perhaps the most useful wired action that can be targeted at a Flash track is kAction-FlashTrackSetFlashVariable, which allows us to interact with ActionScripts attached to Flash elements. We can also use this wired action to dynamically set the text of a text item in a Flash track, without any assistance from Flash ActionScripts.

We've also seen how to embed wired actions in Flash files. We've walked through the steps involved in adding wired actions to a button, and similar code can be used to add wired actions to a frame in a Flash animation.

Big

Playing Movies Full-Screen

Introduction

It's sometimes remarked that when QuickTime was first introduced, it was able to play movies that were only about the size of a postage stamp. It turns out that this isn't quite true. The very first QuickTime CDs distributed to software developers contained a number of sample movies that were 320-by-240 pixels, or just under 4.5 by 3.5 inches (which is significantly larger than any postage stamp I've ever seen). What *is* true is that certain kinds of movies—in particular, full-motion movies encoded using the video compressor—had to be kept small in order to achieve a reasonable frame rate during playback. These kinds of movies typically had to be somewhere on the order of 160-by-120 pixels to get a playback rate of about 12 fps. Not great, but pretty good for a software-only movie playback system on a Mac II in 1991.

Since then, computer hardware and software technologies have advanced to the point that QuickTime can achieve smooth playback for much larger movies, at frames rates of 24 to 30 fps (or even greater). From QuickTime version 2.1 onward, it has also been possible to play QuickTime movies back *full-screen* so that the movie occupies an entire monitor. Figure 8.1 shows a frame of a movie being played back full-screen; as you can see, there is no menu bar and the window that contains the movie does not have a window frame or title bar. In addition, the control strip (on classic Mac operating systems), the dock (on Mac OS X), or the taskbar (on Windows operating systems) is hidden while a movie is playing full-screen. At its natural proportions, this movie does not completely fill the screen, so it's centered horizontally with the edges drawn in black. Full-screen movie playback is fairly common in games, especially for the cut scenes that occur between game levels. It has also recently become popular for many of the movie trailers posted to the Web in QuickTime format.

Figure 8.1 A QuickTime movie played full-screen.

Figure 8.2 The Test menu of QTBigScreen.

In this chapter, we're going to learn how to play QuickTime movies full-screen. I mentioned in Chapter 6, "The Flash," that full-screen movie play-back is accomplished primarily using the two functions `BeginFullScreen` and `EndFullScreen`. When using these functions to integrate full-screen playback into our sample applications, however, we'll need to pay attention to a number of issues, including saving and restoring the state of our movie windows and their associated movie controllers. We'll also take a look at the wired action introduced in QuickTime 5.0.1 that a movie can use to begin and end full-screen playback. Along the way, we'll touch on a few topics of general interest to QuickTime developers, including time base callback functions.

Our sample application for this chapter is called QTBigScreen. As usual, it's based on the QTShell sample application and adds support for entering and exiting full-screen mode. The Test menu of QTBigScreen is shown in Figure 8.2; it contains just one item, which allows the user to put the front-most movie window into full-screen mode.

There is no menu item for exiting full-screen mode; instead, we'll follow the example of QuickTime Player and return to the normal windowed mode when the user types the Escape key or when a noninteractive and non-looped movie reaches the end.

The Theory

Let's begin by taking a look at the `BeginFullScreen` and `EndFullScreen` functions. As I mentioned, things tend to get a tad lengthy when we use these calls in a real-life application, so it's good to have a firm grasp on how they work before we try to do that. In this chapter, we are going to focus on using these functions to play QuickTime movies full-screen, but they can, in fact, be used to display *any* kind of content in a full-screen window. Moreover, we can use these functions simply to change the resolution of a screen, without wanting to take over the entire screen. In short, there's a lot going on with these two functions that we need to understand clearly before we attempt to use them in our applications.

Entering and Exiting Full-Screen Mode

The `BeginFullScreen` function is declared essentially like this:

```
OSErr BeginFullScreen (
        Ptr *restoreState,
        GDHandle whichGD,
        short *desiredWidth,
        short *desiredHeight,
        WindowRef *newWindow,
        RGBColor *eraseColor,
        long flags);
```

The key input parameters are `desiredWidth` and `desiredHeight`, which are pointers to the width and height of the movie (or image, or other content) that we want to display full-screen. `BeginFullScreen` creates a new window that is at least that large and returns a window pointer for that window in the location pointed to by the `newWindow` parameter. `BeginFullScreen` also erases the screen (using the color specified by the `eraseColor` parameter) and (depending on the value of the `flags` parameter, which we'll consider in a moment) hides the menu bar and control strip. The `whichGD` parameter indicates which graphics device we want to put into full-screen mode; we shall always pass the value `NULL` to select the main screen.

`BeginFullScreen` also returns, through the `restoreState` parameter, a pointer to a block of memory that contains information on how to return from full-screen mode to normal windowed mode. We exit full-screen mode by passing that pointer to `EndFullScreen`, which is declared like this:

```
OSErr EndFullScreen (Ptr fullState, long flags);
```

Note that the restoreState (or fullState) pointer is opaque and is owned by QuickTime; we shouldn't do anything with it except pass it to End-FullScreen when we are ready to exit full-screen mode. Similarly, the newWindow window pointer is owned by QuickTime, which will dispose of it after we call EndFullScreen.

The flags parameter passed to EndFullScreen is unused and should be set to 0. The flags parameter passed to BeginFullScreen controls several aspects of full-screen mode. Currently, we can use these constants to set the value of this parameter:

```
enum {
    fullScreenHideCursor                    = 1L << 0,
    fullScreenAllowEvents                   = 1L << 1,
    fullScreenDontChangeMenuBar             = 1L << 2,
    fullScreenPreflightSize                 = 1L << 3
};
```

The fullScreenHideCursor flag indicates that BeginFullScreen should hide the cursor while the screen is in full-screen mode. This is useful if we just want to play a movie full-screen from start to finish, but it's less useful for interactive movies played full-screen. In QTBigScreen, we will not set this flag when we call BeginFullScreen. The fullScreenAllowEvents flag indicates that our application intends to allow other open applications to receive processing time; in general, we should set this flag. The fullScreenDontChangeMenuBar flag indicates that BeginFullScreen should not hide the menu bar.

The fullScreenPreflightSize flag is of particular interest. If we set this flag, then BeginFullScreen does not change any screen settings and does not return a new window to us. Instead, it returns, through the desiredWidth and desiredHeight parameters, the width and height that the screen would have been set to if the fullScreenPreflightSize flag had not been set. We can use that flag to determine the size of the full-screen window without actually entering full-screen mode.

Changing the Screen Resolution

Why is this useful? Recall that BeginFullScreen will create a window that is at least as large as the height and width we pass it. In addition, BeginFullScreen will change the screen resolution to the closest resolution that contains that window. If, for instance, the main screen is originally set to a resolution of 1024 by 768 and if we pass a width and height of (say) 762 and 560, then BeginFullScreen will change the resolution of the screen to 800 by 600 (assuming that the monitor supports that resolution).

We can exploit this behavior in several ways. First, we can use BeginFullScreen to determine the current screen resolution. If we set 0 to be the value pointed to by both the desiredWidth and desiredHeight parameters, then BeginFullScreen leaves the dimensions of the screen unchanged but returns to us the current dimensions of the screen in the locations pointed to by those parameters. If we also pass the fullScreenPreflightSize flag, then BeginFullScreen doesn't change any of the current screen settings. The end result is that we are given the current height and width of the screen (that is, its resolution). Listing 8.1 defines the function QTUtils_GetScreenResolution, which retrieves the current resolution of the main screen.

Listing 8.1 Getting the current resolution of the main screen.

```
OSErr QTUtils_GetScreenResolution (short *thePixelsHoriz, short *thePixelsVert)
{
  Ptr        myDummyPtr = NULL;
  OSErr      myErr = noErr;

  if ((thePixelsHoriz == NULL) || (thePixelsVert == NULL))
    return(paramErr);

  *thePixelsHoriz = 0;
  *thePixelsVert = 0;

  myErr = BeginFullScreen(&myDummyPtr, NULL, thePixelsHoriz, thePixelsVert,
            NULL, NULL, fullScreenPreflightSize);

  return(myErr);
}
```

Notice that we need to pass the address of a variable of type Ptr as the first parameter to BeginFullScreen, even though it does not return an actual pointer in that location. If we look at the value of myDummyPtr after calling BeginFullScreen here, we'll see that it's still NULL. So there is no need to call EndFullScreen to dispose of that pointer.

We can also use BeginFullScreen to change the screen resolution without hiding the menu bar. We simply pass in the desired height and width, and we set the flags parameter so that the menu bar is not hidden. In this case, we need to pass the value NULL for the newWindow parameter, indicating that we don't want a new window to be created. Here's how we could set the main screen to a resolution of 800 by 600:

```
myHorizPixels = 800;
myVertPixels = 600;

myErr = BeginFullScreen(&gRestoreState, NULL, &myHorizPixels,
          &myVertPixels, NULL, NULL, fullScreenDontChangeMenuBar);
```

We need to keep track of the restore state so that we can undo the resolution change at some future time. You should keep in mind that there is no way to suppress the hiding of the control strip (or dock or taskbar) when you call `BeginFullScreen`. If you want the control strip (or dock or taskbar) to remain visible after you adjust the resolution, you'll need to programmatically reshow it. (For instance, on Windows you could call the QTML function `ShowHideTaskBar` to reshow the taskbar.) It might be nice if QuickTime defined a flag that would allow us to request that the control strip (or its ilk) remain visible after a call to `BeginFullScreen`.

Scaling the Movie

In QTBigScreen, we don't want the resolution of the main screen to be changed when we play a movie full-screen. We can accomplish this by scaling the movie so that the requested size is large enough to occupy all or almost all of the main screen at its current resolution. So we're going to end up calling `BeginFullScreen` twice, once to get the current resolution (as we did in Listing 8.1) and again to put a movie window into full-screen mode. But before we call `BeginFullScreen` the second time, we need to do a little mathematics to figure out how to scale the movie so that it retains its original aspect ratio but fills as much of the screen as possible.

We begin by calling `BeginFullScreen` to get the current resolution of the screen:

```
short           myScreenWidth = 0;
short           myScreenHeight = 0;

myErr = BeginFullScreen(&(**myAppData).fRestoreState, NULL, &myScreenWidth,
          &myScreenHeight, NULL, NULL, fullScreenPreflightSize);
```

As you can see, we are storing the restore state in the application data record. Ultimately, we're going to have to maintain about a dozen pieces of data in that record (which we'll encounter shortly). Once we've retrieved the current resolution, let's make a copy of that information:

```
myOrigScreenHeight = myScreenHeight;
myOrigScreenWidth = myScreenWidth;
```

Now we need to get the natural size of the movie we want to play full-screen. We can do this by calling `GetMovieNaturalBoundsRect`:

```
GetMovieNaturalBoundsRect(myMovie, &myRect);
MacOffsetRect(&myRect, -myRect.left, -myRect.top);

myMovieWidth = myRect.right;
myMovieHeight = myRect.bottom;
```

(Calling GetMovieBox here wouldn't work quite right, since the user might have resized the movie window before putting it into full-screen mode.)

And now we can calculate the aspect ratios of the screen and the movie:

```
myMovieRatio = FixRatio(myMovieWidth, myMovieHeight);
myScreenRatio = FixRatio(myScreenWidth, myScreenHeight);
```

We use these ratios to determine which dimension of the movie should be scaled to completely fill the corresponding dimension of the screen. The math required is simple:

```
if (myMovieRatio > myScreenRatio) {
  myMovieHeight = (myScreenWidth * myMovieHeight) / myMovieWidth;
  myMovieWidth = myScreenWidth;
} else {
  myMovieWidth = (myScreenHeight * myMovieWidth) / myMovieHeight;
  myMovieHeight = myScreenHeight;
}
```

At this point, we know the desired size of the movie and hence we can call BeginFullScreen once again:

```
myScreenWidth = myMovieWidth;
myScreenHeight = myMovieHeight;
myErr = BeginFullScreen(&(**myAppData).fRestoreState, NULL, &myScreenWidth,
         &myScreenHeight, &(**myAppData).fFullScreenWindow,
         &myColor, fullScreenAllowEvents);
```

If BeginFullScreen returns successfully, then (**myAppData).fFullScreenWindow contains a window pointer to the new full-screen window and myScreenWidth and myScreenHeight point to the actual width and height of that window. If the aspect ratio of the movie does not exactly match that of the screen, then we need to move the movie down or to the right so that it is centered in the full-screen window (see Figure 8.1 again). First we set the movie's rectangle:

```
MacSetRect(&myRect, 0, 0, myMovieWidth, myMovieHeight);
```

And then we nudge the movie down or to the right to center it on the screen:

```
MacOffsetRect(&myRect, (myScreenWidth - myMovieWidth) / 2,
                        (myScreenHeight - myMovieHeight) / 2);
SetMovieBox(myMovie, &myRect);
```

There is one final "gotcha" we need to watch out for. Although we scaled the movie up so that one of its dimensions extends for the full width or height of the screen, it's possible that the expanded movie size exactly matches a screen resolution that is not the same as the original screen resolution. Suppose, for instance, that our movie has a natural size of 480-by-360 pixels. This movie, when scaled up, will exactly fill a screen that is 1024 by 768. However, the "megawide" screen on the Titanium PowerBook has a natural resolution of 1152 by 768, and it also supports the resolution of 1024 by 768 (by blanking 64 pixels on the left and right sides of the screen). If we play this movie full-screen on that PowerBook, our existing code will result in the screen resolution being changed to 1024 by 768; in that case, there is no need to nudge the movie down or to the right.

So before we adjust the movie's rectangle, we should check to see whether the screen resolution did in fact change. We cleverly saved the original screen resolution, and our second call to BeginFullScreen gives us back the current screen resolution; we can compare the current with the original and then nudge the movie only if the resolution has not changed:

```
if ((myScreenWidth == myOrigScreenWidth) &&
    (myScreenHeight == myOrigScreenHeight))
   MacOffsetRect(&myRect, (myScreenWidth - myMovieWidth) / 2,
    (myScreenHeight - myMovieHeight) / 2);
```

Once again, it might be nice if BeginFullScreen supported a flag that instructed it not to change the screen resolution.

The Practice

So, we now understand how to use BeginFullScreen and EndFullScreen to enter and exit full-screen mode. We've seen how to request a full-screen window size that makes our movie as large as possible while preserving its original aspect ratio and also preventing changes in the screen resolution (whenever possible). And we've seen how to adjust the movie box—the rectangle in which the movie is drawn inside its window—so that the movie is nicely centered in the full-screen window. Aren't we done yet?

No. There are still a couple of issues we need to address. Our basic sample application framework was not developed with the intention of supporting full-screen movie playback, so a couple of our framework functions need some minor tweaking. More important, we need to keep track of some information (including the restore information and the new window pointer) for each movie window we put into full-screen mode. And, of course, we need to make sure that events get passed to a movie playing full-screen. In this section, we'll tackle these issues.

Initializing the Movie Window Data

Ideally, we'd like the user to be able to put any of our application's movie windows into full-screen mode and then back into normal mode. We therefore need to keep track of the restore state information and the new window pointer returned by BeginFullScreen, as well as a few other pieces of information. We'll define a custom application data record, like this:

```
typedef struct ApplicationDataRecord {
    WindowReference         fOrigWindow;
    WindowPtr               fFullScreenWindow;
    Ptr                     fRestoreState;
    GWorldPtr               fOrigMovieGWorld;
    Rect                    fOrigMovieRect;
    Rect                    fOrigControllerRect;
    Boolean                 fOrigControllerVis;
    Boolean                 fOrigControllerAttached;
    QTCallBack              fCallBack;
    QTCallBackUPP           fCallBackUPP;
    Boolean                 fEndFullscreenNeeded;
    Boolean                 fDestroyWindowNeeded;
} ApplicationDataRecord, *ApplicationDataPtr, **ApplicationDataHdl;
```

The fOrigWindow field will contain the original window reference—that is, a reference to the window that the user puts into full-screen mode. (Remember that the actual type of this object varies; on Macintosh systems, it's of type WindowPtr, while on Windows systems it's of type HWND.) The fRestoreState and fFullScreenWindow fields hold the restore state and window pointer returned by BeginFullScreen. The next five fields hold information about the state of the movie window at the time it's put into full-screen mode; for instance, the fOrigMovieRect field holds the movie rectangle, and fOrigControllerVis indicates whether the controller bar was visible when we called BeginFullScreen. We'll need these pieces of information when we restore the movie to its normal windowed state.

The `fCallBack` and `fCallBackUPP` fields hold information related to a time base callback function; we use this function to automatically return a movie from full-screen state to normal state when the movie reaches the end, to mimic the behavior of QuickTime Player. (I personally don't like this behavior, but it's useful to know how to implement it. I've conditionalized the callback code using the compiler flag END_FULLSCREEN_AT_MOVIE_END, so it's easy enough to turn off.)

The last two fields of our application data structure are Boolean values that indicate whether the associated movie window should be returned from full-screen mode to normal mode and whether the associated movie window should be closed. Later, we'll see why we need these fields.

I'm also going to introduce a global variable that holds the window object for the window that is currently in full-screen mode:

```
WindowObject                    gFullScreenWindowObject = NULL;
```

It would be possible to determine which, if any, movie window is in full-screen mode by iterating through all open movie windows and checking their application data record (to see if fFullScreenWindow is non-NULL), but using a global variable will simplify our code.

When we first open a movie window, we'll call QTBig_InitWindowData (Listing 8.2) to create this custom application data record and initialize its fields.

Listing 8.2 Initializing application-specific window data.

```
ApplicationDataHdl QTBig_InitWindowData (WindowObject theWindowObject)
{
  ApplicationDataHdl        myAppData = NULL;

  // if we already have some window data, dump it
  myAppData = (ApplicationDataHdl)QTFrame_GetAppDataFromWindowObject(theWindowObject);
  if (myAppData != NULL)
    QTBig_DumpWindowData(theWindowObject);

  // allocate a new application data handle
  myAppData = (ApplicationDataHdl)NewHandleClear(sizeof(ApplicationDataRecord));

  return(myAppData);
}
```

And when we close a movie window, we want to deallocate the application data record. For this, we call the function QTBig_DumpWindowData, defined in Listing 8.3. Notice that we first check to see whether the window is in full-screen mode; if it is, we call our function `QTBig_StopFullscreen` to return it to normal mode.

Listing 8.3 Destroying application-specific window data.

```
void QTBig_DumpWindowData (WindowObject theWindowObject)
{
  ApplicationDataHdl     myAppData = NULL;

  myAppData = (ApplicationDataHdl)QTFrame_GetAppDataFromWindowObject(theWindowObject);
  if (myAppData != NULL) {
    if ((**myAppData).fFullScreenWindow != NULL)
      QTBig_StopFullscreen(theWindowObject);

    DisposeHandle((Handle)myAppData);
    (**theWindowObject).fAppData = NULL;
  }
}
```

Entering Full-Screen Mode

Let's revisit for a moment our basic scheme for opening movie windows and keeping track of window-specific data. On Macintosh systems, we call `NewCWindow` to obtain a window pointer to a new window. We allocate a new window object record and store a handle to that record as the window reference constant (by calling `SetWRefCon`). This allows us to retrieve our window-specific data (the movie being displayed in the window, the movie controller associated with the movie, and so forth) if we are given the window pointer. On Windows operating systems, we call `CreateWindowEx` to create a new window and `SetWindowLong` to store a handle to the window record in the window's data. (See Volume One, Chapter 1, for a more complete account of all this.)

Now, our entire application framework assumes that each window displayed by our application is associated with a window object record. We need the data in that record to know which movie or image is contained in the window, whether the movie or image has been changed since it was last saved, and similar information. So, when `BeginFullScreen` returns to us a new full-screen window, we need to attach a window object to that window. We could, of course, create a new window object and attach it to the window, but things actually work much better if we borrow the window object from the movie window we want to put into full-screen mode. We'll do that like this:

```
#if TARGET_OS_MAC
    SetWRefCon((**myAppData).fFullScreenWindow, (long)theWindowObject);
#endif
#if TARGET_OS_WIN32
    SetWindowLong(GetPortNativeWindow(
      (GrafPtr)(**myAppData).fFullScreenWindow), GWL_USERDATA,
      (LPARAM)theWindowObject);
#endif
```

The Macintosh code is straightforward: simply set the reference constant of the window created by `BeginFullScreen` to the window object passed to `QTBig_StartFullscreen`. The Windows code is a little more involved, since `BeginFullScreen` returns to us a window pointer (of type `WindowPtr`) but our Windows application expects a movie window to be of type `HWND`. Accordingly, we need to call `GetPortNativeWindow` to get the native window (of type `HWND`) that is associated with the window pointer. This window was created automatically by QuickTime when it created the full-screen window.

Keep in mind that we now have *two* windows to worry about: the original movie window (which is either of type `WindowPtr` or `HWND`, depending on the native operating system), and a full-screen window (which is always of type `WindowPtr` but which on Windows is also associated with a window of type `HWND`). We are attaching the window object associated with the original movie window to the full-screen window; this lets us know which movie to play full-screen and how to control that movie; it's also important to have a window object available when we want to pass events to the full-screen movie (as we'll see shortly).

It seems reasonable that once we've created the full-screen window, we should hide the original movie window; after all, we won't be able to redraw the original movie window or let the user move it around. We can hide the movie window like this:

```
QTFrame_SetWindowVisState(theWindowObject, false);
```

The `QTFrame_SetWindowVisState` function is a new function that we need to add to our framework; it's defined in Listing 8.4.

Listing 8.4 Showing or hiding a movie window.

```
void QTFrame_SetWindowVisState (WindowObject theWindowObject, Boolean theState)
{
  // make sure we have a non-NULL window object and window
  if (theWindowObject == NULL)
    return;

  if ((**theWindowObject).fWindow == NULL)
    return;
```

```
  // set the visibility state of the window
#if TARGET_OS_MAC
  if (theState)
    MacShowWindow((**theWindowObject).fWindow);
  else
    HideWindow((**theWindowObject).fWindow);
#endif
#if TARGET_OS_WIN32
  ShowWindow((**theWindowObject).fWindow, theState);
#endif
}
```

(It's interesting to note that QuickTime Player does not hide the original movie window after putting it into full-screen mode. What's up with that?)

There is one final set of tasks we need to attend to when putting a movie window into full-screen mode. As we've seen, we are using the same movie and movie controller in the new full-screen window that we use in the original movie window. But, of course, the full-screen window has a different graphics world and a different size. So we need to save the graphics world, size, and a few other pieces of information before we go into full-screen mode; later we'll restore them when we return to normal mode. QTBig_ StartFullscreen contains these lines to save the relevant information in our application data record:

```
GetMovieGWorld(myMovie, &(**myAppData).fOrigMovieGWorld, NULL);
GetMovieBox(myMovie, &(**myAppData).fOrigMovieRect);
MCGetControllerBoundsRect(myMC, &(**myAppData).fOrigControllerRect);
(**myAppData).fOrigControllerVis = MCGetVisible(myMC);
(**myAppData).fOrigControllerAttached = MCIsControllerAttached(myMC);
(**myAppData).fOrigWindow = (**theWindowObject).fWindow;
```

Once we've successfully entered full-screen mode, we need to set the movie graphics world, movie controller bounds, and so forth for the new full-screen window:

```
SetGWorld(GetWindowPort((**myAppData).fFullScreenWindow), NULL);
SetMovieGWorld(myMovie, GetWindowPort((**myAppData).fFullScreenWindow),
    NULL);
MCSetControllerPort(myMC, GetWindowPort((**myAppData).fFullScreenWindow));
MCSetControllerAttached(myMC, false);
MCSetControllerBoundsRect(myMC, &myRect);

MCSetVisible(myMC, false);
MCActivate(myMC, (**myAppData).fFullScreenWindow, true);
```

We also need to set the fWindow field of the window object record to the new full-screen window:

```
(**theWindowObject).fWindow = QTFrame_GetWindowReferenceFromWindow(
                                 (**myAppData).fFullScreenWindow);
```

And we want to keep track of the full-screen window in a global variable:

```
gFullScreenWindowObject = theWindowObject;
```

We are finally ready to take a look at the complete definition of QTBig_StartFullscreen, shown in Listing 8.5.

Listing 8.5 Entering full-screen mode.

```
OSErr QTBig_StartFullscreen (WindowObject theWindowObject)
{
  MovieController       myMC = NULL;
  Movie                 myMovie = NULL;
  ApplicationDataHdl    myAppData = NULL;
  long                  myFlags = fullScreenAllowEvents;
  OSErr                 myErr = paramErr;

  if (theWindowObject == NULL)
    goto bail;

  myAppData = (ApplicationDataHdl)QTFrame_GetAppDataFromWindowObject(theWindowObject);
  myMovie = (**theWindowObject).fMovie;
  myMC = (**theWindowObject).fController;

  if ((myAppData == NULL) || (myMovie == NULL) || (myMC == NULL))
    goto bail;

  if ((**myAppData).fFullScreenWindow == NULL) {
    short         myOrigScreenWidth = 0;
    short         myOrigScreenHeight = 0;
    short         myNewScreenWidth = 0;
    short         myNewScreenHeight = 0;
    short         myScreenWidth = 0;
    short         myScreenHeight = 0;
    short         myMovieWidth = 0;
    short         myMovieHeight = 0;
    Fixed         myScreenRatio;
    Fixed         myMovieRatio;
    Rect          myRect;
    RGBColor      myColor = {0x0000, 0x0000, 0x0000};     // black
```

```
// remember some of the current state
GetMovieGWorld(myMovie, &(**myAppData).fOrigMovieGWorld, NULL);
GetMovieBox(myMovie, &(**myAppData).fOrigMovieRect);
MCGetControllerBoundsRect(myMC, &(**myAppData).fOrigControllerRect);
(**myAppData).fOrigControllerVis = MCGetVisible(myMC);
(**myAppData).fOrigControllerAttached = MCIsControllerAttached(myMC);
(**myAppData).fOrigWindow = (**theWindowObject).fWindow;

// get the current screen resolution
myErr = BeginFullScreen(&(**myAppData).fRestoreState, NULL,
          &myScreenWidth, &myScreenHeight, NULL, NULL, fullScreenPreflightSize);
if (myErr != noErr)
  goto bail;

// keep track of the original screen resolution
myOrigScreenHeight = myScreenHeight;
myOrigScreenWidth = myScreenWidth;

// calculate the destination rectangle
GetMovieNaturalBoundsRect(myMovie, &myRect);
MacOffsetRect(&myRect, -myRect.left, -myRect.top);

myMovieWidth = myRect.right;
myMovieHeight = myRect.bottom;

myMovieRatio = FixRatio(myMovieWidth, myMovieHeight);
myScreenRatio = FixRatio(myScreenWidth, myScreenHeight);

// scale the movie rectangle to fit the screen ratio
if (myMovieRatio > myScreenRatio) {
  myMovieHeight = (myScreenWidth * myMovieHeight) / myMovieWidth;
  myMovieWidth = myScreenWidth;
} else {
  myMovieWidth = (myScreenHeight * myMovieWidth) / myMovieHeight;
  myMovieHeight = myScreenHeight;
}

MacSetRect(&myRect, 0, 0, myMovieWidth, myMovieHeight);

myScreenWidth = myMovieWidth;
myScreenHeight = myMovieHeight;

// begin full-screen display
myErr = BeginFullScreen(&(**myAppData).fRestoreState, NULL,
          &myScreenWidth, &myScreenHeight, &(**myAppData).fFullScreenWindow,
          &myColor, myFlags);
if (myErr != noErr)
  goto bail;
```

```
    // determine whether the resolution changed; if it has changed, we must have
    // passed in a supported resolution, so we want the movie to fill the screen;
    // otherwise, we need to offset the movie to center it in the screen
    if ((myScreenWidth == myOrigScreenWidth) && (myScreenHeight == myOrigScreenHeight))
      MacOffsetRect(&myRect,
        (myScreenWidth - myMovieWidth) / 2, (myScreenHeight - myMovieHeight) / 2);

#if TARGET_OS_WIN32
    // on Windows, set a window procedure for the new window
    QTMLSetWindowWndProc((**myAppData).fFullScreenWindow, QTBig_HandleMessages);
#endif

    // hide the original window
    QTFrame_SetWindowVisState(theWindowObject, false);

    // attach the existing window object to the new window
#if TARGET_OS_MAC
    SetWRefCon((**myAppData).fFullScreenWindow, (long)theWindowObject);
#endif
#if TARGET_OS_WIN32
    SetWindowLong(GetPortNativeWindow((GrafPtr)(**myAppData).fFullScreenWindow),
      GWL_USERDATA, (LPARAM)theWindowObject);
#endif

    // set the movie and movie controller state to the new window and rectangle
    SetGWorld(GetWindowPort((**myAppData).fFullScreenWindow), NULL);
    SetMovieGWorld(myMovie, GetWindowPort((**myAppData).fFullScreenWindow), NULL);
    MCSetControllerPort(myMC, GetWindowPort((**myAppData).fFullScreenWindow));
    MCSetControllerAttached(myMC, false);
    MCSetControllerBoundsRect(myMC, &myRect);

    SetMovieBox(myMovie, &myRect);
    MCSetVisible(myMC, false);
    MCActivate(myMC, (**myAppData).fFullScreenWindow, true);

    (**theWindowObject).fWindow = QTFrame_GetWindowReferenceFromWindow(
                                    (**myAppData).fFullScreenWindow);

#if TARGET_API_MAC_CARBON
    HiliteWindow((**myAppData).fFullScreenWindow, true);
#endif
```

```
#if END_FULLSCREEN_AT_MOVIE_END
    // install a callback procedure to return linear, nonlooping movies
    // to normal mode at the end of the movie
    if (QTBig_MovieIsStoppable(myMC))
      QTBig_InstallCallBack(theWindowObject);
#endif
  }

  gFullScreenWindowObject = theWindowObject;

bail:
  return(myErr);
}
```

You'll notice a few lines of code we haven't discussed yet. The Windows-only call to QTMLSetWindowWndProc is necessary to handle messages targeted at the full-screen window, as we'll see in the next section. The Carbon-only call to HiliteWindow ensures that the window returned by BeginFullScreen is highlighted. (Apparently, in some circumstances, that window is occasionally unhighlighted, which blocks any interactivity in the movie.) And the code selected by the END_FULLSCREEN_AT_MOVIE_END flag installs a time base callback function that returns a noninteractive, nonlooping movie to normal mode when the movie reaches its end. We'll delve into that issue toward the end of this chapter.

Handling Events for the Full-Screen Window

Now we've created a full-screen window, attached a movie and movie controller to it, and positioned the movie box so that the movie appears centered in the full-screen window. We've also set the movie and movie controller graphics ports to the full-screen window and hidden the original movie window. So things are looking great. We'd also like them to start *acting* great. That is, we want the full-screen movie to respond in the normal ways to mouse movements, mouse clicks, and key presses, and we want it to jump out of full-screen mode if the user presses the Escape key.

This Escape key behavior is quite easy to implement. Our application framework contains a stub function QTApp_HandleKeyPress that we can use to intercept key presses. In QTBigScreen, QTApp_HandleKeyPress is defined as shown in Listing 8.6. As you can see, we look for presses on the Escape key while a full-screen window is active; if we find one, we call QTBig_StopFullscreen.

Listing 8.6 Handling key presses.

```
Boolean QTApp_HandleKeyPress (char theCharCode)
{
  Boolean                 isHandled = false;

  switch (theCharCode) {
    // Escape key during full-screen display restores the window to its original state
    case kEscapeCharCode:
      if (gFullScreenWindowObject != NULL)
        isHandled = (QTBig_StopFullscreen(gFullScreenWindowObject) == noErr);
      break;
  }

  return(isHandled);
}
```

All the other important behaviors we care about are provided by the movie controller. So we need to make sure that we call MCIsPlayerEvent for any events our application receives while there is a full-screen movie. Again, we'll insert some code into another application function, QTApp_HandleEvent:

```
if ((**myAppData).fFullScreenWindow != NULL)
  return(MCIsPlayerEvent((**myWindowObject).fController, theEvent));
```

On the Macintosh, this is pretty much all we need to do to make the full-screen movie behave as expected. That's because our Mac framework calls QTApp_HandleEvent for every event it receives, and it calls QTApp_HandleKey-Press on every key event. On Windows, things are a bit trickier. Our Windows framework calls these functions only for MDI child movies—that is, windows using the QTFrame_MovieWndProc window procedure. But the full-screen window is not an MDI child window. The easy solution here is to define a custom window procedure for the full-screen window that calls QTApp_HandleEvent and QTApp_HandleKeyPress at the appropriate times. (We install this window procedure by calling QTMLSetWindowWndProc, as you saw in Listing 8.5.) Listing 8.7 shows our definition of QTBig_HandleMessages.

Listing 8.7 Handling full-screen window messages.

```
LRESULT CALLBACK QTBig_HandleMessages (HWND theWnd, UINT theMessage,
                UINT wParam, LONG lParam)
{
  MovieController      myMC = NULL;
  Movie                myMovie = NULL;
  WindowObject         myWindowObject = NULL;
```

```
   MSG                     myMsg = {0};
   EventRecord             myMacEvent;
   LONG                    myPoints = GetMessagePos();
   BOOL                    myIsHandled = false;

   if (gFullScreenWindowObject == NULL)
     goto bail;

   // make sure we don't get called while the movie is returning to normal state
   if (gEndingFullScreen)
     goto bail;

   // get the window object, movie, and movie controller for this window
   myWindowObject = gFullScreenWindowObject;
   myMC = (**myWindowObject).fController;
   myMovie = (**myWindowObject).fMovie;

   // give the movie controller this message first
   if (myMC != NULL) {
     LONG                  myPoints = GetMessagePos();

     myMsg.hwnd = theWnd;
     myMsg.message = theMessage;
     myMsg.wParam = wParam;
     myMsg.lParam = lParam;
     myMsg.time = GetMessageTime();
     myMsg.pt.x = LOWORD(myPoints);
     myMsg.pt.y = HIWORD(myPoints);

     // translate a Windows event to a Mac event
     WinEventToMacEvent(&myMsg, &myMacEvent);

     // let the application-specific code have a chance to intercept the event
     myIsHandled = QTApp_HandleEvent(&myMacEvent);
   }

   switch (theMessage) {
     case WM_CHAR:
       // do any application-specific key press handling
       myIsHandled = QTApp_HandleKeyPress((char)wParam);
       break;
   }

bail:
   return(DefWindowProc(theWnd, theMessage, wParam, lParam));
}
```

There's nothing too extravagant here. Notice, however, that we look at the gEndingFullScreen global variable to see whether we got this message during a call to EndFullScreen. If so, we don't want to pass the event to the movie controller.

We need to make a couple of other small changes to get everything working satisfactorily, now that our application has to support full-screen windows. For instance, in the function QTFrame_SizeWindowToMovie, we use code like the following to get the size of a movie that is associated with a movie controller:

```
if (myMC != NULL)
  if (MCGetVisible(myMC))
    MCGetControllerBoundsRect(myMC, &myRect);
```

This assumes that the controller is attached to the movie, which is always true for our movie windows but false for our full-screen movie. So we need to revise that code like so:

```
if (myMC != NULL)
  if (MCGetVisible(myMC))
    if (MCIsControllerAttached(myMC))
      MCGetControllerBoundsRect(myMC, &myRect);
```

Exiting Full-Screen Mode

Returning from full-screen mode to normal windowed mode is a breeze. The main step is, of course, to call EndFullScreen. To prevent QTBig_Handle-Messages from being called while EndFullScreen is executing, we bracket our call with setting and unsetting the gEndingFullScreen global variable:

```
gEndingFullScreen = true;
myErr = EndFullScreen((**myAppData).fRestoreState, 0L);
gEndingFullScreen = false;
```

We also need to restore the settings we saved previously, such as the movie and movie controller graphics ports and the visibility state of the controller bar. It's all pretty much what you'd expect (Listing 8.8).

Listing 8.8 Returning to normal window mode.

```
OSErr QTBig_StopFullscreen (WindowObject theWindowObject)
{
  ApplicationDataHdl      myAppData = NULL;
  OSErr                   myErr = paramErr;
```

```
    if (theWindowObject == NULL)
      goto bail;

  myAppData = (ApplicationDataHdl)QTFrame_GetAppDataFromWindowObject(theWindowObject);
  if (myAppData != NULL) {
    if ((**myAppData).fFullScreenWindow != NULL) {

      // restore the original settings
      (**theWindowObject).fWindow = (**myAppData).fOrigWindow;

      MacSetPort(QTFrame_GetPortFromWindowReference((**theWindowObject).fWindow));

      SetMovieGWorld((**theWindowObject).fMovie, (CGrafPtr)(**myAppData).fOrigMovieGWorld,
        GetGWorldDevice((CGrafPtr)(**myAppData).fOrigMovieGWorld));
      SetMovieBox((**theWindowObject).fMovie, &(**myAppData).fOrigMovieRect);

      MCSetControllerPort((**theWindowObject).fController,
        (CGrafPtr)(**myAppData).fOrigMovieGWorld);
      MCSetControllerAttached((**theWindowObject).fController,
        (**myAppData).fOrigControllerAttached);
      MCSetVisible((**theWindowObject).fController, (**myAppData).fOrigControllerVis);
      MCSetControllerBoundsRect((**theWindowObject).fController,
        &(**myAppData).fOrigControllerRect);

      gEndingFullScreen = true;

      // end full-screen playback
      myErr = EndFullScreen((**myAppData).fRestoreState, 0L);

      gEndingFullScreen = false;

      // empty out the data structures and global variables
      (**myAppData).fOrigWindow = NULL;
      (**myAppData).fFullScreenWindow = NULL;
      (**myAppData).fRestoreState = NULL;
      (**myAppData).fOrigMovieGWorld = NULL;

      gFullScreenWindowObject = NULL;

#if END_FULLSCREEN_AT_MOVIE_END
      // dispose of the CallMeWhen callback and the callback UPP
      if ((**myAppData).fCallBack != NULL)
        DisposeCallBack((**myAppData).fCallBack);

      if ((**myAppData).fCallBackUPP != NULL)
        DisposeQTCallBackUPP((**myAppData).fCallBackUPP);
```

```
      (**myAppData).fCallBack = NULL;
      (**myAppData).fCallBackUPP = NULL;
#endif

      // make sure the movie window is the correct size and then show it again
      QTFrame_SizeWindowToMovie(theWindowObject);
      QTFrame_SetWindowVisState(theWindowObject, true);
    }
  }

bail:
  return(myErr);
}
```

For now, don't worry about the code in the END_FULLSCREEN_AT_MOVIE_END block; we'll discuss that a bit later.

▶ Flash Application Messages

In Chapter 6, "The Flash," we learned that Flash movies can send messages to the playback application requesting that it perform specific actions such as quitting or launching some other application. Of the five standard *Flash application messages*, or FSCommands, one is relevant to our current concern: fullscreen. This command can have one of two arguments, either true or false. If the argument is true, then the playback application should put the window containing the Flash movie into full-screen mode; if it's false, then the application should put the window into normal mode. We are now able to upgrade the sample application we built in that chapter, QTFlash, to support the fullscreen application message.

QuickTime's Flash media handler intercepts Flash application messages and repackages them into movie controller actions of type mcActionDoScript, which are then sent to the application's movie controller action filter function. In QTFlash, we responded to those actions by calling the application function QTFlash_DoFSCommand, like so:

```
case mcActionDoScript:
  isHandled = QTFlash_DoFSCommand(theMC,
              (QTDoScriptPtr)theParams, myWindowObject);
  break;
```

QTFlash_DoFSCommand, in turn, inspected the command and argument fields of the specified QTDoScriptRecord to determine which command to perform. We can now add the lines in Listing 8.9 to support entering and exiting full-screen mode:

Listing 8.9 Handling the `fullscreen` application message.

```
if (strcmp(theScriptPtr->command, "fullscreen") == 0) {
  if (strcmp(theScriptPtr->arguments, "true") == 0)
    QTBig_StartFullscreen(theWindowObject);

  if (strcmp(theScriptPtr->arguments, "false") == 0)
    QTBig_StopFullscreen(theWindowObject);

  isHandled = true;
}
```

As you can see, we call our new functions `QTBig_StartFullscreen` and `QTBig_StopFullscreen`. Of course, we also need to add to QTFlash all the additional code in QTBigScreen that handles full-screen mode (such as the code in `QTApp_HandleEvent`).

QuickTime Application Messages

QuickTime 5.0.1 introduced a mechanism for sending messages from a QuickTime movie to the playback application that is strongly reminiscent of the FSCommand capability in Flash movies. These *QuickTime application messages* provide a way for a movie to request full-screen mode for the window containing the movie, close the window containing the movie, and perform several other tasks.

The standard way to send an application message from a QuickTime movie to the playback application is by using the `kActionSendAppMessage` wired action. This action requires one parameter, which is of type `long` and which specifies the message to send to the application. Currently, Quick-Time defines five public application messages (in the file `Movies.h`):

```
enum {
    kQTAppMessageSoftwareChanged            = 1,
    kQTAppMessageWindowCloseRequested       = 3,
    kQTAppMessageExitFullScreenRequested    = 4,
    kQTAppMessageDisplayChannels            = 5,
    kQTAppMessageEnterFullScreenRequested   = 6
};
```

The `kQTAppMessageSoftwareChanged` message indicates that some part of the QuickTime software has been updated, and the `kQTAppMessageDisplay-Channels` message requests that the QuickTime Player application display its user interface for selecting one of the QuickTime channels; neither of these messages is relevant to our sample applications, and we shall blithely ignore

them. The kQTAppMessageEnterFullScreenRequested and kQTAppMessageExit-
FullScreenRequested messages request that the playback application put the
associated movie window into full-screen or normal mode, and the kQTApp-
MessageWindowCloseRequested message requests that the playback application
close the window containing the movie.

We insert one of these application messages into a movie by inserting a
wired action in the standard manner. For instance, Listing 8.10 shows how
we can make a mouse click on a sprite close the movie that contains it.

Listing 8.10 Adding a window-close request to a sprite.

```
myErr = QTInsertChild(mySpriteAtom, kParentAtomIsContainer, kQTEventType,
        kQTEventMouseClickEndTriggerButton, 1, 0, NULL, &myEventAtom);
if (myErr != noErr)
  goto bail;

// add an action atom to the event handler
myErr = QTInsertChild(mySpriteAtom, myEventAtom, kAction, 0, 0, 0, NULL, &myActionAtom);
if (myErr != noErr)
  goto bail;

myAction = EndianU32_NtoB(kActionSendAppMessage);
myErr = QTInsertChild(mySpriteAtom, myActionAtom, kWhichAction, 1, 1,
        sizeof(myAction), &myAction, NULL);
if (myErr != noErr)
  goto bail;

// add a parameter atom to specify which action to perform
myMsg = EndianU32_NtoB(kQTAppMessageWindowCloseRequested);
myErr = QTInsertChild(mySpriteAtom, myActionAtom, kActionParameter,0, 1,
        sizeof(myMsg), &myMsg, NULL);
```

Here we add an event atom whose atom ID is kQTEventMouseClickEnd-
TriggerButton to the sprite atom (mySpriteAtom). Then we insert an action
atom into that event atom. The action atom is given two children, one of type
kWhichAction whose atom data is kActionSendAppMessage, and one of type
kActionParameter whose atom data is kQTAppMessageWindowCloseRequested.

Keep in mind that a movie controller cannot handle these application messages by itself. The actions requested here (entering or exiting full-screen
mode, and closing the window containing a movie) require assistance from
the playback application. Accordingly, the movie controller informs the application of the request by sending it a movie controller action of type mcAction-
AppMessageReceived. The application is free to act on that request or ignore it
entirely. In this section, we'll see how to handle the full-screen and close-
window application messages.

Handling Full-Screen Messages

It's fairly simple to add support for the kQTAppMessageEnterFullScreen-Requested and kQTAppMessageExitFullScreenRequested application messages to QTBigScreen. Listing 8.11 shows the code we'll add to our movie controller action filter procedure to handle these messages.

Listing 8.11 Handling application messages.

```
case mcActionAppMessageReceived:
  switch ((long)theParams) {
    case kQTAppMessageEnterFullScreenRequested:
      QTBig_StartFullscreen(myWindowObject);
      isHandled = true;
      break;

    case kQTAppMessageExitFullScreenRequested:
      QTBig_StopFullscreen(myWindowObject);
      isHandled = true;
      break;
  }

  break;
```

Handling Close-Window Messages

Now let's see how to handle the kQTAppMessageWindowCloseRequested application message. It's tempting perhaps to handle this message by adding these few lines of code to the switch statement in Listing 8.11:

```
case kQTAppMessageWindowCloseRequested:
  QTFrame_DestroyMovieWindow((**myWindowObject).fWindow);
  isHandled = true;
  break;
```

Here, we simply call the framework function QTFrame_DestroyMovieWindow to close the window associated with the specified movie. This function checks to see whether the movie has been changed since it was opened or last saved and, if so, prompts the user to save or discard any changes; once the changes have been saved or discarded, QTFrame_DestroyMovieWindow calls QTFrame_CloseWindowObject to close the movie file and dispose of the movie and movie controller. Then QTFrame_DestroyMovieWindow calls DisposeWindow (on Macintosh systems) or SendMessage with the WM_MDIDESTROY message (on Windows systems) to actually close and destroy the movie window.

There is a problem with this simple approach, however. As noted, QTFrame_CloseWindowObject disposes of the movie controller associated with the movie, and experience tells me that this is definitely a bad thing to do inside of a movie controller action filter procedure. So we need to adopt a different approach: in response to the kQTAppMessageWindowCloseRequested message, we'll set a flag in our application data record that indicates that we need to destroy the window object. Listing 8.12 shows the code we'll add.

Listing 8.12 Handling close-window messages.

```
case kQTAppMessageWindowCloseRequested:
  myAppData = (ApplicationDataHdl)QTFrame_GetAppDataFromWindowObject(myWindowObject);
  if (myAppData != NULL)
    (**myAppData).fDestroyWindowNeeded = true;
  isHandled = true;
  break;
```

Later, in the QTApp_HandleEvent function, we'll need to cycle through all open movie windows to see whether any of them needs to be closed. We'll add a while loop, as shown in Listing 8.13.

Listing 8.13 Looking for windows to close.

```
myWindow = QTFrame_GetFrontMovieWindow();
while (myWindow != NULL) {
  myNextWindow = QTFrame_GetNextMovieWindow(myWindow);

  myAppData = (ApplicationDataHdl)QTFrame_GetAppDataFromWindow(myWindow);
  if (myAppData != NULL) {
    if ((**myAppData).fDestroyWindowNeeded) {
      (**myAppData).fDestroyWindowNeeded = false;
      QTFrame_DestroyMovieWindow(myWindow);
    }
  }

  myWindow = myNextWindow;
}
```

Presentation Movie User Data

A QuickTime movie file can contain a piece of movie user data of type 'ptv ' that specifies that the movie should be *presented*—that is, displayed at a certain size against a solid black background. When a movie is presented, it's drawn without the normal window frame or controller bar. Most often, this feature is used to put a movie into full-screen mode automatically when the movie file is opened. QuickTime Player looks for and interprets this user data item; in this section, we'll see how to handle it in QTBigScreen (at least in part).

The data contained in a 'ptv' user data item occupies 8 bytes; we can exhibit the structure of this data using a QTPFSDataRec structure, defined like this:

```
typedef struct {
  UInt16          fSize;
  UInt16          fUnused1;
  UInt16          fUnused2;
  Boolean         fPlaySlideShow;
  Boolean         fPlayOnOpen;
} QTPFSDataRec;
```

This structure is defined in our file QTBigScreen.h; there is no 'ptv' item structure defined in any of the public QuickTime header files. (By the way, "ptv" stands for "print to video"; the presenting capability was intended also to provide a nonwindowed version of a movie that could be written out to videotape.)

The fSize field contains a 16-bit integer that specifies the desired size of the presented movie. The value 0 indicates that the movie should be presented at its normal size. The value 1 indicates that the movie should be presented at twice its normal size. The value 2 indicates that the movie should be presented at half its normal size. The value 3 indicates that the movie should be presented full-screen. QuickTime Player calls BeginFullScreen with the appropriate width and height to present the movie. As we've seen, however, this can cause the resolution of the screen to be changed, in which case the actual size of the presented movie might not be what we would expect. To force QuickTime Player to present the movie at its normal size, we can specify the value 4. We'll define these constants for the fSize field:

```
enum {
  kSizeNormal           = 0,
  kSizeDouble           = 1,
  kSizeHalf             = 2,
  kSizeFullScreen       = 3,
  kSizeCurrent          = 4
};
```

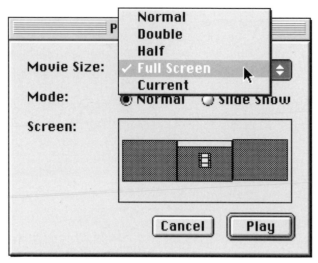

Figure 8.3 QuickTime Player's Present Movie dialog box.

The values of these constants appear to derive from the order of the items in the Movie Size pop-up menu in the dialog box displayed by QuickTime Player when the user selects the Present Movie item in the Movie menu (shown in Figure 8.3).

The fPlaySlideShow field contains a Boolean value that indicates whether the movie should be played in *slideshow mode*; in slideshow mode, the movie advances to another frame only when the user presses the right-arrow or left-arrow key (which move the movie forward one frame or backward one frame, respectively). Any sound tracks in the movie are ignored during slide-show mode. Finally, the fPlayOnOpen field contains a Boolean value that indicates whether the movie should begin playing automatically when the movie is presented.

Listing 8.14 defines a function that we can use to add a 'ptv ' user data item to a movie.

Listing 8.14 Adding a play-fullscreen item to a movie.

```
#define kPTVItemType                    FOUR_CHAR_CODE('ptv ')

OSErr QTBig_AddPTVItemToMovie (Movie theMovie)
{
  UserData         myUserData = NULL;
  short            myCount = 0;
  QTPFSDataRec     myPFSData;
  OSErr            myErr = noErr;
```

```
// get the movie's user data list
myUserData = GetMovieUserData(theMovie);
if (myUserData == NULL)
  return(paramErr);

// we want to end up with at most one user data item of type 'ptv ',
// so let's remove any existing ones
myCount = CountUserDataType(myUserData, kPTVItemType);
while (myCount--)
  RemoveUserData(myUserData, kPTVItemType, 1);

// add a new user data item of type 'ptv '
myPFSData.fSize = EndianU16_NtoB(kSizeFullScreen);
myPFSData.fUnused1 = 0;
myPFSData.fUnused2 = 0;
myPFSData.fPlaySlideShow = false;
myPFSData.fPlayOnOpen = true;
myErr = SetUserDataItem(myUserData, &myPFSData, sizeof(myPFSData), kPTVItemType, 0);

return(myErr);
}
```

QTBig_AddPTVItemToMovie adds to the specified movie a 'ptv ' user data item that requests that the movie be played back full-screen and that the movie start playing as soon as it's opened. (It's worth mentioning that a movie can also contain a user data item of type 'ptvc', whose data is an RGB-Color structure that specifies the background color of a presented movie.)

Now, when QTBigScreen opens a movie file that contains a movie user data item of type 'ptv ' and the value in the fSize field is kSizeFullScreen, we want to call our function QTBig_StartFullscreen to play it full-screen. We also want to inspect the fPlayOnOpen field to see whether the movie should begin playing immediately. We'll add the lines of code in Listing 8.15 to our framework function QTFrame_OpenMovieInWindow.

Listing 8.15 Processing a 'ptv ' user data item.

```
UserData           myUserData = NULL;
QTPFSDataRec       myRec;
OSErr              myErr = paramErr;
```

```
// get the movie's user data list
myUserData = GetMovieUserData(myMovie);
if (myUserData != NULL) {
  myErr = GetUserDataItem(myUserData, &myRec, sizeof(myRec), FOUR_CHAR_CODE('ptv '), 0);
  if (myErr == noErr) {
    myRec.fSize = EndianU16_BtoN(myRec.fSize);

    if (myRec.fSize == kSizeFullScreen)
      MCDoAction(myMC, mcActionAppMessageReceived,
            (void *)kQTAppMessageEnterFullScreenRequested);

    if (myRec.fPlayOnOpen)
      MCDoAction(myMC, mcActionPrerollAndPlay, (void *)GetMoviePreferredRate(myMovie));
  }
}
```

Notice that we don't call QTBig_StartFullscreen directly; instead, we issue a movie controller action of type mcActionAppMessageReceived with the parameter kQTAppMessageEnterFullScreenRequested, which (as we've seen) causes QTBigScreen to call QTBig_StartFullscreen. Notice also that we ignore all size values except kSizeFullScreen; I'll leave it as an exercise for the motivated reader to modify QTBigScreen so that it can present a movie in any of the currently defined sizes.

Time Base Callback Functions

We noted earlier that QuickTime Player automatically returns from full-screen mode to normal mode when it reaches the end of a noninteractive, nonlooped movie. We can achieve this same behavior in QTBigScreen by installing a *time base callback function*, a function that is executed when a specific time in a movie is reached or when some other event related to the movie's time base occurs.

You may recall from Volume One that a movie's time base controls the direction and speed of movie playback, as well as its looping state and current movie time. A time base (of type TimeBase) is automatically created when we load a movie; we can retrieve a movie's time base at any time by calling the GetMovieTimeBase function. We can attach to a time base one or more callback functions that are triggered when a specific *callback event* occurs. Currently, five types of callback events are defined; we indicate a specific type of callback event using these constants:

```
enum {
    callBackAtTime                     = 1,
    callBackAtRate                     = 2,
    callBackAtTimeJump                 = 3,
    callBackAtExtremes                 = 4,
    callBackAtTimeBaseDisposed         = 5
};
```

The callBackAtTime event causes a callback function to be called when a specific time value in the movie is reached (for instance, when the movie reaches the 2 second mark). The callBackAtRate event causes a callback function to be called when the movie begins to play at a specified rate (for instance, when the movie is played at twice the normal speed). The callBackAtTimeJump event causes a callback function to be called when a jump in time occurs; this means that the callback function is called whenever the movie time is set to a time different from what it would be under normal movie playback (for instance, if the user clicks in the movie controller bar to select a different movie time, or if a wired action changes the current movie time). The callBackAtTimeBaseDisposed event causes a callback function to be called when the time base is about to be disposed.

For present purposes, we are interested in the callBackAtExtremes event, which occurs at either the beginning or the end of the movie. As we'll see in a moment, we indicate that we want our callback function to be called at the end of the movie by passing a specific value when we activate the time base callback.

In QTBigScreen, we call the QTBig_InstallCallBack function to install a time base callback function to return from full-screen mode to normal mode at the end of the movie. We add these lines of code to QTBig_StartFull-screen:

```
#if END_FULLSCREEN_AT_MOVIE_END
    if (QTBig_MovieIsStoppable(myMC))
        QTBig_InstallCallBack(theWindowObject);
#endif
```

The definition of QTBig_MovieIsStoppable is quite simple; we just call MCGetControllerInfo to determine whether the movie is looping or interactive, as shown in Listing 8.16.

Listing 8.16 *Determining whether a movie should be stopped.*

```
Boolean QTBig_MovieIsStoppable (MovieController theMC)
{
   long      myFlags = 0L;

   MCGetControllerInfo(theMC, &myFlags);

   if ((myFlags & mcInfoIsLooping) || (myFlags & mcInfoMovieIsInteractive))
      return(false);
   else
      return(true);
}
```

Now we need to install a time base callback function and respond when the callback function is triggered.

Installing a Time Base Callback Function

To install a time base callback function, we create a *time base callback* and then activate it. We create a time base callback by calling the NewCallBack function, like this:

```
myCallBack = NewCallBack(GetMovieTimeBase((**theWindowObject).fMovie),
               callBackAtExtremes);
```

As you can see, the first parameter here is the movie's time base, and the second parameter is a constant that indicates the kind of callback we wish to create. We can set one or both of the two high-order bits in the second parameter to indicate that our callback function can be called at interrupt time or at deferred task time, using these constants:

```
enum {
   callBackAtInterrupt               = 0x8000,
   callBackAtDeferredTask            = 0x4000
};
```

Setting these bits results in more accurate timing, but the callBackAt-Interrupt flag requires that the callback function be interrupt-safe (in particular, that it not cause any memory to be allocated or moved). We don't need extremely accurate timing in returning the movie from full-screen to normal mode, so we'll leave these bits clear when we call NewCallBack.

To activate a time base callback function, we call the CallMeWhen function, which is declared essentially like this:

```
OSErr CallMeWhen (QTCallBack cb, QTCallBackUPP callBackProc, long refCon,
                  long param1, long param2, long param3);
```

Here, cb is the callback we created by calling NewCallBack, and callBackProc is a universal procedure pointer for the callback function. The refCon parameter is a reference constant that is passed to the callback function; as you might have guessed, we'll pass the window object for the full-screen window as the refCon parameter. The last three parameters to CallMeWhen contain additional information required for the callback and vary depending on the type of the callback. For a callback of type callBackAtExtremes, only the param1 parameter is used; it indicates which movie extreme we want to target. We can use these constants to specify a movie extreme:

```
enum {
  triggerAtStart                          = 0x0001,
  triggerAtStop                           = 0x0002
};
```

In QTBigScreen, we want to keep track of the callback and the callback UPP. Accordingly, we'll add a couple of fields to the application data record (defined in the file ComApplication.h):

```
QTCallBack                    fCallBack;
QTCallBackUPP                 fCallBackUPP;
```

Finally, we can look at the definition of the QTBig_InstallCallBack function (Listing 8.17). It calls NewCallBack and CallMeWhen, and it stores the callback identifier and the callback UPP in the application data record.

Listing 8.17 Installing a time base callback function.

```
void QTBig_InstallCallBack (WindowObject theWindowObject)
{
  ApplicationDataHdl            myAppData = NULL;
  QTCallBack                    myCallBack = NULL;

  if (theWindowObject == NULL)
    return;

  if ((**theWindowObject).fMovie == NULL)
    return;

  myAppData = (ApplicationDataHdl)QTFrame_GetAppDataFromWindowObject(theWindowObject);
  if (myAppData == NULL)
    return;
```

```
myCallBack = NewCallBack(GetMovieTimeBase((**theWindowObject).fMovie),
        callBackAtExtremes);
if (myCallBack != NULL) {
  (**myAppData).fCallBack = myCallBack;
  (**myAppData).fCallBackUPP = NewQTCallBackUPP(QTBig_FullscreenCallBack);
  CallMeWhen(myCallBack, (**myAppData).fCallBackUPP, (long)theWindowObject,
    triggerAtStop, 0, 0);
  }
}
```

Handling a Time Base Callback

Now our callback is primed and ready to fire when the movie reaches its end. At that point, the function QTBig_FullscreenCallBack is executed. QTBig_FullscreenCallBack is declared like this:

```
PASCAL_RTN void QTBig_FullscreenCallBack
                (QTCallBack theCallBack, long theRefCon);
```

The first parameter is the callback identifier; the second parameter is the reference constant we passed to CallMeWhen, which is of course the window object for the full-screen window. In general, it's best to keep callback functions short and sweet; the recommended practice is simply to set some flag that is inspected elsewhere in the application. Listing 8.18 gives our definition of QTBig_FullscreenCallBack.

Listing 8.18 Handling a time base callback.

```
PASCAL_RTN void QTBig_FullscreenCallBack (QTCallBack theCallBack, long theRefCon)
{
  WindowObject          myWindowObject = (WindowObject)theRefCon;
  ApplicationDataHdl    myAppData = NULL;
  QTCallBack            myCallBack = NULL;

  if (myWindowObject == NULL)
    return;

  myAppData = (ApplicationDataHdl)QTFrame_GetAppDataFromWindowObject(myWindowObject);
  if (myAppData == NULL)
    return;

  if ((**myAppData).fCallBack != theCallBack)
    return;
```

```
  // mark this window for ending full-screen mode
  (**myAppData).fEndFullscreenNeeded = true;

  // clean up the callback stuff
  if ((**myAppData).fCallBack != NULL)
    DisposeCallBack((**myAppData).fCallBack);

  if ((**myAppData).fCallBackUPP != NULL)
    DisposeQTCallBackUPP((**myAppData).fCallBackUPP);

  (**myAppData).fCallBack = NULL;
  (**myAppData).fCallBackUPP = NULL;
}
```

First, we cast the theRefCon parameter to be of type WindowObject and make sure that we are given a non-NULL window object. Then we extract the application data associated with that window object and verify that the callback passed to the callback function (theCallBack) is the same as the callback stored in the application data record ((**myAppData).fCallBack). If everything checks out OK, we set the fEndFullscreenNeeded field to true. We'll add some code to the QTApp_HandleEvent function that checks this field and returns a window to normal mode if it is true. Remember that we already go looking for any windows that are marked for closing, so we can rework the while loop as shown in Listing 8.19.

Listing 8.19 Looking for windows to return to normal mode.

```
myWindow = QTFrame_GetFrontMovieWindow();
while (myWindow != NULL) {
  myNextWindow = QTFrame_GetNextMovieWindow(myWindow);

  myAppData = (ApplicationDataHdl)QTFrame_GetAppDataFromWindow(myWindow);
  if (myAppData != NULL) {

    if ((**myAppData).fEndFullscreenNeeded) {
      (**myAppData).fEndFullscreenNeeded = false;
      QTBig_StopFullscreen(QTFrame_GetWindowObjectFromWindow(myWindow));
    }

    if ((**myAppData).fDestroyWindowNeeded) {
      (**myAppData).fDestroyWindowNeeded = false;
      QTFrame_DestroyMovieWindow(myWindow);
    }
  }

  myWindow = myNextWindow;
}
```

Finally, since we are done with the callback, we call `DisposeCallBack` to dispose of the callback and `DisposeQTCallBackUPP` to dispose of the callback UPP. We finish up by clearing out the fields in the application data record that store the callback and callback UPP.

Conclusion

Let's quickly recap what we've learned here. A movie can contain a movie user data item of type 'ptv ' that (usually) requests that the movie be played back full-screen. A wired movie can issue an application message of type `kQTAppMessageEnterFullScreenRequested`, and a Flash movie can issue a Flash application message of type `fullscreen` with the argument `true`. In all these cases, or in response to the user selecting the Play Fullscreen menu item, our application QTBigScreen calls the QuickTime function `BeginFullScreen` to put the movie into full-screen mode. The movie remains in full-screen mode until it reaches its end (if it's a noninteractive, nonlooping movie), until the user presses the Escape key, or until our application receives an application message that requests normal mode. At that point, we exit full-screen mode by calling `EndFullScreen`.

Event Horizon

Using Carbon Events in a QuickTime Application

**Introduction**

Up to now, we've used an application called QTShell as the basis for our explorations into the QuickTime APIs. QTShell provides the basic Macintosh or Windows application services (start-up, shutdown, event or message handling, menu and window management, and so forth), and it provides stub routines that we use for our application-specific code. For instance, in the previous chapter, we saw how to add code to QTShell to allow it to play movies full-screen.

The main problem with QTShell as it stands today is that its Macintosh code uses an event-handling model that is about 20 years old and sorely in need of a tune-up. Our Macintosh code is indeed already fully Carbonized; that is, it uses only Carbon APIs and hence can run both under "classic" Macintosh systems that support CarbonLib (Mac OS 8 and 9) and under Mac OS X. But it still uses a couple of functions that result in less than optimal performance, especially under Mac OS X. In particular, it calls WaitNext-Event to retrieve events for the application, and it uses ModalDialog to handle events while its About box is displayed to the user.

What's wrong with using WaitNextEvent and ModalDialog is that we need to continually poll the operating system to see whether any events have arrived for the application. If our application isn't doing anything (for instance, no movies are playing and the user has gone to get a cup of coffee), we are wasting valuable processor time that could be used by other open applications. It would be better if the operating system would just inform us when an event arrives for our application. This is the fundamental idea behind the *Carbon Event Manager*.

In this chapter, we're going to learn how to replace our calls to the "classic" Event Manager with calls to the Carbon Event Manager. As we'll see, this mostly involves writing a few *event callback functions* (or *event handlers*) that are executed when specific types of events occur. In effect, our application is transformed from a nagging kid ("Are we there yet? Are we there yet?...") into a polite child who waits patiently for instructions. We'll also need to write a *Carbon event loop timer callback function* to allow us to task our open movies periodically. (To *task* or *idle* a movie is to grant its data handlers and media handlers some time to do their work.) Now, in fact, this obviates some of the good work we'll do in moving away from WaitNext-Event, since the Carbon event loop timer is going to fire periodically even if our application has no work to do. (The nagging child has been replaced by a nagging parent: "Clean your room! Clean your room!....") We can work around this by using the *movie tasking interval* functions—new to QuickTime 6—to determine when our application should next task the movie. Armed with that information, we can then reset the event timer accordingly. Toward the end of this chapter, we'll also see how to work with the *Carbon movie control*, a custom control introduced in QuickTime 6 that we can use in Carbon applications on Mac OS X to display and control movies. The Carbon movie control automatically handles all the event and tasking interval management associated with displaying a movie in a window and, hence, frees us from having to write callback functions or timer routines for this. Very nice.

A few words of caution before we begin: the Carbon movie control provides an elegant way to put a QuickTime movie into a window, but it's available only under Mac OS X and only under QuickTime 6 or later; as a result, we'll retain our existing code for managing movies and isolate the new code with the USE_CARBON_MOVIE_CONTROL compiler flag. Similarly, we'll use the USE_TASK_MGMT compiler flag to set off the code that uses QuickTime's new tasking interval management APIs. In both cases, we really ought to replace the compiler flags with runtime checking of the system software and Quick-Time versions and just do the right thing. I'll leave that refinement as an exercise for the reader.

More important, we still want to be able to build non-Carbon versions of QTShell-based applications and versions that don't use Carbon events. (These can sometimes be useful, for instance, in tracking down bugs.) So we'll introduce yet a third new compiler flag, USE_CARBON_EVENTS, to enclose the code that handles Carbon events. We run the risk of ending up with unreadable code with all these flags, but in fact the damage is fairly minor. Indeed, seeing the Carbon Event Manager code side by side with the corresponding "classic" Event Manager code can be instructive, as we'll soon see.

Carbon Events Overview

Let's think back to 1984. The Macintosh operating system popularized the idea of *event-driven programming*, where an application is structured so that it is guided by events reporting the user's actions with the mouse and keyboard (and other occurrences in the computer). An application is driven by its *event loop*, a block of code that retrieves events from the Event Manager and dispatches them to the appropriate event-handling routine. Listing 9.1 shows a typical event loop.

Listing 9.1 Retrieving and dispatching events.

```
static void QTFrame_MainEventLoop (void)
{
  EventRecord        myEvent;
  long               myDuration = kWNEMinimumSleep;

  while (!gShuttingDown) {
    // get the next event in the queue
    WaitNextEvent(everyEvent, &myEvent, myDuration, NULL);

    // handle the event
    QTFrame_HandleEvent(&myEvent);
  }
}
```

We call WaitNextEvent to retrieve an event from the Event Manager and then QTFrame_HandleEvent to handle the event. The myDuration parameter to WaitNextEvent specifies the number of ticks that our application is willing to suspend processing if no events (other than null events) are pending for it. This allows other applications and services to use the processor while we don't need it. If an event arrives for our application before the specified duration elapses, WaitNextEvent returns immediately with that event. Otherwise, when the duration elapses, WaitNextEvent returns with a null event. We can use this steady stream of null events as a trigger to perform periodic actions.

The QTFrame_HandleEvent function is essentially a big switch statement that branches on the type of the event, as shown in Listing 9.2.

Listing 9.2 Handling events.

```
switch (theEvent->what) {
  case mouseDown:
    // handle mouse-down events here
    break;

  case updateEvt:
    // handle update events here
    break;

  // cases for other event types

  case nullEvent:
    // handle null events here
    break;
}
```

When we throw QuickTime into the mix, we need to make a very simple adjustment to QTFrame_HandleEvent: before stepping into the switch statement, we'll see whether the event should be handled by a movie controller attached to one of our open movie windows. We do this by calling QTFrame_CheckMovieControllers, which loops through all our application's open movie windows and calls MCIsPlayerEvent until it finds a movie controller that handles the event. So, in outline, our event handling function now looks like this:

```
isEventHandled = QTFrame_CheckMovieControllers(theEvent);
if (isEventHandled)
  return;

switch (theEvent->what) {

}
```

The Carbon Event Manager changes this model in several key ways. First, as we've seen, we don't continually poll for events by calling WaitNextEvent. Rather, we install one or more event callback functions (we'll see how to do this shortly); the Carbon Event Manager sends particular events directly to those callback functions, which then handle the events as appropriate. We enable this dispatching by calling RunApplicationEventLoop. Listing 9.3 shows our revised version of QTFrame_MainEventLoop.

Listing 9.3 Retrieving and dispatching events (revised).

```
static void QTFrame_MainEventLoop (void)
{
#if USE_CARBON_EVENTS
   RunApplicationEventLoop();
#else
   EventRecord       myEvent;
   long              myDuration = kWNEMinimumSleep;

   while (!gShuttingDown) {
      // get the next event in the queue
      WaitNextEvent(everyEvent, &myEvent, myDuration, NULL);

      // handle the event
      QTFrame_HandleEvent(&myEvent);

   } // while (!gShuttingDown)
#endif
}
```

RunApplicationEventLoop processes and dispatches events until we call QuitApplicationEventLoop. As you would guess, we call QuitApplication-EventLoop in our application shutdown function QTFrame_QuitFramework.

The second main change is that the Carbon Event Manager redefines the kinds of events our application can receive. The original or "classic" Event Manager can handle only a limited number of event types:

```
enum {
   nullEvent            = 0,
   mouseDown            = 1,
   mouseUp              = 2,
   keyDown              = 3,
   keyUp                = 4,
   autoKey              = 5,
   updateEvt            = 6,
   diskEvt              = 7,
   activateEvt          = 8,
   osEvt                = 15,
   kHighLevelEvent      = 23
};
```

The Macintosh system software folks could, of course, add new event types to this list, but they would be limited to 16 total event types by the size of the event mask (a 16-bit value that determines which events our application receives when it calls WaitNextEvent).

The Carbon Event Manager uses a much larger set of events, called *Carbon events*. A Carbon event is uniquely specified by its *event class* and its *event kind*. For instance, the Carbon event that corresponds to the classic event keyDown is of class kEventClassKeyboard and kind kEventRawKeyDown. And the Carbon event that corresponds to the classic event updateEvt is of class kEventClassWindow and kind kEventWindowUpdate. Here are the event classes we shall be concerned with in QTShell:

```
enum {
    kEventClassKeyboard                 = FOUR_CHAR_CODE('keyb'),
    kEventClassApplication              = FOUR_CHAR_CODE('appl'),
    kEventClassMenu                     = FOUR_CHAR_CODE('menu'),
    kEventClassWindow                   = FOUR_CHAR_CODE('wind'),
    kEventClassControl                  = FOUR_CHAR_CODE('cntl'),
    kEventClassCommand                  = FOUR_CHAR_CODE('cmds')
};
```

But the Carbon Event Manager doesn't just reshuffle the classic events into new classes; in addition, it defines a large number of new kinds of events. For instance, our application can register to receive an event of class kEventClassWindow and kind kEventWindowClose when the user clicks in a window's close box. Gone are the days when we got just a mouse click and had to determine where the click occurred and perhaps then track the click until the user released the mouse button; instead, we get higher-level indications of what the user is trying to accomplish. We really don't care about the mouse-down event per se; rather, we care that the user clicked in the window's close box.

This ties in with yet another significant advantage of the Carbon Event Manager: it provides default event handlers for many event classes. The default handler for window events, for instance, knows how to handle clicks in the close box and the zoom box, as well as drag-clicks in the window's title bar. And the default handler for controls knows how to handle control clicks and tracking. Our application needs to get involved only when we want to override or augment the behaviors provided by the default handlers. For instance, before we allow the user to close a movie window, we need to check to see whether any of the data associated with the window has changed and give the user the opportunity to save any changes. So we'll install an event handler that receives window close events.

We install an event handler by calling InstallEventHandler. In theory, we could write one big event handler for all the event classes and kinds we care about, but in practice it's better to write one event handler for each type of event target. An *event target* is an opaque object that corresponds to an object in the application that can receive events, such as a control, a window, or the application itself. The Carbon Event Manager provides a handful of routines for obtaining event targets; for example, we can call `GetWindow-EventTarget` to get the event target associated with a particular window.

In summary, we implement support for the Carbon Event Manager by defining and installing an event handler for each event target our application cares about. Depending on the type of target, we may need to explicitly install the default (or standard) event handler. And we make it all go by calling `RunApplicationEventLoop`, as we saw in Listing 9.2.

Document Windows

As you know, QTShell can open movies and images in standard document windows. We'll take advantage of the default behaviors provided by the Carbon Event Manager's standard window event handler and restrict our window event handler to those events that have special meaning for QuickTime or for our application.

Specifying Events

We specify one or more events by creating an array of *event type specifications*, defined by the `EventTypeSpec` data type:

```
struct EventTypeSpec {
  UInt32              eventClass;
  UInt32              eventKind;
};
```

If a window contains a movie, we need to pass to the associated movie controller any key events that are not command-key events (which might therefore be menu item shortcuts); we also need to pass the movie controller any mouse clicks inside the movie rectangle. In addition, our application needs to know when the window is being closed, activated, or deactivated, and when it needs to be redrawn. We'll specify the events that should be sent to our window event handler like this:

```
EventTypeSpec           myEventSpec[] = {
  {kEventClassKeyboard, kEventRawKeyDown},
  {kEventClassKeyboard, kEventRawKeyRepeat},
  {kEventClassKeyboard, kEventRawKeyUp},
  {kEventClassWindow, kEventWindowUpdate},
```

```
  {kEventClassWindow, kEventWindowDrawContent},
  {kEventClassWindow, kEventWindowActivated},
  {kEventClassWindow, kEventWindowDeactivated},
  {kEventClassWindow, kEventWindowHandleContentClick},
  {kEventClassWindow, kEventWindowClose}
};
```

Notice that a single event target can receive more than one class of event; in this case, our document window event handler is to be sent both keyboard events and window events.

Installing Event Handlers

In our Macintosh code, we create a movie or image window by calling NewCWindow. We can attach the standard event handler to that new window by calling the InstallStandardEventHandler function, like this:

```
InstallStandardEventHandler(GetWindowEventTarget(myWindow));
```

The GetWindowEventTarget function returns an event target associated with the specified window. It's worth noting that if we had called CreateNewWindow to create the window, then we should install the standard event handler by setting a window attribute, like this:

```
ChangeWindowAttributes(myWindow, kWindowStandardHandlerAttribute, 0);
```

We use the InstallEventHandler function to install our custom window event handler:

```
if (gWinEventHandlerUPP != NULL)
  InstallEventHandler(GetWindowEventTarget(myWindow), gWinEventHandlerUPP,
    GetEventTypeCount(myEventSpec), myEventSpec,
    QTFrame_GetWindowObjectFromWindow(myWindow), NULL);
```

The first parameter is, of course, the event target—which corresponds to our new window. The second parameter is a universal procedure pointer to the event callback function, which we can create by calling NewEventHandlerUPP:

```
EventHandlerUPP    gWinEventHandlerUPP = NULL;

gWinEventHandlerUPP = NewEventHandlerUPP(QTFrame_CarbonEventWindowHandler);
```

The third parameter is the number of event type specifications contained in the fourth parameter. As you can see, we use the Carbon Event Manager function GetEventTypeCount to get that number. The fifth parameter is a reference constant that is passed to the event handler when it is called. In this case, we want to pass a handle to the application-specific data attached to the window. The last parameter to `InstallEventHandler` is the address of a variable of type `EventHandlerRef`; this is an opaque type that refers to the newly installed event handler. We don't need that reference, so we pass NULL.

Listing 9.4 shows our revised version of `QTFrame_CreateMovieWindow`.

Listing 9.4   Creating a movie window (revised).

```
WindowReference QTFrame_CreateMovieWindow (void)
{
  WindowReference      myWindow = NULL;

  // create a new window to display the movie in
  myWindow = NewCWindow(NULL, &gWindowRect, gWindowTitle, false, noGrowDocProc,
            (WindowPtr)-1L, true, 0);

  // create a new window object associated with the new window
  QTFrame_CreateWindowObject(myWindow);

#if USE_CARBON_EVENTS
{
  EventTypeSpec        myEventSpec[] = {
    {kEventClassKeyboard, kEventRawKeyDown},
    {kEventClassKeyboard, kEventRawKeyRepeat},
    {kEventClassKeyboard, kEventRawKeyUp},
    {kEventClassWindow, kEventWindowUpdate},
    {kEventClassWindow, kEventWindowDrawContent},
    {kEventClassWindow, kEventWindowActivated},
    {kEventClassWindow, kEventWindowDeactivated},
    {kEventClassWindow, kEventWindowHandleContentClick},
    {kEventClassWindow, kEventWindowClose}
  };

  // install Carbon event handlers for this window
  InstallStandardEventHandler(GetWindowEventTarget(myWindow));
  if (gWinEventHandlerUPP != NULL)
    InstallEventHandler(GetWindowEventTarget(myWindow), gWinEventHandlerUPP,
      GetEventTypeCount(myEventSpec), myEventSpec,
      QTFrame_GetWindowObjectFromWindow(myWindow), NULL);
}
#endif

  return(myWindow);
}
```

Handling Window Events

Now, when the Carbon Event Manager receives an event of a kind we want to handle for a document window, it calls QTFrame_CarbonEventWindowHandler, which is declared like this:

```
PASCAL_RTN OSStatus QTFrame_CarbonEventWindowHandler
        (EventHandlerCallRef theCallRef, EventRef theEvent,
         void *theRefCon);
```

The event handler is passed the reference constant we specified when we called InstallEventHandler, as well as an event reference and an event handler call reference. The *event reference* is an opaque data structure that contains information about the event, such as its class, its kind, and any additional parameters for the event. We can use the GetEventClass and GetEventKind functions to extract the event class and kind from the event reference:

```
myClass = GetEventClass(theEvent);
myKind = GetEventKind(theEvent);
```

And we can use GetEventParameter to retrieve any additional event parameters. For instance, when the event class is kEventClassWindow and the event kind is kEventWindowHandleContentClick, then the direct object parameter is a window pointer for the target window; we can retrieve that information like this:

```
WindowRef   myWindow = NULL;
myErr = GetEventParameter(theEvent, kEventParamDirectObject, typeWindowRef,
            NULL, sizeof(myWindow), NULL, &myWindow);
```

Recall that with the "classic" Event Manager, the amount of information associated with an event was limited to what could be stuffed into an event record; with the Carbon Event Manager, any number of event parameters can be associated with a particular event type.

The theCallRef parameter passed to QTFrame_CarbonEventWindowHandler is a reference to the next event handler in the event handler sequence for the associated event target. The Carbon Event Manager arranges handlers into a sequence (technically, a stack) and calls each handler in turn until one of them handles the event. This scheme allows us to override certain behaviors of a standard event handler but perhaps not all. For example, when we receive the kEventWindowClose event, we can prompt the user to save or discard any changes to the movie data in a window and then fall through to the standard event handler to actually close the window. (We can avoid this "fall through" by returning any result code other than eventNotHandledErr.) And if we want to invoke the next event handler in the stack *before* we do our custom processing, we can call CallNextEventHandler with the event handler call reference passed to our own event handler. In QTShell we won't use this event handler call reference since we shall completely handle any events we are registered to receive or else fall through to the standard handlers.

Let's take a look at how we handle a few of the events targeted at a document window. It turns out that some of these events can be directly translated into classic events and then processed using our existing function QTFrame_HandleEvent. We can use the function ConvertEventRefToEventRecord to convert a Carbon event into its corresponding classic event:

```
EventRecord     myEvent;
ConvertEventRefToEventRecord(theEvent, &myEvent);
```

ConvertEventRefToEventRecord returns a Boolean value that indicates whether it successfully converted the Carbon event into a classic event; so we can process our keyboard events like this:

```
case kEventClassKeyboard:
  switch (myKind) {
    case kEventRawKeyDown:
    case kEventRawKeyRepeat:
    case kEventRawKeyUp:
      if (ConvertEventRefToEventRecord(theEvent, &myEvent))
        QTFrame_HandleEvent(&myEvent);
      myErr = noErr;
      break;
  }
  break;
```

However, ConvertEventRefToEventRecord appears to work only for a small number of Carbon events, namely, those that have an exactly equivalent classic event. In the cases in which it doesn't work, we need to construct an event record manually. For example, we can handle the kEventWindowHandle-ContentClick event by explicitly retrieving the relevant event parameters and assigning them to the fields of the event record, as shown in Listing 9.5.

Listing 9.5 Handling document window events.

```
PASCAL_RTN OSStatus QTFrame_CarbonEventWindowHandler
        (EventHandlerCallRef theCallRef, EventRef theEvent, void *theRefCon)
{
#pragma unused(theCallRef)
  UInt32              myClass, myKind;
  UInt32              myModifiers;
  WindowRef           myWindow = NULL;
  EventRecord         myEvent;
  WindowObject        myWindowObject = (WindowObject)theRefCon;
  OSStatus            myErr = eventNotHandledErr;

  myClass = GetEventClass(theEvent);
  myKind = GetEventKind(theEvent);

  switch (myClass) {
    case kEventClassKeyboard:
      switch (myKind) {
        case kEventRawKeyDown:
        case kEventRawKeyRepeat:
        case kEventRawKeyUp:
          if (ConvertEventRefToEventRecord(theEvent, &myEvent))
            QTFrame_HandleEvent(&myEvent);
          myErr = noErr;
          break;
      }
      break;

    case kEventClassWindow:
      switch (myKind) {
        case kEventWindowUpdate:
        case kEventWindowDrawContent:
        case kEventWindowActivated:
        case kEventWindowDeactivated:
          if (ConvertEventRefToEventRecord(theEvent, &myEvent))
            QTFrame_HandleEvent(&myEvent);
          myErr = noErr;
          break;

        case kEventWindowHandleContentClick:
          myErr = GetEventParameter(theEvent, kEventParamDirectObject,
                    typeWindowRef, NULL, sizeof(myWindow), NULL, &myWindow);
          if (myErr == noErr) {
```

```
          GetEventParameter(theEvent, kEventParamKeyModifiers, typeUInt32, NULL,
            sizeof(myModifiers), NULL, &myModifiers);
          GetEventParameter(theEvent, kEventParamMouseLocation, typeQDPoint, NULL,
            sizeof(Point), NULL, &myEvent.where);

          myEvent.what = mouseDown;
          myEvent.message = (long)myWindow;
          myEvent.modifiers = myModifiers;
          myEvent.when = EventTimeToTicks(GetCurrentEventTime());

          QTFrame_HandleEvent(&myEvent);
          myErr = noErr;
        }
        break;

    case kEventWindowClose:
      if (myWindowObject != NULL) {
        QTFrame_DestroyMovieWindow((**myWindowObject).fWindow);
        myErr = noErr;
      }
      break;

    default:
      break;
    }
    break;
  }

  return(myErr);
}
```

Notice that we set the when field of the event record by calling GetCurrent-EventTime and converting the value it returns into ticks (using the utility macro EventTimeToTicks); this is the Carbon event replacement for good old TickCount.

Menus

Currently, we handle Macintosh menu selections in the standard "classic" fashion: we call MenuSelect when we get a mouse-down event in the menu bar. MenuSelect drops down the menus and tracks events in them until the user releases the mouse button; then it returns a 32-bit long integer whose high-order 16-bit word is the ID of the menu and whose low-order 16-bit word is the menu item index. Our function `QTFrame_HandleMenuCommand` inspects that long integer and reacts appropriately.

On Windows, a menu item is specified by a single 16-bit "menu item identifier," which is an arbitrary value that we associate with the menu item. Because the value on Windows is arbitrary, we've constructed it by setting the high-order 8 bits to the Macintosh menu ID and the low-order 8 bits to the index of the menu item in the menu. Here are the values we use for the File menu items:

```
#define IDM_FILENEW                          33025
#define IDM_FILEOPEN                         33026
#define IDM_FILECLOSE                        33027
#define IDM_FILESAVE                         33028
#define IDM_FILESAVEAS                       33029
#define IDM_EXIT                             33031
```

We've designed our menu-handling functions (`QTFrame_HandleFileMenuItem`, `QTFrame_HandleEditMenuItem`, and `QTApp_HandleMenu`) to accept these 16-bit values, and we've defined several macros to help us construct and deconstruct a menu item identifier:

```
#define MENU_IDENTIFIER(menuID,menuItem)    ((menuID<<8)+(menuItem))
#define MENU_ID(menuIdentifier)             ((menuIdentifier&0xff00)>>8)
#define MENU_ITEM(menuIdentifier)           ((menuIdentifier&0x00ff))
```

The Carbon Event Manager greatly simplifies our menu handling. The default application event handler processes all events in the menu bar and in menus; our application is called only when a menu state needs to be adjusted or when the user actually selects a menu item. Notifications of menu selections are sent to an application's event callback function that handles command events. The event class is `kEventClassCommand` and the event kind is `kEventCommandProcess`.

Defining Command IDs

When our menu event callback function is called, we determine which menu item was selected by looking at the *command ID* associated with the event. A command ID is a 32-bit value; we are free to associate any value with any menu item, but the Carbon Event Manager defines a set of IDs for some of the standard menu items. For instance, it defines these constants for the Edit menu items:

```
enum {
  kHICommandUndo                          = FOUR_CHAR_CODE('undo'),
  kHICommandRedo                          = FOUR_CHAR_CODE('redo'),
  kHICommandCut                           = FOUR_CHAR_CODE('cut '),
  kHICommandCopy                          = FOUR_CHAR_CODE('copy'),
  kHICommandPaste                         = FOUR_CHAR_CODE('past'),
  kHICommandClear                         = FOUR_CHAR_CODE('clea'),
  kHICommandSelectAll                     = FOUR_CHAR_CODE('sall')
};
```

And the Carbon Event Manager defines this constant for the Quit item in the File menu (on Mac OS 8 and 9) or the Application menu (on Mac OS X):

```
enum {
  kHICommandQuit                          = FOUR_CHAR_CODE('quit')
};
```

We're going to keep using our custom menu item identifiers, but we also need to assign command IDs to the menu items when we are using the Carbon Event Manager. We'll define the COMMAND_ID macro to convert a 16-bit menu item identifier into a 32-bit command ID:

```
#define COMMAND_ID(menuIdentifier) \
  ((MENU_ID(menuIdentifier)<<16)+(MENU_ITEM(menuIdentifier)))
```

When QTShell starts up, we need to call SetMenuItemCommandID to associate command IDs with menu items. Listing 9.6 shows the code we'll call.

Listing 9.6 Defining the framework command IDs.

```
#if USE_CARBON_EVENTS
  myMenu = GetMenuHandle(kAppleMenuResID);
  SetMenuItemCommandID(myMenu, kAboutMenuItem,
    COMMAND_ID(MENU_IDENTIFIER(kAppleMenuResID,kAboutMenuItem)));

  myMenu = GetMenuHandle(kFileMenuResID);
  SetMenuItemCommandID(myMenu, MENU_ITEM(IDM_FILENEW), COMMAND_ID(IDM_FILENEW));
  SetMenuItemCommandID(myMenu, MENU_ITEM(IDM_FILEOPEN), COMMAND_ID(IDM_FILEOPEN));
  SetMenuItemCommandID(myMenu, MENU_ITEM(IDM_FILECLOSE), COMMAND_ID(IDM_FILECLOSE));
  SetMenuItemCommandID(myMenu, MENU_ITEM(IDM_FILESAVE), COMMAND_ID(IDM_FILESAVE));
  SetMenuItemCommandID(myMenu, MENU_ITEM(IDM_FILESAVEAS), COMMAND_ID(IDM_FILESAVEAS));
  SetMenuItemCommandID(myMenu, MENU_ITEM(IDM_EXIT), COMMAND_ID(IDM_EXIT));
```

```
      myMenu = GetMenuHandle(kEditMenuResID);
      SetMenuItemCommandID(myMenu, MENU_ITEM(IDM_EDITUNDO), COMMAND_ID(IDM_EDITUNDO));
      SetMenuItemCommandID(myMenu, MENU_ITEM(IDM_EDITCUT), COMMAND_ID(IDM_EDITCUT));
      SetMenuItemCommandID(myMenu, MENU_ITEM(IDM_EDITCOPY), COMMAND_ID(IDM_EDITCOPY));
      SetMenuItemCommandID(myMenu, MENU_ITEM(IDM_EDITPASTE), COMMAND_ID(IDM_EDITPASTE));
      SetMenuItemCommandID(myMenu, MENU_ITEM(IDM_EDITCLEAR), COMMAND_ID(IDM_EDITCLEAR));
      SetMenuItemCommandID(myMenu, MENU_ITEM(IDM_EDITSELECTALL),
        COMMAND_ID(IDM_EDITSELECTALL));
      SetMenuItemCommandID(myMenu, MENU_ITEM(IDM_EDITSELECTNONE),
        COMMAND_ID(IDM_EDITSELECTNONE));
#endif
```

Of course, applications built on top of QTShell may have additional menus, and we need to define command IDs for items in those menus as well. Listing 9.7 shows how we can set up command IDs for items in the Test menu.

Listing 9.7   Defining the application-specific command IDs.

```
#if USE_CARBON_EVENTS
  MenuRef           myMenu = NULL;

  myMenu = GetMenuHandle(kTestMenuResID);
  SetMenuItemCommandID(myMenu, MENU_ITEM(IDM_CONTROLLER), COMMAND_ID(IDM_CONTROLLER));
  SetMenuItemCommandID(myMenu, MENU_ITEM(IDM_SPEAKER_BUTTON),
    COMMAND_ID(IDM_SPEAKER_BUTTON));
#endif
```

It's worth noting that we could instead embed command IDs in our application's resources. The 'xmnu' resource type contains extended menu information, including a command ID to be associated with a particular menu item. In QTShell, we'll use SetMenuItemCommandID, as just shown. (It's also worth noting that we could specify command IDs in a .nib file, if we were using .nib files instead of resources to define our application's user interface.)

Adjusting Menus

Our application receives an event of class kEventClassCommand and kind kEventCommandUpdateStatus when the menus need to be adjusted. We can handle that event by calling our function QTFrame_AdjustMenus:

```
case kEventCommandUpdateStatus:
  myErr = GetEventParameter(theEvent, kEventParamDirectObject,
          typeHICommand, NULL, sizeof(myCommand), NULL, &myCommand);
  if ((myErr == noErr) &&
      ((myCommand.attributes & kHICommandFromMenu) != 0))
    QTFrame_AdjustMenus(FrontWindow(), NULL, 0L);
  break;
```

We adjust the menus only if the command ID is being sent to us as the result of some event involving a menu (that is, if the kHICommandFromMenu bit is set in the command attributes).

Handling Menu Selections

When the user selects one of our application's menu items, the Carbon Event Manager sends us an event of class kEventClassCommand and kind kEventCommandProcess. Once again, we check that the command arises from a menu selection; then we call our existing function QTFrame_HandleMenu-Command:

```
case kEventCommandProcess:
  myErr = GetEventParameter(theEvent, kEventParamDirectObject,
          typeHICommand, NULL, sizeof(myCommand), NULL, &myCommand);
  if ((myErr == noErr) &&
      ((myCommand.attributes & kHICommandFromMenu) != 0))
    myErr = QTFrame_HandleMenuCommand(myCommand.commandID) ?
            noErr : eventNotHandledErr;
  break;
```

Remember that an event handler should return eventNotHandledErr when we want the event to be propagated to other handlers in the call chain. I've reworked QTFrame_HandleMenuCommand (and the menu handlers it calls) so that it returns a Boolean value indicating whether the menu command was handled by the application. We return noErr if we handle the event.

Listing 9.8 shows our complete application event handler QTFrame_Carbon-EventAppHandler, which handles command events.

Listing 9.8 Handling commands.

```
PASCAL_RTN OSStatus QTFrame_CarbonEventAppHandler
        (EventHandlerCallRef theCallRef, EventRef theEvent, void *theRefCon)
{
#pragma unused(theCallRef, theRefCon)
  UInt32          myClass, myKind;
  HICommand       myCommand;
  OSStatus        myErr = eventNotHandledErr;

  myClass = GetEventClass(theEvent);
  myKind = GetEventKind(theEvent);

  switch (myClass) {
    case kEventClassCommand:
      switch (myKind) {
        case kEventCommandProcess:
          myErr = GetEventParameter(theEvent, kEventParamDirectObject, typeHICommand,
                    NULL, sizeof(myCommand), NULL, &myCommand);
          if ((myErr == noErr) && ((myCommand.attributes & kHICommandFromMenu) != 0))
            myErr = QTFrame_HandleMenuCommand(myCommand.commandID)
                      ? noErr : eventNotHandledErr;
          break;

        case kEventCommandUpdateStatus:
          myErr = GetEventParameter(theEvent, kEventParamDirectObject, typeHICommand,
                    NULL, sizeof(myCommand), NULL, &myCommand);
          if ((myErr == noErr) && ((myCommand.attributes & kHICommandFromMenu) != 0))
            QTFrame_AdjustMenus(FrontWindow(), NULL, OL);
          break;
      }
      break;

    case kEventClassMenu:
      switch (myKind) {
        case kEventMenuBeginTracking:
          gMenuIsTracking = true;
          break;

        case kEventMenuEndTracking:
          gMenuIsTracking = false;
          break;
      }
      break;
  }
```

```
        return(myErr);

}
```

As you can see, toward the end of QTFrame_CarbonEventAppHandler we also handle two commands in the kEventClassMenu event class; these commands are sent to our handler when the user begins and ends tracking a menu. In effect, the gMenuIsTracking global variable indicates whether a menu is currently being displayed. We'll use that global variable a bit later, when we see how to task our QuickTime movies.

Installing the Application Event Handler

Of course, we still need to install our application event handler, by calling InstallEventHandler. The Carbon Event Manager automatically installs a standard application event handler, so we don't need to do that. Listing 9.9 shows the code we add to QTFrame_InitMacEnvironment to install our application event handler.

Listing 9.9 Installing an application event handler.

```
EventTypeSpec      myEventSpec[] = {
    {kEventClassMenu, kEventMenuBeginTracking},
    {kEventClassMenu, kEventMenuEndTracking},
    {kEventClassCommand, kEventCommandProcess},
    {kEventClassCommand, kEventCommandUpdateStatus}
};

gAppEventHandlerUPP = NewEventHandlerUPP(QTFrame_CarbonEventAppHandler);
if (gAppEventHandlerUPP != NULL)
  InstallEventHandler(GetApplicationEventTarget(), gAppEventHandlerUPP,
    GetEventTypeCount(myEventSpec), myEventSpec, NULL, NULL);
```

▶ Modal Windows

Now it's time to wean ourselves of ModalDialog. Happily, our application calls it only once, when we display our About box (Figure 9.1). The Carbon Event Manager provides the function RunAppModalLoopForWindow, which we can use instead of ModalDialog to put our application into a modal state. When the application is in a modal state, only events targeted at a specified

Figure 9.1 The About box of QTShell.

window (or at any window in front of it) are processed by the Carbon Event Manager. The application remains in a modal state until it calls QuitApp-ModalLoopForWindow.

Handling Events for the About Box

Our About box is pretty simple. We'll install the standard window event handler for it, to obtain all the usual window behaviors:

```
myWindow = GetDialogWindow(myDialog);
InstallStandardEventHandler(GetWindowEventTarget(myWindow));
```

The only thing our application needs to handle explicitly is a user click on the OK button or a keyboard shortcut for a click on that button. We can call SetWindowDefaultButton to map keyboard events to the OK button:

```
GetDialogItem(myDialog, kStdOkItemIndex, &myItemKind, &myItemHandle,
  &myItemRect);
if (myItemHandle != NULL)
  SetWindowDefaultButton(myWindow, (ControlHandle)myItemHandle);
```

And we handle user clicks on the OK button by installing an event handler that processes events of class kEventClassControl and kind kEvent-ControlHit. Listing 9.10 shows the main segment of QTFrame_ShowAboutBox. Notice that we also register to receive draw events for the dialog window.

Listing 9.10 Displaying the application's About box.

```
#if USE_CARBON_EVENTS
  EventTypeSpec    myEventSpec[] = {
      {kEventClassWindow, kEventWindowDrawContent},
      {kEventClassControl, kEventControlHit}
  };

  // install a window handler for the dialog window
  GetDialogItem(myDialog, kStdOkItemIndex, &myItemKind, &myItemHandle, &myItemRect);
  if (myItemHandle != NULL)
    SetWindowDefaultButton(myWindow, (ControlHandle)myItemHandle);

  InstallStandardEventHandler(GetWindowEventTarget(myWindow));
  if (gWinEventModalHandlerUPP != NULL)
    InstallEventHandler(GetWindowEventTarget(myWindow), gWinEventModalHandlerUPP,
      GetEventTypeCount(myEventSpec), myEventSpec, (void *)myDialog, NULL);

  // display and handle events in the dialog box until the user clicks OK
  RunAppModalLoopForWindow(myWindow);
#else
  // display and handle events in the dialog box until the user clicks OK
  do {
    ModalDialog(gModalFilterUPP, &myItem);
  } while (myItem != kStdOkItemIndex);
#endif
```

We specify the dialog pointer of the About box as the reference constant when we call InstallEventHandler. This allows us to know which dialog box to draw when we get the kEventWindowDrawContent event. Listing 9.11 shows our definition of our modal dialog event handler, QTFrame_CarbonEventModal-WindowHandler.

Listing 9.11 Handling events for the About box.

```
PASCAL_RTN OSStatus QTFrame_CarbonEventModalWindowHandler
        (EventHandlerCallRef theCallRef, EventRef theEvent, void *theRefCon)
{
#pragma unused(theCallRef)
  UInt32        myClass, myKind;
  DialogPtr     myDialog = (DialogPtr)theRefCon;
  OSStatus      myErr = eventNotHandledErr;
```

```
myClass = GetEventClass(theEvent);
myKind = GetEventKind(theEvent);

switch (myClass) {
  case kEventClassWindow:
    switch (myKind) {
      case kEventWindowDrawContent:
        if (myDialog != NULL)
          DrawDialog(myDialog);
        myErr = noErr;
        break;
    }
    break;

  case kEventClassControl:
    switch (myKind) {
      case kEventControlHit:
        if (myDialog != NULL)
          myErr = QuitAppModalLoopForWindow(GetDialogWindow(myDialog));
        break;
    }
    break;
}

return(myErr);
}
```

We call `QuitAppModalLoopForWindow`, and hence leave the modal state, when the user clicks the OK button.

Handling Nondocument Windows

Let's digress briefly to fix a bug that can arise when QTShell or one of its descendants is running on Mac OS X and we display a help tag. A *help tag* is a message that can appear when the cursor is left motionless over some interface element (typically a window, a control, or a menu item) for a pre-set amount of time. Figure 9.2 shows a help tag associated with our About box.

It's fairly simple to add help tags to a Carbon application. Listing 9.12 shows some code we can add to `QTFrame_ShowAboutBox` to display the help tag illustrated in Figure 9.2. (The application's resources include two strings with the specified 'STR#' resource ID and indices.)

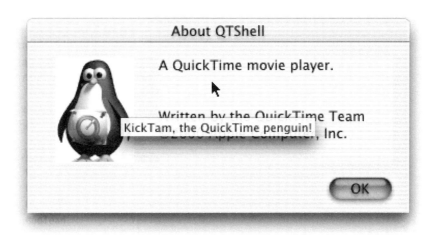

Figure 9.2 A help tag.

Listing 9.12 Adding a help tag to the About box.

```
HMHelpContentRec     myContent;

myContent.version = kMacHelpVersion;
myContent.tagSide = kHMAbsoluteCenterAligned;

myContent.content[0].contentType = kHMStringResContent;
myContent.content[0].u.tagStringRes.hmmResID = 128;
myContent.content[0].u.tagStringRes.hmmIndex = 1;

myContent.content[1].contentType = kHMStringResContent;
myContent.content[1].u.tagStringRes.hmmResID = 128;
myContent.content[1].u.tagStringRes.hmmIndex = 2;

MacSetRect(&myContent.absHotRect, 0, 0, 0, 0);

HMSetWindowHelpContent(myWindow, &myContent);
```

The problem arises because a help tag is drawn inside of a small yellow window (as the drop shadow in Figure 9.2 indicates) and our existing code is unable to distinguish that window from our movie or image windows. Currently, we determine whether a window is an application window (that is, a movie or image window) by calling QTFrame_IsAppWindow, defined in Listing 9.13.

Listing 9.13 Finding application windows.

```
Boolean QTFrame_IsAppWindow (WindowReference theWindow)
{
  if (theWindow == NULL)
    return(false);

#if TARGET_OS_MAC
  return(GetWindowKind(theWindow) >= kApplicationWindowKind);
#endif
#if TARGET_OS_WIN32
  return(true);
#endif
}
```

The trouble is that—lo and behold—help tag windows also have the window kind kApplicationWindowKind. So the Macintosh code in QTFrame_Is-AppWindow will decide that help tag windows are application windows; eventually, our framework code will retrieve the window's reference constant and later doubly dereference it to get the associated window object data. On Mac OS X, where the operating system is rather strict about memory accesses, we'll get an access fault.

There are several ways to avoid this problem. Perhaps the best solution is to rework QTFrame_IsAppWindow so that it winnows out help tag windows. We can do this by inspecting the *window class* of the window passed in, as shown in Listing 9.14.

Listing 9.14 Finding application windows (revised).

```
Boolean QTFrame_IsAppWindow (WindowReference theWindow)
{
#if TARGET_OS_MAC
  UInt32        myClass = 0;
  OSStatus      myErr = noErr;

  if (theWindow == NULL)
    return(false);

  myErr = GetWindowClass(theWindow, &myClass);
  if (myErr != noErr)
    return(false);
  else
    return(myClass == kDocumentWindowClass);
```

```
#endif
#if TARGET_OS_WIN32
  return(theWindow != NULL);
#endif
}
```

Here we look at the window class (which we retrieve by calling GetWindow-
Class). Our movie and image windows have a window class of kDocumentWin-
dowClass, while help tag windows have a window class of kHelpWindowClass.
Problem solved.

It's worth noting that this problem has nothing to do with Carbon events;
rather, it arises from the fact that our original code considers a help tag to be
an application window, with a bona fide window object attached to it. It's
also worth noting that the problem can arise even if our application doesn't
display its own help tags; on Mac OS X, the Open File dialog box will display a help tag if the cursor remains motionless for the appropriate amount
of time over a filename that's too long to fit in a column. Compare Figures
9.3 and 9.4.

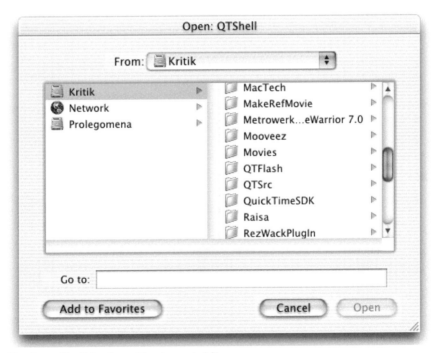

Figure 9.3 The Open File dialog box with a truncated filename.

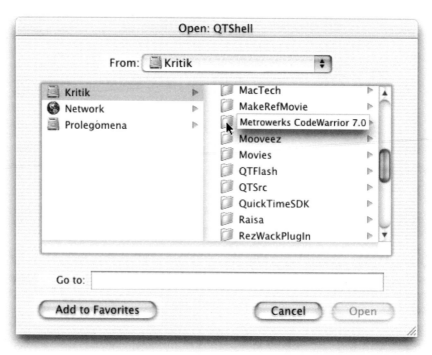

Figure 9.4 A help tag in the Open File dialog box.

Event Loop Timers

Because our applications play QuickTime movies, we need to call `MCIsPlayerEvent` periodically to make sure that QuickTime can process events for any open movies. When using the classic event model, we rely on the fact that our application will receive a steady stream of null events; since our call to `MCIsPlayerEvent` is contained inside of `QTFrame_HandleEvent`, `MCIsPlayerEvent` will be called often enough to keep any open movies playing smoothly.

The Carbon Event Manager does not issue null events. To ensure that an open QuickTime movie is tasked periodically, we can install an event loop timer. We create a universal procedure pointer to our timer callback routine by calling `NewEventLoopTimerUPP`:

```
gWinTimerHandlerUPP = NewEventLoopTimerUPP(QTFrame_CarbonEventWindowTimer);
```

Then we create a new timer and attach it to a window by calling `Install-EventLoopTimer`:

```
if (gWinTimerHandlerUPP != NULL)
  InstallEventLoopTimer(GetMainEventLoop(), 0,
    TicksToEventTime(kWNEMinimumSleep), gWinTimerHandlerUPP,
    myWindowObject, &(**myWindowObject).fTimerRef);
```

The first parameter specifies the event loop to which we want to attach the timer; in QTShell we have only one event loop, which we get by calling GetMainEventLoop. The third parameter indicates the desired period between timer calls. The fifth parameter is a reference constant that's passed to the timer callback when it is executed; here, we pass the window object associated with the window so that we can use the window-specific data contained in it. An *event loop timer reference* is returned in the last parameter, which here is &(**myWindowObject).fTimerRef. We need to keep track of this reference so that we can later remove the event loop timer when the window is closed:

```
if ((**myWindowObject).fTimerRef != NULL)
  RemoveEventLoopTimer((**myWindowObject).fTimerRef);
```

As you can see, we've added a field fTimerRef to the window object record to hold the event loop timer reference.

We'll use our event loop timer callback function, QTFrame_CarbonEvent-WindowTimer, to call MCIdle on the window's movie controller, as you can see in Listing 9.15.

Listing 9.15 Handling event loop timer callbacks.

```
PASCAL_RTN void QTFrame_CarbonEventWindowTimer
        (EventLoopTimerRef theTimer, void *theRefCon)
{
#pragma unused(theTimer)
  WindowObject    myWindowObject = (WindowObject)theRefCon;

  // just pretend a null event has been received...
  if ((myWindowObject != NULL) && ((**myWindowObject).fController != NULL))
    if (!gMenuIsTracking || gRunningUnderX)
      MCIdle((**myWindowObject).fController);
}
```

We don't call MCIdle if the menu is being tracked and we're running on Mac OS 8 or 9; this is to prevent QuickTime from drawing on top of the dropped-down menus.

Notice that we install a separate event loop timer for each open movie window. As an alternative, we could install a single application-wide event loop timer whose callback function loops through all open movie windows and calls MCIdle on each window's movie controller. This alternate strategy would require a small amount of extra code (principally to make sure we don't have an active timer if no movie windows are open), but might result in better efficiency (since we are using only one event loop timer). I'm told, however, that any efficiency gains are likely to be minimal; as a result, I've chosen to use one event loop timer per movie window.

Tasking Interval Management

We use an event loop timer to call MCIdle to task an open movie. This works great, except that the timer fires at the specified interval even if none of the movie's data handlers or media handlers has any work to do. QuickTime 6 introduced several functions that we can use to manage these tasking intervals. The key new function is QTGetTimeUntilNextTask, which we can use to find out when we next need to call MCIsPlayerEvent or MCIdle. For instance:

```
QTGetTimeUntilNextTask(&myDuration, 60);
```

QTGetTimeUntilNextTask returns, in the first parameter, the length of time until a QuickTime movie needs to be tasked next. The second parameter indicates the desired time scale of that duration. Passing 60 means that we want QTGetTimeUntilNextTask to give us a duration in ticks. Passing 1000 would give us a duration in milliseconds.

Adjusting the Classic Event Loop Interval

We can use QTGetTimeUntilNextTask to adjust the interval we pass to Wait-NextEvent in our classic event loop. Listing 9.16 shows our final version of QTFrame_MainEventLoop.

Listing 9.16 Retrieving and dispatching events (final).

```
static void QTFrame_MainEventLoop (void)
{
#if USE_CARBON_EVENTS
  RunApplicationEventLoop();
#else
  EventRecord        myEvent;
  long               myDuration = kWNEMinimumSleep;
```

```
    while (!gShuttingDown) {

#if USE_TASK_MGMT
    // get the number of ticks until QuickTime's next task
    QTGetTimeUntilNextTask(&myDuration, 60);

    if (myDuration == 0)
      myDuration = kWNEMinimumSleep;
#endif

    // get the next event in the queue
    WaitNextEvent(everyEvent, &myEvent, myDuration, NULL);

    // handle the event
    QTFrame_HandleEvent(&myEvent);

    } // while (!gShuttingDown)
#endif
}
```

QTGetTimeUntilNextTask can return a duration of 0, which means that QuickTime wants to be called immediately. It's generally a bad idea to pass a sleep time of 0 to WaitNextEvent, so we enforce a minimum sleep of kWNE-MinimumSleep ticks (kWNEMinimumSleep is set to 1).

Adjusting the Carbon Event Loop Timer Interval

We can also use QTGetTimeUntilNextTask to adjust the period of our event loop timer. Each time our timer callback function is called, we can determine the interval to the next time we need to call MCIdle and then reset the timer interval accordingly. Here, we want to work in milliseconds:

```
QTGetTimeUntilNextTask(&myDuration, 1000);
if (theTimer != NULL)
  SetEventLoopTimerNextFireTime(theTimer,
    myDuration * kEventDurationMillisecond);
```

Listing 9.17 shows our event loop timer with the tasking management code in place.

Listing 9.17 Handling event loop timer callbacks (revised).

```
PASCAL_RTN void QTFrame_CarbonEventWindowTimer
        (EventLoopTimerRef theTimer, void *theRefCon)
{
  WindowObject    myWindowObject = (WindowObject)theRefCon;

#if USE_TASK_MGMT
  long            myDuration = 0L;

  // get the number of milliseconds until QuickTime's next task
  QTGetTimeUntilNextTask(&myDuration, 1000);

  if (myDuration == 0)
    myDuration = kMinAppTaskInMillisecs;

  // set the timer to fire at that time
  if (theTimer != NULL)
    SetEventLoopTimerNextFireTime(theTimer, myDuration * kEventDurationMillisecond);
#endif

  // just pretend a null event has been received...
  if ((myWindowObject != NULL) && ((**myWindowObject).fController != NULL))
    if (!gMenuIsTracking || gRunningUnderX)
      MCIdle((**myWindowObject).fController);
}
```

If `QTGetTimeUntilNextTask` returns the value 0, we'll once again peg the delay to a predefined minimum to avoid swamping the processor with our QuickTime tasks.

Handling Task-Sooner Notifications

What happens if QuickTime needs to be tasked before the event loop timer fires next? To handle that possibility, we can install a *task-sooner* callback function. QuickTime calls this function if our application needs to task one of its movies before a specified event loop timer is scheduled to fire. We call `QTInstallNextTaskNeededSoonerCallback` to install our callback function:

```
#if USE_TASK_MGMT
gQTTaskSoonerUPP = NewQTNextTaskNeededSoonerCallbackUPP
                      (QTFrame_NextTaskNeededSoonerProcedure);
if ((gQTTaskSoonerUPP != NULL) && (gAppEventLoopTimerRef != NULL))
  QTInstallNextTaskNeededSoonerCallback(gQTTaskSoonerUPP, 1000, 0,
    (void *)(**myWindowObject).fTimerRef);
#endif
```

The callback function is quite simple. It calls SetEventLoopTimerNextFire-Time to reset the event loop timer (Listing 9.18).

Listing 9.18 Handling task-sooner notifications.

```
PASCAL_RTN void QTFrame_NextTaskNeededSoonerProcedure
        (TimeValue theDuration, unsigned long theFlags, void *theRefCon)
{
#pragma unused(theFlags)

  EventLoopTimerRef      myTimer = (EventLoopTimerRef)theRefCon;

  if (myTimer != NULL)
    SetEventLoopTimerNextFireTime(myTimer, theDuration * kEventDurationMillisecond);
}
```

Of course, when our application is quitting, we want to dispose of the callback function UPP:

```
if (gQTTaskSoonerUPP != NULL)
    DisposeQTNextTaskNeededSoonerCallbackUPP(gQTTaskSoonerUPP);
```

▶ The Carbon Movie Control

Now, wouldn't it be great if there were a way to display a movie in a window without having to worry about all this tasking and timer interval resetting and event handling? That is precisely what is provided by the *Carbon movie control*, introduced in QuickTime 6 on Mac OS X. The Carbon movie control is a custom control that displays and manages a QuickTime movie. We create the control by calling CreateMovieControl, like this:

```
CreateMovieControl(theWindow, &myRect, theMovie, myFlags, &myControl);
```

The first parameter is the window that is to contain the new control. The second parameter is the control rectangle (in local coordinates); in our case, we'll use the entire movie window. The third parameter is the movie to be displayed using the movie control, a handle to which is returned in the fifth parameter.

The fourth parameter to CreateMovieControl specifies a set of flags that modify the behavior of the new movie control. Currently, these flags are defined:

```
enum {
    kMovieControlOptionHideController          = (1L << 0),
    kMovieControlOptionLocateTopLeft           = (1L << 1),
    kMovieControlOptionEnableEditing           = (1L << 2),
    kMovieControlOptionHandleEditingHI         = (1L << 3),
    kMovieControlOptionSetKeysEnabled          = (1L << 4),
    kMovieControlOptionManuallyIdled           = (1L << 5)
};
```

In QTShell, we'll use these flags:

```
myFlags = kMovieControlOptionSetKeysEnabled |
          kMovieControlOptionLocateTopLeft |
          kMovieControlOptionEnableEditing;
```

The kMovieControlOptionManuallyIdled flag indicates that we want to task the movie ourselves (presumably with our own event loop timer). If this flag is clear, the movie control uses its own event loop timer to task the movie.

The movie control created by CreateMovieControl is associated with a movie controller; this movie controller is always attached to the movie and will be initially visible unless we set the kMovieControlOptionHideController flag. If we want to call movie controller functions, we can retrieve the movie controller by calling GetControlData:

```
myErr = GetControlData(myControl, kControlEntireControl,
        kMovieControlDataMovieController, sizeof(myMC),
        (void *)&myMC, NULL);
```

To appreciate just how cool the Carbon movie control is, try this: take some sample code that uses the Carbon event model but knows nothing about QuickTime. Add the few lines of code you need to open a movie file and create a movie from that file. Add the preceding line of code that uses CreateMovieControl in the appropriate spot. Add the necessary QuickTime libraries to your project. Compile and link. Voilà, you now have a QuickTime-savvy application. It can't get any easier than that. But it *can* get better: the Carbon movie control supports the basic movie controller editing operations, and it also adjusts the Edit menu items as appropriate to the state of the movie, if the kMovieControlOptionHandleEditingHI flag is set.

▶ Conclusion

Let's wrap things up. We've managed to bring QTShell into the 21st century by replacing its "classic" Event Manager underpinnings with the more elegant and more efficient machinery of the Carbon Event Manager. To accomplish this, we wrote and installed a few event handlers and a timer callback function, and we set the whole thing in motion by calling `RunApplication-EventLoop`. The Carbon Event Manager then sends our application events as they become available, and it invokes our timer callback function periodically so that we can call `MCIdle` to task our open movies.

We also saw how to use the tasking interval management functions introduced in QuickTime 6 to adjust the interval between timer callbacks. It's important to understand that we need to use these functions only in Carbon event–savvy applications that install their own timer callback functions or in any Macintosh applications that use the "classic" event model. On Windows, or in Cocoa applications that use the `NSMovie` and `NSMovieView` classes, the tasking intervals are managed internally. Also, if we use the Carbon movie control (available on Mac OS X in QuickTime 6 and later versions), we don't need to worry about handling events or timer intervals at all.

QTShell still contains a few loose ends. In theory, there is no need for our About box to be a modal window. It could just as easily be implemented as a document window with a special window class. This would allow us to keep the About box open while the user operates on an open movie window. I'll leave this as an exercise for the interested reader.

Virtuosity

Programming with QuickTime VR

▶ Introduction

QuickTime VR (or, more briefly, *QTVR*) is the part of QuickTime that allows users to interactively explore and examine photorealistic, three-dimensional virtual worlds and objects. A QuickTime VR movie is a collection of one or more *nodes*; each node is either a *panoramic node* (also known as a *panorama*) or an *object node* (also known as an *object*). Figure 10.1 shows a view of a sample panoramic node, and Figure 10.2 shows a view of an object node. (When a QuickTime VR movie consists of a single node, folks often refer to it as a *panorama movie* or an *object movie*, depending on the type of node it contains.)

QuickTime VR movies are managed by the *QuickTime VR movie controller*, a movie controller component that knows how to interpret user actions in a QuickTime VR movie. The QuickTime VR movie controller also displays a controller bar with buttons that are appropriate to QuickTime VR movies. From left to right, the five buttons allow the user to go back to the previous node, zoom out, zoom in, show the visible hotspots, and translate an object in the movie window. The QuickTime VR movie controller automatically disables any buttons that are not appropriate for the current node type or movie state. For instance, the back button is disabled in Figure 10.2 because the movie is a single-node movie. Similarly, the translate button is disabled in Figure 10.1 because the current node is a panoramic node, not an object node.

QuickTime has supported QuickTime VR movie creation and playback since mid-1995. In early 1997, Apple released QuickTime VR version 2.0, which (in addition to numerous other improvements) provided a C programming interface to QuickTime VR. This interface, called the *QuickTime VR Manager*, provides an extensive set of functions for controlling QuickTime VR movies. In this chapter, we'll take a look at the QuickTime VR Manager.

Figure 10.1 A QuickTime VR panorama movie.

Figure 10.2 A QuickTime VR object movie.

The QuickTime VR movie controller also allows QuickTime VR movies to send and receive wired actions. We could, for instance, use buttons in a Flash track to control a QTVR movie, as illustrated in Figure 10.3. Here the Flash buttons in the lower-left corner of the movie are configured to send the appropriate QuickTime wired actions to pan, tilt, or zoom the panorama. (We saw how to attach wired actions to Flash track buttons in Chapter 7, "The Flash II.")

We'll take a look at the actions that can be targeted at a QuickTime VR movie, and we'll also see how to attach wired actions to elements in a QuickTime VR movie. We can attach wired actions to a particular node or to a particular hotspot in a node. For example, we can wire a hotspot to launch the user's Web browser and navigate to a particular website when the user clicks that hotspot. Or, we can have some actions triggered when the user enters a node. We won't learn how to build QuickTime VR movies in this chapter, but we will need to understand some of the structure of these movies in order to learn how to attach wired actions to nodes and hotspots.

Figure 10.3 A Flash track controlling a QuickTime VR movie.

▶ The QuickTime VR Manager

The QuickTime VR Manager provides a large number of capabilities that we can use to customize and extend the user's virtual experience of panoramas and objects. Here, we'll summarize the basic capabilities of the QuickTime VR Manager. Then, in the following sections, we'll illustrate how to use some of them. The QuickTime VR Manager provides these main capabilities:

- **Positioning.** A QuickTime VR movie file contains a *scene*, which is a collection of one or more nodes. Each node is uniquely identified by its node ID. Within a panoramic node, the user's view is determined by three factors: the pan angle, the tilt angle, and the vertical field of view (sometimes also called the *zoom angle*). For objects, the view is also determined by the view center (the position of the center of the object in the movie window). The QuickTime VR Manager provides functions to get and set any of these properties. For instance, we can programmatically spin an object around by repeatedly incrementing the current pan angle.

- **Hotspot handling.** We can use the QuickTime VR Manager to manage any hotspots in a panorama or object. For instance, we can trigger a hotspot programmatically (that is, simulate a click on the hotspot), enable and disable hotspots, determine whether the cursor is over a hotspot, find all visible hotspots, and so forth. We can also install a callback routine that is called whenever the cursor is over an enabled hotspot.

- **Custom node-entering and node-leaving behaviors.** The QuickTime VR Manager allows us to perform actions whenever the user enters a new node or leaves the current node. For instance, we might use a node-entering procedure to play a sound when the user enters a particular node. Or, we can use a node-leaving procedure to prevent the user from leaving a node until some task has been accomplished.

- **Getting information.** We can use the QuickTime VR Manager to get information about a scene or about a specific node. For instance, we might want to determine the ID and type of the current node. Much of the information about scenes and nodes is stored in atoms in the movie file. To get information about a scene or node that isn't provided directly by the QuickTime VR Manager, we'll need to use the QuickTime atom container functions to extract information from those atoms.

- **Intercepting QuickTime VR Manager functions.** We can intercept calls to some QuickTime VR Manager functions in order to augment or modify their behavior. For example, to assign behaviors to custom hotspots, we can install an intercept routine that is called whenever a hotspot is triggered. Our intercept routine might check the type of the triggered hotspot and then perform the actions appropriate for that type.

Another typical use of intercept routines is to intercept positioning functions (changing the pan, tilt, and field of view) and adjust environmental factors accordingly. For instance, we can adjust the balance and volume of a sound as the pan angle changes in a panorama, thereby making it appear that the sound is localized within the panorama.

■ **Accessing the prescreen buffer.** QuickTime VR maintains an offscreen buffer for each panorama, called the *prescreen buffer*. The prescreen buffer contains the image that is about to be copied to the screen. We can use QuickTime VR Manager functions to access the prescreen buffer, perhaps to draw a graphic image over the panorama.

This list is not exhaustive. The QuickTime VR Manager provides many other capabilities as well.

QuickTime VR Movie Playback

Our existing sample applications, such as QTShell, are already able to open and display QuickTime VR movies. The QuickTime VR movie controller handles the basic click-and-drag navigation, keyboard input, and controller bar events. We need to use the QuickTime VR Manager only if we want to exploit some of the capabilities just described.

Initializing the QuickTime VR Manager

Before we can call the QuickTime VR Manager, however, we need to do a little setting up (over and above what's required for using QuickTime). First, we need to ensure that the QuickTime VR Manager is available in the current operating environment. There are several Gestalt selectors that we can use to see whether the QuickTime VR Manager is available and what features it has. Listing 10.1 shows the definition of the QTVRUtils_IsQTVRMgr-Installed function, which indicates whether the QuickTime VR Manager is available in the current operating environment.

Listing 10.1 Determining whether the QuickTime VR Manager is available.

```
Boolean QTVRUtils_IsQTVRMgrInstalled (void)
{
  Boolean      myQTVRAvail = false;
  long         myAttrs;
  OSErr        myErr = noErr;
```

```
    myErr = Gestalt(gestaltQTVRMgrAttr, &myAttrs);
    if (myErr == noErr)
      if (myAttrs & (1L << gestaltQTVRMgrPresent))
        myQTVRAvail = true;

    return(myQTVRAvail);
}
```

For simplicity, we'll introduce a global variable to keep track of whether the QuickTime VR Manager is available:

```
gQTVRMgrIsPresent = QTVRUtils_IsQTVRMgrInstalled();
```

On Windows operating systems, we need to call the InitializeQTVR function to initialize the QuickTime VR Manager, like this:

```
#if TARGET_OS_WIN32
  InitializeQTVR();
#endif
```

Calling any other QuickTime VR Manager functions before calling InitializeQTVR will result in an error on Windows.

We also need to close our connection to the QuickTime VR Manager before our application terminates:

```
#if TARGET_OS_WIN32
  TerminateQTVR();
#endif
```

Getting the QTVR Instance

The QuickTime VR Manager keeps track of QuickTime VR movies using an identifier called a *QTVR instance* (of data type QTVRInstance), defined like this:

```
typedef struct OpaqueQTVRInstance*    QTVRInstance;
```

Virtually all QuickTime VR Manager functions operate on QTVR instances. You can think of an instance as representing what's in a QuickTime VR movie file, that is, a scene or (more common) a single node.

We obtain a QTVR instance by calling the QTVRGetQTVRInstance function. QTVRGetQTVRInstance takes a reference to a QTVR track, which we can obtain by calling QTVRGetQTVRTrack. Listing 10.2 shows our definition of QTApp_Set-upWindowObject, which we call for every movie we open.

Listing 10.2 Getting a QTVR instance.

```
void QTApp_SetupWindowObject (WindowObject theWindowObject)
{
  Track                  myQTVRTrack = NULL;
  Movie                  myMovie = NULL;
  MovieController        myMC = NULL;
  QTVRInstance           myInstance = NULL;

  if (theWindowObject == NULL)
    return;

  // make sure we can safely call the QTVR API
  if (!gQTVRMgrIsPresent)
    return;

  // find the QTVR track, if there is one
  myMC = (**theWindowObject).fController;
  myMovie = (**theWindowObject).fMovie;
  myQTVRTrack = QTVRGetQTVRTrack(myMovie, 1);

  QTVRGetQTVRInstance(&myInstance, myQTVRTrack, myMC);
  (**theWindowObject).fInstance = myInstance;

  // do any QTVR window configuration
  if (myInstance != NULL) {
    // set unit to radians
    QTVRSetAngularUnits(myInstance, kQTVRRadians);
  }
}
```

Notice that we keep track of the QTVR instance by storing it in the fInstance field of the window object associated with the movie (here, theWindowObject). This gives us an easy way to determine whether a given movie window contains a QuickTime VR movie. Notice also that we call the QTVRSetAngularUnits function to set our preferred angular units to radians. The QuickTime VR Manager allows us to work with either degrees or radians when specifying angular measurements (for instance, when we call QTVRGetPanAngle). The default angular unit type is degrees. Internally, however, the QuickTime VR Manager always uses radians, and in some situations it gives us measurements in radians no matter what the current angular unit is set to. In general, therefore, I find it easier to work in radians most of the time, so I've reset the angular unit type to radians. (Your prefer-ence may vary.) We can define some simple macros to allow us to convert between degrees and radians:

```
#define kVRPi                           ((float)3.1415926535898)
#define kVR2Pi                          ((float)(2.0 * 3.1415926535898))
#define QTVRUtils_DegreesToRadians(x)   ((float)((x) * kVRPi / 180.0))
#define QTVRUtils_RadiansToDegrees(x)   ((float)((x) * 180.0 / kVRPi))
```

We don't need to explicitly release or dispose of a QTVR instance; the value we obtain by calling QTVRGetQTVRInstance remains valid until we dis-pose of the associated movie controller.

Controlling View Angles

Finally, we're ready to use the QuickTime VR Manager to do some real work. The most basic way to use the API is to control the view angles of a node—the pan, tilt, and field of view angles. Listing 10.3 defines a function that gradually increments the pan angle through 360°. With panoramas, this has the effect of making the user seem to spin a full circle (as if the user were spinning on a rotating stool). With objects, this has the effect of mak-ing the object spin around a full circle (as if the object were spinning on a turntable).

Listing 10.3 Spinning a node around once.

```
void SpinAroundOnce (QTVRInstance theInstance)
{
   float        myOrigPanAngle, myCurrPanAngle;

   myOrigPanAngle = QTVRGetPanAngle(theInstance);

   for (myCurrPanAngle = myOrigPanAngle;
        myCurrPanAngle <= myOrigPanAngle + kVR2Pi;
        myCurrPanAngle += QTVRUtils_DegreesToRadians(10.0)) {
      QTVRSetPanAngle(theInstance, myCurrPanAngle);
      QTVRUpdate(theInstance, kQTVRCurrentMode);
   }
}
```

The idea here is simple: get the starting pan angle (by calling QTVRGet-PanAngle) and then repeatedly increment the pan angle by a certain amount (here, 10°) until a full circle has been traversed. Note that we need to call the QTVRUpdate function after we set a new pan angle to make sure the updated view is displayed on the screen.

Drawing on a Panorama

Suppose we want to draw a logo or other graphic element on top of a panorama (as seems to be in vogue on broadcast television channels these days). As we learned earlier, we can draw into a panorama's prescreen buffer before that buffer is copied to the screen. (Object nodes don't have prescreen buffers, so this technique won't work for those kinds of nodes.) We exploit this capability by installing a *prescreen buffer imaging completion procedure*, which is called by the QuickTime VR Manager each time the prescreen buffer is about to be copied to the screen. We install our procedure using the QTVRSetPrescreenImagingCompleteProc function:

```
ImagingCompleteUPP                          myImagingProc;

myImagingProc = NewImagingCompleteProc(MyPrescreenRoutine);
QTVRSetPrescreenImagingCompleteProc(myInstance, myImagingProc,
  (SInt32)theWindowObject, 0);
```

The QTVRSetPrescreenImagingCompleteProc function takes four parameters, which are the QTVR instance, a universal procedure pointer to the imaging complete procedure, a 4-byte reference constant, and a 4-byte flags parameter. In this case, we pass the window object reference as the third parameter so that the imaging complete procedure can access any data associated with the window.

Our prescreen buffer imaging completion procedure is called after Quick-Time VR has finished drawing into the prescreen buffer. When it's called, the current graphics port is set to the prescreen buffer. All we need to do is draw a picture at the appropriate spot, as shown in Listing 10.4.

Listing 10.4 Drawing a picture on top of a panorama.

```
pascal OSErr MyPrescreenRoutine (QTVRInstance theInstance, WindowObject theWindowObject)
{
#pragma unused(theInstance)

    ApplicationDataHdl      myAppData;
    Rect                    myMovieRect;
    Rect                    myPictRect;
```

```
  // get the application-specific data associated with the window
  myAppData = (ApplicationDataHdl)GetAppDataFromWindowObject(theWindowObject);
  if (myAppData == NULL)
    return(paramErr);

  // if there is no picture to display, just return
  if ((**myAppData).fPicture == NULL)
    return(noErr);

  // get the current size of the movie
  GetMovieBox((**theWindowObject).fMovie, &myMovieRect);

  // set the size and position of the overlay rectangle
  MacSetRect(&myPictRect, 0, 0, 32, 32);
  MacOffsetRect(&myPictRect,
    myMovieRect.right - (myPictRect.right + 5),
    myMovieRect.bottom - (myPictRect.bottom + 5));

  // draw the picture
  DrawPicture((**myAppData).fPicture, &myPictRect);

  return(noErr);
}
```

There's nothing very complicated in this prescreen buffer imaging completion procedure. Essentially, it just figures out where in the buffer to draw the picture and then draws it. We assume that a handle to the picture data is stored in the fPicture field of the application data record.

Intercepting QuickTime VR Manager Functions

Suppose we want to play a sound every time the user clicks (that is, triggers) a hotspot. The easiest way to do this is to install an *intercept procedure* that is called each time a hotspot is triggered. The intercept procedure simply plays the sound and then returns, whereupon QuickTime VR processes the hotspot click as usual. Listing 10.5 shows a simple hotspot triggering intercept procedure.

Listing 10.5 Playing a sound on hotspot clicks.

```
pascal void MyInterceptRoutine (QTVRInstance theInstance, QTVRInterceptPtr theMsg,
            WindowObject theWindowObject, Boolean *cancel)
{
#pragma unused(theInstance, theWindowObject)

  Boolean              myCancelInterceptedProc = false;

  switch (theMsg->selector) {
    case kQTVRTriggerHotSpotSelector:
      MyPlaySound();
      break;
  }

  *cancel = myCancelInterceptedProc;
}
```

An intercept routine is executed whenever the intercepted routine is called, either programmatically or by a user action. On entry, the QuickTime VR Manager provides three pieces of information: the relevant QTVR instance, a pointer to an *intercept record*, and an application-defined reference constant, which we use here to pass in the window object. The intercept record (pointed to by the theMsg parameter) has this structure:

```
struct QTVRInterceptRecord {
  SInt32              reserved1;
  SInt32              selector;
  SInt32              reserved2;
  SInt32              reserved3;
  SInt32              paramCount;
  void               *parameter[6];
};
```

For present purposes, we need to inspect only the selector field, which contains a value that indicates which intercepted routine is being called. As you can see in Listing 10.5, we look for any calls to QTVRTriggerHotSpot and call the application-defined function MyPlaySound when we get one.

We install an intercept procedure by calling the QTVRInstallInterceptProc function, as shown in Listing 10.6.

Listing 10.6 Installing an intercept routine.

```
void MyInstallInterceptRoutine (QTVRInstance theInstance, WindowObject theWindowObject)
{
  QTVRInterceptUPP      myInterceptProc;

  myInterceptProc = NewQTVRInterceptProc(MyInterceptRoutine);

  QTVRInstallInterceptProc(theInstance, kQTVRTriggerHotSpotSelector, myInterceptProc,
    (SInt32)theWindowObject, 0);
}
```

The QuickTime VR File Format

A QuickTime VR movie always contains several tracks. A panorama movie, for instance, contains a *panorama image track* (which holds the image data for the panorama), a *panorama track* (which contains information about the panoramic node), and a *QTVR track* (which maintains general information about the movie, such as the default imaging properties). Similarly, an object movie contains an *object image track* (which holds the image data for the object), an *object track* (which contains information about the object node), and a *QTVR track*. For multinode movies, the QTVR track also contains a list of the nodes in the movie and an indication of which node is the default node. Movies with hotspots also contain a *hotspot image track* (a video track in which the hotspots are designated by colored regions).

Usually this structure is important to us only when we want to create a QuickTime VR movie. But it's also useful when we want to alter an existing movie or extract information not provided by the available QuickTime VR Manager functions.

Working with Node Information

A QTVR track maintains general information about a QuickTime VR movie. Each individual sample in the QTVR track's media is an atom container called a *node information atom container*. This atom container holds a *node header atom*, which contains information about a single node, such as the node's type, ID, and name. The node information atom container can also hold a *hotspot parent atom* if the node has any hotspots in it. The QuickTime VR Manager provides the QTVRGetNodeInfo function that we can use to get a copy of a particular node information atom container or of any of its children. Listing 10.7 defines a function that we can use to get a copy of a node header atom for a specified node ID.

Listing 10.7 Finding the node header atom data.

```
OSErr QTVRUtils_GetNodeHeaderAtomData (QTVRInstance theInstance, UInt32 theNodeID,
        QTVRNodeHeaderAtomPtr theNodeHdrPtr)
{
  QTAtomContainer       myNodeInfo;
  QTAtom                myAtom;
  OSErr                 myErr = noErr;

  // get the node information atom container for the specified node
  myErr = QTVRGetNodeInfo(theInstance, theNodeID, &myNodeInfo);
  if (myErr != noErr)
    return(myErr);

  // get the single node header atom in the node information atom container
  myAtom = QTFindChildByID(myNodeInfo, kParentAtomIsContainer,
              kQTVRNodeHeaderAtomType, 1, NULL);
  if (myAtom != 0)
    myErr = QTCopyAtomDataToPtr(myNodeInfo, myAtom, false,
                sizeof(QTVRNodeHeaderAtom), theNodeHdrPtr, NULL);
  else
    myErr = cannotFindAtomErr;

  QTDisposeAtomContainer(myNodeInfo);
  return(myErr);
}
```

As you can see, we call QTVRGetNodeInfo to get the node information atom container for the specified node ID; then we call QTFindChildByID to find the single node header atom inside that container. If we find that atom, we call QTCopyAtomDataToPtr to make a copy of its data. A node header atom has this structure:

```
struct QTVRNodeHeaderAtom {
    UInt16              majorVersion;
    UInt16              minorVersion;
    OSType              nodeType;
    QTAtomID            nodeID;
    QTAtomID            nameAtomID;
    QTAtomID            commentAtomID;
    UInt32              reserved1;
    UInt32              reserved2;
};
```

Listing 10.8 defines the function QTVRUtils_GetNodeType, which reads the nodeType field of a node header atom to determine the node type. (In fact, the QuickTime VR Manager provides the QTVRGetNodeType function to get a node's type; I'm presenting QTVRUtils_GetNodeType simply to show another way of getting that information.)

Listing 10.8   Getting a node type.

```
OSErr QTVRUtils_GetNodeType (QTVRInstance theInstance, UInt32 theNodeID,
        OSType *theNodeType)
{
  QTVRNodeHeaderAtom        myNodeHeader;
  OSErr                     myErr = noErr;

  // make sure we always return some meaningful value
  *theNodeType = kQTVRUnknownType;

  // get the node header atom data
  myErr = QTVRUtils_GetNodeHeaderAtomData(theInstance, theNodeID, &myNodeHeader);
  if (myErr == noErr)
    *theNodeType = EndianU32_BtoN(myNodeHeader.nodeType);

  return(myErr);
}
```

Here there is no need to deallocate the block of data returned by QTVRUtils_GetNodeHeaderAtomData because it is allocated on the stack in a local variable.

Working with a VR World

All samples in a QTVR track use a single sample description. The data field of that sample description holds a *VR world atom container*, which holds general information about the scene contained in the QuickTime VR movie. This information includes the name of the entire scene, the default node ID, and the default imaging properties. We can use the QTVRGetVRWorld function to retrieve a copy of a movie's VR world atom container. Listing 10.9 illustrates one way to use this function.

Listing 10.9 Finding the VR world atom data.

```
OSErr QTVRUtils_GetVRWorldHeaderAtomData (QTVRInstance theInstance,
        QTVRWorldHeaderAtomPtr theVRWorldHdrAtomPtr)
{
  QTAtomContainer          myVRWorld;
  QTAtom                   myAtom;
  OSErr                    myErr = noErr;

  // get the VR world
  myErr = QTVRGetVRWorld(theInstance, &myVRWorld);
  if (myErr != noErr)
    return(myErr);

  // get the single VR world header atom in the VR world
  myAtom = QTFindChildByIndex(myVRWorld, kParentAtomIsContainer, kQTVRWorldHeaderAtomType,
            1, NULL);
  if (myAtom != 0)
    myErr = QTCopyAtomDataToPtr(myVRWorld, myAtom, false, sizeof(QTVRWorldHeaderAtom),
              theVRWorldHdrAtomPtr, NULL);
  else
    myErr = cannotFindAtomErr;

  QTDisposeAtomContainer(myVRWorld);
  return(myErr);
}
```

A VR world atom container contains (perhaps among other things) a single *VR world header atom*, whose structure is defined by the QTVRWorldHeader-Atom data type:

```
struct QTVRWorldHeaderAtom {
    UInt16              majorVersion;
    UInt16              minorVersion;
    QTAtomID            nameAtomID;
    UInt32              defaultNodeID;
    UInt32              vrWorldFlags;
    UInt32              reserved1;
    UInt32              reserved2;
};
```

We can use this information to determine the node ID of a scene's default node, as shown in Listing 10.10.

Listing 10.10 Finding a scene's default node.

```
UInt32 QTVRUtils_GetDefaultNodeID (QTVRInstance theInstance)
{
  QTVRWorldHeaderAtom       myVRWorldHeader;
  UInt32                    myNodeID = kQTVRCurrentNode;
  OSErr                     myErr = noErr;

  myErr = QTVRUtils_GetVRWorldHeaderAtomData(theInstance, &myVRWorldHeader);
  if (myErr == noErr)
    myNodeID = EndianU32_BtoN(myVRWorldHeader.defaultNodeID);

  return(myNodeID);
}
```

QTVRUtils_GetDefaultNodeID can be useful if we need to know the ID of a movie's default node, since there is no QuickTime VR Manager function that returns this information directly.

▶ Wired Actions and QuickTime VR

We've seen how to work with QuickTime wired actions in conjunction with sprite tracks, text tracks, and Flash tracks. We use wired actions to attach dynamic, interactive behaviors to elements in a QuickTime movie and to allow different elements in those movies (and indeed in different movies) to communicate with one another. In this section, we'll investigate how to work with wired actions and QuickTime VR movies.

Sending Actions to QuickTime VR Movies

Let's begin by taking a look at the wired actions that can be targeted at a QuickTime VR movie. When action wiring was first introduced, in Quick-Time 3, these five wired actions were supported:

```
enum {
  kActionQTVRSetPanAngle            = 4096,
  kActionQTVRSetTiltAngle           = 4097,
  kActionQTVRSetFieldOfView         = 4098,
  kActionQTVRShowDefaultView        = 4099,
  kActionQTVRGoToNodeID             = 4100
};
```

The first three actions allow us to set a new pan angle, tilt angle, or field of view in a QuickTime VR movie. Each of these actions takes a single parameter, a value of type float that specifies the desired new angle. This value should be specified in degrees (not radians) and is by default an absolute angle to pan, tilt, or zoom to. It's often useful to specify a relative value instead; we can indicate that the parameter value is relative by inserting into the action atom an atom of type kActionFlags whose atom data is a long integer with (at least) the kActionFlagActionIsDelta flag set. Listing 10.11 shows how we can build an atom container holding a wired atom that pans the target QuickTime VR movie 1° to the left each time it gets an idle event. (We'll see later how to make sure the movie is sent idle events.)

Listing 10.11 Panning a QuickTime VR movie during idle events.

```
static OSErr AddVRAct_CreateIdleActionContainer (QTAtomContainer *theActions)
{
  QTAtom        myEventAtom = 0;
  QTAtom        myActionAtom = 0;
  long          myAction;
  float         myPanAngle = 1.0;
  UInt32        myFlags;
  OSErr         myErr = noErr;

  myErr = QTNewAtomContainer(theActions);
  if (myErr != noErr)
    goto bail;

  myErr = QTInsertChild(*theActions, kParentAtomIsContainer, kQTEventIdle, 1, 1, 0,
          NULL, &myEventAtom);
  if (myErr != noErr)
    goto bail;

  myErr = QTInsertChild(*theActions, myEventAtom, kAction, 1, 1, 0, NULL, &myActionAtom);
  if (myErr != noErr)
    goto bail;

  myAction = EndianS32_NtoB(kActionQTVRSetPanAngle);
  myErr = QTInsertChild(*theActions, myActionAtom, kWhichAction, 1, 1, sizeof(long),
          &myAction, NULL);
  if (myErr != noErr)
    goto bail;

  AddVRAct_ConvertFloatToBigEndian(&myPanAngle);
  myErr = QTInsertChild(*theActions, myActionAtom, kActionParameter, 1, 1, sizeof(float),
          &myPanAngle, NULL);
  if (myErr != noErr)
    goto bail;
```

```
myFlags = EndianU32_NtoB(kActionFlagActionIsDelta | kActionFlagParameterWrapsAround);
myErr = QTInsertChild(*theActions, myActionAtom, kActionFlags, 1, 1, sizeof(UInt32),
        &myFlags, NULL);

bail:
  return(myErr);
}
```

The action kActionQTVRShowDefaultView sets the current node to its default
view (that is, the view that is displayed when the node is first entered). The
kActionQTVRGoToNodeID action takes a single parameter that specifies a node
ID; when the action is executed, the node with that ID becomes the current
node. QuickTime 3 also introduced four wired action operands, which we
can use to get information about the current state of a QuickTime VR
movie:

```
enum {
    kOperandQTVRPanAngle                    = 4096,
    kOperandQTVRTiltAngle                   = 4097,
    kOperandQTVRFieldOfView                 = 4098,
    kOperandQTVRNodeID                      = 4099
};
```

QuickTime 5 added three more actions that we can send to a QuickTime VR
movie:

```
enum {
    kActionQTVREnableHotSpot                = 4101,
    kActionQTVRShowHotSpots                 = 4102,
    kActionQTVRTranslateObject              = 4103
};
```

The kActionQTVREnableHotSpot action enables or disables a hotspot. This
action requires two parameters, a long integer that specifies a hotspot ID
and a Boolean value that specifies whether to enable (true) or disable (false)
the hotspot. The kActionQTVRShowHotSpots action shows or hides all hotspots
in a node, depending on the Boolean value in the parameter atom. The
kActionQTVRTranslateObject action sets the view center of an object node to
the values specified in the action's two parameters. To allow us to retrieve
the current hotspot visibility state and the current view center, QuickTime 5
introduced three additional operands:

```
enum {
  kOperandQTVRHotSpotsVisible                    = 4100,
  kOperandQTVRViewCenterH                        = 4101,
  kOperandQTVRViewCenterV                        = 4102
};
```

There is currently no operand that will allow us to determine whether a particular hotspot is enabled.

Adding Actions to QuickTime VR Movies

We can wire actions to a particular node and to a particular hotspot in a node. Examples of node-specific actions are setting the pan and tilt angles when the user first enters the node and performing some actions periodically when the movie gets an idle event. An example of a hotspot action might be playing a sound when the cursor is moved over a hotspot.

All QuickTime VR wired actions are attached to a particular node, so the atom containers holding the actions are placed in the node information atom container that is contained in the media sample for that node in the QTVR track. So, our job here boils down to finding a media sample in the QTVR track, constructing some atom containers for our desired actions, placing those action containers into the appropriate places in the media sample, and then writing the modified media sample back into the QTVR track. We'll also need to put an atom into the media property atom container of the QTVR track to enable wired action and idle event processing.

Adding Actions to a Hotspot

Let's begin by seeing how to attach some wired actions to a particular hotspot in a node. Let's suppose that we know both the node ID and the hotspot ID and that we have already constructed the atom container that holds the wired actions. Recall that a QTVR track contains one media sample for each node in the movie and that that media sample is a node information atom container. For simplicity, we'll assume that we want to wire a hotspot in a single-node QuickTime VR movie. As a result, we can get the media sample by calling GetMediaSample, like this:

```
GetMediaSample(myMedia, mySample, 0, NULL, myMediaTime, NULL,
  &mySampleDuration, (SampleDescriptionHandle)myQTVRDesc,
  NULL, 1, NULL, &mySampleFlags);
```

If GetMediaSample returns successfully, then mySample will be the atom container that holds the atoms we want to modify.

At this point, we'll call an application function AddVRAct_SetWiredActions-ToHotSpot to add our wired actions to the specified hotspot:

```
AddVRAct_SetWiredActionsToHotSpot(mySample, myHotSpotID, myActions);
```

The first thing we need to do in AddVRAct_SetWiredActionsToHotSpot is find the hotspot parent atom inside the node information atom container:

```
myHotSpotParentAtom = QTFindChildByIndex(theSample, kParentAtomIsContainer,
                kQTVRHotSpotParentAtomType, 1, NULL);
```

A hotspot parent atom contains a *hotspot atom* (of type kQTVRHotSpotAtomType) for each hotspot in the node. The ID of the hotspot atom is the same as the ID of the hotspot, so we can find the appropriate hotspot atom like this:

```
myHotSpotAtom = QTFindChildByID(theSample, myHotSpotParentAtom,
                kQTVRHotSpotAtomType, theHotSpotID, NULL);
```

We add wired actions to a hotspot by inserting an event atom (that is, an atom of type kQTEventType) into the hotspot atom:

```
QTInsertChildren(theSample, myHotSpotAtom, theActions);
```

Listing 10.12 shows our complete definition of AddVRAct_SetWiredActionsTo-HotSpot.

Listing 10.12 Adding wired actions to a hotspot.

```
static OSErr AddVRAct_SetWiredActionsToHotSpot
        (Handle theSample, long theHotSpotID, QTAtomContainer theActions)
{
  QTAtom          myHotSpotParentAtom = 0;
  QTAtom          myHotSpotAtom = 0;
  short           myCount, myIndex;
  OSErr           myErr = paramErr;

  myHotSpotParentAtom = QTFindChildByIndex(theSample, kParentAtomIsContainer,
                        kQTVRHotSpotParentAtomType, 1, NULL);
  if (myHotSpotParentAtom == NULL)
    goto bail;
```

```
myHotSpotAtom = QTFindChildByID(theSample, myHotSpotParentAtom,
                kQTVRHotSpotAtomType, theHotSpotID, NULL);
if (myHotSpotAtom == NULL)
  goto bail;

// see how many events are already associated with the specified hotspot
myCount = QTCountChildrenOfType(theSample, myHotSpotAtom, kQTEventType);

for (myIndex = myCount; myIndex > 0; myIndex--) {
  QTAtom        myTargetAtom = 0;

  // remove all the existing events
  myTargetAtom = QTFindChildByIndex(theSample, myHotSpotAtom,
                kQTEventType, myIndex, NULL);
  if (myTargetAtom != 0) {
    myErr = QTRemoveAtom(theSample, myTargetAtom);
    if (myErr != noErr)
      goto bail;
  }
}

if (theActions) {
  myErr = QTInsertChildren(theSample, myHotSpotAtom, theActions);
  if (myErr != noErr)
    goto bail;
}

bail:
  return(myErr);
}
```

You'll notice that we look to see whether the hotspot atom already contains any event atoms; if so, we remove them from the hotspot atom. This ensures that the event atom we pass to AddVRAct_SetWiredActionsToHotSpot is the only one in the hotspot atom.

Adding Actions to a Node

We add wired actions to a node by inserting children into the node information atom container for that node. The type of a child atom for a wired action should be the same as the event type, and the ID should be 1. Listing 10.13 defines the AddVRAct_SetWiredActionsToNode function, which we use to add a wired atom to a particular node. The first parameter is assumed to be the node information atom container.

Listing 10.13 Adding wired actions to a node.

```
static OSErr AddVRAct_SetWiredActionsToNode
        (Handle theSample, QTAtomContainer theActions, UInt32 theActionType)
{
  QTAtom          myEventAtom = 0;
  QTAtom          myTargetAtom = 0;
  OSErr           myErr = noErr;

  // look for an event atom in the specified actions atom container
  if (theActions != NULL)
    myEventAtom = QTFindChildByID(theActions, kParentAtomIsContainer,
                    theActionType, 1, NULL);

  // look for an event atom in the node information atom container
  myTargetAtom = QTFindChildByID(theSample, kParentAtomIsContainer,
                    theActionType, 1, NULL);
  if (myTargetAtom != 0) {
    // if there is already an event atom in the node information atom container,
    // then either replace it with the one we were passed or remove it
    if (theActions != NULL)
      myErr = QTReplaceAtom(theSample, myTargetAtom, theActions, myEventAtom);
    else
      myErr = QTRemoveAtom(theSample, myTargetAtom);
  } else {
    // there is no event atom in the node information atom container,
    // so add in the one we were passed
    if (theActions != NULL)
      myErr = QTInsertChildren(theSample, kParentAtomIsContainer, theActions);
  }

  return(myErr);
}
```

We can add an idle event handler to a node like this:

```
AddVRAct_SetWiredActionsToNode(mySample, myActions, kQTEventIdle);
```

And we can add a frame-loaded event handler to a node like this:

```
AddVRAct_SetWiredActionsToNode(mySample, myActions, kQTEventFrameLoaded);
```

Other event types (such as kQTEventMouseClick or kQTEventKey) might not make sense for a node-based wired action.

Updating the Media Property Atom

When we add some wiring to a sprite track, we need to include in the track's media property atom an atom of type kSpriteTrackPropertyHas-Actions whose atom data is set to true. (See Volume One, Chapter 16.) This atom tells the movie controller that the sprite track has wiring associated with it. If, in addition, any of the wired sprites employs the kQTEventIdle event, we also need to add an atom of type kSpriteTrackPropertyQTIdle-EventsFrequency whose atom data indicates the desired idle event frequency, in ticks. We need to add these same atoms to the media property atom when we wire a QuickTime VR movie. Listing 10.14 defines the function AddVRAct_WriteMediaPropertyAtom, which we use to add the appropriate atoms.

Listing 10.14 Adding atoms to the media property atom.

```
static OSErr AddVRAct_WriteMediaPropertyAtom (Media theMedia, long thePropertyID,
          long thePropertySize, void *theProperty)
{
  QTAtomContainer       myPropertyAtom = NULL;
  QTAtom                myAtom = 0;
  OSErr                 myErr = noErr;

  // get the current media property atom
  myErr = GetMediaPropertyAtom(theMedia, &myPropertyAtom);
  if (myErr != noErr)
    goto bail;

  // if there isn't one yet, then create one
  if (myPropertyAtom == NULL) {
    myErr = QTNewAtomContainer(&myPropertyAtom);
    if (myErr != noErr)
      goto bail;
  }

  // see if there is an existing atom of the specified type; if not, then create one
  myAtom = QTFindChildByID(myPropertyAtom, kParentAtomIsContainer,
            thePropertyID, 1, NULL);
  if (myAtom == NULL) {
    myErr = QTInsertChild(myPropertyAtom, kParentAtomIsContainer,
              thePropertyID, 1, 0, 0, NULL, &myAtom);
    if ((myErr != noErr) || (myAtom == NULL))
      goto bail;
  }
```

```
  // set the data of the specified atom to the data passed in
  myErr = QTSetAtomData(myPropertyAtom, myAtom, thePropertySize, (Ptr)theProperty);
  if (myErr != noErr)
    goto bail;

  // write the new atom data out to the media property atom
  myErr = SetMediaPropertyAtom(theMedia, myPropertyAtom);

bail:
  if (myPropertyAtom != NULL)
    QTDisposeAtomContainer(myPropertyAtom);

  return(myErr);
}
```

To indicate that the QuickTime VR movie has wired actions embedded in it, we can call AddVRAct_WriteMediaPropertyAtom like this:

```
myHasActions = true;
AddVRAct_WriteMediaPropertyAtom(myMedia, kSpriteTrackPropertyHasActions,
    sizeof(Boolean), &myHasActions);
```

And we can set the idle frequency like this:

```
myFrequency = EndianU32_NtoB(30);
AddVRAct_WriteMediaPropertyAtom(myMedia,
    kSpriteTrackPropertyQTIdleEventsFrequency, sizeof(UInt32), &myFrequency);
```

Saving the Modified Media Data

So far, we've added some wired atoms to a node information atom container or to a hotspot atom inside of a node information atom container, and we've updated the media property atom of the QTVR track. To save these changes, we need to replace the appropriate sample in the QTVR track media and then update the movie atom. Listing 10.15 shows the complete definition of the AddVRAct_AddWiredActionsToQTVRMovie function, which we use to wire a QuickTime VR movie.

Listing 10.15 Adding wired actions to a QuickTime VR movie.

```
static void AddVRAct_AddWiredActionsToQTVRMovie (FSSpec *theFSSpec)
{
  short                       myResID = 0;
  short                       myResRefNum = -1;
  Movie                       myMovie = NULL;
  Track                       myTrack = NULL;
  Media                       myMedia = NULL;
  TimeValue                   myTrackOffset;
  TimeValue                   myMediaTime;
  TimeValue                   mySampleDuration;
  TimeValue                   mySelectionDuration;
  TimeValue                   myNewMediaTime;
  QTVRSampleDescriptionHandle myQTVRDesc = NULL;
  Handle                      mySample = NULL;
  short                       mySampleFlags;
  Fixed                       myTrackEditRate;
  QTAtomContainer             myActions = NULL;
  Boolean                     myHasActions;
  long                        myHotSpotID = 0L;
  UInt32                      myFrequency;
  OSErr                       myErr = noErr;

  // open the movie file and get the QTVR track from the movie

  // open the movie file for reading and writing
  myErr = OpenMovieFile(theFSSpec, &myResRefNum, fsRdWrPerm);
  if (myErr != noErr)
    goto bail;

  myErr = NewMovieFromFile(&myMovie, myResRefNum, &myResID, NULL, newMovieActive, NULL);
  if (myErr != noErr)
    goto bail;

  // find the first QTVR track in the movie
  myTrack = GetMovieIndTrackType(myMovie, 1, kQTVRQTVRType, movieTrackMediaType);
  if (myTrack == NULL)
    goto bail;

  // get the first media sample in the QTVR track
  myMedia = GetTrackMedia(myTrack);
  if (myMedia == NULL)
    goto bail;
```

```
myTrackOffset = GetTrackOffset(myTrack);
myMediaTime = TrackTimeToMediaTime(myTrackOffset, myTrack);

// allocate some storage to hold the sample description for the QTVR track
myQTVRDesc = (QTVRSampleDescriptionHandle)NewHandle(4);
if (myQTVRDesc == NULL)
  goto bail;

mySample = NewHandle(0);
if (mySample == NULL)
  goto bail;

myErr = GetMediaSample(myMedia, mySample, 0, NULL, myMediaTime, NULL,
          &mySampleDuration, (SampleDescriptionHandle)myQTVRDesc,
          NULL, 1, NULL, &mySampleFlags);
if (myErr != noErr)
  goto bail;

// add idle actions

// create an action container for idle actions
myErr = AddVRAct_CreateIdleActionContainer(&myActions);
if (myErr != noErr)
  goto bail;

// add idle actions to sample
myErr = AddVRAct_SetWiredActionsToNode(mySample, myActions, kQTEventIdle);
if (myErr != noErr)
  goto bail;

myErr = QTDisposeAtomContainer(myActions);
if (myErr != noErr)
  goto bail;

// add frame-loaded actions

// create an action container for frame-loaded actions
myErr = AddVRAct_CreateFrameLoadedActionContainer(&myActions);
if (myErr != noErr)
  goto bail;

// add frame-loaded actions to sample
myErr = AddVRAct_SetWiredActionsToNode(mySample, myActions, kQTEventFrameLoaded);
if (myErr != noErr)
  goto bail;
```

```
myErr = QTDisposeAtomContainer(myActions);
if (myErr != noErr)
  goto bail;

// add hotspot actions

// find the first hotspot in the selected node; don't bail if there are no hotspots
myErr = AddVRAct_GetFirstHotSpot(mySample, &myHotSpotID);
if ((myErr == noErr) && (myHotSpotID != 0)) {
  // create an action container for hotspot actions
  myErr = AddVRAct_CreateHotSpotActionContainer(&myActions);
  if (myErr != noErr)
    goto bail;

  // add hotspot actions to sample
  myErr = AddVRAct_SetWiredActionsToHotSpot(mySample, myHotSpotID, myActions);
  if (myErr != noErr)
    goto bail;
}

// replace sample in media
myTrackEditRate = GetTrackEditRate(myTrack, myTrackOffset);
if (GetMoviesError() != noErr)
  goto bail;

GetTrackNextInterestingTime(myTrack, nextTimeMediaSample | nextTimeEdgeOK,
  myTrackOffset, fixed1, NULL, &mySelectionDuration);
if (GetMoviesError() != noErr)
  goto bail;

myErr = DeleteTrackSegment(myTrack, myTrackOffset, mySelectionDuration);
if (myErr != noErr)
  goto bail;

myErr = BeginMediaEdits(myMedia);
if (myErr != noErr)
  goto bail;

myErr = AddMediaSample(myMedia, mySample, 0, GetHandleSize(mySample),
        mySampleDuration, (SampleDescriptionHandle)myQTVRDesc, 1, mySampleFlags,
        &myNewMediaTime);
if (myErr != noErr)
  goto bail;

myErr = EndMediaEdits(myMedia);
if (myErr != noErr)
  goto bail;
```

```
    // add the media to the track
    myErr = InsertMediaIntoTrack(myTrack, myTrackOffset, myNewMediaTime,
              mySelectionDuration, myTrackEditRate);
    if (myErr != noErr)
      goto bail;

    // set the media property atom to enable wired action and idle-time processing
    myHasActions = true;
    myErr = AddVRAct_WriteMediaPropertyAtom(myMedia, kSpriteTrackPropertyHasActions,
              sizeof(Boolean), &myHasActions);
    if (myErr != noErr)
      goto bail;

    myFrequency = EndianU32_NtoB(1);
    myErr = AddVRAct_WriteMediaPropertyAtom(myMedia,
              kSpriteTrackPropertyQTIdleEventsFrequency, sizeof(UInt32), &myFrequency);
    if (myErr != noErr)
      goto bail;

    // update the movie resource
    myErr = UpdateMovieResource(myMovie, myResRefNum, myResID, NULL);

bail:
    // close the movie file
    CloseMovieFile(myResRefNum);

    if (myActions != NULL)
      QTDisposeAtomContainer(myActions);

    if (mySample != NULL)
      DisposeHandle(mySample);

    if (myQTVRDesc != NULL)
      DisposeHandle((Handle)myQTVRDesc);

    if (myMovie != NULL)
      DisposeMovie(myMovie);
}
```

▶ Conclusion

In this chapter, we've learned how to work with the QuickTime VR Manager to control the operation of QuickTime VR movies programmatically. We've seen how to adjust pan, tilt, and zoom angles, how to alter the displayed image by drawing into a panorama's prescreen buffer, and how to intercept some QuickTime QTVR Manager functions. As usual, these few examples of using the QTVR APIs are just the tip of the iceberg; with just a little bit more time and energy, we can develop some truly impressive interactive applications using QuickTime VR.

We've also taken a look at QuickTime VR and wired actions, first reviewing how to send actions to VR movies and then (more important) learning how to embed wired actions into QuickTime VR movies. We haven't yet learned how to actually build QuickTime VR movies from scratch, but we do have a preliminary idea of how they are put together.

Trading Places

Working with Alternate Tracks and Alternate Movies

 Introduction

QuickTime's original designers understood very clearly that QuickTime movies would be played back in quite varied environments—on monitors with different pixel depths, on faster or slower machines, in Quebec or in Cupertino. They developed a mechanism by which QuickTime can choose one track from a group of tracks in a movie according to some characteristic of the playback environment. For instance, a movie might contain two sound tracks, one with an English narration and one with a French narration. At playback time, QuickTime selects the sound track whose language code matches that of the current operating system.

The group of tracks from which QuickTime selects is called an *alternate track group*, and a track in this group is called an *alternate track*. An alternate track is selected based on the language of the track's media or the quality of the track's media. The media quality is a relative indication of the track's sound or video quality (poor, good, better, or best). In addition, for visual media types, this media quality can specify the pixel depths for which the track is appropriate. Alternate track groups provide a simple but effective way to tailor a QuickTime movie for playback in different languages and on computers with different sound and video hardware.

QuickTime 3 introduced a way to tailor the movie data displayed to the user according to a much wider array of environmental characteristics, including the speed of the user's connection to the Internet, the version of QuickTime that is installed on the user's machine, and the availability or version of certain software components. This magic is accomplished not with alternate tracks but with *alternate movies*. An alternate movie is any one of a set of movies that contain media data appropriate for a specific characteristic or set of characteristics. For instance, one alternate movie might contain highly compressed video and monophonic sound, while a second alternate movie might contain higher-quality video and stereo sound. Because it is smaller in size, the first alternate movie would be appropriate for users with relatively slow Internet connections; the second movie would be appropriate for users with faster Internet connections. Similarly, one alternate movie might be appropriate for playback under QuickTime 6 and another might be appropriate for playback under all earlier versions of QuickTime.

Alternate movies are associated with one another using a movie file that contains data references to all of the alternate movies as well as information about the criteria by which QuickTime should select one of those alternate movies when that movie file is opened. This other movie file is called an *alternate reference movie file* (or, more briefly, a *reference movie*), since it refers to a set of alternate movies. When the principal selection criterion is the user's Internet connection speed, this movie is sometimes also called an *alternate data rate movie*.

In this chapter, we're going to take a look at alternate tracks and alternate movies. We'll see how to create alternate track groups in a movie and how to interact with QuickTime's alternate track selection either programmatically or using wired actions. Then we'll see how to create alternate reference movie files.

Alternate Tracks

As we've seen, tracks in a movie can be sorted into alternate track groups. At any time, at most one track in an alternate track group is enabled and the remaining tracks in the group are disabled. This enabling and disabling is called *auto-alternating* and is performed automatically by the Movie Toolbox, based either on the language of the tracks or the quality of the tracks. Tracks in an alternate track group can be of the same type (for example, all video tracks) or they can be of different types. Figure 11.1 shows a frame of a movie played on a computer with English system software. Figure 11.2 shows a frame of the very same movie when played on a computer with French system software. This movie contains two text tracks that are grouped into an alternate track group.

Figure 11.1 An English alternate track.

Figure 11.2 A French alternate track.

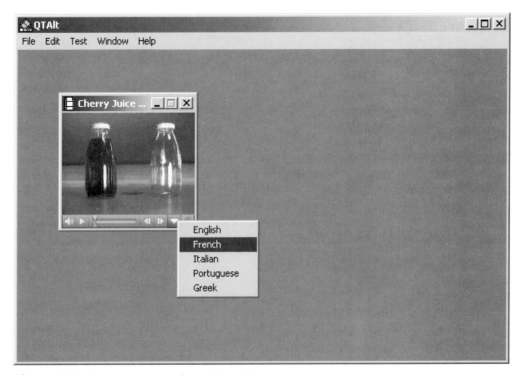

Figure 11.3 The custom pop-up language menu.

The Movie Toolbox provides about a dozen functions that we can use to work with alternate groups and with a media's language and quality. For instance, we can use these functions to create an alternate track group in a movie and to dynamically switch languages during movie playback. We can also use these functions to control QuickTime's alternate track selection process. We'll exercise some of these functions by adding a pop-up menu to the controller bar that allows the user to select from among the languages used in the movie. Figure 11.3 shows this pop-up menu at work.

Getting and Setting a Media's Language

A media's language is specified using a 16-bit language code. (This is also sometimes called the *region code*.) Here are a few of the language codes defined in the header file Script.h:

```
enum {
    langEnglish                     = 0,
    langFrench                      = 1,
    langGerman                      = 2,
    langItalian                     = 3,
    langDutch                       = 4,
    langSwedish                     = 5,
    langSpanish                     = 6,
    langDanish                      = 7,
    langPortuguese                  = 8,
    langNorwegian                   = 9,
    langHebrew                      = 10,
    langJapanese                    = 11
};
```

When we create a new media (typically by calling NewTrackMedia), the language is set to 0, or langEnglish. We can, however, change the language by calling SetMediaLanguage. To set a media's language to French, we could use this line of code:

```
SetMediaLanguage(myMedia, langFrench);
```

When the movie's metadata is written to the movie file (typically by calling AddMovieResource or UpdateMovieResource), the language setting is saved in an atom (in particular, in the media header atom).

At playback time, we can call the GetMediaLanguage function to determine the language of a track's media, like this:

```
myLanguage = GetMediaLanguage(myMedia);
```

Listing 11.1 defines a function that calls GetMediaLanguage for each track in a movie to determine which languages are used in a movie. If a language is used in the movie, the corresponding element in the array fLanguageMask is set to 1. (We'll use this array to determine which languages to put in our custom pop-up menu.)

Listing 11.1 Finding languages used in a movie.

```c
static OSErr QTAlt_UpdateMovieLanguageMask (WindowObject theWindowObject)
{
  ApplicationDataHdl      myAppData = NULL;
  Movie                   myMovie = NULL;
  Track                   myTrack = NULL;
  Media                   myMedia = NULL;
  short                   myTrackCount, myIndex;
  OSErr                   myErr = noErr;

  myAppData = (ApplicationDataHdl)QTFrame_GetAppDataFromWindowObject(theWindowObject);
  if (myAppData == NULL)
    return(paramErr);

  myMovie = (**theWindowObject).fMovie;
  if (myMovie == NULL)
    return(paramErr);

  // clear out the existing mask
  for (myIndex = 0; myIndex < kNumLanguages; myIndex++)
    (**myAppData).fLanguageMask[myIndex] = 0;

  // get the language of each track in the movie
  myTrackCount = GetMovieTrackCount(myMovie);
  for (myIndex = 1; myIndex <= myTrackCount; myIndex++) {
    myTrack = GetMovieIndTrack(myMovie, myIndex);
    if (myTrack != NULL) {
      short             myLanguage;

      myMedia = GetTrackMedia(myTrack);
      myLanguage = GetMediaLanguage(myMedia);
      if ((myLanguage >= 0) && (myLanguage < kNumLanguages))
        (**myAppData).fLanguageMask[myLanguage] = 1;
    }
  }

  return(myErr);
}
```

Notice that we use the language code as the index into the fLanguageMask array. This allows us to walk through that array to find the items that should be in the language pop-up menu, as illustrated by the QTAlt_GetMenuItem-IndexForLanguageCode function (defined in Listing 11.2).

Listing 11.2 Finding a menu item index for a given language.

```
UInt16 QTAlt_GetMenuItemIndexForLanguageCode (WindowObject theWindowObject, short theCode)
{
   ApplicationDataHdl      myAppData = NULL;
   short                   myCount = 0;
   short                   myIndex = 0;

   myAppData = (ApplicationDataHdl) QTFrame_GetAppDataFromWindowObject(theWindowObject);
   if (myAppData == NULL)
      return(myIndex);

   QTAlt_UpdateMovieLanguageMask(theWindowObject);

   for (myCount = 0; myCount <= theCode; myCount++) {
      if ((**myAppData).fLanguageMask[myCount] == 1)
         myIndex++;
   }

   return(myIndex);
}
```

Getting and Setting a Media's Quality

A track's media also has a quality, which is specified using a 16-bit value. Figure 11.4 shows how this value is interpreted. The high-order byte is currently unused. Bits 6 and 7 of the low-order byte represent a relative quality. The Movie Toolbox defines these constants that we can use to get the relative quality from the entire quality value:

```
enum {
   mediaQualityDraft                       = 0x0000,
   mediaQualityNormal                      = 0x0040,
   mediaQualityBetter                      = 0x0080,
   mediaQualityBest                        = 0x00C0
};
```

Bits 0 through 5 of the low-order byte indicate, for visual media types, the pixel depths at which the track can be displayed. If bit n is set to 1, then the track can be displayed at pixel depth 2^n. Thus, these 6 bits can indicate pixel depths from 1 bit (that is, 2^0) to 32 bits (2^5). More than one bit can be set, indicating that the track can be displayed at multiple pixel depths.

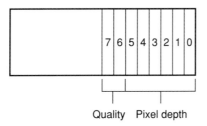

Quality   Pixel depth

Figure 11.4   A media quality value.

The Movie Toolbox provides two functions, GetMediaQuality and SetMedia-Quality, which we can use to get and set a media's quality value. Here's an example of setting a video track's quality to display at 16- and 32-bit pixel depths, at the highest quality:

```
short       myQuality = mediaQualityBest + 32 + 16;
SetMediaQuality(myMedia, myQuality);
```

If two or more tracks could be selected from a given alternate group (that is, their languages are the same and they are both valid at the current bit depth), QuickTime selects the track with the highest relative quality.

Creating Alternate Groups

Suppose now that we've assigned appropriate languages and quality values to some of the tracks in a movie. At this point, we can group these tracks into alternate track groups by calling SetTrackAlternate, which is declared essentially like this:

```
void SetTrackAlternate (Track theTrack, Track alternateT);
```

The first parameter, theTrack, is the track we want to add to a track group. The second parameter, alternateT, is a track that is already in that group. If theTrack is not already in a group and alternateT is in a group, then theTrack is added to the group that contains alternateT. If theTrack is already in a group but alternateT is not, then alternateT is added to the group that contains theTrack. If both theTrack and alternateT are already in groups, then the two groups are combined into one group. If neither the-Track nor alternateT is in a group, then a new group is created to hold them both. Finally, if alternateT is NULL, then theTrack is removed from the group that contains it.

In practice, this is actually much easier than it may sound from that description. For instance, if myTrack1 and myTrack2 are two video tracks with different media languages, we can group them into an alternate track group like this:

```
SetTrackAlternate(myTrack1, myTrack2);
```

And we can remove myTrack1 from its group like this:

```
SetTrackAlternate(myTrack1, NULL);
```

If we want to find all tracks in a particular alternate track group, we can use the GetTrackAlternate function, which is declared like this:

```
Track GetTrackAlternate (Track theTrack);
```

GetTrackAlternate returns the track identifier of the next track in the alternate track group. For instance, GetTrackAlternate(myTrack1) would return myTrack2, and GetTrackAlternate(myTrack2) would return myTrack1. As you can see, calling GetTrackAlternate repeatedly will eventually return the track identifier we started with. And if there is only one track in an alternate track group, GetTrackAlternate will return the track identifier we pass it.

Getting and Setting a Movie's Language

Recall that when a movie file is first opened and prepared for playback, QuickTime selects the alternate track whose language code matches that of the current operating system. We can dynamically modify the language used by a movie by calling the SetMovieLanguage function. For instance, we can execute this code to set the language to French:

```
SetMovieLanguage(myMovie, (long)langFrench);
```

QuickTime inspects all alternate track groups in the movie and enables the track in each group that has that language. If no track in any alternate group has the specified language code, then the movie's language is not changed.

Interestingly, QuickTime does not provide a GetMovieLanguage function, even though it might sometimes be useful for us to know the current language being used in a movie. We can define our own function, however, to get this information. Listing 11.3 defines the QTUtils_GetMovieLanguage function, which looks at each enabled track and inspects the language of that track's media.

Listing 11.3 Finding a movie's current language.

```
short QTUtils_GetMovieLanguage (Movie theMovie)
{
   Track              myTrack = NULL;
   Media              myMedia = NULL;
   short              myTrackCount, myIndex;
   short              myLanguage = -1;                  // an invalid language code

   myTrackCount = GetMovieTrackCount(theMovie);
   for (myIndex = 1; myIndex <= myTrackCount; myIndex++) {
      myTrack = GetMovieIndTrack(theMovie, myIndex);
      if ((myTrack != NULL) && GetTrackEnabled(myTrack)) {
         Track        myAltTrack = NULL;

         myAltTrack = GetTrackAlternate(myTrack);
         if ((myAltTrack != NULL) && (myAltTrack != myTrack)) {
            myMedia = GetTrackMedia(myTrack);
            myLanguage = GetMediaLanguage(myMedia);
            break;
         }
      }
   }

   return(myLanguage);
}
```

You'll notice that we don't simply get the language of the first enabled track's media; rather, we call GetTrackAlternate to make sure that the track is contained in an alternate track group that contains at least two tracks. (A media's language is ignored by the Movie Toolbox if the corresponding track is not part of any alternate track group.)

Listing 11.4 shows the QTAlt_HandleCustomButtonClick function, which we use to handle user clicks on the custom button in the controller bar. We've encountered code like this before, so I'll be content here to just show the code.

Listing 11.4 Handling clicks on the custom controller bar button.

```
void QTAlt_HandleCustomButtonClick (MovieController theMC,
      EventRecord *theEvent, long theRefCon)
{
   MenuHandle               myMenu = NULL;
   WindowObject             myWindowObject = (WindowObject)theRefCon;
   ApplicationDataHdl       myAppData = NULL;
   StringPtr                myMenuTitle = QTUtils_ConvertCToPascalString(kMenuTitle);
   UInt16                   myCount = 0;
```

```
   // make sure we got valid parameters
   if ((theMC == NULL) || (theEvent == NULL) || (theRefCon == NULL))
     goto bail;

   myAppData = (ApplicationDataHdl)QTFrame_GetAppDataFromWindowObject(myWindowObject);
   if (myAppData == NULL)
     goto bail;

   // create a new menu
   myMenu = NewMenu(kCustomButtonMenuID, myMenuTitle);
   if (myMenu != NULL) {
     long            myItem = 0;
     Point           myPoint;

     // add all track languages in the current movie to the pop-up menu
     myCount = QTAlt_AddMovieLanguagesToMenu(myWindowObject, myMenu);

     if (((**myAppData).fCurrMovieIndex > 0) && ((**myAppData).fCurrMovieIndex <= myCount))
       MacCheckMenuItem(myMenu, (**myAppData).fCurrMovieIndex, true);

     // insert the menu into the menu list
     MacInsertMenu(myMenu, hierMenu);

     // find the location of the mouse click;
     // the top-left corner of the pop-up menu is anchored at this point
     myPoint = theEvent->where;
     LocalToGlobal(&myPoint);

     // display the pop-up menu and handle the item selected
     myItem = PopUpMenuSelect(myMenu, myPoint.v, myPoint.h, myItem);
     if (myItem > 0) {
       (**myAppData).fCurrMovieIndex = myItem;
       SetMovieLanguage(MCGetMovie(theMC),
         QTAlt_GetLanguageCodeForMenuItemIndex(myWindowObject, myItem));
       UpdateMovie(MCGetMovie(theMC));
     }

     // remove the menu from the menu list
     MacDeleteMenu(GetMenuID(myMenu));

     // dispose of the menu
     DisposeMenu(myMenu);
   }

bail:
   free(myMenuTitle);
}
```

We've already seen all of the application-defined functions used here, except for QTAlt_AddMovieLanguagesToMenu. Listing 11.5 shows our implementation of this function.

Listing 11.5 Adding languages to the pop-up menu.

```
static UInt16 QTAlt_AddMovieLanguagesToMenu (WindowObject theWindowObject,
            MenuHandle theMenu)
{
  ApplicationDataHdl      myAppData = NULL;
  Movie                   myMovie = NULL;
  Track                   myTrack = NULL;
  Media                   myMedia = NULL;
  short                   myIndex;
  UInt16                  myCount = 0;

  myAppData = (ApplicationDataHdl)QTFrame_GetAppDataFromWindowObject(theWindowObject);
  if (myAppData == NULL)
    goto bail;

  // update the mask of movie languages
  QTAlt_UpdateMovieLanguageMask(theWindowObject);

  // add menu items
  for (myIndex = 0; myIndex < kNumLanguages; myIndex++) {
    if ((**myAppData).fLanguageMask[myIndex] == 1) {
      StringPtr   myItemText = QTUtils_ConvertCToPascalString(gLanguageArray[myIndex]);

      MacAppendMenu(theMenu, myItemText);
      free(myItemText);
      myCount++;
    }
  }

bail:
  return(myCount);
}
```

Enabling and Disabling Alternate Track Selection

The selection of alternate tracks based on the media language and quality occurs automatically when a movie file is first opened. We can override this default behavior, however, by passing the newMovieDontAutoAlternates flag when we call NewMovieFromFile or NewMovieFromDataRef (or any of the other

NewMovieFrom calls). Similarly, we can change the state of auto-alternating dynamically using the SetAutoTrackAlternatesEnabled function. For instance, we can turn off auto-alternating for a specific movie like this:

```
SetAutoTrackAlternatesEnabled(myMovie, false);
```

When auto-alternating is on, the Movie Toolbox re-scans alternate track groups whenever we execute a function that might change one of the relevant selection criteria. For instance, if we change the movie's language (by calling SetMovieLanguage), the Movie Toolbox re-scans all alternate track groups to make sure that the correct alternate track in each group is enabled. Likewise, the Movie Toolbox performs this check if we change any of the relevant visual characteristics of the movie (by calling functions like SetMovieGWorld, UpdateMovie, or SetMovieMatrix). Moreover, the alternate track groups are re-scanned if the user performs any action that causes QuickTime to call any of these functions internally, such as moving the movie window from one monitor to another (since the monitors may be set to different pixel depths).

If for some reason we want to explicitly force the Movie Toolbox to re-scan the alternate groups in a movie immediately, we can call the SelectMovieAlternates function, like so:

```
SelectMovieAlternates(myMovie);
```

Note, however, that if all the tracks in a particular alternate track group are disabled when we call SelectMovieAlternates, then none of the tracks in that group will be enabled.

Changing Alternate Tracks with Wired Actions

QuickTime provides a wired action, kActionMovieSetLanguage, which we can use in wired atoms to change a movie's language. This action takes a single parameter, which is a long integer that specifies the desired language. The function WiredUtils_AddMovieSetLanguage, defined in Listing 11.6, shows how we can add these wired actions to an atom container.

Listing 11.6 Adding a set-language action.

```
OSErr WiredUtils_AddMovieSetLanguage
        (QTAtomContainer theContainer, QTAtom theAtom, long theEvent, long theLanguage)
{
  QTAtom          myActionAtom = 0;
  OSErr           myErr = noErr;
```

```
  myErr = WiredUtils_AddQTEventAndActionAtoms(theContainer, theAtom, theEvent,
          kActionMovieSetLanguage, &myActionAtom);
  if (myErr != noErr)
    goto bail;

  theLanguage = EndianS32_NtoB(theLanguage);
  myErr = WiredUtils_AddActionParameterAtom(theContainer, myActionAtom,
          kFirstParam, sizeof(theLanguage), &theLanguage, NULL);

bail:
  return(myErr);
}
```

There is currently no wired action for setting a media's quality, and there are no wired operands for getting a movie's current language or quality. Sigh.

Alternate Movies

Let's turn now to consider alternate movies and alternate reference movies. An alternate reference movie file is a movie file that contains references to a set of alternate movies, together with the information that QuickTime should use to select one of those movies when the alternate reference movie file is opened. This information can rely on a wide range of features of the operating environment, including:

- Internet connection speed
- Language of the operating system software
- CPU speed—a relative ranking, ranging from 1 (slowest) to 5 (fastest)
- Installed version of QuickTime
- Installed version of a specific software component
- Network connection status

To create an alternate reference movie, we need to know which alternate movies it should refer to and what criteria are to be used in selecting a movie from among that collection of alternate movies. Apple provides a utility called MakeRefMovie that is widely used for creating alternate reference movies. Figure 11.5 shows the MakeRefMovie main window, containing several panes that describe the alternate movies and their selection criteria.

Each pane specifies either a local movie file or a URL to a movie file, together with the selection settings for that movie. Notice that each pane

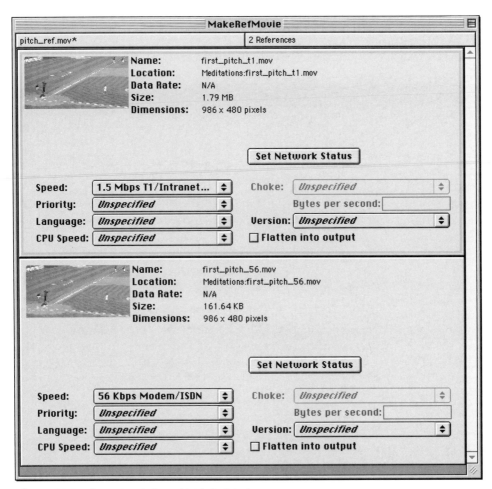

Figure 11.5 The main window of MakeRefMovie.

also contains a checkbox labeled "Flatten into output". If this box is checked (as in Figure 11.6), then the data for the specified movie will be included in toto in the alternate reference movie file. This movie (let's call it the *contained movie*) will be selected if the alternate reference movie file is opened under a version of QuickTime prior to 3 (which is the earliest version that supports alternate reference movies) or if none of the criteria for selecting one of the other alternate movies is met. Clearly, at most one alternate movie should be specified as the contained movie, and MakeRefMovie enforces this restriction by allowing at most one of these boxes to be checked at any one time.

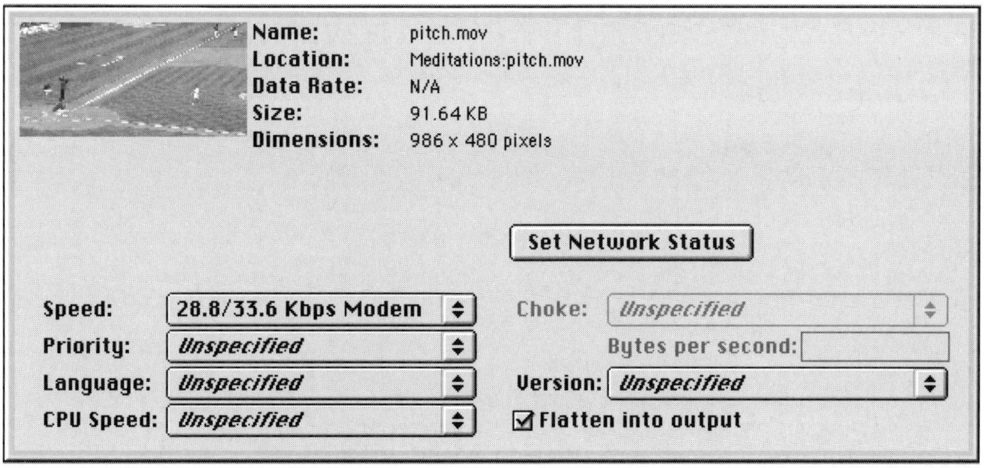

Figure 11.6 An alternate movie pane.

There are also other tools available for creating alternate reference movies. If you like to work with XML, you can use the XMLtoRefMovie utility written by former QuickTime engineer Peter Hoddie. XMLtoRefMovie converts a text file containing an XML-based description of alternate movies and selection criteria into an alternate reference movie file. Listing 11.7 shows the XML data for the information shown in Figure 11.5.

Listing 11.7 Specifying an alternate reference movie using XML.

```
<qtrefmovie>
  <refmovie src="first_pitch_56.mov" data-rate="56k modem" />
  <refmovie src="first_pitch_t1.mov" data-rate="t1" />
</qtrefmovie>
```

Listing 11.8 shows the XML data for an alternate reference movie that has a contained movie (or *default movie*, in XMLtoRefMovie parlance).

Listing 11.8 Including a contained movie using XML.

```
<qtrefmovie>
  <default-movie src="file:///Meditations/pitch.mov" />
  <refmovie src="first_pitch_56.mov" data-rate="56k modem" />
  <refmovie src="first_pitch_t1.mov" data-rate="t1" />
</qtrefmovie>
```

In the rest of this section, I'll assume that we already know which set of movies to use as alternate movies and what the selection criteria are. We want to see how to take that information and create a final alternate reference movie file.

Creating Alternate Reference Movies

We've learned in Volume One that a QuickTime movie file is structured as a series of atoms. Each atom contains some data prefixed by a header. The header is 8 bytes long and specifies the length of the entire atom (header included) and the type of the atom. All of this data (header and atom data) is stored in big-endian format.

A typical QuickTime movie file contains a movie atom (of type MovieAID, or 'moov'), which contains a movie header atom (of type 'mvhd') and one or more track atoms (of type 'trak'). A self-contained movie file also contains a movie data atom (of type 'mdat'). Figure 11.7 illustrates this structure. The movie atom contains the movie header atom and the track atom, so its total length is the lengths of those atoms plus the length of the movie atom header (that is, $x = y + z + 8$).

An alternate reference movie file likewise contains a movie atom, but it does not always contain a movie header atom or any track atoms. Instead, when there is no contained movie, the movie atom contains a single *reference movie record atom* (of type ReferenceMovieRecordAID, or 'rmra'); in turn, this reference movie record atom contains one *reference movie descriptor atom* (of type 'rmda') for each alternate movie described by the alternate reference movie. Figure 11.8 shows this general structure.

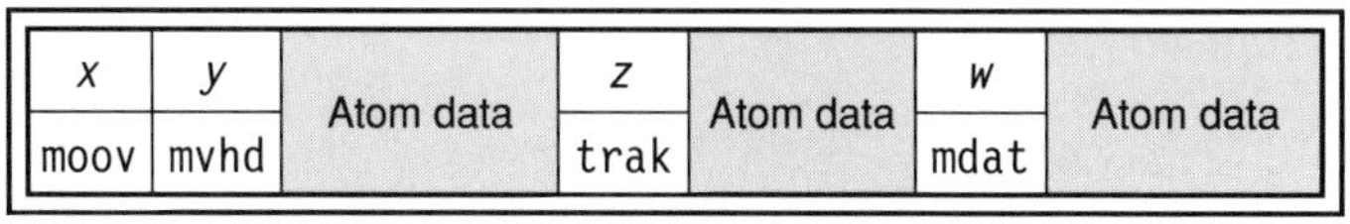

Figure 11.7 The structure of a standard QuickTime movie file.

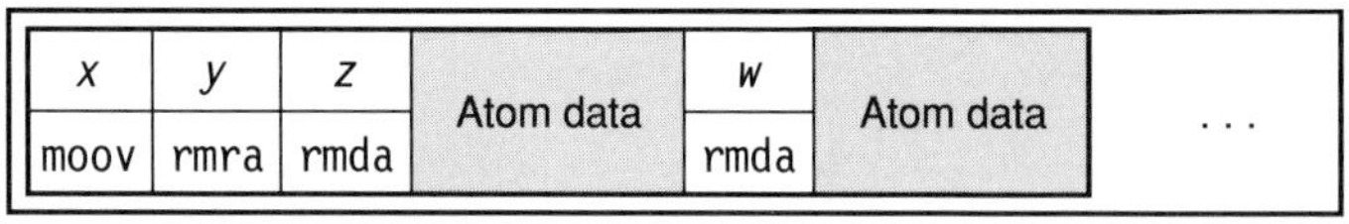

Figure 11.8 The structure of an alternate reference movie file.

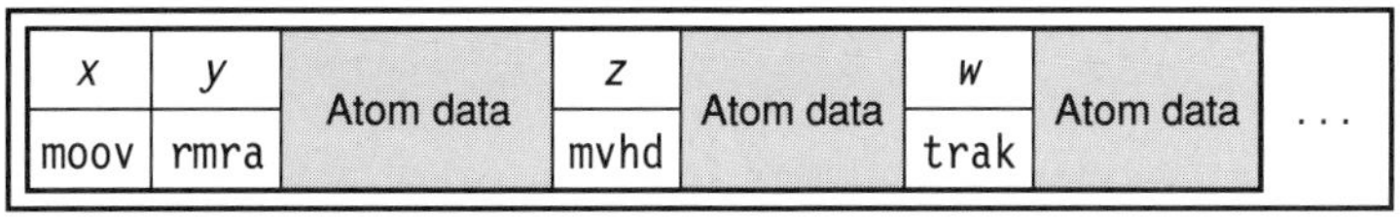

Figure 11.9   An alternate reference movie file with a contained movie.

When an alternate reference movie file does have a contained movie, the movie header atom and the track atoms should follow the reference movie record atom, as shown in Figure 11.9.

A reference movie descriptor atom describes a single alternate movie. It contains other atoms that indicate the selection criteria for that alternate movie, as well as a *data reference atom* that specifies the location of the alternate movie. The header file `MoviesFormat.h` contains a set of atom ID constants that we can use to indicate these atom types:

```
enum {
    ReferenceMovieRecordAID                     = FOUR_CHAR_CODE('rmra'),
    ReferenceMovieDescriptorAID                 = FOUR_CHAR_CODE('rmda'),
    ReferenceMovieDataRefAID                     = FOUR_CHAR_CODE('rdrf'),
    ReferenceMovieVersionCheckAID               = FOUR_CHAR_CODE('rmvc'),
    ReferenceMovieDataRateAID                   = FOUR_CHAR_CODE('rmdr'),
    ReferenceMovieComponentCheckAID             = FOUR_CHAR_CODE('rmcd'),
    ReferenceMovieQualityAID                     = FOUR_CHAR_CODE('rmqu'),
    ReferenceMovieLanguageAID                   = FOUR_CHAR_CODE('rmla'),
    ReferenceMovieCPURatingAID                  = FOUR_CHAR_CODE('rmcs'),
    ReferenceMovieAlternateGroupAID             = FOUR_CHAR_CODE('rmag'),
    ReferenceMovieNetworkStatusAID              = FOUR_CHAR_CODE('rnet')
};
```

Specifying an Alternate Movie

A reference movie descriptor atom must contain a single data reference atom, which specifies an alternate movie. The atom data for the data reference atom is a *reference movie data reference record*, which has this structure:

```
struct ReferenceMovieDataRefRecord {
    long            flags;
    OSType          dataRefType;
    long            dataRefSize;
    char            dataRef[1];
};
```

Currently, this value is defined for the flags field:

```
enum {
  kDataRefIsSelfContained                    = (1 << 0)
};
```

If the flags field is kDataRefIsSelfContained, then the other fields are ignored and QuickTime searches for the movie data in the alternate reference movie itself (as shown in Figure 11.9). Otherwise, if the flags field is 0, QuickTime uses the data reference contained in the dataRef field, using the dataRefType and dataRefSize fields to determine the type and size of that data reference.

The dataRef field can contain any kind of data reference supported by QuickTime, but usually it's either a file data reference or a URL data reference. (See Volume One, Chapter 9, for more information about data references.) Listing 11.9 shows some code that builds a data reference atom, based on information stored in an application data structure associated with a pane.

Listing 11.9   Creating a data reference atom.

```
ReferenceMovieDataRefRecord    myDataRefRec;
AliasHandle                    myAlias = NULL;
Ptr                            myData = NULL;
long                           myFlags;

switch((**myAppData).fPaneType) {
  case kMRM_MoviePaneType:
    // create an alias record for the movie
    myErr = NewAlias(&gRefMovieSpec, &(**myWindowObject).fFileFSSpec, &myAlias);
    if (myErr != noErr)
      goto bailLoop;

    if ((**myAppData).fCurrentFlat == kMRM_FlatCheckOn)
      myFlags = kDataRefIsSelfContained;
    else
      myFlags = 0;

    myDataRefRec.flags = EndianU32_NtoB(myFlags);
    myDataRefRec.dataRefType = EndianU32_NtoB(kMRM_DataRefTypeAlias);
    myDataRefRec.dataRefSize = EndianU32_NtoB(GetHandleSize((Handle)myAlias));

    // allocate a data block and copy the data reference record and alias record into it
    myData = NewPtrClear(sizeof(ReferenceMovieDataRefRecord)
             + GetHandleSize((Handle)myAlias) - 1);
    if (myData == NULL)
      goto bailLoop;
```

```
  HLock((Handle)myAlias);
  BlockMove(&myDataRefRec, myData,
    sizeof(ReferenceMovieDataRefRecord) - sizeof(char) - 1);
  BlockMove(*myAlias, (Ptr)(myData + sizeof(ReferenceMovieDataRefRecord)
    - sizeof(char) - 1), GetHandleSize((Handle)myAlias));
  HUnlock((Handle)myAlias);
  break;

case kMRM_URLPaneType:
  myDataRefRec.flags = EndianU32_NtoB(0L);
  myDataRefRec.dataRefType = EndianU32_NtoB(kMRM_DataRefTypeURL);
  myDataRefRec.dataRefSize = EndianU32_NtoB(strlen((**myAppData).fURL) + 1);

  // allocate a data block and copy the data reference record and URL into it
  myData = NewPtrClear(sizeof(ReferenceMovieDataRefRecord)
            + strlen((**myAppData).fURL) - 1);

  if (myData == NULL)
    goto bailLoop;

  BlockMove(&myDataRefRec, myData, sizeof(ReferenceMovieDataRefRecord) -
    sizeof(char) - 1);
  BlockMove((**myAppData).fURL, (Ptr)(myData + sizeof(ReferenceMovieDataRefRecord)
    - sizeof(char) - 1), strlen((**myAppData).fURL) + 1);

  break;
}
```

Keep in mind that the ReferenceMovieDataRefRecord structure contains as its final field a single character, which is a placeholder for the actual data reference; this means that we generally need to subtract sizeof(char) from sizeof(ReferenceMovieDataRefRecord) to get the "real" size of the record.

Specifying Selection Criteria

A reference movie descriptor atom can contain one or more atoms that indicate the selection criteria for the movie specified in the data reference atom. To indicate that that movie should be selected based on the user's Internet connection speed, we add a *data rate atom*, of type ReferenceMovieData-RateAID. The atom data for the data rate atom is an *alternate data rate record*, which has this structure:

```
struct QTAltDataRateRecord {
    long                    flags;
    long                    dataRate;
};
```

The flags field is currently always 0, and the dataRate field should contain one of these constants:

```
enum {
    kDataRate144ModemRate               = 1400L,
    kDataRate288ModemRate               = 2800L,
    kDataRateISDNRate                   = 5600L,
    kDataRateDualISDNRate               = 11200L,
    kDataRate256kbpsRate                = 25600L,
    kDataRate384kbpsRate                = 38400L,
    kDataRate512kbpsRate                = 51200L,
    kDataRate768kbpsRate                = 76800L,
    kDataRate1MbpsRate                  = 100000L,
    kDataRateT1Rate                     = 150000L,
    kDataRateInfiniteRate               = 0x7FFFFFFF
};
```

Figure 11.10 shows the atom data of a reference movie descriptor atom for a movie that is appropriate for downloading across a connection whose speed is 56 K/sec.

When an alternate reference movie file is opened, QuickTime looks for a reference movie descriptor atom whose data rate atom matches the connection speed specified in the Connection Speed pane of the QuickTime control panel. If no data rate atom exactly matches that speed preference, then the movie with the highest data rate that is less than that preference will be selected. Further, if no data rate atom specifies a data rate that is less than the user's preference, then the alternate movie with the lowest data rate will be selected.

To indicate that an alternate movie should be selected based on the operating system's language, we add a *language atom* (of type ReferenceMovie-LanguageAID) to the reference movie descriptor atom. The atom data for the language atom is an *alternate language record*, which has this structure:

Figure 11.10 A connection speed reference movie descriptor atom.

```
struct QTAltLanguageRecord {
    long                flags;
    short               language;
};
```

The flags field is once again always 0, and the language field should contain a language code. Listing 11.10 shows a chunk of code that creates a language atom.

Listing 11.10 Adding a language atom.

```
if ((**myAppData).fCurrLangIndex > 0) {
  QTAltLanguageRecord        myLanguageRec;
  long                       myAtomHeader[2];

  myLanguageRec.flags = 0L;
  myLanguageRec.language = EndianS16_NtoB((**myAppData).fCurrLang);

  // concatenate the header for the language atom
  myAtomHeader[0] = EndianU32_NtoB(sizeof(myLanguageRec) + myAtomHeaderSize);
  myAtomHeader[1] = EndianU32_NtoB(ReferenceMovieLanguageAID);
  myErr = PtrAndHand(myAtomHeader, myRefMovieDescAtom, myAtomHeaderSize);
  if (myErr != noErr)
    goto bail;

  // concatenate the language data onto the end of the reference movie descriptor atom
  myErr = PtrAndHand(&myLanguageRec, myRefMovieDescAtom, sizeof(myLanguageRec));
  if (myErr != noErr)
    goto bail;
}
```

To indicate that an alternate movie should be selected based on the movie quality, we can add an atom of type ReferenceMovieQualityAID to the reference movie descriptor atom. In this case, the atom data is simply a signed long integer as shown in Figure 11.11. If two alternate movies meet all other listed selection criteria, then QuickTime uses the quality atom to break the tie; the alternate movie with the higher specified quality is selected.

Figure 11.11 A quality reference movie descriptor atom.

Adding a Contained Movie

It's relatively straightforward to build an alternate reference movie file if there is no contained movie; as we've seen, we simply need to add the appropriate atoms to the movie file (and we've had plenty of practice doing that by now). Things get a bit more complicated when we want to build an alternate reference movie file that holds a contained movie, since we need to merge the contained movie with the alternate movie data to obtain the file shown in Figure 11.9. This actually isn't all that complicated, thanks to the fact that the FlattenMovieData function will happily append the flattened data to an existing movie file if we tell it to do so. Let's see how to exploit that capability to create an alternate reference movie file with a contained movie.

Suppose we have created an alternate reference movie atom structure in memory, which has the structure shown in Figure 11.8. Suppose also that we have opened the movie that is to be flattened into the alternate reference movie file. We'll begin by creating a file that is the size of the reference movie record atom that's contained in the existing alternate reference movie atom:

```
myErr = FSpCreate(&gRefMovieSpec, FOUR_CHAR_CODE('TVOD'), MovieFileType, 0);
myErr = FSpOpenDF(&gRefMovieSpec, fsRdWrPerm, &myRefNum);
myMovAtomSize = GetHandleSize(theMovieAtom);
myRefAtomSize = myMovAtomSize - myAtomHeaderSize;
*(long *)myData = EndianU32_NtoB(myRefAtomSize);
*(long *)(myData + sizeof(long)) = EndianU32_NtoB(FreeAtomType);

SetFPos(myRefNum, fsFromStart, 0);
FSWrite(myRefNum, &myCount, myData);
```

As you can see, this new file contains all zeros, except for the 8-byte atom header; the atom type is set to FreeAtomType (that is, 'free'). Figure 11.12 shows the new file at this point.

Now we'll call FlattenMovieData to append the data for the contained movie onto the end of this file:

Figure 11.12 Step 1: Space for the reference movie record atom.

```
myMovie = FlattenMovieData(theMovie,
        flattenAddMovieToDataFork |
        flattenForceMovieResourceBeforeMovieData,
        &gRefMovieSpec,
        FOUR_CHAR_CODE('TVOD'),
        smSystemScript,
        0L);
```

Notice that we pass the flag flattenAddMovieToDataFork to append the data to the existing file and flattenForceMovieResourceBeforeMovieData to ensure that the movie atom is written out at the beginning of the appended data. At this point, the file has the structure shown in Figure 11.13. We reopen the file and read the size of the 'moov' atom:

```
myErr = FSpOpenDF(&gRefMovieSpec, fsRdWrPerm, &myRefNum);

SetFPos(myRefNum, fsFromStart, myRefAtomSize);
myCount = 8;
myErr = FSRead(myRefNum, &myCount, &(myAtom[0]));
myAtom[0] = EndianU32_BtoN(myAtom[0]);
```

Now we know what the size of the entire movie file should be, and we allocate a block of memory large enough to hold the file data:

```
myData = NewPtrClear(myRefAtomSize + myAtom[0]);
```

We write a 'moov' atom header into this new block of data:

```
*(long *)myData = EndianU32_NtoB(myRefAtomSize + myAtom[0]);
*(long *)(myData + sizeof(long)) = EndianU32_NtoB(MovieAID);
```

Then we copy the reference movie record atom into place:

```
BlockMoveData(*theMovieAtom + myAtomHeaderSize, myData + myAtomHeaderSize,
    myRefAtomSize);
```

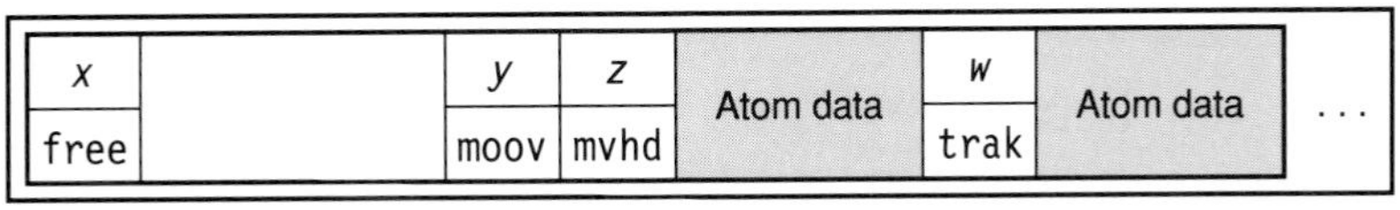

Figure 11.13 Step 2: The flattened data of the contained movie.

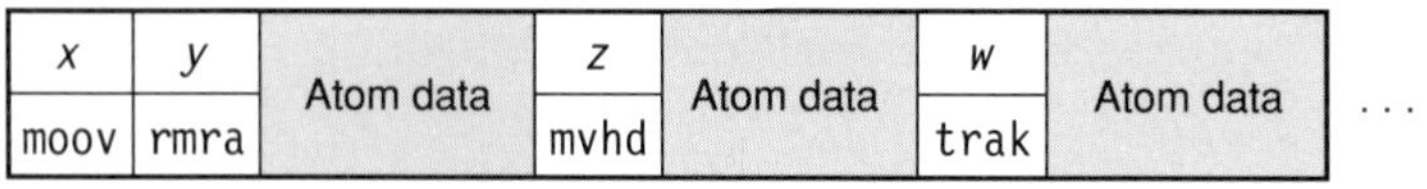

Figure 11.14 Step 3: The movie data in memory.

And then we read the flattened movie data out of our existing movie file into the appropriate spot in our block of data:

```
myCount = myAtom[0] - myAtomHeaderSize;
myErr = FSRead(myRefNum, &myCount, myData + myAtomHeaderSize +
        myRefAtomSize);
```

We're almost done; the block of memory now looks like Figure 11.14. All we need to do now is write this block of data back into the movie file, over-writing its existing data.

```
myCount = myRefAtomSize + myAtom[0];

SetFPos(myRefNum, fsFromStart, 0);
myErr = FSWrite(myRefNum, &myCount, myData);
```

And we're done! The complete definition of MRM_MakeReferenceMovie is shown in Listing 11.11.

Listing 11.11 Adding a contained movie to an alternate reference movie.

```
void MRM_MakeReferenceMovie (Movie theMovie, Handle theMovieAtom)
{
  Movie          myMovie = NULL;
  short          myRefNum = -1;
  long           myAtom[2];
  Ptr            myData = NULL;
  long           myCount;                 // the number of bytes to read or write
  long           myMovAtomSize;           // size of the entire movie atom
  long           myRefAtomSize;           // size of the reference movie atom
  unsigned long  myAtomHeaderSize = 2 * sizeof(long);
  OSErr          myErr = noErr;

  // create and open the output file
  myErr = FSpCreate(&gRefMovieSpec, FOUR_CHAR_CODE('TVOD'), MovieFileType, 0);
  if (myErr != noErr) {
    // if the file already exists, we want to delete it and re-create it
    if (myErr == dupFNErr) {
      myErr = FSpDelete(&gRefMovieSpec);
```

```
      if (myErr == noErr)
        myErr = FSpCreate(&gRefMovieSpec, FOUR_CHAR_CODE('TVOD'), MovieFileType, 0);
   }

   if (myErr != noErr)
     goto bail;
}

myErr = FSpOpenDF(&gRefMovieSpec, fsRdWrPerm, &myRefNum);
if (myErr != noErr)
  goto bail;

myMovAtomSize = GetHandleSize(theMovieAtom);
myRefAtomSize = myMovAtomSize - myAtomHeaderSize;

HLock(theMovieAtom);

// if there is no contained movie to flatten into the output file,
// we can skip most of this code and just go ahead and write the data
if (theMovie == NULL) {
  myData = *theMovieAtom;
  myCount = myMovAtomSize;
  goto writeData;
}

// write a free atom at the start of the file so that FlattenMovieData adds the new
// movie resource and media data far enough into the file to allow room for the
// reference movie atom
myCount = myRefAtomSize;
myData = NewPtrClear(myRefAtomSize);
if (myData == NULL) {
  myErr = MemError();
  goto bail;
}

*(long *)myData = EndianU32_NtoB(myRefAtomSize);
*(long *)(myData + sizeof(long)) = EndianU32_NtoB(FreeAtomType);

SetFPos(myRefNum, fsFromStart, 0);
FSWrite(myRefNum, &myCount, myData);

DisposePtr(myData);
myData = NULL;

// close the file, so that FlattenMovieData can open it
FSClose(myRefNum);
myRefNum = -1;
```

```
// flatten the contained movie into the output file;
// because the output file already exists and because we're not deleting it,
// the flattened movie data is *appended* to the existing data
myMovie = FlattenMovieData(theMovie,
            flattenAddMovieToDataFork |
            flattenForceMovieResourceBeforeMovieData,
            &gRefMovieSpec,
            FOUR_CHAR_CODE('TVOD'),
            smSystemScript,
            0L);
myErr = GetMoviesError();
if (myErr != noErr)
    goto bail;

// open the output file again and read the movie atom
myErr = FSpOpenDF(&gRefMovieSpec, fsRdWrPerm, &myRefNum);
if (myErr != noErr)
  goto bail;

SetFPos(myRefNum, fsFromStart, myRefAtomSize);
// should put us at the 'moov' atom
myCount = 8;
myErr = FSRead(myRefNum, &myCount, &(myAtom[0]));
if (myErr != noErr)
  goto bail;

// swap the size and type data so that we can use it here
myAtom[0] = EndianU32_BtoN(myAtom[0]);
myAtom[1] = EndianU32_BtoN(myAtom[1]);

if (myAtom[1] != MovieAID) {     // this should never happen
  myErr = paramErr;
  goto bail;
}

myData = NewPtrClear(myRefAtomSize + myAtom[0]);
if (myData == NULL) {
  myErr = MemError();
  goto bail;
}

// merge the movie atom that FlattenMovieData created with the reference movie atom
*(long *)myData = EndianU32_NtoB(myRefAtomSize + myAtom[0]);
*(long *)(myData + sizeof(long)) = EndianU32_NtoB(MovieAID);
```

```
    // insert the reference movie atom
    BlockMoveData(*theMovieAtom + myAtomHeaderSize, myData + myAtomHeaderSize,
       myRefAtomSize);

    // read original movie atom
    myCount = myAtom[0] - myAtomHeaderSize;
    myErr = FSRead(myRefNum, &myCount, myData + myAtomHeaderSize + myRefAtomSize);
    if (myErr != noErr)
        goto bail;

    myCount = myRefAtomSize + myAtom[0];

writeData:
    // write the final movie to disk
    SetFPos(myRefNum, fsFromStart, 0);
    myErr = FSWrite(myRefNum, &myCount, myData);

bail:
    if (myData != NULL)
      DisposePtr(myData);

    if (myRefNum != -1)
      FSClose(myRefNum);

    if (myMovie != NULL)
      DisposeMovie(myMovie);

    HUnlock(theMovieAtom);
}
```

▶ Conclusion

Alternate track groups provide a simple but effective way to tailor a Quick-Time movie for playback in different languages and on computers with different sound and video hardware. They do, however, have their limitations. For one thing, adding lots of alternate tracks can increase the size of the movie file to the point that it's too bulky for easy Web deployment. More important, alternate tracks can be selected based only on the quality or language of the track. For these reasons, it's generally more useful to use alternate reference movies to select one from a set of alternate movies.

12

A Bug's Life
Retrieving Errors in QuickTime Applications

▶ Introduction

Termites happen. So do errors in QuickTime-savvy applications—often for reasons other than mere sloppy programming. Network connections can fail in the middle of downloading a movie file or other data. System resources (memory, disk space, and so forth) can get depleted while an application runs. Components necessary for the playback of some media data might not be available on a particular machine. In short, lots of unpredictable occurrences can lead to the failure of QuickTime functions. How you deal with those failures is up to you. You might throw an exception, which (hopefully) is caught by an exception handler. Or you might just return an error code to your caller and expect it to handle the error gracefully. This is all part of the theory and practice of error handling, which is often the subject of heated debates among programmers. But before you even begin to *handle* an error, you first need to discover that it has occurred in the first place. That's the subject of this chapter: how to determine that a QuickTime function has failed to do what you wanted it to do.

At first glance, this might seem like a fairly trivial topic. After all, many QuickTime functions return a result code that indicates the success or failure of the operation. But, in fact, things are not always that simple. For starters, not all QuickTime functions return a result code directly to the caller. Many of them, particularly Movie Toolbox calls, return a result code only indirectly, and we need to do a little work to retrieve that result code. We'll begin this chapter by looking at how to do that. Also, it's easy to misinterpret some of these result codes, so we'll investigate one or two of the pitfalls lurking here. Toward the end of the chapter, we'll take a look at a bug in our sample applications that I inadvertently added a few chapters ago.

▶ Error-Reporting Functions

A large number of QuickTime functions return a result code directly to the caller as their function result. For instance, the EnterMovies function is declared pretty much like this:

```
OSErr EnterMovies (void);
```

If a call to EnterMovies fails, QuickTime tells us so by returning a nonzero result code. The main reason that EnterMovies can fail is insufficient memory available for QuickTime to do the necessary initialization, so the result code is very likely to be memFullErr. No matter what the error here, however, our sample applications all quit almost immediately after they get one, first informing the user of the error. Listing 12.1 shows a portion of our application start-up code on the Macintosh.

Listing 12.1 Initializing the Movie Toolbox (Macintosh).

```
myErr = EnterMovies();
if (myErr != noErr) {
  QTFrame_ShowWarning("\pCould not initialize QuickTime. Exiting.", myErr);
  ExitToShell();
}
```

Listing 12.2 shows the corresponding code in our Windows applications.

Listing 12.2 Initializing the Movie Toolbox (Windows).

```
myErr = EnterMovies();
if (myErr != noErr) {
  MessageBox(NULL, "Could not initialize QuickTime. Exiting.", gAppName,
    MB_OK | MB_APPLMODAL);
  return(0);
}
```

But a significant number of QuickTime functions do not return a result. A good example is StartMovie, which is declared like this:

```
void StartMovie (Movie theMovie);
```

As you can see, StartMovie returns no function result at all. Some other functions do return function results but they are not of type OSErr. An example here is GetMovieActive, which returns a result of type Boolean:

```
Boolean GetMovieActive (Movie theMovie);
```

To handle cases like these, QuickTime provides a set of error-reporting functions. Let's see how they work.

Getting the Current Error

We can use the Movie Toolbox function GetMoviesError to retrieve the *current error value* (or *current error*), which is the result code of the most recently executed QuickTime function. GetMoviesError is declared like this:

```
OSErr GetMoviesError (void);
```

We can use GetMoviesError to get the result code for those functions that do not return a result code as their function result. (GetMoviesError also returns the result code for functions that *do* return an OSErr, but it's redundant in those cases.) Here's a typical use of GetMoviesError:

```
myTrack = NewMovieTrack(myMovie, myWidth, myHeight, 0);
myErr = GetMoviesError();
if (myErr != noErr)
  goto bail;
```

We could just as easily have checked to see whether myTrack is equal to NULL after the call to NewMovieTrack, but calling GetMoviesError gives us a result code that we can return to our caller, if so desired.

It's worth noting that GetMoviesError (and GetMoviesStickyError, which we'll consider in a moment) are global to an application and are not thread-specific. This means that an error that occurs in one thread can be reported to another thread. (Just something to keep in mind if you are writing multi-threaded applications.)

Getting the Sticky Error

QuickTime also maintains an error value called the *sticky error value* (or *sticky error*), which is the first nonzero result code of a Movie Toolbox function that was generated since the last time the sticky error was cleared. We retrieve the sticky error value by calling GetMoviesStickyError, and we clear the sticky error by calling ClearMoviesStickyError. Here are the function prototypes:

```
OSErr GetMoviesStickyError (void);
void ClearMoviesStickyError (void);
```

When our application first starts up, the sticky error is 0. If all our Movie Toolbox function calls succeed, the sticky error remains set to 0. But as soon as any Movie Toolbox function encounters an error, the appropriate error value is copied into the sticky error value. We can call GetMoviesStickyError at any time to retrieve the sticky error value. This value does not change, even if subsequent Movie Toolbox calls fail, until we explicitly reset it to 0 by calling ClearMoviesStickyError.

The sticky error value is useful when we want to execute a series of Movie Toolbox functions but don't particularly want to check for errors after each Movie Toolbox call. Listing 12.3 shows a situation in which GetMoviesStickyError might be used. The function VRObject_ImportVideoTrack copies a video track from one movie (the source) into a second movie (the destination).

Listing 12.3 Importing a video track from one movie into another.

```
OSErr VRObject_ImportVideoTrack (Movie theSrcMovie, Movie theDstMovie,
        Track *theImageTrack)
{
    Track        mySrcTrack = NULL;
    Media        mySrcMedia = NULL;
    Track        myDstTrack = NULL;
    Media        myDstMedia = NULL;
    Fixed        myWidth, myHeight;
    OSType       myType;
    OSErr        myErr = noErr;

    ClearMoviesStickyError();

    // get the first video track in the source movie
    mySrcTrack = GetMovieIndTrackType(theSrcMovie, 1, VideoMediaType, movieTrackMediaType);
    if (mySrcTrack == NULL)
      return(paramErr);

    // get the track's media and dimensions
    mySrcMedia = GetTrackMedia(mySrcTrack);
    GetTrackDimensions(mySrcTrack, &myWidth, &myHeight);

    // create a destination track
    myDstTrack = NewMovieTrack(theDstMovie, myWidth, myHeight, GetTrackVolume(mySrcTrack));
```

```
// create a destination media
GetMediaHandlerDescription(mySrcMedia, &myType, 0, 0);
myDstMedia = NewTrackMedia(myDstTrack, myType, GetMediaTimeScale(mySrcMedia), 0, 0);

// copy the entire track
InsertTrackSegment(mySrcTrack, myDstTrack, 0, GetTrackDuration(mySrcTrack), 0);
CopyTrackSettings(mySrcTrack, myDstTrack);
SetTrackLayer(myDstTrack, GetTrackLayer(mySrcTrack));

// an object video track should always be enabled
SetTrackEnabled(myDstTrack, true);

if (theImageTrack != NULL)
  *theImageTrack = myDstTrack;

return(GetMoviesStickyError());
}
```

As you can see, we call ClearMoviesStickyError at the beginning of this function and then return to our caller the value returned by GetMovies-StickyError. The idea here is that our caller will care only about the first error we encounter while executing this function, which will of course be the sticky error (since we cleared the sticky error at the beginning).

Another case where we may want to access the sticky error is when we know or suspect that a call to a QuickTime function will report an error, but we don't really care about that error. Listing 12.4 defines a function, QTUtils_GetFrameCount, which returns the number of frames in a specified track. We use GetTrackNextInterestingTime to step through the track's samples.

Listing 12.4 Counting the frames in a track.

```
long QTUtils_GetFrameCount (Track theTrack)
{
  long          myCount = -1;
  short         myFlags;
  TimeValue     myTime = 0;
  OSErr         myErr = noErr;

  if (theTrack == NULL)
    goto bail;

  myErr = GetMoviesStickyError();

  // we want to begin with the first frame (sample) in the track
  myFlags = nextTimeMediaSample + nextTimeEdgeOK;
```

```
  while (myTime >= 0) {
    myCount++;

    // look for the next frame in the track; when there are no more frames,
    // myTime is set to -1, so we'll exit the while loop
    GetTrackNextInterestingTime(theTrack, myFlags, myTime, fixed1, &myTime, NULL);

    // after the first interesting time, don't include the time we're currently at
    myFlags = nextTimeStep;
  }

  if (myErr == noErr)
    ClearMoviesStickyError();

bail:
  return(myCount);
}
```

GetTrackNextInterestingTime returns, in the sixth parameter, the first time value it finds that satisfies the search criteria specified in the flags parameter. When it cannot find a time value that satisfies those criteria, it sets that parameter to –1. For all we know, it's possible that GetTrackNextInterestingTime also sets an error value; if so, we want to clear that value by calling ClearMoviesStickyError (but only if the sticky error on entry to our function was noErr).

▶ Error Notification Functions

QuickTime provides the SetMoviesErrorProc function, which we can use to install an *error notification function* (or, more briefly, *error function*). An error notification function is called whenever QuickTime encounters a nonzero result code during the execution of a Movie Toolbox function. SetMoviesErrorProc is declared like this:

```
void SetMoviesErrorProc (MoviesErrorUPP errProc, long refcon);
```

The first parameter is a universal procedure pointer to our custom error notification function; the second parameter is a 4-byte reference constant that is passed to our error function when it is called. The error notification function is declared like this:

```
void MyMoviesErrorProc (OSErr theErr, long theRefcon);
```

The first parameter is the nonzero result code that was just encountered, and the second parameter is the reference constant we specified when we called SetMoviesErrorProc.

An error notification function is useful during application development or debugging, as it provides a single location where all errors are reported. This keeps us from having to put breakpoints all through our code as we track down problems.

Mysterious Errors

While we're on the topic of retrieving errors in QuickTime-savvy applications, it's worth discussing an issue that trips people up occasionally. This is the issue of mysterious QuickTime errors like –32766, which can occur when we execute some code like this:

```
OSErr        myErr = GraphicsExportSetDepth(myComponent, 32);
```

When this code is executed, then for certain graphics exporters, myErr is set to –32766. If we look in the file MacErrors.h, we won't find any such error. What's going on?

The explanation is surprisingly straightforward: GraphicsExportSetDepth and many other QuickTime functions that work with components return a function result of type ComponentResult, which is declared like this:

```
typedef long              ComponentResult;
```

On the other hand, the OSErr data type is declared like this:

```
typedef SInt16            OSErr;
```

When we try to fit a ComponentResult into an OSErr, we get only the low-order 16 bits, interpreted as a signed value. When the ComponentResult is noErr, this truncation is unproblematic. But several component errors use the full 32 bits of the long word, in which case the truncation will give us the mysterious errors described. In particular, if a component does not support a particular action, then it will return the value badComponentSelector, which is defined as 0x80008002. Truncating 0x80008002 to a 16-bit signed quantity gives us –32766. That's what's happening with the call to Graphics-ExportSetDepth that we just considered: the particular component specified by the myComponent parameter does not support setting the export bit depth, in which case it returns badComponentSelector.

The lesson here is simple: pay attention to the data type of a function's return value and make sure you have enough space to hold that value. More specifically: don't use a variable of type OSErr to hold the return value of a component-related function whose return value is of type ComponentResult. But don't feel bad if you slip up occasionally. It happens to the best of us. Indeed, this mix-up is so common that the file MacErrors.h contains some helpful comments:

```
/* ComponentError codes*/
enum {
  badComponentInstance = (long)0x80008001,/* when cast to an OSErr this
                                           is -32767*/
  badComponentSelector = (long)0x80008002 /* when cast to an OSErr this
                                           is -32766*/
};
```

▶ A Framework Bug

Let's close this chapter by squashing a particularly nasty bug that I introduced into our sample applications a few chapters back, when we updated our Macintosh code to use Carbon events instead of "classic" events. (See Chapter 9, "Event Horizon.") Recall that we added a Carbon event loop timer to each open movie window, so that we can periodically task the movie controller (by calling MCIsPlayerEvent or MCIdle). Unfortunately, our existing application can crash—at least on Mac OS 9—if we do something as simple as open a movie window and then later close it. That's not good.

Fixing the Bug

The problematic code turns out to be in the Macintosh version of the QTFrame_CreateMovieWindow function, shown in Listing 12.5. Here we create a new window and window object. Then we attach standard and custom Carbon event handlers to the window. Finally, we call InstallEventLoopTimer to attach a timer to the window.

Listing 12.5 Creating a movie window.

```
WindowReference QTFrame_CreateMovieWindow (void)
{
  WindowReference            myWindow = NULL;

  // create a new window to display the movie in
  myWindow = NewCWindow(NULL, &gWindowRect, gWindowTitle, false, noGrowDocProc,
            (WindowPtr)-1L, true, 0);
```

```
  // create a new window object associated with the new window
  QTFrame_CreateWindowObject(myWindow);

#if USE_CARBON_EVENTS
{
  EventTypeSpec       myEventSpec[] = {
    {kEventClassKeyboard, kEventRawKeyDown},
    {kEventClassKeyboard, kEventRawKeyRepeat},
    {kEventClassKeyboard, kEventRawKeyUp},
    {kEventClassWindow, kEventWindowUpdate},
    {kEventClassWindow, kEventWindowDrawContent},
    {kEventClassWindow, kEventWindowActivated},
    {kEventClassWindow, kEventWindowDeactivated},
    {kEventClassWindow, kEventWindowHandleContentClick},
    {kEventClassWindow, kEventWindowClose}
  };

  // install Carbon event handlers for this window
  InstallStandardEventHandler(GetWindowEventTarget(myWindow));
  if (gWinEventHandlerUPP != NULL)
    InstallEventHandler(GetWindowEventTarget(myWindow), gWinEventHandlerUPP,
      GetEventTypeCount(myEventSpec), myEventSpec,
      QTFrame_GetWindowObjectFromWindow(myWindow), NULL);
}
  if (gWinTimerHandlerUPP != NULL)
    InstallEventLoopTimer(GetMainEventLoop(), 0, TicksToEventTime(kWNEMinimumSleep),
      gWinTimerHandlerUPP, myWindowObject, &(**myWindowObject).fTimerRef);
#endif

  return(myWindow);
}
```

It turns out that InstallEventLoopTimer can move memory, which might invalidate its last parameter, &(**myWindowObject).fTimerRef. If the window object indeed moves, then InstallEventLoopTimer will write the timer reference into the previous location of the window object. That's bad enough, but it gets worse when you realize that the window object, in its new memory location, now won't contain the timer reference returned by Install-EventLoopTimer. Rather, (**myWindowObject).fTimerRef will still be NULL. The event loop timer indeed gets installed, but we don't have a reference to it.

This in itself isn't a problem until we try to remove the event loop timer when the window is closed. Here's the code we use to do that:

```
if ((**myWindowObject).fTimerRef != NULL)
  RemoveEventLoopTimer((**myWindowObject).fTimerRef);
```

Since (**myWindowObject).fTimerRef is indeed NULL, RemoveEventLoopTimer isn't called, and the timer continues firing even after the movie window has disappeared. Listing 12.6 shows our event loop timer callback function.

Listing 12.6 Handling event loop timer callbacks.

```
PASCAL_RTN void QTFrame_CarbonEventWindowTimer
              (EventLoopTimerRef theTimer, void *theRefCon)
{
#pragma unused(theTimer)
  WindowObject    myWindowObject = (WindowObject)theRefCon;

  // just pretend a null event has been received...
  if ((myWindowObject != NULL) && ((**myWindowObject).fController != NULL))
    if (!gMenuIsTracking || gRunningUnderX)
      MCIdle((**myWindowObject).fController);
}
```

If the window object has been disposed of, then reading any of its fields (in this case, fController) will likely result in a segmentation fault or other error.

This is a classic case of using a *dangling pointer*, the address of a block of memory whose contents have moved. You can get the full details on this type of problem in the book *Inside Macintosh: Memory,* 2nd ed. (Apple Computer, Inc. 1992), which I am presently chagrined to admit I myself wrote a decade ago. There are several solutions to this type of problem. A standard solution is to lock the window object before calling InstallEventLoopTimer and then unlock it afterwards:

```
HLock((Handle)myWindowObject);
if (gWinTimerHandlerUPP != NULL)
  InstallEventLoopTimer(GetMainEventLoop(), 0,
    TicksToEventTime(kWNEMinimumSleep),
    gWinTimerHandlerUPP, myWindowObject, &(**myWindowObject).fTimerRef);
HUnlock((Handle)myWindowObject);
```

Or, even more simply, we can just use a temporary variable to hold the timer reference:

```
EventLoopTimerRef      myTimerRef;

if (gWinTimerHandlerUPP != NULL)
  InstallEventLoopTimer(GetMainEventLoop(), 0,
    TicksToEventTime(kWNEMinimumSleep),
    gWinTimerHandlerUPP, myWindowObject, &myTimerRef);
(**myWindowObject).fTimerRef = myTimerRef;
```

Adding Some More Protections

Let's take this opportunity to tinker with the Carbon event loop timer callback function QTFrame_CarbonEventWindowTimer (see Listing 12.6). First of all, we should add a check at the top of the function to make sure we got a non-NULL window object:

```
if (myWindowObject == NULL)
  return;
```

And, we should make sure that we are passed the same timer reference we are storing in the window object:

```
if ((**myWindowObject).fTimerRef != theTimer)
  return;
```

More important, I want to change the call to MCIdle into a call to MCIs-PlayerEvent. We can achieve this end by building a null event and passing it to our framework function QTFrame_HandleEvent as shown in Listing 12.7.

Listing 12.7 Handling event loop timer callbacks (revised).

```
PASCAL_RTN void QTFrame_CarbonEventWindowTimer
        (EventLoopTimerRef theTimer, void *theRefCon)
{
  WindowObject           myWindowObject = (WindowObject)theRefCon;

  if (myWindowObject == NULL)
    return;

  // sanity check: make sure it's our timer
  if ((**myWindowObject).fTimerRef != theTimer)
    return;
```

```
  // just issue a null event to our event-handling routine...
  if (!gMenuIsTracking || gRunningUnderX) {
    EventRecord               myEvent;

    myEvent.what = nullEvent;
    myEvent.message = 0;
    myEvent.modifiers = 0;
    myEvent.when = EventTimeToTicks(GetCurrentEventTime());
    QTFrame_HandleEvent(&myEvent);
  }
}
```

I prefer this revised approach to tasking our movie controllers because it
routes null events through our existing event-handling routine QTFrame_
HandleEvent. This, in turn, will make it easier to modify our code to handle
movies that need to be tasked but that don't yet have a movie controller
attached to them. In the next chapter, we'll see how this can happen.

▶ Conclusion

Of the four new QuickTime functions we've encountered in this chapter
(GetMoviesError, GetMoviesStickyError, ClearMoviesStickyError, and SetMovies-
ErrorProc), we're most likely to need to use GetMoviesError in our daily programming, as it provides our only means of retrieving the result codes for a
large number of QuickTime functions. I generally find the sticky error less
useful, but there are times we might want to take a look at it. The error procedure is, to my knowledge, largely unused. I can, however, imagine that a
clever programmer could find some useful applications for it, so it's good to at
least know it exists.

13

Loaded
Loading Movies Asynchronously

▶ **Introduction**

Typically, we use the `NewMovieFromFile` function to load a QuickTime movie from a file stored locally. In Volume One, when we were investigating data references, we saw how to use the `NewMovieFromDataRef` function to load a movie specified by a URL that picks out a file located on a remote server (see Chapter 9). In all cases, we have called these functions synchronously. This means that we wait until the function completes and returns a movie to us before we continue on to attach a movie controller to the movie, create a window to hold the movie and the movie controller bar, size and position the movie window appropriately, and so forth.

The drawback with opening movies synchronously is that there may be a perceptible lag as QuickTime retrieves the movie data from the specified location, especially if the data is on a remote server and the user has a relatively slow connection to the network. In version 4.1, QuickTime introduced a mechanism for loading movies asynchronously. In this case, the movie-loading functions (`NewMovieFromFile`, `NewMovieFromDataRef`, and their siblings) return almost immediately with a valid movie identifier. This movie, however, might be empty or incomplete, if its data is still being retrieved from a remote location (or a particularly slow local storage device). Before we can actually *do* anything with the newly opened movie, we need to wait until at least the movie atom has become available. We can determine this by continually checking the *movie load state*, an indication of the state of the loading process and hence what operations we can safely perform on the movie. When the movie load state reaches a particular threshold, we can continue on with our standard procedure for displaying the movie in a window on the screen and allowing the user to interact with the movie.

In this chapter, we're going to learn how to load movies asynchronously. We'll see how to modify our calls to the NewMovieFrom... functions and how to check the movie load state as the movie data loads. The end result of this tinkering should be a more responsive application, since the user will no longer have to wait until a movie is sufficiently loaded for our application to continue processing. Instead, the user can work with any movies that are already open, or indeed open still other movies.

We'll also take the opportunity to add a few bells and whistles to our application. In particular, we'll see how to display a progress bar that indicates how much of the movie data has become available, as shown in Figure 13.1. (The bar grows from left to right in proportion to the amount of movie data loaded.) We do this by drawing on top of each movie frame, using a *movie drawing-complete procedure*. Inside this procedure, we call the GetMaxLoadedTimeInMovie function to determine how much of the movie has loaded, and then we scale the progress bar accordingly.

It's also possible for a QuickTime movie to provide its own loading progress bar without any assistance from the playback application. We can accomplish this by adding a wired sprite track or a wired Flash track to the movie. The key element here is the kOperandMaxLoadedTimeInMovie wired operand, which returns the same information as the GetMaxLoadedTimeIn-Movie function. Figure 13.2 shows a QuickTime movie that draws its own loading progress bar; here the loading progress bar is a sprite whose horizontal position changes based on the movie load time.

Figure 13.1 An application movie loading progress bar.

Figure 13.2 A sprite movie loading progress bar.

Test

Open URL...	⌘1
Add Sprite Loader Track	⌘2
Export with QTVR Preview Track...	⌘3

Figure 13.3 The Test menu of QTAsynchLoad.

Our sample application for this chapter is called QTAsynchLoad; it's based on the version of QTShell that uses Carbon events (which we developed in Chapter 9, "Event Horizon"). Figure 13.3 shows the Test menu of QTAsynchLoad. The first menu item prompts the user for a URL and then opens the movie file picked out by that URL. (I borrowed the code for this directly from the QTDataRef application we developed in Volume One, Chapter 9.) This is useful for testing that our new code really does load remote movies asynchronously. The second menu item adds to an existing movie a sprite track that displays the movie loading progress bar shown in Figure 13.2. The third menu item exports a QuickTime VR panorama movie as a Fast Start movie file with a low-resolution image track; this track is loaded first and acts as a kind of preview track for the entire panorama, as we'll see later.

⏵ Asynchronous Movie Loading

Let's begin by reviewing our current movie loading strategy. When a user selects the Open item in the File menu, we present a file-opening dialog box and then pass the selected file to the `OpenMovieFile` function, like this:

```
myErr = OpenMovieFile(&myFSSpec, &myRefNum, fsRdWrPerm);
```

`OpenMovieFile` opens the file with the specified access permissions (here, with read-write access). If it's successful, we then call `NewMovieFromFile` to load the movie in that file:

```
myErr = NewMovieFromFile(&myMovie, myRefNum, &myResID, NULL,
        newMovieActive, NULL);
```

If `NewMovieFromFile` is successful, we then perform these actions:

- Create a window to hold the movie and movie controller bar.
- Create a window object to hold information about the movie and movie window.
- Set the movie graphics world to the new movie window.
- Create a new movie controller for the new movie.
- Resize the window to exactly fit the movie and movie controller bar.
- Set the window position from information stored in the movie user data.
- Make the window visible.
- Start the movie playing, if it's an auto-play movie.

Currently, all this is accomplished inside of our framework function `QTFrame_OpenMovieInWindow`.

Allowing Asynchronous Movie Loading

The important point here is that our call to `NewMovieFromFile` will not return until enough of the movie is available that QuickTime considers the movie to be configurable and playable. We can override this default behavior by including the `newMovieAsyncOK` flag when we call `NewMovieFromFile`, like this:

```
myErr = NewMovieFromFile(&myMovie, myRefNum, &myResID, NULL,
        newMovieActive + newMovieAsyncOK, NULL);
```

The newMovieAsyncOK flag tells NewMovieFromFile that it should create a new movie and return it to the caller as quickly as possible, even if the new movie is empty (that is, contains no tracks, no movie atom, no user data, or the like). In general, for local movie files the new movie is a fully valid movie, complete with tracks and movie user data. That is to say, the movie loading occurs exactly as if the newMovieAsyncOK flag had not been specified. This flag simply grants permission to QuickTime to use asynchronous loading if possible; it does not force the movie to be loaded asynchronously.

Therefore, the more interesting case is when we open a movie stored remotely, which we can do by passing a URL to the QTDR_GetMovieFromURL function we defined in Volume One, Chapter 9. To enable asynchronous movie loading, we once again add the newMovieAsyncOK flag, as shown in Listing 13.1.

Listing 13.1   Opening a movie specified by a URL.

```
Movie QTDR_GetMovieFromURL (char *theURL)
{
  Movie        myMovie = NULL;
  Handle       myDataRef = NULL;
  short        myFlags = newMovieActive;

#if ALLOW_ASYNCH_LOADING
  myFlags += newMovieAsyncOK;
#endif

  myDataRef = QTDR_MakeURLDataRef(theURL);
  if (myDataRef != NULL) {
    NewMovieFromDataRef(&myMovie, myFlags, NULL, myDataRef, URLDataHandlerSubType);
    DisposeHandle(myDataRef);
  }

  return(myMovie);
}
```

You'll notice the ALLOW_ASYNCH_LOADING compiler flag; once again, I'm going to try to rework our source code so that the existing synchronous movie-loading behavior can be re-enabled by changing the value of that flag.

Checking the Movie Load State

Since the movie returned by NewMovieFromDataRef (or its siblings) may be empty, we can't just launch into our standard sequence of calls for creating and configuring a new movie window. Instead, we need to wait until the movie reaches the proper load state. We can get the current load state by calling GetMovieLoadState like this:

```
myLoadState = GetMovieLoadState(myMovie);
```

GetMovieLoadState currently returns one of these values:

```
enum {
  kMovieLoadStateError               = -1L,
  kMovieLoadStateLoading             = 1000,
  kMovieLoadStateLoaded              = 2000,
  kMovieLoadStatePlayable            = 10000,
  kMovieLoadStatePlaythroughOK       = 20000,
  kMovieLoadStateComplete            = 100000L
};
```

If GetMovieLoadState returns kMovieLoadStateError, then an error has occurred during the movie load process. This probably means that a URL could not be successfully resolved, but it could also mean that the indicated file is not a QuickTime movie file (or other file type that can be imported as a QuickTime movie).

If GetMovieLoadState returns kMovieLoadStateLoading, then QuickTime has found the specified file (or data stream) and is searching for the movie atom in it. If GetMovieLoadState returns kMovieLoadStateLoaded, then QuickTime has found the movie atom, but there may not be enough media data available to begin playing the movie. (It's not clear to me that GetMovieLoadState ever actually returns kMovieLoadStateLoaded; I suspect that this state has fallen into disuse.)

When a movie's load state reaches kMovieLoadStatePlayable, the movie atom is available and enough of the media data is available that the movie can be prerolled and started. This is the threshold that is most interesting to us, since we can then look at the movie user data (which is stored in the movie atom) to determine the desired window location of the movie window; we can also make Movie Toolbox calls like GetMovieTrackCount to determine the number of tracks in the movie or GetMovieBox to determine the size of the movie.

GetMovieLoadState returns kMovieLoadStatePlaythroughOK when Quick-Time thinks that it has enough of the media data that the entire movie can be played through to the end without stopping. Finally, GetMovieLoadState returns kMovieLoadStateComplete when all of the movie's media data is available.

Modifying the Application Framework

If we allow a movie to be opened asynchronously, then we need to wait until the movie reaches at least the kMovieLoadStatePlayable load state before we assign a movie controller to it and undertake any other configuration of the movie or movie controller. The first thing we need to do, then, is revise our framework function QTFrame_OpenMovieInWindow. Listing 13.2 shows the relevant portions of our new version of this function. As you can see, we open a new, invisible window, allocate a new window object, and set the movie (or graphics importer) graphics world to the new window. Then, if the user is opening an image file instead of a movie file, we proceed to set up the image window, as we did previously.

Listing 13.2 Opening a movie in a new window.

```
// create a new window in which to display the movie
myWindow = QTFrame_CreateMovieWindow();
if (myWindow == NULL)
  goto bail;

myWindowObject = QTFrame_GetWindowObjectFromWindow(myWindow);
if (myWindowObject == NULL)
  goto bail;

// set the window title
QTFrame_SetWindowTitleFromFSSpec(myWindow, &myFSSpec, true);

// make sure the movie or image file uses the window GWorld
if (myMovie != NULL)
  SetMovieGWorld(myMovie, (CGrafPtr)QTFrame_GetPortFromWindowReference(myWindow), NULL);
if (myImporter != NULL)
  GraphicsImportSetGWorld(myImporter,
    (CGrafPtr)QTFrame_GetPortFromWindowReference(myWindow), NULL);

// store movie information in the window record
(**myWindowObject).fMovie = myMovie;
(**myWindowObject).fController = NULL;
(**myWindowObject).fGraphicsImporter = myImporter;
(**myWindowObject).fFileResID = myResID;
(**myWindowObject).fFileRefNum = myRefNum;
(**myWindowObject).fCanResizeWindow = true;
(**myWindowObject).fIsDirty = false;
(**myWindowObject).fIsQTVRMovie = false;
(**myWindowObject).fInstance = NULL;
```

```
(**myWindowObject).fAppData = NULL;
(**myWindowObject).fFileFSSpec = myFSSpec;

if ((**myWindowObject).fGraphicsImporter != NULL) {
  Point          myPoint = {kDefaultWindowX, kDefaultWindowY};

  // do any application-specific window object initialization
  QTApp_SetupWindowObject(myWindowObject);

  // size the window to fit the image
  QTFrame_SizeWindowToMovie(myWindowObject);

  // show the window
  QTFrame_ShowWindowAtPoint(myWindow, &myPoint);
}
```

Mostly we've just removed our movie-specific processing, which we need to defer until we know the movie is playable. We've also added a call to the QTFrame_ShowWindowAtPoint function, which makes the image or movie window visible. Listing 13.3 shows our definition of QTFrame_ShowWindowAtPoint.

Listing 13.3 Making a window visible.

```
void QTFrame_ShowWindowAtPoint (WindowReference theWindow, Point *thePoint)
{
#if TARGET_OS_MAC
  Rect          myRect;
#endif

  if ((theWindow == NULL) || (thePoint == NULL))
    return;

#if TARGET_OS_MAC
  MoveWindow(theWindow, thePoint->h, thePoint->v, false);
  MacShowWindow(theWindow);
  SelectWindow(theWindow);
  InvalWindowRect(theWindow, GetWindowPortBounds(theWindow, &myRect));
#endif
#if TARGET_OS_WIN32
  SetWindowPos(theWindow, 0, thePoint->h, thePoint->v, 0, 0, SWP_NOZORDER | SWP_NOSIZE);
  ShowWindow(theWindow, SW_SHOW);
  UpdateWindow(theWindow);
#endif
}
```

At this point, we need to decide where in our application code we want to call GetMovieLoadState. On Macintosh operating systems, our applications call QTFrame_CheckMovieControllers to give each open movie controller a chance to handle an event. This is also a good place to check the current load state of a movie and to respond to any changes in the movie load state. Listing 13.4 shows our current version of QTFrame_CheckMovieControllers.

Listing 13.4 Checking the movie controllers (original).

```
static Boolean QTFrame_CheckMovieControllers (EventRecord *theEvent)
{
  WindowPtr              myWindow = NULL;
  MovieController        myMC = NULL;

  myWindow = QTFrame_GetFrontMovieWindow();
  while (myWindow != NULL) {
    myMC = QTFrame_GetMCFromWindow(myWindow);
    if (myMC != NULL)
      if (MCIsPlayerEvent(myMC, theEvent))
        return(true);

    myWindow = QTFrame_GetNextMovieWindow(myWindow);
  }

  return(false);
}
```

Listing 13.5 shows our revised version of QTFrame_CheckMovieControllers. We've added a call to QTFrame_CheckMovieLoadState, and we've revised the looping so that QTFrame_CheckMovieLoadState can safely destroy the movie window if it determines that an error has occurred in the movie loading (that is, if GetMovieLoadState returns kMovieLoadStateError).

Listing 13.5 Checking the movie controllers (revised).

```
static Boolean QTFrame_CheckMovieControllers (EventRecord *theEvent)
{
  WindowPtr              myWindow = NULL;
  MovieController        myMC = NULL;

  myWindow = QTFrame_GetFrontMovieWindow();
  while (myWindow != NULL) {
    WindowPtr              myNextWindow = QTFrame_GetNextMovieWindow(myWindow);
```

```
QTFrame_CheckMovieLoadState(QTFrame_GetWindowObjectFromWindow(myWindow));
myMC = QTFrame_GetMCFromWindow(myWindow);
if (myMC != NULL)
  if (MCIsPlayerEvent(myMC, theEvent))
    return(true);

  myWindow = myNextWindow;
}

return(false);
}
```

On Windows operating systems, messages are sent directly to the window procedure of a movie window, where we translate the message into a Mac-style event. Here we'll call QTFrame_CheckMovieLoadState from within QTFrame_MovieWndProc, as shown in Listing 13.6.

Listing 13.6 Checking the movie controller (Windows).

```
// translate a Windows event to a Mac event
WinEventToMacEvent(&myMsg, &myMacEvent);

// let the application-specific code have a chance to intercept the event
myIsHandled = QTApp_HandleEvent(&myMacEvent);

if (myWindowObject != NULL) {
  QTFrame_CheckMovieLoadState(myWindowObject);
  if (myWindowObject == NULL)
    return(0);
  myMC = (**myWindowObject).fController;            // refresh our local variable
}

// pass the Mac event to the movie controller
if (!myIsHandled)
  if (myMC != NULL)
    if (!IsIconic(theWnd))
      myIsHandled = MCIsPlayerEvent(myMC, (EventRecord *)&myMacEvent);
```

As you can see, we call QTFrame_CheckMovieLoadState and then immediately check to see whether the window object has been destroyed. Again, this is to protect ourselves in case an error occurs when attempting to load the movie. Also, we refresh the local variable myMC, since QTFrame_Check-MovieLoadState might have created a new movie controller for the movie.

Handling Load State Changes

So, all we need to do now is define the function QTFrame_CheckMovieLoad-State. This function calls GetMovieLoadState and then inspects the returned movie load state to determine how to proceed. As I've already mentioned, we want to close the movie window that we created in QTFrame_OpenMovieIn-Window if the movie load state is kMovieLoadStateError. Listing 13.7 shows the code we execute in this case.

Listing 13.7 Handling a movie load error.

```
if (myLoadState <= kMovieLoadStateError) {
  // close the movie window
  if ((**theWindowObject).fWindow != NULL)
    QTFrame_DestroyMovieWindow((**theWindowObject).fWindow);

  myErr = invalidMovie;
}
```

Here we test to see whether the movie load state is less than or equal to kMovieLoadStateError. Apple has reserved the right to define other movie load states in the future, so all that really matters is whether the load state has reached a certain threshold. That's why we'll test for ranges of values in our code.

When an error has not occurred, we next want to see whether we've reached the playable state. If not, we need to task the movie so that it gets time to load:

```
else if (myLoadState < kMovieLoadStatePlayable) {
  MoviesTask(myMovie, 1);
}
```

The first stage at which we can do something interesting is when the movie is playable. At this point, we need to create and configure a movie controller if it has not already been created. Here's where we'll put most of the code that we cut out of our synchronous version of QTFrame_OpenMovie-InWindow. Listing 13.8 shows our complete definition of QTFrame_CheckMovie-LoadState.

Listing 13.8 Checking the movie load state.

```
OSErr QTFrame_CheckMovieLoadState (WindowObject theWindowObject)
{
  Movie             myMovie = NULL;
  MovieController    myMC = NULL;
```

```
   long                  myLoadState = 0L;
   long                  myPrevState = 0L;
   OSErr                 myErr = noErr;

   if (theWindowObject == NULL)
     return(paramErr);

   // if the window contains an image, we can return
   if ((**theWindowObject).fGraphicsImporter != NULL)
     return(noErr);

   // if the window does not contain a movie, we can return
   myMovie = (**theWindowObject).fMovie;
   if (myMovie == NULL)
     return(paramErr);

#if TARGET_OS_WIN32
   // if we are adjusting the window location or size, don't go any farther
   if (gWeAreSizingWindow)
     return(noErr);
#endif

   myMC = (**theWindowObject).fController;

#if ALLOW_ASYNCH_LOADING
   // get the previous load state
   myPrevState = (**theWindowObject).fLoadState;
#endif

   // if we're already fully loaded and configured, we can return
   if ((myPrevState >= kMovieLoadStateComplete) && (myMC != NULL))
     return(noErr);

   // get the current load state
   myLoadState = GetMovieLoadState(myMovie);

#if ALLOW_ASYNCH_LOADING
   // remember the new state
   (**theWindowObject).fLoadState = myLoadState;
#endif

   // process the movie according to its current load state
   if (myLoadState <= kMovieLoadStateError) {

     // an error occurred while attempting to load the movie; close the movie window
     if ((**theWindowObject).fWindow != NULL)
       QTFrame_DestroyMovieWindow((**theWindowObject).fWindow);
```

```
      myErr = invalidMovie;

} else if (myLoadState < kMovieLoadStatePlayable) {

   // we're not playable yet; task the movie so it gets time to load
   MoviesTask(myMovie, 1);

} else {

   // we are now playable;
   // if we haven't set up the movie and movie controller, do so now
   if (myMC == NULL) {
      WindowReference    myWindow = (**theWindowObject).fWindow;
      Point              myPoint;

      if (myWindow == NULL)
         return(paramErr);

      // set the default progress procedure for the movie
      SetMovieProgressProc(myMovie, (MovieProgressUPP)-1, 0);

      // make sure that the movie is active
      SetMovieActive(myMovie, true);

      // create and configure the movie controller
      myMC = QTFrame_SetupController(myMovie, myWindow, true);

      (**theWindowObject).fController = myMC;
      (**theWindowObject).fIsQTVRMovie = QTUtils_IsQTVRMovie(myMovie);

      // do any application-specific window object initialization
      QTApp_SetupWindowObject(theWindowObject);

      // size the window to fit the movie and controller
      QTFrame_SizeWindowToMovie(theWindowObject);

      // set the movie's play hints to allow dynamic resizing
      SetMoviePlayHints(myMovie, hintsAllowDynamicResize, hintsAllowDynamicResize);

      // set the movie's position, if it has a 'WLOC' user data atom
      QTUtils_GetWindowPositionFromFile(myMovie, &myPoint);

      // show the window
      QTFrame_ShowWindowAtPoint(myWindow, &myPoint);

      if (myMC != NULL) {
         // if the movie is a play-all-frames movie, tell the movie controller
         if (QTUtils_IsPlayAllFramesMovie(myMovie))
            MCDoAction(myMC, mcActionSetPlayEveryFrame, (void *)true);
```

```
#if !ALLOW_ASYNCH_LOADING
        // if the movie is an autoplay movie, then start it playing immediately
        if (QTUtils_IsAutoPlayMovie(myMovie))
          MCDoAction(myMC, mcActionPrerollAndPlay,
                (void *)GetMoviePreferredRate(myMovie));
#endif
      }
    }

#if ALLOW_ASYNCH_LOADING
    // if we can play through to the end and we have an autoplay movie, start it playing
    if (myLoadState >= kMovieLoadStatePlaythroughOK) {
      if ((myPrevState < kMovieLoadStatePlaythroughOK) && (myMC != NULL)) {
        // if the movie is an autoplay movie, then start it playing immediately
        if (QTUtils_IsAutoPlayMovie(myMovie))
          MCDoAction(myMC, mcActionPrerollAndPlay,
                (void *)GetMoviePreferredRate(myMovie));
      }
    }
#endif
  }

  // do any application-specific processing
  if (myErr == noErr)
    myErr = QTApp_CheckMovieLoadState(theWindowObject, myLoadState, myPrevState);

  return(myErr);
}
```

You'll notice that, on Windows, we check the global variable gWeAre-
SizingWindow to see whether we are in the middle of resizing a movie window; if so, we don't continue. This helps us avoid problems when we call
QTFrame_ShowWindowAtPoint (which, on Windows, will cause several messages
to get sent to the movie, which will eventually trigger a stack overflow).

Notice also that, near the end of QTFrame_CheckMovieLoadState, we call the
function QTApp_CheckMovieLoadState, which is defined in the file ComApplica-
tion.c. This provides an easy way for us to implement application-specific
movie loading behaviors without having to change the underlying framework. In a moment, we'll see how to use this function to control the loader
progress bar we draw on top of loading movies.

Adjusting Menu Items

There is one final change we should make to support asynchronous movie
loading: we need to prevent the user from exporting or saving a movie file if

the movie is not yet fully loaded. That is to say, we should count a movie as savable only if all the media data is available. So we'll add a few lines of code to the QTFrame_AdjustMenus function. Listing 13.9 shows the segment of QTFrame_AdjustMenus that adjusts the Save and Save As menu items.

Listing 13.9 Adjusting the Save and Save As menu items.

```
if (myWindowObject != NULL) {
  QTFrame_SetMenuItemState(myMenu, IDM_FILESAVEAS, kEnableMenuItem);
  QTFrame_SetMenuItemState(myMenu, IDM_FILESAVE,
    (**myWindowObject).fIsDirty ? kEnableMenuItem : kDisableMenuItem);

#if ALLOW_ASYNCH_LOADING
  // a movie is savable only if it's completely loaded
  if ((**myWindowObject).fMovie != NULL) {
    if (GetMovieLoadState((**myWindowObject).fMovie) < kMovieLoadStateComplete) {
      QTFrame_SetMenuItemState(myMenu, IDM_FILESAVEAS, kDisableMenuItem);
      QTFrame_SetMenuItemState(myMenu, IDM_FILESAVE, kDisableMenuItem);
    }
  }
#endif
} else {
  QTFrame_SetMenuItemState(myMenu, IDM_FILESAVEAS, kDisableMenuItem);
  QTFrame_SetMenuItemState(myMenu, IDM_FILESAVE, kDisableMenuItem);
}
```

If your application supports other menu items that require all the media data to be available (such as Export or Publish), you should adjust those items as well.

▶ Movie Drawing-Complete Procedures

We've learned how to load QuickTime movies asynchronously on both Macintosh and Windows operating systems. Now let's see how to add the movie loading progress bar we illustrated earlier in Figure 13.1. Figure 13.4 shows another example of the progress bar at work.

You might have noticed that the standard movie controller already gives us this information by filling in the time slider rectangle in the movie controller bar. Our progress bar is somewhat more general, however, since it also works for movies that use the QuickTime VR movie controller or the no-interface movie controller. Figure 13.5 shows our load progress bar drawn on top of a QuickTime VR movie.

Figure 13.4 A movie load progress bar on a QuickTime movie.

It's actually quite simple to determine the size of the progress bar while a movie is downloading, using the GetMaxLoadedTimeInMovie function. This function returns the duration of the part of the movie that has already downloaded. For example:

```
GetMaxLoadedTimeInMovie(theMovie, &myTimeValue);
```

Here, myTimeValue will contain the duration, in movie time units, of the part of the movie that is available. For example, if the movie's duration is 18000 (say, 30 seconds long with a time scale of 600), then GetMaxLoaded-TimeInMovie will return 4500 if the movie is one-fourth downloaded. So if we know the dimensions of the movie (myMovieRect), we can calculate the rectangle for the progress bar like this:

```
myLoadRect.left = myMovieRect.left;
myLoadRect.bottom = myMovieRect.bottom;
myLoadRect.top = myLoadRect.bottom - kLoaderBarHeight;
myLoadRect.right = myLoadRect.left +
  (((myMovieRect.right - myMovieRect.left) *
  myTimeValue) / GetMovieDuration(theMovie));
```

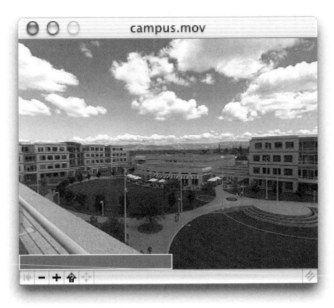

Figure 13.5   A movie load progress bar on a QuickTime VR movie.

GetMaxLoadedTimeInMovie returns positive values only once the movie has become playable. If the movie load state is less than kMovieLoadStatePlayable, the returned value is always 0. And, of course, once the load state reaches kMovieLoadStateComplete, the returned value will be the duration of the movie.

Drawing on Top of a Movie

We can draw our progress bar on top of a movie using a *movie drawing-complete procedure*. This is a callback function that is executed whenever QuickTime has finished drawing a new frame of a movie. A movie drawing-complete procedure can do all sorts of fun things. In the present case, we'll just fill the progress bar rectangle with a solid color:

```
PaintRect(&myLoadRect);
```

Then we'll outline the rectangle with a different color:

```
MacFrameRect(&myLoadRect);
```

Our movie drawing-complete procedure is declared like this:

```
PASCAL_RTN OSErr QTAL_MovieDrawingCompleteProc
             (Movie theMovie, long theRefCon);
```

The first parameter is the movie, of course, and the second parameter is an application-specific reference constant. As usual, we'll specify the movie's window object as the reference constant. Listing 13.10 shows our movie drawing-complete procedure.

Listing 13.10 Drawing on top of a movie.

```
PASCAL_RTN OSErr QTAL_MovieDrawingCompleteProc (Movie theMovie, long theRefCon)
{
  Rect              myMovieRect;
  Rect              myLoadRect;
  TimeValue         myTimeValue = 0L;
  RGBColor          myOrigColor;
  RGBColor          myLoadColor = {0x6666, 0x6666, 0xcccc};
  RGBColor          myRectColor = {0xeeee, 0xeeee, 0xeeee};
  GrafPtr           mySavedPort;
  WindowObject      myWindowObject = (WindowObject)theRefCon;

  if (myWindowObject == NULL)
    return(paramErr);

  if ((**myWindowObject).fWindow == NULL)
    return(paramErr);

  GetPort(&mySavedPort);
  MacSetPort(QTFrame_GetPortFromWindowReference((**myWindowObject).fWindow));

  GetMovieBox(theMovie, &myMovieRect);
  if (!EmptyRect(&myMovieRect)) {
    GetForeColor(&myOrigColor);
    RGBForeColor(&myLoadColor);

    GetMaxLoadedTimeInMovie(theMovie, &myTimeValue);

    // calculate the loading progress bar rectangle
    myLoadRect.left = myMovieRect.left;
    myLoadRect.bottom = myMovieRect.bottom;
    myLoadRect.top = myLoadRect.bottom - kLoaderBarHeight;
    myLoadRect.right = myLoadRect.left +
      (((myMovieRect.right - myMovieRect.left) *
      myTimeValue) / GetMovieDuration(theMovie));
    PaintRect(&myLoadRect);

    RGBForeColor(&myRectColor);
    MacFrameRect(&myLoadRect);
```

```
    RGBForeColor(&myOrigColor);
  }

  MacSetPort(mySavedPort);
  return(noErr);
}
```

We take the trouble to set the current graphics port (first saving and later restoring the current graphics port) to ensure that we're drawing into our movie's graphics port. In all likelihood, the current port when our procedure is called is indeed the movie's graphics port; however, the documentation doesn't guarantee this, so it's good to be careful.

Installing a Drawing-Complete Procedure

Now we need to see how to activate and deactivate our movie drawing-complete procedure. To activate our procedure, we'll call the `SetMovieDrawingCompleteProc` function, passing it the movie identifier, a flag, a universal procedure pointer for our procedure, and the desired reference constant:

```
(**myAppData).fDrawCompleteUPP =
  NewMovieDrawingCompleteUPP(QTAL_MovieDrawingCompleteProc);

SetMovieDrawingCompleteProc(myMovie, movieDrawingCallAlways,
  (**myAppData).fDrawCompleteUPP, (long)theWindowObject);
```

The second parameter indicates how often we want our drawing-complete procedure to be called; it should be one of these two values:

```
enum {
  movieDrawingCallWhenChanged                    = 0,
  movieDrawingCallAlways                         = 1
};
```

The `movieDrawingCallAlways` flag indicates that we want QuickTime to call our procedure every time the movie is tasked (that is, every time our application calls `MoviesTask`, either directly or indirectly). The `movieDrawingCallWhenChanged` flag indicates that we want QuickTime to call our procedure only when the movie has changed (that is, when something new was actually drawn into the movie's graphics world). As you can see, we use the `movieDrawingCallAlways` flag so that our procedure is called as often as possible, whether or not the movie image has changed.

We want to install our movie drawing-complete procedure when the movie first becomes playable, and we want to uninstall it when the movie data is finished downloading. We can do all of this inside our application-specific function QTApp_CheckMovieLoadState, as shown in Listing 13.11.

Listing 13.11 Installing and uninstalling the movie drawing-complete procedure.

```
OSErr QTApp_CheckMovieLoadState
        (WindowObject theWindowObject, long theLoadState, long thePrevState)
{
#pragma unused(thePrevState)
  ApplicationDataHdl      myAppData = NULL;
  Movie                   myMovie = NULL;
  Rect                    myRect;
  OSErr                   myErr = noErr;

  if (theWindowObject == NULL)
    return(paramErr);

  myMovie = (**theWindowObject).fMovie;
  if (myMovie == NULL)
    return(paramErr);

  myAppData = (ApplicationDataHdl)(**theWindowObject).fAppData;
  if (myAppData == NULL)
    return(paramErr);

  // we don't care about the early stages
  if (theLoadState < kMovieLoadStatePlayable)
    return(noErr);

#if ALLOW_ASYNCH_LOADING
  // display a load progress bar, until the movie is completely loaded
  if (theLoadState < kMovieLoadStateComplete) {
    if ((**myAppData).fDrawCompleteUPP == NULL) {
      (**myAppData).fDrawCompleteUPP = NewMovieDrawingCompleteUPP
              (QTAL_MovieDrawingCompleteProc);

      SetMovieDrawingCompleteProc(myMovie, movieDrawingCallAlways,
        (**myAppData).fDrawCompleteUPP, (long)theWindowObject);
    }
  } else {
    if ((**myAppData).fDrawCompleteUPP != NULL) {
      // make sure the loading progress bar reaches the end
      QTAL_MovieDrawingCompleteProc(myMovie, (long)theWindowObject);
```

```
            // remove the drawing-complete procedure
            SetMovieDrawingCompleteProc(myMovie, 0L, NULL, 0L);

            DisposeMovieDrawingCompleteUPP((**myAppData).fDrawCompleteUPP);
            (**myAppData).fDrawCompleteUPP = NULL;

            // erase the loading progress bar, now that we are at the end
            GetMovieBox(myMovie, &myRect);
            myRect.top = myRect.bottom - kLoaderBarHeight;
#if TARGET_OS_MAC
            InvalWindowRect(
                QTFrame_GetWindowFromWindowReference((**theWindowObject).fWindow), &myRect);
#endif
#if TARGET_OS_WIN32
            {
                RECT        myWinRect;

                QTFrame_ConvertMacToWinRect(&myRect, &myWinRect);
                InvalidateRect((**theWindowObject).fWindow, &myWinRect, false);
            }
#endif
        }
    }
#endif

    return(myErr);
}
```

Once the movie data is completely downloaded, we remove the movie drawing-complete procedure and then erase the progress bar rectangle. Otherwise, the progress bar would remain visible until the movie was next redrawn.

You should be aware that some of the media handlers used to play back a movie may need to use less efficient code paths when a movie drawing-complete procedure is installed. In the current case, since we are waiting for the movie's media data to download and are probably not playing the movie yet, this is less of a concern.

Loader Tracks

Now let's see how we can attach a progress bar to a movie so that it displays its own status as the movie data is downloaded to the user's computer. The basic idea is extremely simple: we'll create a new sprite track that contains a

Figure 13.6 The sprite image for the loader sprite.

single wired sprite. The image for this sprite is just the progress bar shown in Figure 13.6. We'll set the sprite's initial position so that the right side of the loader bar is at the left edge of the movie box. Then we'll attach some wiring to the sprite that, on idle events, checks the amount of movie data currently loaded and moves the sprite to the right by the appropriate amount. Finally, when the movie data is fully downloaded, the sprite will deactivate its own track so that the loader sprite disappears.

Creating the Sprite Track

We've had plenty of experience creating sprite tracks and adding wired actions to them, so we can be brief here. We create the sprite track by calling NewMovieTrack and NewTrackMedia, using the dimensions of the original movie to determine the size of the sprite track:

```
GetMovieBox(theMovie, &myRect);
myWidth = Long2Fix(myRect.right - myRect.left);
myHeight = Long2Fix(kLoaderBarHeight);
```

Then we adjust the sprite track matrix so that the progress bar is drawn at the bottom of the movie box:

```
GetTrackMatrix(myTrack, &myMatrix);
TranslateMatrix(&myMatrix, 0, Long2Fix(myRect.bottom - kLoaderBarHeight));
SetTrackMatrix(myTrack, &myMatrix);
```

At this point, we call an application function to add the sprite samples to the new sprite media:

```
myErr = QTAL_AddSpriteLoaderSamplesToMedia(myMedia, myDuration,
            myRect.right - myRect.left);
```

Then we call InsertMediaIntoTrack, as usual, to add the new media samples to the track. We finish up by adjusting the sprite track properties so that the new sprite track is the frontmost track (that is, has the lowest track layer) and so that that track is loaded before any other tracks in the movie:

```
QTAL_SetTrackProperties(myMedia, 15);

SetTrackLayer(myTrack, kMaxLayerNumber);
SetTrackLayer(myTrack, QTAL_GetLowestLayerInMovie(theMovie) - 1);
myErr = QTAL_SetTrackToPreload(myTrack);
```

QTAL_SetTrackProperties and QTAL_GetLowestLayerInMovie are versions of functions that we've encountered previously. QTAL_SetTrackToPreload is a very simple function that sets the specified track to *preload*—that is, to be loaded entirely into memory when the movie is opened. This by itself isn't such a big deal, as our sprite loader track will be fairly small (barely a thousand bytes) and would probably have been loaded entirely into RAM anyway. The main advantage to setting a track to preload is that FlattenMovie-Data places the data for any tracks marked to preload before the data for other tracks in the movie. This means that our sprite loader track will be downloaded first and hence able to display its progress bar as early as possible. Listing 13.12 shows our definition of QTAL_SetTrackToPreload.

Listing 13.12 Setting a track to preload.

```
OSErr QTAL_SetTrackToPreload (Track theTrack)
{
   TimeValue      myTime = 0L;
   TimeValue      myDuration = 0L;
   long           myFlags = 0L;
   long           myHints = 0L;
   OSErr          myErr = noErr;

   if (theTrack == NULL)
     return(invalidTrack);

   // get the current track load settings
   GetTrackLoadSettings(theTrack, &myTime, &myDuration, &myFlags, &myHints);
   myErr = GetMoviesError();
   if (myErr != noErr)
     goto bail;

   myFlags = preloadAlways;
   myTime = -1;

   // set the new track load settings
   SetTrackLoadSettings(theTrack, myTime, myDuration, myFlags, myHints);
   myErr = GetMoviesError();

bail:
   return(myErr);
}
```

The key step here is calling SetTrackLoadSettings with the myFlags parameter set to include the preloadAlways flag.

Adding the Loader Sprite Image

The QTAL_AddSpriteLoaderSamplesToMedia function performs two main tasks: it adds the progress bar image to the sprite sample, and it adds wiring to the loader sprite. Let's tackle the first task here.

When we've previously constructed sprite tracks, we've usually read the sprite images from an existing location (typically, the application's resource fork). In this case, however, we don't know the width of the sprite image in advance, so we'll need to create it dynamically, once we know the width of the movie we are adding the loader track to. We'll adapt the existing utility ICUtils_RecompressPictureWithTransparency to fit our needs; the resulting function, QTAL_AddLoaderBarPICTToKeyFrameSample, is shown in Listing 13.13. Parts of this function will remind you of QTAL_MovieDrawingCompleteProc (Listing 13.10).

Listing 13.13 Adding the image for the loader bar sprite.

```
OSErr QTAL_AddLoaderBarPICTToKeyFrameSample (QTAtomContainer theKeySample,
        long theBarWidth, RGBColor *theKeyColor, QTAtomID theID,
        FixedPoint *theRegistrationPoint, StringPtr theImageName)
{
  Rect                    myRect;
  RGBColor                myOrigColor;
  RGBColor                myLoadColor = {0x6666, 0x6666, 0xcccc};
  RGBColor                myRectColor = {0xeeee, 0xeeee, 0xeeee};
  PicHandle               myPicture = NULL;
  Handle                  myCompressedPicture = NULL;
  ImageDescriptionHandle  myImageDesc = NULL;
  OSErr                   myErr = noErr;

  // set up the PICT rectangle
  myRect.top = 0;
  myRect.left = 0;
  myRect.right = theBarWidth;
  myRect.bottom = kLoaderBarHeight;

  // create the loader bar PICT
  myPicture = OpenPicture(&myRect);
  if (myPicture != NULL) {
    GetForeColor(&myOrigColor);
    RGBForeColor(&myLoadColor);
```

```
    PaintRect(&myRect);

    RGBForeColor(&myRectColor);
    MacFrameRect(&myRect);

    RGBForeColor(&myOrigColor);

    ClosePicture();

    // convert it to image data compressed by the animation compressor
    myErr = ICUtils_RecompressPictureWithTransparency(myPicture, theKeyColor, NULL,
            &myImageDesc, &myCompressedPicture);
    if (myErr != noErr)
      goto bail;

    // add it to the key sample
    HLock(myCompressedPicture);
    myErr = SpriteUtils_AddCompressedImageToKeyFrameSample(theKeySample, myImageDesc,
            GetHandleSize(myCompressedPicture), *myCompressedPicture, theID,
            theRegistrationPoint, theImageName);
  }

bail:
  if (myPicture != NULL)
    KillPicture(myPicture);

  if (myCompressedPicture != NULL)
    DisposeHandle(myCompressedPicture);

  if (myImageDesc != NULL)
    DisposeHandle((Handle)myImageDesc);

  return(myErr);
}
```

Wiring the Loader Sprite

All that remains is to add the appropriate wiring to the sprite, to cause it to
move gradually to the right as the media data is downloaded; we also need
to disable the sprite track once the media data is fully downloaded. In
pseudocode, our wiring will look like this:

```
if kOperandMaxLoadedTimeInMovie < kOperandMovieDuration
   TranslateSprite xPos, 0, true
else
   EnableTrack false
```

Here, the horizontal position of the sprite (or xPos, in the pseudocode) is calculated like this:

$$xPos = (kOperandMaxLoadedTimeInMovie / myDurPerPixel) - theWidth)$$

where myDurPerPixel is simply the movie duration divided by the movie width. Listing 13.14 shows the portion of QTAL_AddSpriteLoaderSamplesTo-Media that constructs the wired action atom.

Listing 13.14 Adding actions to the loader bar sprite.

```
WiredUtils_AddQTEventAndActionAtoms(mySpriteData, kParentAtomIsContainer, kQTEventIdle,
  kActionCase, &myActionAtom);
if (myActionAtom != 0) {
  QTAtom           myParamAtom = 0;
  QTAtom           myConditionalAtom = 0;
  QTAtom           myExpressionAtom = 0;

  // add a parameter atom to the kActionCase action atom; this will serve as a parent to
  // hold the expression and action atoms
  WiredUtils_AddActionParameterAtom(mySpriteData, myActionAtom, kFirstParam, 0, NULL,
    &myParamAtom);
  if (myParamAtom != 0) {

    // if...
    WiredUtils_AddConditionalAtom(mySpriteData, myParamAtom, 1, &myConditionalAtom);
    if (myConditionalAtom != 0) {
      WiredUtils_AddExpressionContainerAtomType(mySpriteData, myConditionalAtom,
        &myExpressionAtom);
      if (myExpressionAtom != 0) {
        QTAtom          myOperatorAtom = 0;

        // ...kOperandMaxLoadedTimeInMovie < kOperandMovieDuration
        myErr = WiredUtils_AddOperatorAtom(mySpriteData, myExpressionAtom,
                  kOperatorLessThan, &myOperatorAtom);
        if (myOperatorAtom != 0) {
          WiredUtils_AddOperandAtom(mySpriteData, myOperatorAtom,
            kOperandMaxLoadedTimeInMovie, 1, NULL, 0);
          WiredUtils_AddOperandAtom(mySpriteData, myOperatorAtom,
            kOperandMovieDuration, 2, NULL, 0);
        }
      }

      //      TranslateSprite...
      WiredUtils_AddActionListAtom(mySpriteData, myConditionalAtom, &myActionListAtom);
      if (myActionListAtom != 0) {
```

```
WiredUtils_AddActionAtom(mySpriteData, myActionListAtom, kActionSpriteTranslate,
  &myNewActionAtom);
if (myNewActionAtom != 0) {
  QTAtom      myNewParamAtom = 0;
  long        myDurPerPixel = theDuration / theWidth;

  // first parameter: (kOperandMaxLoadedTimeInMovie / myDurPerPixel)
  // - theWidth
  WiredUtils_AddActionParameterAtom(mySpriteData, myNewActionAtom,
    kFirstParam, 0, NULL, &myNewParamAtom);
  if (myNewParamAtom != 0) {

    QTAtom      myExpressionAtomSub = 0;
    QTAtom      myExpressionAtomMin = 0;
    QTAtom      myOperatorAtomSub = 0;
    QTAtom      myOperatorAtomDiv = 0;
    QTAtom      myOperandAtom = 0;
    QTAtom      myNewOperandAtom = 0;

    WiredUtils_AddExpressionContainerAtomType(mySpriteData, myNewParamAtom,
      &myExpressionAtomSub);
    if (myExpressionAtomSub != 0) {

      WiredUtils_AddOperatorAtom(mySpriteData, myExpressionAtomSub,
        kOperatorSubtract, &myOperatorAtomSub);
      if (myOperatorAtomSub != 0) {

        // the minuend
        QTInsertChild(mySpriteData, myOperatorAtomSub, kOperandAtomType, 1, 1,
          0, NULL, &myOperandAtom);
        if (myOperandAtom != 0) {

          QTInsertChild(mySpriteData, myOperandAtom, kOperandExpression,
            1, 1, 0, NULL, &myNewOperandAtom);

          WiredUtils_AddExpressionContainerAtomType(mySpriteData,
            myNewOperandAtom, &myExpressionAtomMin);
          if (myExpressionAtomMin != 0) {
            WiredUtils_AddOperatorAtom(mySpriteData, myExpressionAtomMin,
              kOperatorDivide, &myOperatorAtomDiv);
            if (myOperatorAtomDiv != 0) {
              WiredUtils_AddOperandAtom(mySpriteData, myOperatorAtomDiv,
                kOperandMaxLoadedTimeInMovie, 1, NULL, 0);
              WiredUtils_AddOperandAtom(mySpriteData, myOperatorAtomDiv,
                kOperandConstant, 2, NULL, (float)myDurPerPixel);
            }
          }
        }
```

```
            // the subtrahend
            WiredUtils_AddOperandAtom(mySpriteData, myOperatorAtomSub,
              kOperandConstant, 2, NULL, (float)theWidth);
          }
        }
      }

      // second parameter: 0
      myFixed = EndianU32_NtoB(0);
      WiredUtils_AddActionParameterAtom(mySpriteData, myNewActionAtom,
        kSecondParam, sizeof(Fixed), &myFixed, NULL);

      // third parameter: true
      myBoolean = true;
      WiredUtils_AddActionParameterAtom(mySpriteData, myNewActionAtom,
        kThirdParam, sizeof(myBoolean), &myBoolean, NULL);
    }
  }
}

// else if...
WiredUtils_AddConditionalAtom(mySpriteData, myParamAtom, 2, &myConditionalAtom);
if (myConditionalAtom != 0) {

  // ... (1)
  WiredUtils_AddExpressionContainerAtomType(mySpriteData, myConditionalAtom,
    &myExpressionAtom);
    if (myExpressionAtom != 0)
      WiredUtils_AddOperandAtom(mySpriteData, myExpressionAtom, kOperandConstant, 1,
        NULL, 1.0);

  // kActionTrackSetEnabled false
  WiredUtils_AddActionListAtom(mySpriteData, myConditionalAtom, &myActionListAtom);
  if (myActionListAtom != 0)
    WiredUtils_AddTrackSetEnabledAction(mySpriteData, myActionListAtom,
      0, 0, NULL, 0, false);
  }
 }
}
```

▶ QuickTime VR Movie Loading

Before we close, let's take a quick look at one additional topic related to loading movies: how to specify a preview track in a QuickTime VR panoramic movie. As you know (at least if you read Chapter 10, "Virtuosity"), the image data for a panorama is contained in a panorama image track inside a QuickTime VR movie file. Each sample in the panorama image track represents one section, or *tile*, of the image data. For cylindrical panoramas, a tile is a vertical slice of the image. For cubic panoramas, a tile is usually an entire face of the cube. Chopping the panorama image data into tiles allows QuickTime VR to display parts of the panorama to the user without having the entire image data in memory.

This is relevant to us now because QuickTime downloads a panoramic movie one tile at a time. This means that, on suitably slow network connections and with suitably narrow tiles, the panorama image data that's been downloaded at some point might fill only part of the movie window. By default, QuickTime fills the remainder of the movie window with a black and gray grid pattern, as shown in Figure 13.7. (This pattern is sometimes called the *holodeck* pattern, after a similar grid effect seen in some *Star Trek* episodes.) As new tiles are downloaded, they overlay the grid.

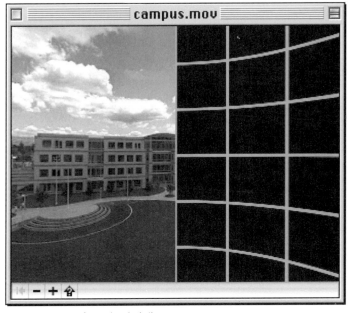

Figure 13.7 The grid pattern for unloaded tiles.

It's possible to achieve a better user experience by including a *low-resolution image track* in the panorama. This is a video track that (typically) shows the same location as the full-resolution track but occupies a small fraction of the space of the full-resolution track. The low-resolution image track is loaded fairly quickly and is hence often called a *low-resolution preview track* (or just *preview track*). As the high-resolution tiles arrive, they are drawn on top of the low-resolution track, in just the same way that the high-resolution tiles are drawn on top of the grid. Figure 13.8 shows a low-resolution image track (on the left) and the high-resolution tiles (on the right).

Hotspots in the panorama will be active under the low-resolution track but inactive under the grid pattern. For this reason at least, it's usually best to include a low-resolution image track in any panoramas we create. Most QuickTime VR authoring tools provide some means of attaching these low-resolution tracks to a movie, but it's easy enough to do it ourselves. If we've got a panorama that does not contain a low-resolution image track, we can add one to it by exporting the movie using the *QuickTime VR flattener*. This is a movie export component that prepares a QuickTime VR movie for Fast Start downloading and provides the option of including a low-resolution image track. Listing 13.15 shows our definition of the QTVRUtils_Flatten-MovieForStreaming function, which exports the specified movie into a new file. (See Volume One, Chapter 5, for a more extensive discussion of movie exporting.)

Figure 13.8 A low-resolution image track and some high-resolution tiles.

Listing 13.15 Flattening a QuickTime VR movie.

```
OSErr QTVRUtils_FlattenMovieForStreaming (Movie theMovie, FSSpecPtr theFSSpecPtr)
{
  ComponentDescription    myCompDesc;
  MovieExportComponent    myExporter = NULL;
  long                    myFlags = createMovieFileDeleteCurFile | showUserSettingsDialog
                                                                 | movieFileSpecValid;
  ComponentResult         myErr = badComponentType;

  // find and open a movie exporter that can flatten a QuickTime VR movie file
  myCompDesc.componentType = MovieExportType;
  myCompDesc.componentSubType = MovieFileType;
  myCompDesc.componentManufacturer = kQTVRFlattenerManufacturer;
  myCompDesc.componentFlags = 0;
  myCompDesc.componentFlagsMask = 0;
  myExporter = OpenComponent(FindNextComponent(NULL, &myCompDesc));
  if (myExporter == NULL)
    goto bail;

  // use the default progress procedure
  SetMovieProgressProc(theMovie, (MovieProgressUPP)-1L, 0);

  // export the movie into a file
  myErr = ConvertMovieToFile(theMovie, NULL, theFSSpecPtr, MovieFileType, sigMoviePlayer,
          smSystemScript, NULL, myFlags, myExporter);

bail:
  // close the movie export component
  if (myExporter != NULL)
    CloseComponent(myExporter);

  return((OSErr)myErr);
}
```

Since we include the showUserSettingsDialog flag in the myFlags parameter passed to ConvertMovieToFile, the user will be presented with the Export Settings dialog box, shown in Figure 13.9. If the user clicks the Options button, the dialog box shown in Figure 13.10 will be presented, allowing the user to determine the resolution of the preview track and whether it is blurred or pixilated. If the user unchecks the Create Preview button, no preview track is created.

Figure 13.9 The Export Settings dialog box.

Figure 13.10 The Options dialog box.

 Conclusion

The focus of this chapter was on loading QuickTime movies. We've learned how to modify our basic QuickTime movie playback application to support loading movies asynchronously. The changes required here are indeed fairly simple, but they pay big dividends. First and foremost, our application can now continue processing while a movie is being loaded. Also, we've now got the machinery in place to do application-specific processing while a movie loads, such as displaying a progress bar showing how much of the movie is loaded.

We've also taken a look at a couple of ways to enhance a movie's own loading behavior. We saw how to add a sprite track that displays a loader bar, and we saw how to add a low-resolution preview track to a QuickTime VR panorama.

Human Resources
Adding Macintosh Resources to a Windows Application

▶ Introduction

Macintosh applications use resources in a wide variety of ways. A few of these include: to specify their menus and menu items, to define the appearance of windows and dialog boxes displayed by the applications, to hold strings and other localizable data, and to store fonts, sounds, pictures, custom cursors, and icons. These resources—let's call them *Macintosh resources*—are stored in the application's resource fork, which is automatically opened when the application is launched. The application can retrieve a particular resource by calling Resource Manager functions like GetResource and GetIcon.

Windows applications also use things called resources for many of the same purposes, but these resources are not the same as Macintosh resources. These resources—let's call them *Windows resources*—are stored inside the executable file (the .exe file) and can be loaded programmatically using functions like LoadResource and LoadIcon. Typically, an application's Windows resources are defined using a *resource script* (a file whose name ends in .rc) and are automatically inserted into the executable file when the application is built.

As we've seen in many previous chapters, it's often useful to use Macintosh resources in our QuickTime applications, whether those applications run on Macintosh or Windows computers. For instance, when we once wanted to elicit a URL from the user, we called GetNewDialog to display a dialog box defined by the application's resources; then we called ModalDialog to handle user actions in the dialog box. Figure 14.1 shows the dialog box on Macintosh systems, and Figure 14.2 shows the dialog box on Windows systems.

Let's consider another example. Recently I added a properties panel to QuickTime Player to display information about movie tracks. I constructed the panel on a Macintosh computer using a text description that is converted

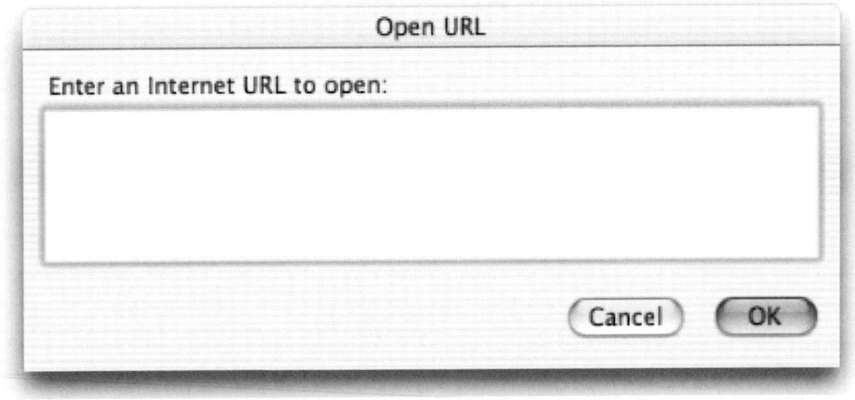

Figure 14.1 The Open URL dialog box (Macintosh).

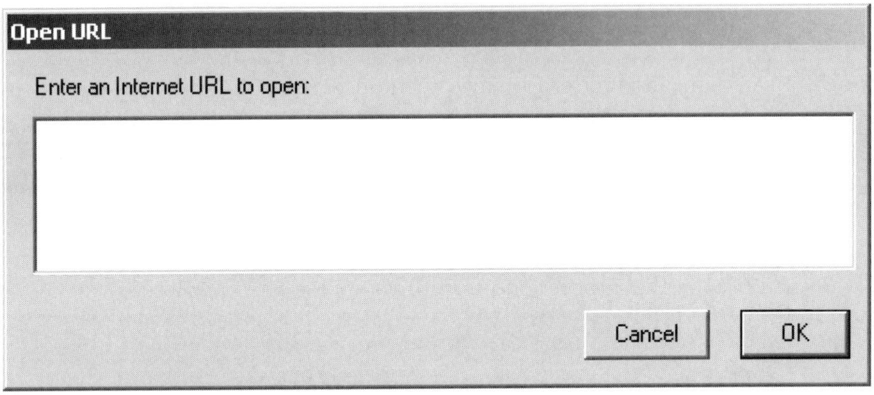

Figure 14.2 The Open URL dialog box (Windows).

by the tool Rez into a Macintosh resource. Figure 14.3 shows the panel on the Mac OS 9, and Figure 14.4 shows the panel on Windows. (This panel is not included with any shipping version of QuickTime Player, so don't bother looking for it.)

The main advantage to using Macintosh resources for dialog boxes on both operating systems is that we can use the exact same resource description on both systems, and we can use the exact same code to display and manage the dialog boxes. On Windows, this magic is provided by the *Quick-Time Media Layer* (*QTML*), which we have considered before (see, for example, Volume One, Chapter 12). In this chapter, I want to focus on how to attach Macintosh resources to a Windows application. We got a preliminary taste of doing this in that earlier chapter, where we saw how to use the tools Rez and RezWack on Windows to convert a resource description into a

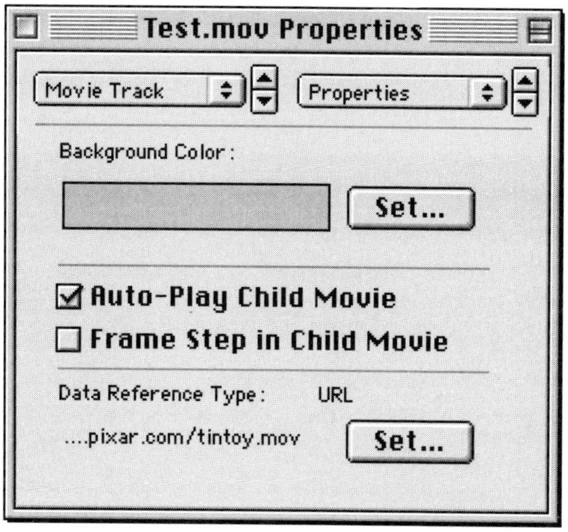

Figure 14.3 The Movie Track Properties panel (Mac OS 9).

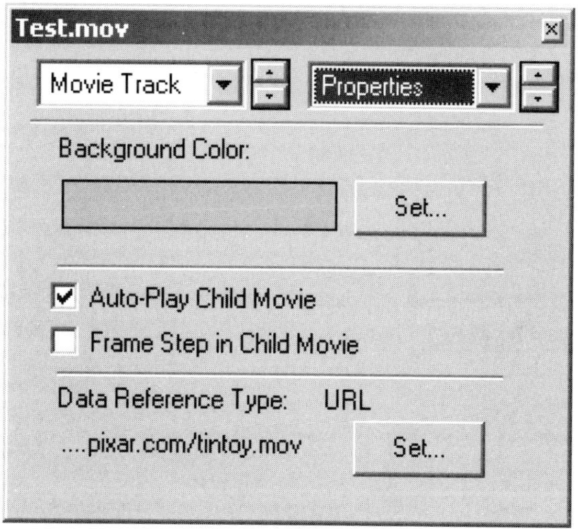

Figure 14.4 The Movie Track Properties panel (Windows).

resource file and attach it to an application. Here, I want to investigate this process in a bit greater detail and to show how to configure our Windows development environment, Microsoft Visual Studio, to perform these steps automatically each time we build our application.

Some programmers, of course, prefer to do most of their software development on Macintosh computers, so it's useful to see how to perform these steps on a Mac. The CodeWarrior integrated development environment (IDE) for Macintosh (from Metrowerks) supplies compilers and linkers for

Windows targets; moreover, the QuickTime SDK provides CodeWarrior projects configured to build Windows applications for virtually all of the sample code applications. All that's missing is a Macintosh version of the RezWack tool. In this chapter, we'll see how to fill in that gap. First, we'll develop a stand-alone application that does this, and then we'll see how to construct a plug-in for the CodeWarrior IDE that performs the RezWack step as part of the build process. By the end of this chapter, you'll know how to create complete Windows applications that contain Macintosh resources, whether you prefer to program on Macintosh or Windows systems.

Before we begin, I should mention that having a single resource description for *all* of our target platforms is a wonderful goal that is not always achievable in practice, at least if we want to pay attention to Apple's human interface guidelines. The reason for this is simply that the Aqua appearance on Mac OS X has different layout requirements than the "classic" Mac OS 8 and 9 appearance. For instance, button labels are usually larger under Aqua than under earlier systems, so we need to make our buttons larger. Figure 14.5 shows the Movie Track Properties panel when displayed on a computer running Mac OS X. Here the entire dialog box is bigger to be able to contain the larger controls and other dialog items.

Figure 14.5   The Movie Track Properties panel (Mac OS X).

Creating Resource Files

Suppose, then, that we're writing a QuickTime application that is to run on Windows and we want to do our development on Windows using the Visual Studio environment. To make things as easy as possible, we'll construct our Macintosh resources by creating a text file that contains a resource description. For instance, Listing 14.1 shows the resource description of the 'DITL' resource for the dialog box shown in Figures 14.3 and 14.4.

Listing 14.1 Resource description for the Movie Track Properties panel.

```
resource 'DITL' (kResourceID) {
  {  /* array DITLarray: 12 elements */
    /* [1] */
    {8, 10, 25, 132},
    StaticText {
      disabled,
      "Background Color:"
    },
    /* [2] */
    {29, 12, 51, 138},
    UserItem {
      enabled
    },
    /* [3] */
    {30, 146, 50, 207},
    Button {
      enabled,
      "Set…"
    },
    /* [4] */
    {16, 7, 60, 214},
    UserItem {
      enabled
    },
    /* [5] */
    {74, 7, 90, 214},
    CheckBox {
      enabled,
      "Auto-Play Child Movie"
    },
    /* [6] */
```

```
        {94, 7, 110, 214},
        CheckBox {
          enabled,
          "Frame Step in Child Movie"
        },
        /* [7] */
        {120, 10, 136, 132},
        StaticText {
          disabled,
          "Data Reference Type: "
        },
        /* [8] */
        {120, 132, 136, 207},
        StaticText {
          disabled,
          "URL"
        },
        /* [9] */
        {140, 12, 156, 132},
        StaticText {
          enabled,
          ""
        },
        /* [10] */
        {138, 146, 158, 207},
        Button {
          enabled,
          "Set…"
        },
        /* [11] */
        {67, 10, 68, 215},
        UserItem {
          disabled
        },
        /* [12] */
        {115, 10, 116, 215},
        UserItem {
          disabled
        }
      }
};
```

The QuickTime SDK for Windows provides the tool Rez, which converts a resource description into a resource file. We can execute this line of code in a DOS console window to create a resource file:

```
QuickTimeSDK\QTDevWin\Tools\Rez
        -i "QuickTimeSDK\QTDevWin\RIncludes" -i .
        MIAMProperties.r -o MIAMProperties.qtr
```

Here, Rez converts the resource descriptions in the file MIAMProperties.r into resources in the resource file MIAMProperties.qtr. Rez looks in the current directory (.) and in the directory QuickTimeSDK\QTDevWin\RIncludes for any included .r files. (Of course, your paths may differ, depending on where you install the QuickTime SDK tools and .r files.)

The suffix .qtr is the preferred filename extension on Windows for files that contain Macintosh resources. When we are building an application, say, QTWiredActions.exe, we should therefore name the resource file "QTWired-Actions.qtr". In our application code, we need to explicitly open that resource file; to do this, we can use the code in Listing 14.2.

Listing 14.2 Opening an application's resource file.

```
myLength = GetModuleFileName(NULL, myFileName, MAX_PATH);
if (myLength != 0) {
  NativePathNameToFSSpec(myFileName, &gAppFSSpec, kFullNativePath);

  gAppResFile = FSpOpenResFile(&gAppFSSpec, fsRdWrPerm);
  if (gAppResFile != kInvalidFileRefNum)
    UseResFile(gAppResFile);
}
```

Note that we do not need this code in our Macintosh applications; as we noted earlier, on the Mac an application's resource fork is automatically opened when the application is launched.

Embedding Resource Files in an Application

When developing and testing an application, it's OK to have to work with two files (the application file and the Macintosh resource file). But when we want to distribute an application, it's desirable to combine these two files into a single executable file. This is the job that RezWack is designed to accomplish. RezWack creates a new file that appends the resource data to the data in the executable file (and also appends some additional data to alert QTML to the fact that the .exe file contains some Macintosh resource data). We can call RezWack like this:

```
QuickTimeSDK\QTDevWin\Tools\RezWack -d QTWiredActions.exe
        -r QTWiredActions.qtr -o TempName.exe
del QTWiredActions.exe
ren TempName.exe QTWiredActions.exe
```

RezWack does not allow us to overwrite either of the two input files, so we need to save the executable file under a temporary name, delete the original .exe file, and then rename the output file to the desired name. Once we've executed these commands, the file QTWiredActions.exe contains the original executable code and the Macintosh resources that were contained in the file QTWiredActions.qtr.

Even if we have inserted the resource data into the executable file using RezWack, we still need to explicitly open the resource file at runtime; so our Windows applications should always include the code in Listing 14.2, whether the resource data is in a separate file or is included in the executable file.

Adding a Post-link Step

It would get tedious really fast to have to type the preceding Rez and RezWack commands in a DOS console window every time we rebuild our application. We can simplify our work by creating a batch file that contains these commands and by executing the batch file automatically as a custom post-link step. Listing 14.3 shows the batch file that we use when building the debug version of the application QTWiredActions.

Listing 14.3 Rezzing and RezWacking an application's resources.

```
REM *** batch program to embed our Macintosh
REM *** resources into our application file
..\..\QTDevWin\Tools\Rez -i "..\..\QTDevWin\RIncludes" -i .
        QTWiredActions.r -o QTWiredActions.qtr
..\..\QTDevWin\Tools\RezWack -d .\Debug\QTWiredActions.exe
        -r QTWiredActions.qtr -o .\Debug\TEMP.exe -f
del .\Debug\QTWiredActions.exe
REM *** now rename new file to previous name
ren .\Debug\TEMP.exe QTWiredActions.exe
```

You'll notice that the paths to the Rez and RezWack tools are relative to the location of the batch file, which we keep in the same folder as the Visual Studio project file; you may need to edit this file to set the correct paths for your particular folder arrangement.

We can tell Visual Studio to execute this file as a custom post-link step by adjusting the project settings. Figure 14.6 shows the appropriate settings panel.

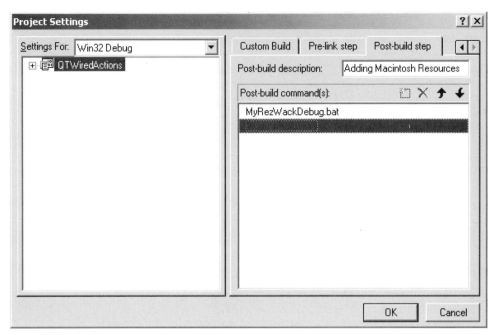

Figure 14.6 Setting a custom post-link step.

Development on Macintosh

So what does RezWack actually *do*? We already know that it adds Macintosh resource data to a Windows executable file. But we need to uncover a bit more detail here if we are to be able to write a tool that performs resource wacking on Macintosh computers. Here's the essential information: RezWack creates a new file that begins with the data in the Windows executable file, followed immediately by the Macintosh resource data, padded to the nearest 4-Kbyte boundary; this is all followed by some *RezWack tag data*. Figure 14.7 illustrates the structure of a file created by RezWack; let's call this a *wacked file*.

The RezWack tag data is a 36-byte block of data that describes the layout of the wacked file. It specifies the offset of the executable data from the beginning of the file (which is usually 0) and the size of the executable data; it also specifies the offset of the resource data from the beginning of the file and the size of the resource data. The tag data ends with this 12-byte identifier: "mkQuickTime™". (What's the "mk"? I strongly suspect that they are the initials of the engineer who implemented the RezWack tool.)

The idea here is that QuickTime can look at the last 12 bytes of a Windows executable file to determine whether it contains any Macintosh resources. If it does, then QuickTime can look at the last 36 bytes of the file

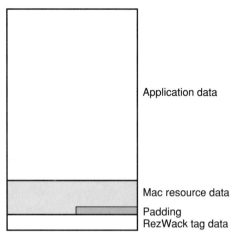

Application data

Mac resource data

Padding
RezWack tag data

Figure 14.7 The structure of a wacked file.

to get the offset into the file of those resources and the size of the resource data.

Let's define a couple of constants that we can use to help us in the wacking process:

```
#define kRezWackTag                              "mkQuickTime™"
#define kRezWackTagSize                          12
```

Then we can define this data structure for the RezWack tag data:

```
typedef struct RezWackTagData {
    UInt32      fDataTag;                    // must be 'data'
    UInt32      fDataOffset;                 // offset of binary data
    UInt32      fDataSize;                   // size of binary data
    UInt32      fRsrcTag;                    // must be 'rsrc'
    UInt32      fRsrcOffset;                 // offset of resource data
    UInt32      fRsrcSize;                   // size of resource data
    char        fWackTag[kRezWackTagSize];
} RezWackTagData, *RezWackTagDataPtr;
```

We'll use this later, when we finally get around to building wacked files.

Setting Up a Droplet

Our current goal is to develop a stand-alone application—let's call it *RezWack PPC*—that we can use as a droplet. That is, we'll compile our Windows code using CodeWarrior on the Macintosh and then drag the execut-

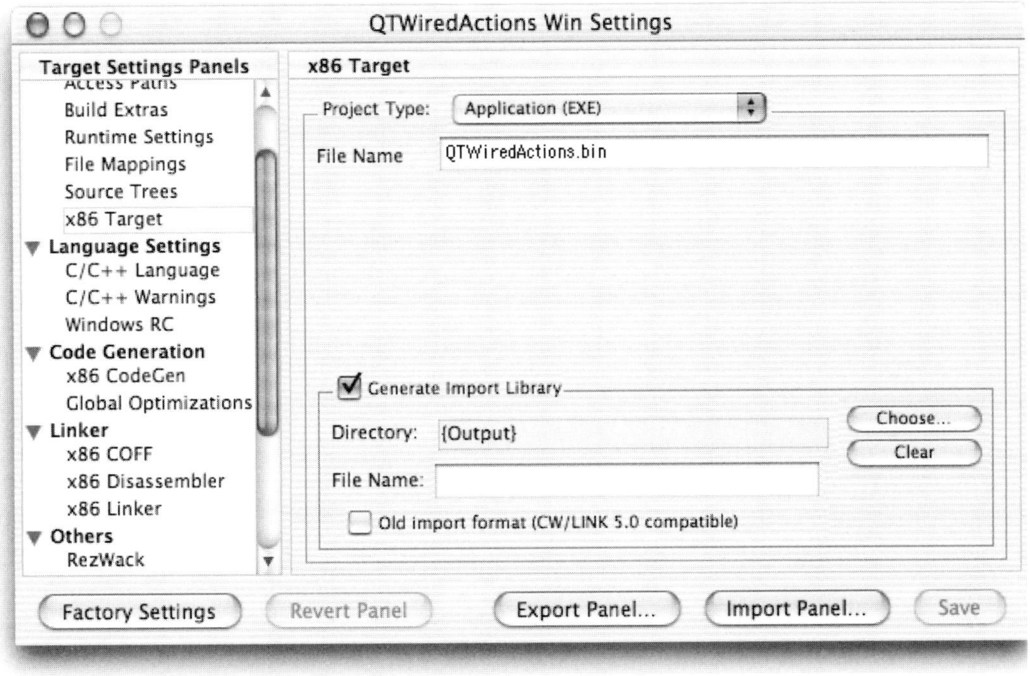

Figure 14.8 Setting the intermediate filename.

able file created by CodeWarrior onto our droplet, which finds the appropriate resource file and creates a new file containing the executable data, the resource data, and the RezWack tag data.

We want the final wacked file to have the standard .exe suffix, so we need to tell CodeWarrior to generate an intermediate executable file with some other suffix. (Remember, RezWack won't overwrite either of its input files and so neither should we.) Let's use the suffix .bin, as shown in Figure 14.8. Our droplet should accept these binary files, look for a resource file with the suffix .qtr, and then create the final wacked file with the .exe suffix. To make RezWack PPC act like a droplet, we need to modify the function QTApp_HandleOpenDocumentAppleEvent. Listing 14.4 shows our new definition of this function.

Listing 14.4 Handling files dropped onto RezWack PPC.

```
PASCAL_RTN OSErr QTApp_HandleOpenDocumentAppleEvent
    (const AppleEvent *theMessage, AppleEvent *theReply, long theRefcon)
{
#pragma unused(theReply, theRefcon)
```

```
   long          myIndex;
   long          myItemsInList;
   AEKeyword     myKeyWd;
   AEDescList    myDocList;
   long          myActualSize;
   DescType      myTypeCode;
   FSSpec        myFSSpec;
   OSErr         myIgnoreErr = noErr;
   OSErr         myErr = noErr;

   // get the direct parameter and put it into myDocList
   myDocList.dataHandle = NULL;
   myErr = AEGetParamDesc(theMessage, keyDirectObject, typeAEList, &myDocList);

   // count the descriptor records in the list
   if (myErr == noErr)
     myErr = AECountItems(&myDocList, &myItemsInList);
   else
     myItemsInList = 0;

   // open each specified file
   for (myIndex = 1; myIndex <= myItemsInList; myIndex++)
     if (myErr == noErr) {
       myErr = AEGetNthPtr(&myDocList, myIndex, typeFSS, &myKeyWd, &myTypeCode,
                 (Ptr)&myFSSpec, sizeof(myFSSpec), &myActualSize);
       if (myErr == noErr) {
         FInfo       myFinderInfo;

         // verify that the file type is kWinBinaryFileType or kWinLibraryFileType
         myErr = FSpGetFInfo(&myFSSpec, &myFinderInfo);
         if (myErr == noErr)
           if ((myFinderInfo.fdType == kWinBinaryFileType)
               || (myFinderInfo.fdType == kWinLibraryFileType))
             QTRW_CreateRezWackedFileFromBinary(&myFSSpec);
       }
     }

   if (myDocList.dataHandle)
     myIgnoreErr = AEDisposeDesc(&myDocList);

   QTFrame_QuitFramework();            // act like a droplet and close automatically
   return(myErr);
}
```

As you can see, we look for files of type kWinBinaryFileType and kWin-LibraryFileType, which have these file types:

```
#define kWinBinaryFileType        FOUR_CHAR_CODE('DEXE')
#define kWinLibraryFileType       FOUR_CHAR_CODE('iDLL')
```

When we find one of these types of files, we call QTRW_CreateRezWacked-FileFromBinary to do the necessary resource wacking. Notice that we call QTFrame_QuitFramework to quit the application once we are done processing the files dropped on it.

Wacking the Resources

Listing 14.5 shows our definition of QTRW_CreateRezWackedFileFromBinary; this function simply configures two additional file system specification records (one for the Macintosh resource file and one for the final wacked file) and then calls another function, QTRW_RezWackWinBinaryAndMacResFile, to do the real work. As just indicated, we assume that the resource file has the same name as the binary file but with the .qtr suffix and that the final wacked file has the same name as the binary file but with the .exe suffix. (I'll leave it as an exercise for the reader to implement less restrictive naming for the three files we need to work with.)

Listing 14.5 Setting up names for the resource and wacked files.

```
OSErr QTRW_CreateRezWackedFileFromBinary (FSSpecPtr theBinFSSpecPtr)
{
  FSSpec          myResSpec;
  FSSpec          myExeSpec;
  OSErr           myErr = paramErr;

  if (theBinFSSpecPtr == NULL)
    goto bail;

  // currently, we suppose that the Macintosh resource file has the same name as the
  // binary, but with .qtr filename extension
  myResSpec = *theBinFSSpecPtr;
  myResSpec.name[myResSpec.name[0] - 2] = 'q';
  myResSpec.name[myResSpec.name[0] - 1] = 't';
  myResSpec.name[myResSpec.name[0] - 0] = 'r';

  // currently, we suppose that the Windows executable file has the same name as the
  // binary, but with .exe filename extension
  myExeSpec = *theBinFSSpecPtr;
```

```
myExeSpec.name[myExeSpec.name[0] - 2] = 'e';
myExeSpec.name[myExeSpec.name[0] - 1] = 'x';
myExeSpec.name[myExeSpec.name[0] - 0] = 'e';

myErr = QTRW_RezWackWinBinaryAndMacResFile(theBinFSSpecPtr, &myResSpec, &myExeSpec);
bail:
  return(myErr);
}
```

QTRW_RezWackWinBinaryAndMacResFile is the key function in RezWack PPC. It takes the binary file created by CodeWarrior and the Macintosh resource file and then creates the desired wacked file. First, it creates an empty file, having the same type and creator as the original binary file:

```
FSpGetFInfo(theBinFSSpecPtr, &myFileInfo);
FSpCreate(theExeFSSpecPtr, myFileInfo.fdCreator, myFileInfo.fdType, 0);
```

Then QTRW_RezWackWinBinaryAndMacResFile opens all three relevant files, using FSpOpenDF to open the binary and wacked files, and FSpOpenRF to open the resource file. Actually, we want our droplet to be a bit more flexible about handling resource files; it's possible for resource data to be stored in a data fork of a file, particularly if the resource data was created on a Windows computer (perhaps using the Rez tool). So, first, we'll attempt to open a resource fork having the appropriate name; if we can't find it or if its length is 0, we'll attempt to open a data fork having the appropriate name. Listing 14.6 shows the code that accomplishes this.

Listing 14.6 Opening the resource file.

```
myErr = FSpOpenRF(theResFSSpecPtr, fsRdPerm, &myResFile);
if (myErr != noErr) {
  myTryDataFork = true;
} else {
  // it's possible that the resource fork exists but is 0-length; if so, try the data fork
  GetEOF(myResFile, &mySizeOfRes);
  if (mySizeOfRes == 0)
    myTryDataFork = true;
}

if (myTryDataFork) {
  // close the open resource file (presumably a 0-length resource fork)
  if (myResFile != -1)
    FSClose(myResFile);
```

```
  myErr = FSpOpenDF(theResFSSpecPtr, fsRdPerm, &myResFile);
  if (myErr != noErr)
    goto bail;
}
```

Once we've got all three files open, it's really quite simple to construct the wacked file. We copy the executable data from the binary file into the output file and copy the resource data from the resource file into the output file. Then we pad the file data to the nearest 4-Kbyte boundary, as shown in Listing 14.7.

Listing 14.7 Padding the executable and resource data.

```
mySizeOfExe = mySizeOfBin + mySizeOfRes;
while ((mySizeOfExe + sizeof(myTagData)) % (4 * 1024) != 0) {
  char     myChar = '\0';

  mySize = 1;
  myErr = FSWrite(myExeFile, &mySize, &myChar);
  if (myErr != noErr)
    goto bail;
  mySizeOfExe++;
}
```

The last thing we need to do is append the RezWack tag data. Listing 14.8 shows the code we use to do this. Notice that the tag data must be in big-endian byte order (as is typical for QuickTime-related data).

Listing 14.8 Appending the RezWack tag data.

```
myTagData.fDataTag = EndianU32_NtoB((long)'data');
myTagData.fDataOffset = 0L;
myTagData.fDataSize = EndianU32_NtoB(mySizeOfBin);
myTagData.fRsrcTag = EndianU32_NtoB((long)'rsrc');
myTagData.fRsrcOffset = EndianU32_NtoB(mySizeOfBin);
myTagData.fRsrcSize = EndianU32_NtoB(mySizeOfRes);
strncpy(myTagData.fWackTag, kRezWackTag, kRezWackTagSize);

mySize = sizeof(myTagData);
myErr = FSWrite(myExeFile, &mySize, &myTagData);
```

And we're done! Listing 14.9 shows the complete definition of QTRW_RezWackWinBinaryAndMacResFile.

Listing 14.9 Creating a wacked file.

```
OSErr QTRW_RezWackWinBinaryAndMacResFile
        (FSSpecPtr theBinFSSpecPtr, FSSpecPtr theResFSSpecPtr, FSSpecPtr theExeFSSpecPtr)
{
  FInfo            myFileInfo;
  short            myBinFile = -1;
  short            myResFile = -1;
  short            myExeFile = -1;
  long             mySizeOfBin = 0L;
  long             mySizeOfRes = 0L;
  long             mySizeOfExe = 0L;
  long             mySize = 0L;
  long             myData = 0L;
  Handle           myHandle = NULL;
  RezWackTagData   myTagData;
  Boolean          myTryDataFork = false;
  OSErr            myErr = paramErr;

  // make sure we are passed three non-NULL FSSpecPtrs
  if ((theBinFSSpecPtr == NULL)
        || (theResFSSpecPtr == NULL)
        || (theExeFSSpecPtr == NULL))
    goto bail;

  // get the creator and file type of the binary file
  myErr = FSpGetFInfo(theBinFSSpecPtr, &myFileInfo);
  if (myErr != noErr)
    goto bail;

  // create the final executable file
  myErr = FSpCreate(theExeFSSpecPtr, myFileInfo.fdCreator, myFileInfo.fdType, 0);
  if ((myErr != noErr) && (myErr != dupFNErr))
    goto bail;

  myErr = FSpOpenDF(theExeFSSpecPtr, fsRdWrPerm, &myExeFile);
  if (myErr != noErr)
    goto bail;

  // open the resource file; it's possible that the resources are stored in the data fork
  // (particularly if the resource file was built on Windows); so make sure we've got a
  // non-0-length resource file
  myErr = FSpOpenRF(theResFSSpecPtr, fsRdPerm, &myResFile);
  if (myErr != noErr) {
    myTryDataFork = true;
  } else {
```

```
  // it's possible that the resource fork exists but is 0-length; if so, try the data
  // fork
  GetEOF(myResFile, &mySizeOfRes);
  if (mySizeOfRes == 0)
    myTryDataFork = true;
}

if (myTryDataFork) {
  // close the open resource file (presumably a 0-length resource fork)
  if (myResFile != -1)
    FSClose(myResFile);

  myErr = FSpOpenDF(theResFSSpecPtr, fsRdPerm, &myResFile);
  if (myErr != noErr)
    goto bail;
}

myErr = FSpOpenDF(theBinFSSpecPtr, fsRdPerm, &myBinFile);
if (myErr != noErr)
  goto bail;

// copy the binary data into the final executable file
myErr = SetEOF(myExeFile, 0);
if (myErr != noErr)
  goto bail;

myErr = GetEOF(myBinFile, &mySizeOfBin);
if (myErr != noErr)
  goto bail;

myHandle = NewHandleClear(mySizeOfBin);
if (myHandle == NULL) {
  myErr = MemError();
  goto bail;
}

myErr = SetFPos(myBinFile, fsFromStart, 0);
if (myErr != noErr)
  goto bail;

myErr = FSRead(myBinFile, &mySizeOfBin, *myHandle);
if (myErr != noErr)
  goto bail;

myErr = SetFPos(myExeFile, fsFromStart, 0);
if (myErr != noErr)
  goto bail;
```

```
myErr = FSWrite(myExeFile, &mySizeOfBin, *myHandle);
if (myErr != noErr)
  goto bail;

FSClose(myBinFile);
DisposeHandle(myHandle);

// copy the resource data into the final executable file
myErr = GetEOF(myResFile, &mySizeOfRes);
if (myErr != noErr)
  goto bail;

myHandle = NewHandleClear(mySizeOfRes);
if (myHandle == NULL) {
  myErr = MemError();
  goto bail;
}

myErr = SetFPos(myResFile, fsFromStart, 0);
if (myErr != noErr)
  goto bail;

myErr = FSRead(myResFile, &mySizeOfRes, *myHandle);
if (myErr != noErr)
  goto bail;

myErr = FSWrite(myExeFile, &mySizeOfRes, *myHandle);
if (myErr != noErr)
  goto bail;

FSClose(myResFile);
DisposeHandle(myHandle);

// pad the final executable file so that it ends on a 4-Kbyte boundary
mySizeOfExe = mySizeOfBin + mySizeOfRes;
while ((mySizeOfExe + sizeof(myTagData)) % (4 * 1024) != 0) {
  char      myChar = '\0';

  mySize = 1;
  myErr = FSWrite(myExeFile, &mySize, &myChar);
  if (myErr != noErr)
    goto bail;
  mySizeOfExe++;
}
```

```
    // add on the special RezWack tag data
    myTagData.fDataTag = EndianU32_NtoB((long)'data');
    myTagData.fDataOffset = 0L;
    myTagData.fDataSize = EndianU32_NtoB(mySizeOfBin);
    myTagData.fRsrcTag = EndianU32_NtoB((long)'rsrc');
    myTagData.fRsrcOffset = EndianU32_NtoB(mySizeOfBin);
    myTagData.fRsrcSize = EndianU32_NtoB(mySizeOfRes);
    strncpy(myTagData.fWackTag, kRezWackTag, kRezWackTagSize);

    mySize = sizeof(myTagData);
    myErr = FSWrite(myExeFile, &mySize, &myTagData);

    FSClose(myExeFile);

bail:
    return(myErr);
}
```

CodeWarrior Plug-Ins

Our RezWack PPC droplet is a great little tool, but things would be even more convenient if we could get CodeWarrior to perform the resource wacking automatically—in the same way that we earlier added a post-link step to our Microsoft Visual Studio projects to run the Rez and RezWack tools automatically each time we build an application that uses Macintosh resources. Indeed, this is possible, but it's significantly more complicated than just writing a batch file containing a few commands that are executed at the proper time. To get the CodeWarrior IDE to do this post-link step for us, we need to write a *CodeWarrior plug-in*, a code module that extends the capabilities of the IDE. We also will want to write a *CodeWarrior settings panel plug-in* to allow us to specify the names of the resource file and the final output file. Figure 14.9 shows our settings panel.

In this section, we'll take a look at the major steps involved in writing a CodeWarrior post-linker plug-in and a settings panel plug-in for wacking Macintosh resources into Windows applications. We won't have space to step through the entire process, but I'll try to touch on the most important points. Thankfully, most of the hard engineering is already done, for two reasons. First, we'll be able to use the QTRW_RezWackWinBinaryAndMacResFile function defined above (Listing 14.9) virtually unchanged within our post-linker plug-in code. And second, Metrowerks provides an SDK for writing CodeWarrior plug-ins that includes extensive documentation and several sample plug-in projects. Most of our work will consist of adapting two of the existing samples to create a RezWack post-linker and setting panel.

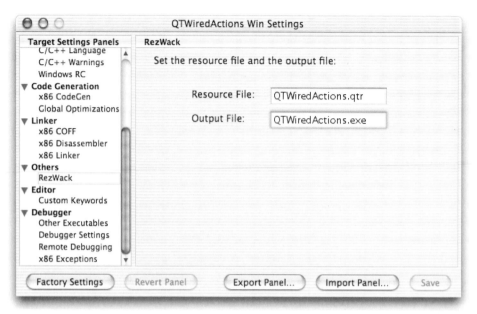

Figure 14.9   The RezWack settings panel.

Writing a Post-linker Plug-In

Let's begin by writing a post-linker plug-in. The first thing to do is download the CodeWarrior SDK from the Metrowerks website. I installed the SDK directly into the Metrowerks CodeWarrior folder on my local machine. Then I duplicated the sample project called Sample_Linker. (There is no sample post-linker project, but it will be easy enough to convert their linker into a post-linker.) Let's call our new project *CWRezWack_Linker*. Once we rename all of the source code files and project files appropriately, we'll have the project shown in Figure 14.10. (The file CWRezWack.rsrc is new and contains a number of string resources that we'll use to report problems that occur during the post-linking; see the section "Handling Post-link Errors" that follows.)

The sample linker project provided by Metrowerks includes both Macintosh and Windows targets, but I have removed the Windows target for simplicity; after all, we don't need a RezWack post-linker on Windows. As you can see, our project contains two source code files, CWRezWack.c and CWRez-WackUtils.cpp. These are just renamed versions of the original Sample_Linker.c and SampleUtils.cpp. We won't modify CWRezWackUtils.cpp further, except to rename the included header file from SampleUtils.h to CWRezWack-Utils.h.

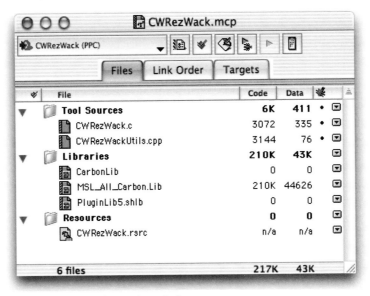

Figure 14.10 The RezWack post-linker project window.

In the file CWRezWack.c, we want to remove any code that supports disassembling. We'll remove the entire definition of the Disassemble function as well as its function declaration near the top of the file. Also, we'll rework the function CWPlugin_GetDropInFlags so that it looks like Listing 14.10.

Listing 14.10 Specifying the plug-in capabilities.

```
CWPLUGIN_ENTRY (CWPlugin_GetDropInFlags) (const DropInFlags** flags, long* flagsSize)
{
  static const DropInFlags sFlags = {
    kCurrentDropInFlagsVersion,
    CWDROPINLINKERTYPE,
    DROPINCOMPILERLINKERAPIVERSION_7,
    isPostLinker | cantDisassemble,                    /* we are a post-linker */
    0,
    DROPINCOMPILERLINKERAPIVERSION
  };

  *flags = &sFlags;
  *flagsSize = sizeof(sFlags);

  return cwNoErr;
}
```

Originally, the fourth line of flags was just linkMultiTargAware; since we're not supporting Windows or disassembling and since we are building a post-linker, I've changed that to isPostLinker | cantDisassemble.

The next important change concerns the routine CWPlugin_GetTargetList, shown in Listing 14.11. As you can see, we indicate that our post-linker applies only to applications built for the Windows operating system, since there is no need to RezWack Macintosh applications.

Listing 14.11 Specifying the plug-in targets.

```
CWPLUGIN_ENTRY (CWPlugin_GetTargetList) (const CWTargetList** targetList)
{
  static CWDataType sCPU = targetCPUAny;
  static CWDataType sOS = targetOSWindows;
  static CWTargetList sTargetList = {kCurrentCWTargetListVersion, 1, &sCPU, 1, &sOS};

  *targetList = &sTargetList;

  return cwNoErr;
}
```

The main function of a CodeWarrior plug-in is largely a dispatcher that calls other functions in the plug-in in response to various requests it receives. Here we need to make just one change to the sample plug-in code, namely, to return an error if our plug-in is asked to disassemble some object code:

```
case reqDisassemble:
  /* disassemble object code for a given project file */
  result = cwErrRequestFailed;
  break;
```

The only request we really need to handle is the reqLink request; in response to this request, we call the Link function defined in Listing 14.12.

Listing 14.12 Handling a link request.

```
static CWResult Link (CWPluginContext context)
{
  CWTargetInfo        targetInfo;
  CWResult            err;
  FSSpec              fileSpec;

  // get the current linker target
  err = CWGetTargetInfo(context, &targetInfo);
```

```
// get an FSSpec from the CWFileSpec
ConvertCWFileSpecToFSSpec(&targetInfo.outfile, &fileSpec);

// add Mac resources to linker target to create final Windows executable
if (err == cwNoErr)
  err = CreateRezWackedFileFromBinary(context, &fileSpec);

return (err);
}
```

CWGetTargetInfo returns information about the link target (that is, the file created by the CodeWarrior linker); we can extract a file system specification from that information using the utility function ConvertCWFileSpecToFSSpec. Then we pass that specification to CreateRezWackedFileFromBinary. Finally, we are on familiar-looking ground once again. The definition of Create-RezWackedFileFromBinary is shown in Listing 14.13.

Listing 14.13 Getting names for the resource and wacked files.

```
OSErr CreateRezWackedFileFromBinary (CWPluginContext context, FSSpecPtr theBinFSSpecPtr)
{
  FSSpec          myResSpec;
  FSSpec          myExeSpec;
  CWMemHandle     prefsHand;
  SamplePref      prefsData;
  SamplePref      *prefsPtr;
  short           errMsgNum;
  CWResult        err;
  OSErr           myErr = paramErr;

  if (theBinFSSpecPtr == NULL)
    goto bail;

  // install a default name for the output file
  myExeSpec = *theBinFSSpecPtr;
  myExeSpec.name[myExeSpec.name[0] - 2] = 'e';
  myExeSpec.name[myExeSpec.name[0] - 1] = 'x';
  myExeSpec.name[myExeSpec.name[0] - 0] = 'e';

  // install a default name for the resource file
  myResSpec = *theBinFSSpecPtr;
  myResSpec.name[myResSpec.name[0] - 2] = 'q';
  myResSpec.name[myResSpec.name[0] - 1] = 't';
  myResSpec.name[myResSpec.name[0] - 0] = 'r';
```

```
// load the panel preferences and get the specified names for the resource and output
// files
err = CWGetNamedPreferences(context, kSamplePanelName, &prefsHand);
if (err == cwNoErr) {
  err = CWLockMemHandle(context, prefsHand, false, (void**)&prefsPtr);
  if (err == cwNoErr) {
    prefsData = *prefsPtr;

    myExeSpec.name[0] = strlen(prefsData.outfile);
    BlockMoveData(prefsData.outfile, myExeSpec.name + 1, myExeSpec.name[0]);

    myResSpec.name[0] = strlen(prefsData.resfile);
    BlockMoveData(prefsData.resfile, myResSpec.name + 1, myResSpec.name[0]);

    CWUnlockMemHandle(context, prefsHand);
  }
}

myErr = RezWackWinBinaryAndMacResFile(theBinFSSpecPtr,
        &myResSpec, &myExeSpec, &errMsgNum);
if (myErr != noErr)
  ReportError(context, errMsgNum);

bail:
  return(myErr);
}
```

The central portion of CreateRezWackedFileFromBinary retrieves the names of the resource file and the desired output file from our custom settings panel; then it calls RezWackWinBinaryAndMacResFile (which is largely just a renamed version of QTRW_RezWackWinBinaryAndMacResFile). In theory, we could omit the code that retrieves the resource filename and the output filename and just use hard-coded extensions as we did in our RezWack PPC droplet. This would relieve us of having to write a settings panel plug-in, but it would provide less flexibility in naming things. Let's do things the right way, even if it means a bit of extra work.

Believe it or not, that's all we need to change in the sample linker to make our RezWack post-linker. We finish up by building the post-linker plug-in and installing it into the appropriate folder in the CodeWarrior plug-in directory. The next time we launch CodeWarrior, we'll be able to select our post-linker in the Target Settings panel of a Windows application project, as shown in Figure 14.11.

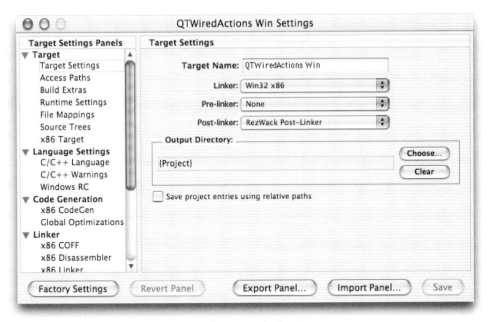

Figure 14.11 The post-linker menu with the RezWack plug-in.

Handling Post-link Errors

You may have noticed, in Listing 14.13, that `RezWackWinBinaryAndMacResFile` returns an error code through the `errMsgNum` parameter. For instance, if the attempt to open the specified resource file fails, then `RezWackWinBinaryAnd-MacResFile` executes this code:

```
if (myErr != noErr) {
  *errMsgNum = kOpenResError;
  goto bail;
}
```

If `CreateRezWackedFileFromBinary` sees that `errMsgNum` is nonzero, then it calls a function `ReportError` to display an error message to the user; a typical error message is shown in Figure 14.12.

The `kOpenResError` constant is defined in our header file `CWRezWack.h`; here's the complete list of error-related constants defined there:

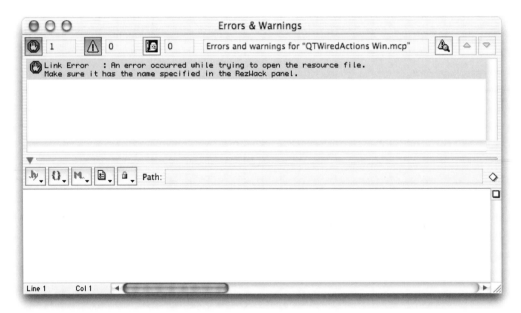

Figure 14.12 A post-linking error message.

```
#define kExeCreateError            1
#define kExeCreateErrorL2          2
#define kOpenExeError              3
#define kOpenExeErrorL2            4
#define kOpenResError              5
#define kOpenResErrorL2            6
#define kOpenBinError              7
#define kOpenBinErrorL2            8
#define kGetMemError               9
#define kGetMemErrorL2            10
#define kWriteExeError            11
#define kWriteExeErrorL2          12
```

These are simply indices into a resource of type 'STR#' that is contained in the file CWRezWack.rsrc. Notice that each error has *two* corresponding string resources (for instance, kOpenResError and kOpenResErrorL2). These two strings provide the messages on the two lines of each error message in the Errors & Warnings window (for instance, "An error occurred while trying to open the resource file." and "Make sure it has the name specified in the RezWack panel.").

Listing 14.14 shows our definition of ReportError. The key ingredient here is the CWReportMessage function, which takes two strings and displays them to the user in the Errors & Warnings window.

Listing 14.14 Reporting a post-linking error to the user.

```
void ReportError (CWPluginContext context, short errMsgNum)
{
  Str255      pErrorMsg;
  char        cErrorMsgL1[256];
  char        cErrorMsgL2[256];

  GetIndString(pErrorMsg, kErrorStrID, errMsgNum);
  if (pErrorMsg[0] != 0)
  {
    BlockMoveData(&pErrorMsg[1], &cErrorMsgL1, pErrorMsg[0]);
    cErrorMsgL1[pErrorMsg[0]] = 0;
  }

  GetIndString(pErrorMsg, kErrorStrID, errMsgNum + 1);
  if (pErrorMsg[0] != 0)
  {
    BlockMoveData(&pErrorMsg[1], &cErrorMsgL2, pErrorMsg[0]);
    cErrorMsgL2[pErrorMsg[0]] = 0;
  }

  CWReportMessage(context, NULL, (char*)&cErrorMsgL1,
    (char*)&cErrorMsgL2, messagetypeError, 0);
}
```

Writing a Settings Panel Plug-In

The final thing we need to do is construct our settings panel plug-in (also called a *preference panel plug-in*), which displays the panel we saw earlier (Figure 14.9) and communicates the settings in that panel to our post-linker when it calls CWGetNamedPreferences (as in Listing 14.13). Once again, we'll clone the sample settings panel project and rename things appropriately, to obtain the project window shown in Figure 14.13.

The layout of the settings panel is determined by a resource of type 'PPob' in the resource file RezWack.rsrc. Figure 14.14 shows the RezWack panel as it appears in the Constructor application. Our RezWack settings panel contains only five items, which we can identify in our code using these constants:

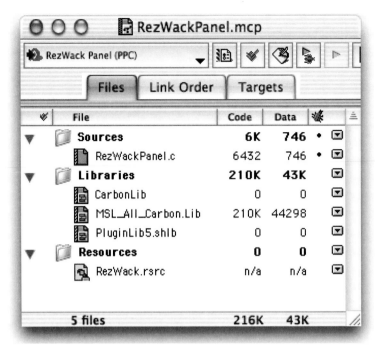

Figure 14.13 The RezWack settings panel project window.

```
enum {
  kStaticText              = 1,
  kResFileLabel,
  kResFileEditBox,
  kOutputFileLabel,
  kOutputFileEditBox
};
```

Most of the changes required in the sample settings panel plug-in code involve removing unneeded routines, which I won't discuss further. The two key functions are the PutData and GetData routines, which transfer data between the onscreen settings panel and an in-memory handle of settings data. For our RezWack settings panel, the data in memory has this structure:

```
typedef struct SamplePref {
  short      version;
  char       outfile[kFileNameSize];
  char       resfile[kFileNameSize];
} SamplePref, **SamplePrefHandle;
```

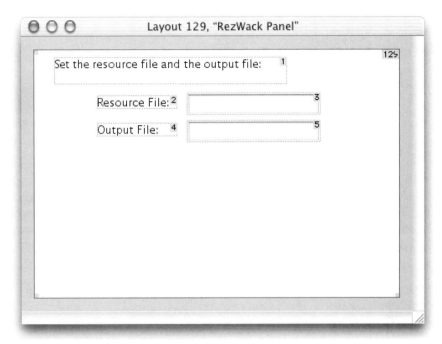

Figure 14.14 The RezWack settings panel in Constructor.

(Take a look back at Listing 14.13 to see how we use the `outfile` and `resfile` fields when building a wacked file.)

Listing 14.15 shows our version of the `PutData` function, which copies settings information from the handle of settings data to the settings panel.

Listing 14.15 Copying settings data into the settings panel.

```
static CWResult PutData (CWPluginContext context)
{
  CWResult          result = cwNoErr;
  CWMemHandle       memHandle = NULL;
  SamplePref        thePreferences;

  try
  {
    // Get a pointer to the current preferences
    result = (GetThePreferences(context, &thePreferences));
    THROW_IF_ERR(result);
    // Stuff data into the preference dialog

    CWPanelSetItemText(context, kOutputFileEditBox, thePreferences.outfile);
```

```
      CWPanelSetItemText(context, kResFileEditBox, thePreferences.resfile);
    }
    catch (CWResult thisErr)
    {
      result = thisErr;
    }

    // Relinquish our pointer to the preferences data
    if (memHandle)
      CWUnlockMemHandle(context, memHandle);        // error is ignored

    return (result);
}
```

And Listing 14.16 shows our version of the GetData function, which copies data from the panel to the handle of settings data.

Listing 14.16 Copying settings data out of the settings panel.

```
static CWResult GetData (CWPluginContext context)
{
  CWResult              result = cwNoErr;
  CWMemHandle           memHandle = NULL;
  SamplePref            thePreferences;              // local copy of preference data
  char *                outname = (char *)malloc(255);
  char *                resname = (char *)malloc(255);
  short                 i, j;

  try
  {
    // Get a pointer to the current preferences
    result = (GetThePreferences(context, &thePreferences));
    THROW_IF_ERR(result);

    // Stuff dialog values into the current preferences
    result = CWPanelGetItemText(context, kOutputFileEditBox, outname,
               sizeof(thePreferences.outfile));
    THROW_IF_ERR(result);

    // apparently nonprinting characters can squeeze their way into the dialog box,
    // so winnow them out...
    for (i = 0, j = 0; i < strlen(outname); i++)
      if (isprint(outname[i]))
        thePreferences.outfile[j++] = outname[i];
```

```
      thePreferences.outfile[j] = 0;

      result = CWPanelGetItemText(context, kResFileEditBox, resname,
                 sizeof(thePreferences.resfile));
      THROW_IF_ERR(result);

      // apparently nonprinting characters can squeeze their way into the dialog box,
      // so winnow them out...
      for (i = 0, j = 0; i < strlen(resname); i++)
        if (isprint(resname[i]))
          thePreferences.resfile[j++] = resname[i];

      thePreferences.resfile[j] = 0;

      // Now update the "real" preferences data
      result = (PutThePreferences(context, &thePreferences));
      THROW_IF_ERR(result);

    }
    catch (CWResult thisErr)
    {
      result = thisErr;
    }

    // Relinquish our pointer to the preferences data
    free(outname);
    free(resname);

    return result;

}
```

I have found that nonprinting characters can sometimes make their way into the edit-text boxes in the settings panel, so we explicitly look for them and remove them from the filenames typed by the user.

The settings panel plug-in code contains a handful of other functions that save preferences on disk, restore preferences to their previous settings, and so forth. I'll leave the inspection of those routines to the interested reader. For the rest of us, we can finish up by building the settings panel plug-in and installing it into the correct folder in the CodeWarrior installation.

▶ Conclusion

In this chapter, we've seen how to embed Macintosh resources into a Windows executable file, whether we want to develop our applications on Windows or Macintosh computers. This resource embedding allows us to take advantage of the support provided by the QuickTime Media Layer for those parts of the Macintosh User Interface Toolbox and the Macintosh Operating System that rely heavily on resources, including the Dialog Manager, the Window Manager, the Control Manager, and of course the Resource Manager. This, in turn, makes it easy to write our code once and deliver it on several platforms.

She's Gotta Have It

Using Media Sample References and Data References

 Introduction

Imagine that we've got a couple dozen pictures from a digital camera and that we'd like to create a slideshow movie from those pictures—that is, a QuickTime movie that displays each picture, in a predetermined sequence, for a predetermined amount of time. The first thing we'd need to do, of course, is create a new movie file, track, and media (by calling `CreateMovie-File`, `NewMovieTrack`, and `NewTrackMedia`). Then we might proceed like this: open each picture file, draw the picture data into an offscreen graphics world, compress the data, and add the compressed data as a new media sample by calling `AddMediaSample`. Then we would finish up by calling `InsertMediaIntoTrack` and `AddMovieResource`. Voilà, we've got our slideshow movie.

This strategy involves copying the picture data from the individual picture files into the slideshow movie file, and for some purposes that might be exactly what we want to do. But, if we're going to keep the picture files around anyway or if we're not sure we want to keep the resulting movie, it might be better to have our QuickTime movie file just point to the data in the picture files instead of having it contain a copy of that data. We can do this by inserting into the movie a *media sample reference* (or, more briefly, a *sample reference*) to the picture file data.

In this chapter, we're going to work with media sample references. We'll begin by taking a look at how to create media sample references, by developing a simple droplet application that creates a slideshow movie from a number of picture files as just described. As we'll see, sample references go hand in hand with data references, which we discussed at some length in Volume One, Chapter 9. So we'll take this opportunity to investigate a couple of somewhat more advanced techniques for using data references. In particular, we'll see how to "flatten" a movie that contains a movie track, so that the child movie data is contained within the parent movie file; we'll also see how to create a movie whose media data is contained entirely in memory and then save it into a file.

Media Sample References

In a nutshell, a media sample reference is a reference to some existing media data. The idea is that once we've got some media data stored in some location (a file, an object addressed by a URL, a block of memory, or the like), we can reuse that media data by simply referring to it. That is, we don't need to copy the data in order to get access to it.

It's worth noting that we've bumped into sample references several times previously. In Volume One, when we discussed movie importers and exporters (in Chapter 5), we learned that QuickTime can import some types of files without having to make a copy of the file data. We say that these kinds of files are *imported in place*—meaning that the associated movie importer constructs a movie that directly references the data in the file being imported. Now we can see that a movie importer does this by inserting media sample references into the new movie. Those references point to the data in the imported file. Importing in place, by using media sample references, allows the new movie to be created more quickly and uses less storage space (since the media data does not need to be copied).

We also ran into sample references while we were working with the QuickTime video effects architecture, when we wanted to add a video effect to part of a video track. (See this volume, Chapter 2, "F/X 2.") The standard way to do this is to create a new video track that is a copy of the appropriate segment of the original video track; then we create an effects track that uses the copied track segment as its input, as shown in Figure 15.1. The new video track can contain a copy of the media data in the original video track, or it can contain only references to that media data.

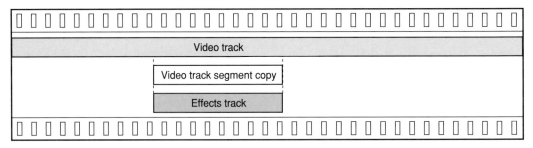

Figure 15.1 A filter applied to part of a video track.

Creating Sample References Indirectly

Let's begin by reviewing the code we used to create the new track that we used as the input to our effects track. Listing 15.1 shows the relevant section of code.

Listing 15.1 Creating a copy of a video track segment.

```
mySrcTrack1 = NewMovieTrack(theMovie, myWidth, myHeight, kNoVolume);
if (mySrcTrack1 == NULL)
  return(paramErr);

mySrcMedia1 = NewTrackMedia(mySrcTrack1, VideoMediaType, myTimeScale, NULL, 0);
if (mySrcMedia1 == NULL)
  return(paramErr);

#if COPY_MOVIE_MEDIA
myErr = BeginMediaEdits(mySrcMedia1);
if (myErr != noErr)
  return(myErr);
#endif

myErr = CopyTrackSettings(myVidTrack1, mySrcTrack1);
myErr = InsertTrackSegment(myVidTrack1, mySrcTrack1, theStartTime, theDuration,
          theStartTime);
if (myErr != noErr)
  return(myErr);

#if COPY_MOVIE_MEDIA
EndMediaEdits(mySrcMedia1);
#endif
```

We call InsertTrackSegment to copy part of the original video track (myVidTrack1) into the track that will be used as the source for the effect (mySrcTrack1). If the compiler flag COPY_MOVIE_MEDIA is set to 0, then we don't call BeginMediaEdits and EndMediaEdits to begin and end a media editing session; in this case, the new track contains references to the media data in the original track, thereby minimizing the resulting file size.

Creating Sample References Directly

So, one way to create sample references is to call InsertTrackSegment without having opened a media editing session (that is, without having called BeginMediaEdits). A more direct way to create sample references is to use the functions AddMediaSampleReference or AddMediaSampleReferences. Both of these functions allow us to add to a media one or more sample references to some existing data (and hence the names are slightly misleading). The main difference between these two functions is that when we are adding a large number of samples to a movie at one time, AddMediaSampleReferences is significantly more efficient than AddMediaSampleReference. In this chapter, we will be adding only one sample reference at a time, so we'll restrict our attention to AddMediaSampleReference, which is declared essentially like this:

```
OSErr AddMediaSampleReference (
        Media theMedia,
        long dataOffset,
        unsigned long size,
        TimeValue durationPerSample,
        SampleDescriptionHandle sampleDescriptionH,
        long numberOfSamples,
        short sampleFlags,
        TimeValue *sampleTime);
```

The parameters here are identical to those for AddMediaSample, with one exception: AddMediaSample also takes a handle to the data that is to be added to the media. With AddMediaSampleReference, we're not adding any data, so we don't need that parameter.

Here's how we might call AddMediaSampleReference to add a single media sample reference to a media:

```
myErr = AddMediaSampleReference(myMedia, myDataOffset, mySize, myDuration,
        myDesc, 1, 0, NULL);
```

As you can see, the numberOfSamples parameter is set to 1, the sampleFlags parameter is set to 0, and the sampleTime parameter is set to NULL (since we don't need to have the new sample time returned to us). The other parameters are set to specific values determined by the application. For example, myDataOffset should specify the offset into the referenced media file (or other storage device) of the desired media data. In our sample slideshow-making application, myDuration will always be set to 600 so that each slide is displayed for one second.

Now, how does AddMediaSampleReference know where the original media data resides? As you know, QuickTime uses data references as its principal means of identifying the location of some data. So we might have expected that AddMediaSampleReference would take a data reference as a parameter. But, alas, you can see in the preceding code that there is no such parameter. Instead, we need to attach the data reference to the media before we call AddMediaSampleReference; we do this by calling the AddMediaDataRef function like this, for example:

```
myErr = AddMediaDataRef(myMedia, &myDataRefIndex,
        (Handle)myAlias, rAliasType);
```

AddMediaDataRef adds the specified data reference to the specified media and returns the index of that data reference in the media's list of data references. Then we assign that index to the dataRefIndex field of the sample description that we pass to AddMediaSampleReference:

```
(**myDesc).dataRefIndex = myDataRefIndex;
```

In this way, we've given AddMediaSampleReference a complete specification of the location of the data for which it will create a sample reference.

Getting Sample References

QuickTime also provides the functions GetMediaSampleReference and Get-MediaSampleReferences, which we can use to get information about one or more samples that are stored in a media data file (or other media storage container). Unlike GetMediaSample, GetMediaSampleReference does not return the actual media data to us; rather, it gives us a handful of pieces of information about the media sample(s), such as the offset within the media container of the sample data, the size of the sample data, and a sample description that specifies the format of that sample data. We just saw that we'll need that offset and size when we call AddMediaSampleReference; we'll also need a sample description when we're building our slideshow movie. So, we'll call GetMediaSampleReference like this:

```
myErr = GetMediaSampleReference(myRefMedia, &myDataOffset, &mySize, 0,
        NULL, NULL, myDesc, NULL, 1, NULL, 0);
```

Here, myRefMedia is the media to which we have a reference. In our slideshow example, it'll be the data in the individual picture files.

▶ Slideshow Movies

Let's illustrate how to work with media sample references by building a slideshow movie from a collection of picture files. We want the user to be able to drop any number of picture files onto our application; when this happens, the application will ask the user to specify a filename and location for the slideshow movie; then, it will create the movie and exit. Let's call this droplet *DropPix*.

Handling Dropped Files

The first thing that DropPix needs to do is assemble a list of the files that the user has dropped onto its icon. In our Macintosh application, we can do this inside of our AppleEvent handler for the Open Document event, as shown in Listing 15.2.

Listing 15.2 Keeping track of dropped files (Macintosh).

```
// open each specified file
for (myIndex = 1; myIndex <= myItemsInList; myIndex++)
  if (myErr == noErr) {
    myErr = AEGetNthPtr(&myDocList, myIndex, typeFSS, &myKeyWd, &myTypeCode,
            (Ptr)&myFSSpec, sizeof(myFSSpec), &myActualSize);
    if (myErr == noErr) {
      gSpecs[myIndex - 1] = myFSSpec;
    }
  }

if (myDocList.dataHandle)
  myIgnoreErr = AEDisposeDesc(&myDocList);

gNumSpecs = myIndex - 1;
DropPix_MakeSlideShow();

QTFrame_QuitFramework();                 // act like a droplet and close automatically
```

You'll notice that we're using two global variables, gSpecs and gNumSpecs, to keep track of the file system specification records for the dropped files. We declare those variables like this:

```
FSSpec          gSpecs[kMaxNumPictureFiles];
short           gNumSpecs;
```

(I'll leave it as an exercise for the enterprising reader to get rid of the hard-coded array size.)

On Windows, we can get a list of the dropped files by reworking some of the code in the QTFrame_OpenCommandLineMovies function (defined in the file WinFramework.c). First, we need to remove the existing call to SHGetFileInfo that restricts our application to opening only QuickTime movie files. Then, once we've finished creating a file system specification record for a dropped file, we can add it to our array and increment our count of dropped files, as shown in Listing 15.3.

Listing 15.3   Keeping track of dropped files (Windows).

```
// make an FSSpec record
NativePathNameToFSSpec(myFileName, &myFSSpec, kFullNativePath);
gSpecs[myFileIndex] = myFSSpec;
myFileIndex++;
```

When we are done collecting the files, we finish up like this:

```
gNumSpecs = myFileIndex;
DropPix_MakeSlideShow();
```

Creating the Slideshow Movie

The `DropPix_MakeSlideShow` function first elicits a movie filename and location from the user so that DropPix knows where to put the output slideshow movie. Then it creates the new movie file:

```
myErr = CreateMovieFile(&myFile, sigMoviePlayer, smCurrentScript,
        myFlags, &myResRefNum, &myMovie);
```

And, as usual, we'll create a new track and media:

```
myTrack = NewMovieTrack(myMovie, myWidth, myHeight, 0);
myMedia = NewTrackMedia(myTrack, VideoMediaType, 600, NULL, 0);
```

The bulk of `DropPix_MakeSlideShow` is a for loop that adds to this new media a sample reference to the data in each of the picture files in gSpecs.

Retrieving the Picture Information

Before we can call `AddMediaSampleReference`, we need to get the offset of the picture data in its file, and we need to add a data reference for that file to the new media. Adding a data reference is easy; first, we create a file data reference:

```
myErr = QTNewAlias((const FSSpec *)&gSpecs[myIndex], &myAlias, true);
```

Then we add it to the media:

```
myErr = AddMediaDataRef(myMedia, &myDataRefIndex,
        (Handle)myAlias, rAliasType);
```

How do we get the offset of the data in the picture file? Earlier, we saw that we can use GetMediaSampleReference to get information about samples that are stored in a media data file. So all we need to do is call NewMovieFrom-DataRef to open the picture file as a movie and then call GetMediaSample-Reference on that movie's media. Listing 15.4 shows the sequence of calls here.

Listing 15.4 Getting information about a picture file.

```
// allocate a sample description
myDesc = (SampleDescriptionHandle)NewHandle(0);
myErr = MemError();
if (myErr != noErr)
  goto bailLoop;

myErr = NewMovieFromDataRef(&myRefMovie, newMovieDontResolveDataRefs, NULL,
        (Handle)myAlias, rAliasType);
if (myErr != noErr)
  goto bailLoop;

// get the first track's media
myRefTrack = GetMovieIndTrack(myRefMovie, 1);
myRefMedia = GetTrackMedia(myRefTrack);
if ((myRefTrack == NULL) || (myRefMedia == NULL))
  goto bailLoop;

myErr = GetMediaSampleReference(myRefMedia, &myDataOffset, &mySize, 0, NULL, NULL, myDesc,
        NULL, 1, NULL, 0);
```

This gives us the data offset and the media sample size. It also gives us a sample description of the image, which we can use (for instance) to determine the size of the video track in the slideshow movie. Our call to New-MovieTrack really looks like this:

```
myTrack = NewMovieTrack(myMovie,
            Long2Fix((**(ImageDescriptionHandle)myDesc).width),
            Long2Fix((**(ImageDescriptionHandle)myDesc).height), kNoVolume);
```

Adding a Sample Reference

Now we're almost finished. We add a sample reference to the data in the picture file like this:

```
             (**myDesc).dataRefIndex = myDataRefIndex;
             myErr = AddMediaSampleReference(myMedia, myDataOffset, mySize, myDuration,
                     myDesc, 1, 0, NULL);
```

Once we've done this for each picture file dropped onto our application, we need to call InsertMediaIntoTrack and AddMovieResource in the usual way. Listing 15.5 shows DropPix_MakeSlideShow in its full glory.

Listing 15.5 Creating a slideshow movie.

```
OSErr DropPix_MakeSlideShow (void)
{
  Movie          myMovie = NULL;
  Track          myTrack = NULL;
  Media          myMedia = NULL;
  FSSpec         myFile;
  Boolean        myIsSelected = false;
  Boolean        myIsReplacing = false;
  StringPtr      myPrompt = QTUtils_ConvertCToPascalString("Save movie as:");
  StringPtr      myFileName = QTUtils_ConvertCToPascalString("Untitled.mov");
  long           myFlags = createMovieFileDeleteCurFile | createMovieFileDontCreateResFile;
  short          myResRefNum = kInvalidFileRefNum;
  short          myResID = movieInDataForkResID;
  short          myIndex;
  OSErr          myErr = noErr;

  if (gNumSpecs <= 0)
    return(paramErr);

  // prompt the user for new filename
  QTFrame_PutFile(myPrompt, myFileName, &myFile, &myIsSelected, &myIsReplacing);
  myErr = myIsSelected ? noErr : userCanceledErr;
  if (myErr != noErr)
    goto bail;

  // delete any existing file of that name
  if (myIsReplacing) {
    myErr = DeleteMovieFile(&myFile);
    if (myErr != noErr)
      goto bail;
  }

  // create a movie file for the destination movie
  myErr = CreateMovieFile(&myFile, sigMoviePlayer, smCurrentScript, myFlags, &myResRefNum,
          &myMovie);
  if (myErr != noErr)
    goto bail;
```

```
// add a sample reference for each image to the new movie
for (myIndex = 0; myIndex < gNumSpecs; myIndex++) {
  short                   myDataRefIndex = 0;
  long                    myDataOffset, mySize;
  SampleDescriptionHandle myDesc = NULL;
  TimeValue               myDuration = 600;
  AliasHandle             myAlias = NULL;
  Movie                   myRefMovie = NULL;
  Track                   myRefTrack = NULL;
  Media                   myRefMedia = NULL;

  myErr = QTNewAlias((const FSSpec *)&gSpecs[myIndex], &myAlias, true);
  if (myErr != noErr)
    goto bailLoop;

  // allocate sample description
  myDesc = (SampleDescriptionHandle)NewHandle(0);
  myErr = MemError();
  if (myErr != noErr)
    goto bailLoop;

  myErr = NewMovieFromDataRef(&myRefMovie, newMovieDontResolveDataRefs,
            NULL, (Handle)myAlias, rAliasType);
  if (myErr != noErr)
    goto bailLoop;

  // get the first track's media
  myRefTrack = GetMovieIndTrack(myRefMovie, 1);
  myRefMedia = GetTrackMedia(myRefTrack);
  if ((myRefTrack == NULL) || (myRefMedia == NULL))
    goto bailLoop;

  myErr = GetMediaSampleReference(myRefMedia, &myDataOffset, &mySize,
            0, NULL, NULL, myDesc, NULL, 1, NULL, 0);
  if (myErr != noErr)
    goto bailLoop;

  if (myTrack == NULL) {
    // create the movie track and media
    myTrack = NewMovieTrack(myMovie,
                Long2Fix((**(ImageDescriptionHandle)myDesc).width),
                Long2Fix((**(ImageDescriptionHandle)myDesc).height),
                kNoVolume);
```

```
          myErr = GetMoviesError();
          if (myErr != noErr)
            goto bail;

          myMedia = NewTrackMedia(myTrack, VideoMediaType, 600, NULL, 0);
          myErr = GetMoviesError();
          if (myErr != noErr)
            goto bail;
        }

        // add a data reference to the media
        myErr = AddMediaDataRef(myMedia, &myDataRefIndex, (Handle)myAlias, rAliasType);
        if (myErr != noErr)
          goto bailLoop;

        (**myDesc).dataRefIndex = myDataRefIndex;

        // add a media sample reference to the media
        myErr = AddMediaSampleReference(myMedia, myDataOffset, mySize, myDuration, myDesc, 1,
                0, NULL);
bailLoop:
        if (myDesc)
          DisposeHandle((Handle)myDesc);
      }

      // add the media to the track
      myErr = InsertMediaIntoTrack(myTrack, 0, 0, GetMediaDuration(myMedia), fixed1);
      if (myErr != noErr)
        goto bail;

      // add the movie atom to the movie file
      myErr = AddMovieResource(myMovie, myResRefNum, &myResID, NULL);

bail:
    if (myResRefNum != kInvalidFileRefNum)
      CloseMovieFile(myResRefNum);

    if (myMovie != NULL)
      DisposeMovie(myMovie);

    free(myPrompt);
    free(myFileName);

    return(myErr);
}
```

As you can see, the size of the slideshow video track is determined by the size of the first picture file in gSpecs. Each remaining image is scaled to fit into that track rectangle, which may result in some distortion of the image. I'll leave it as an exercise for the reader to figure out a way to avoid that distortion.

▶ Movie Tracks

A movie track is a track of type MovieMediaType that effectively embeds one movie inside of another, as illustrated in Figure 15.2. The key feature of using movie tracks—instead of just layering one track on top of another track—is that the parent and child movies can have different time bases, so they can (for instance) have different playback rates and different looping characteristics.

You may recall from our discussion of movie tracks in Volume One (in Chapter 8) that a media sample in a movie track consists of an atom container whose atoms specify the movie that is to be embedded in the main movie as well as some of the playback characteristics of the embedded movie. The media sample does not typically contain the data for the child movie itself; rather, it points to that data using an atom of type kMovieMedia-DataReference; this atom contains a data reference to the child movie data, which is most often a file data reference or a URL data reference.

It would be nice if there were a way to save a movie that contains a movie track such that all the media data—for the parent *and* the child movies—is contained within a single file. In fact, this is quite straightforward

Figure 15.2 A child movie inside of a parent movie.

using a data reference extension. The essential idea is to simply append all of the child movie data to the data reference atom in the appropriate media sample. By suitably reconfiguring the data reference atom, we can force QuickTime to look in the data reference extension for the child movie data instead of resolving the data reference in that atom.

In the process of reconfiguring the data reference atom, we'll need to use a few techniques that are interesting in their own right. We'll need to learn how to get the data for a media sample at a specific movie time, and we'll need to learn how to replace an entire media sample in an existing movie. So let's get started.

Getting the Current Media Sample

A movie track (that is, a track of type MovieMediaType) can have one or more media samples, each of which is an atom container whose atoms pick out a child movie and specify its spatial layout and playback characteristics. We can get the media sample for a given movie time by calling GetMediaSample. The only "gotcha" is that GetMediaSample requires that this time be expressed in the media's time scale. To convert a movie time to the corresponding media time, we can call TrackTimeToMediaTime, as illustrated in Listing 15.6.

Listing 15.6 Getting the current media sample data.

```
Handle                  mySample = NULL;
SampleDescriptionHandle  myDesc = NULL;
TimeValue               myMovieTimeNow = 0;
TimeValue               myMediaTimeNow = 0;
TimeValue               myDuration = 0;

mySample = NewHandleClear(0);
if (mySample == NULL)
  return(MemError());

myDesc = (SampleDescriptionHandle)NewHandleClear(0);
if (myDesc == NULL) {
  myErr = MemError();
  goto bail;
}

myMovieTimeNow = GetMovieTime(myMovie, NULL);
if (myMovieTimeNow == GetMovieDuration(myMovie))
  myMovieTimeNow--;
```

```
myMediaTimeNow = TrackTimeToMediaTime(myMovieTimeNow, myTrack);
if (myMediaTimeNow == -1) {
  myErr = invalidTime;
  goto bail;
}

myErr = GetMediaSample(myMedia, mySample, 0, NULL, myMediaTimeNow, NULL, &myDuration,
          myDesc, NULL, 1, NULL, NULL);
```

TrackTimeToMediaTime returns –1 if there is no media sample in the track at the specified movie time or if the specified movie time is outside the movie's active segment. Since we call GetMovieTime to get the current movie time, we're guaranteed that myMovieTimeNow will be within the active movie segment. (Notice that we decrement the movie time if we happen to be at the end of the movie.)

The time passed to GetMediaSample can be any time within the extent of the media sample. GetMediaSample retrieves the data for that sample and returns it in the handle we pass it (here, mySample). GetMediaSample also returns the duration of the media sample.

Loading the Child Movie Data into Memory

The media data, to repeat, is an atom container that holds at least a data reference atom that picks out the child movie. We can get that atom like this:

```
myAtom = QTFindChildByIndex(mySample, kParentAtomIsContainer,
          kMovieMediaDataReference, 1, NULL);
```

If myAtom is nonzero, then we want to fetch the data in that atom. The data is a data reference prefixed by the data reference type. We can get the data reference and its type like this:

```
QTGetAtomDataPtr(mySample, myAtom, &myDataSize, &myDataPtr);
myDataRefType = EndianU32_BtoN(*(OSType *)myDataPtr);
myErr = PtrToHand(myDataPtr + sizeof(OSType), &myDataRef,
          myDataSize - sizeof(OSType));
```

If all this is successful, then myDataRefType is the data reference type and myDataRef is the data reference itself. Right now, we want to open the child movie specified by that data reference and load it completely into memory. To open the child movie, we can use NewMovieFromDataRef:

```
NewMovieFromDataRef(&myChildMovie, 0, NULL, myDataRef, myDataRefType);
```

To load the movie's media data completely into memory, we can use FlattenMovieData, passing it a handle data reference. (We've used this trick previously, in Volume One, Chapter 9.) Listing 15.7 shows the essential steps.

Listing 15.7 Loading a child movie into memory.

```
DataReferenceRecord         myDataRefRecord;
Handle                      myDataRefHandle = NULL;
Handle                      myHandleDataRef = NULL;

myDataRefHandle = NewHandleClear(0);
if (myDataRefHandle == NULL)
  goto bail;

myHandleDataRef = QTDR_MakeHandleDataRef(myDataRefHandle);
if (myHandleDataRef == NULL)
  goto bail;

myDataRefRecord.dataRefType = HandleDataHandlerSubType;
myDataRefRecord.dataRef = myHandleDataRef;

myMemoryMovie = FlattenMovieData(myChildMovie,
                flattenFSSpecPtrIsDataRefRecordPtr | flattenAddMovieToDataFork,
                (FSSpecPtr)&myDataRefRecord,
                sigMoviePlayer,
                smSystemScript,
                0L);
myErr = GetMoviesError();
if (myErr != noErr)
  goto bail;

DisposeMovie(myChildMovie);
```

Notice that the second parameter passed to FlattenMovieData contains the flattenFSSpecPtrIsDataRefRecordPtr flag, which indicates that the third parameter is a pointer to a data reference record, not a pointer to a file system specification record; it also contains the flattenAddMovieToDataFork flag, which tells FlattenMovieData to write the movie atom as well as the media data into the specified location. If we didn't specify flattenAddMovieToData-Fork, we'd get only the media data in the child movie.

Creating a "Flattened" Child Movie Media Sample

Recall that we want to replace the original data reference in the data reference atom in the child movie media sample by a new data reference that has the child movie data appended to it. That is to say, we want to attach a data reference extension to that original data reference. In this case, the extension is of type kDataRefExtensionInitializationData. Let's call this kind of extension an *initialization data data reference extension*—or, more briefly, an *initialization extension*.

QuickTime uses an initialization extension in one case only: when the data reference is a handle data reference and the specified handle is NULL. When this happens, QuickTime takes the data directly from the initialization extension. In effect, we can use this type of data reference extension to short-circuit the normal data reference resolution that QuickTime would otherwise perform; we're saying: here is the data you're looking for, in this data reference extension.

So our task boils down to this: replace the existing data reference in the atom of type kMovieMediaDataReference by a handle data reference whose associated data is NULL; then append a data reference extension of type kDataRefExtensionInitializationData to that data reference. For this latter task, we'll use the utility function QTDR_AddInitDataDataRefExtension, defined in Listing 15.8.

Listing 15.8 Adding an initialization data data reference extension.

```
OSErr QTDR_AddInitDataDataRefExtension (Handle theDataRef, Ptr theInitDataPtr)
{
    unsigned long       myAtomHeader[2];
    OSErr               myErr = noErr;

    if (theInitDataPtr == NULL)
        return(paramErr);

    myAtomHeader[0] = EndianU32_NtoB(sizeof(myAtomHeader) + GetPtrSize(theInitDataPtr));
    myAtomHeader[1] = EndianU32_NtoB(kDataRefExtensionInitializationData);

    myErr = PtrAndHand(myAtomHeader, theDataRef, sizeof(myAtomHeader));
    if (myErr == noErr)
        myErr = PtrAndHand(theInitDataPtr, theDataRef, GetPtrSize(theInitDataPtr));

    return(myErr);
}
```

Listing 15.9 shows the code we use to replace the original data reference atom by a new data reference atom that contains the data of the child movie.

Listing 15.9 Replacing a data reference atom by a "flattened" atom.

```
// out with the old...
QTRemoveAtom(mySample, myAtom);

// ...and in with the new
myChildDataHandle = NewHandleClear(sizeof(OSType) + sizeof(Handle));
if (myChildDataHandle != NULL) {
  OSType        myType;

  // set the data reference type
  myType = EndianU32_NtoB(HandleDataHandlerSubType);
  BlockMove(&myType, *myChildDataHandle, sizeof(OSType));

  // leave the next four bytes set to 0x00000000;
  // add a filenaming extension and an initialization extension
  myErr = QTDR_AddFilenamingExtension(myChildDataHandle, NULL);
  if (myErr != noErr)
    goto bail;

  HLock(myDataRefHandle);
  myErr = QTDR_AddInitDataDataRefExtension (myChildDataHandle, *myDataRefHandle);
  HUnlock(myDataRefHandle);
  if (myErr != noErr)
    goto bail;

  HLock(myChildDataHandle);
  myErr = QTInsertChild(mySample, kParentAtomIsContainer,
          kMovieMediaDataReference, 1, 1,
          GetHandleSize(myChildDataHandle),
          *myChildDataHandle, NULL);
  HUnlock(myChildDataHandle);
  if (myErr != noErr)
    goto bail;
}
```

Notice that we need to add an empty filenaming extension before we add the initialization extension.

Replacing a Media Sample

One final step remains, namely, to replace the original media sample by the revised media sample. To do this, we first need to delete the track segment corresponding to the original media sample. Then we'll add the new media sample into the media and insert it into the track at that time.

It's easy enough to figure out the start time and duration of a particular media sample. Recall that we already have the current movie time stored in the variable myMovieTimeNow. We can then call GetTrackNextInterestingTime twice, asking it to search backward and then forward for the boundaries of the current media sample:

```
GetTrackNextInterestingTime(myTrack, nextTimeMediaSample | nextTimeEdgeOK,
    myMovieTimeNow, -0x01000, &myMovieStartTime, NULL);
GetTrackNextInterestingTime(myTrack, nextTimeMediaSample | nextTimeEdgeOK,
    myMovieStartTime, 0x01000, NULL, &myMovieDuration);
```

Then we can call DeleteTrackSegment to delete the track segment occupied by the media sample:

```
DeleteTrackSegment(myTrack, myMovieStartTime, myMovieDuration);
```

Then we proceed as usual, opening a media editing session and adding the new media sample to the media. The key step here is a call to AddMedia-Sample:

```
myErr = AddMediaSample(myMedia,
            mySample,
            0,                          // no offset in data
            GetHandleSize(mySample),
            myDuration,                 // frame duration
            (SampleDescriptionHandle)myDesc,
            1,                          // one sample
            0,                          // self-contained samples
            &myNewTime);
```

Finally, we insert the media into the track at the desired time and for the desired duration:

```
myErr = InsertMediaIntoTrack(myTrack, myMovieStartTime, myNewTime,
            myDuration, (Fixed)0x00010000L);
```

And we are done! Listing 15.10 shows the complete process in one handy routine.

Listing 15.10 Flattening a child movie into a parent movie file.

```
OSErr QTMIM_FlattenChildIntoParent (WindowObject theWindowObject)
{
    Movie                     myMovie = NULL;
    Track                     myTrack = NULL;
    Media                     myMedia = NULL;
    Handle                    mySample = NULL;
    SampleDescriptionHandle   myDesc = NULL;
    TimeValue                 myMovieTimeNow = 0;
    TimeValue                 myMediaTimeNow = 0;
    TimeValue                 myDuration = 0;
    QTAtom                    myAtom = 0;
    Ptr                       myDataPtr = NULL;
    Handle                    myDataRef = NULL;
    long                      myDataSize = 0;
    OSType                    myDataRefType;
    Movie                     myChildMovie = NULL;
    Movie                     myMemoryMovie = NULL;
    DataReferenceRecord       myDataRefRecord;
    Handle                    myDataRefHandle = NULL;
    Handle                    myHandleDataRef = NULL;
    Handle                    myChildDataHandle = NULL;
    Fixed                     myRate;
    TimeValue                 myMovieStartTime = 0;
    TimeValue                 myMovieDuration = 0;
    TimeValue                 myNewTime = 0;
    OSErr                     myErr = noErr;

    if (theWindowObject == NULL)
      return(paramErr);

    // round up the usual suspects: the parent movie, movie track, and movie track media

    myMovie = (**theWindowObject).fMovie;
    if (myMovie == NULL)
      return(invalidMovie);

    myTrack = GetMovieIndTrackType(myMovie, 1, MovieMediaType, movieTrackMediaType);
    if (myTrack == NULL)
      return(invalidTrack);

    myMedia = GetTrackMedia(myTrack);
    if (myMedia == NULL)
      return(invalidMedia);
```

```
// get the child movie sample data

// if the parent movie is playing, stop it
myRate = GetMovieRate(myMovie);
SetMovieRate(myMovie, 0);

mySample = NewHandleClear(0);
if (mySample == NULL)
  return(MemError());

myDesc = (SampleDescriptionHandle)NewHandleClear(0);
if (myDesc == NULL) {
  myErr = MemError();
  goto bail;
}

myMovieTimeNow = GetMovieTime(myMovie, NULL);
if (myMovieTimeNow == GetMovieDuration(myMovie))
  myMovieTimeNow--;

myMediaTimeNow = TrackTimeToMediaTime(myMovieTimeNow, myTrack);
if (myMediaTimeNow == -1) {
  myErr = invalidTime;
  goto bail;
}

myErr = GetMediaSample(myMedia, mySample, 0, NULL, myMediaTimeNow, NULL,
          &myDuration, myDesc, NULL, 1, NULL, NULL);
if (myErr != noErr)
  goto bail;

// the media sample is an atom container;
// find the data reference atom inside the media sample

myAtom = QTFindChildByIndex(mySample, kParentAtomIsContainer, kMovieMediaDataReference,
          1, NULL);
if (myAtom != 0) {
  // get the data reference atom data
  QTLockContainer(mySample);

  myErr = QTGetAtomDataPtr(mySample, myAtom, &myDataSize, &myDataPtr);
  if (myErr != noErr)
    goto bail;
```

```
myDataRefType = EndianU32_BtoN(*(OSType *)myDataPtr);
myErr = PtrToHand(myDataPtr + sizeof(OSType),
          &myDataRef, myDataSize - sizeof(OSType));
if (myErr != noErr)
  goto bail;

QTUnlockContainer(mySample);

// open the child movie and flatten it entirely into memory

myErr = NewMovieFromDataRef(&myChildMovie, 0, NULL, myDataRef, myDataRefType);
if (myErr != noErr)
  goto bail;

myDataRefHandle = NewHandleClear(0);
if (myDataRefHandle == NULL)
  goto bail;

myHandleDataRef = QTDR_MakeHandleDataRef(myDataRefHandle);
if (myHandleDataRef == NULL)
  goto bail;

myDataRefRecord.dataRefType = HandleDataHandlerSubType;
myDataRefRecord.dataRef = myHandleDataRef;

myMemoryMovie = FlattenMovieData(myChildMovie,
                  flattenFSSpecPtrIsDataRefRecordPtr |
                  flattenAddMovieToDataFork,
                  (FSSpecPtr)&myDataRefRecord,
                  sigMoviePlayer,
                  smSystemScript,
                  0L);
myErr = GetMoviesError();
if (myErr != noErr)
  goto bail;

DisposeMovie(myChildMovie);

// replace the existing data reference atom by a "flattened" data reference atom

// out with the old...
QTRemoveAtom(mySample, myAtom);

// ...and in with the new
myChildDataHandle = NewHandleClear(sizeof(OSType) + sizeof(Handle));
if (myChildDataHandle != NULL) {
  OSType       myType;
```

```
      // set the data reference type
      myType = EndianU32_NtoB(HandleDataHandlerSubType);
      BlockMove(&myType, *myChildDataHandle, sizeof(OSType));

      // leave the next four bytes set to 0x00000000;
      // add a filenaming extension and an initialization extension
      myErr = QTDR_AddFilenamingExtension(myChildDataHandle, NULL);
      if (myErr != noErr)
        goto bail;

      HLock(myDataRefHandle);
      myErr = QTDR_AddInitDataDataRefExtension(myChildDataHandle, *myDataRefHandle);
      HUnlock(myDataRefHandle);
      if (myErr != noErr)
        goto bail;

      HLock(myChildDataHandle);
      myErr = QTInsertChild(mySample, kParentAtomIsContainer, kMovieMediaDataReference,
              1, 1, GetHandleSize(myChildDataHandle), *myChildDataHandle, NULL);
      HUnlock(myChildDataHandle);
      if (myErr != noErr)
        goto bail;
    }

    // add the new sample to the media

    // determine the bounds of this sample in movie time
    GetTrackNextInterestingTime(myTrack, nextTimeMediaSample | nextTimeEdgeOK,
      myMovieTimeNow, -0x01000, &myMovieStartTime, NULL);
    GetTrackNextInterestingTime(myTrack, nextTimeMediaSample | nextTimeEdgeOK,
      myMovieStartTime, 0x01000, NULL, &myMovieDuration);

    // splice this media over the old one
    DeleteTrackSegment(myTrack, myMovieStartTime, myMovieDuration);

    myErr = BeginMediaEdits(myMedia);
    if (myErr != noErr)
      goto bail;

    // write a new media sample into the track
    myErr = AddMediaSample(myMedia,
              mySample,
              0,                            // no offset in data
              GetHandleSize(mySample),
              myDuration,                   // frame duration
              (SampleDescriptionHandle)myDesc,
```

```
                    1,                    // one sample
                    0,                    // self-contained samples
                    &myNewTime);

        myErr = EndMediaEdits(myMedia);
        if (myErr != noErr)
          goto bail;

        // add the media to the track
        myErr = InsertMediaIntoTrack(myTrack, myMovieStartTime, myNewTime, myDuration,
                (Fixed)0x00010000L);
    } else {
      myErr = cannotFindAtomErr;
    }

bail:
    if (mySample != NULL)
      DisposeHandle(mySample);

    if (myDesc != NULL)
      DisposeHandle((Handle)myDesc);

    if (myDataRef != NULL)
      DisposeHandle(myDataRef);

    if (myDataRefHandle != NULL)
      DisposeHandle(myDataRefHandle);

    if (myHandleDataRef != NULL)
      DisposeHandle(myHandleDataRef);

    if (myChildDataHandle != NULL)
      DisposeHandle(myChildDataHandle);

    // restore the original movie rate
    SetMovieRate(myMovie, myRate);

    return(myErr);
}
```

As written, QTMIM_FlattenChildIntoParent replaces the current movie media sample by a "flattened" sample. It would be easy to adapt this routine to iterate through all samples in the movie track and to flatten each child movie into the parent movie. I'll leave this refinement as an exercise for the reader.

▶ Memory-Based Movies

Let's finish up this chapter by taking a look at a few ways we can create movies or tracks whose media data is contained entirely in memory. This is a useful thing to do in a number of instances. For example, we might generate all of a movie's media data dynamically and not want to have to create a disk file to hold that data. Or, we might want to add a track to an existing movie but don't want the track's media data to be added to the associated movie file unless the user explicitly requests it. In that case, we can tell the track to store its media data in memory, not in the original movie file.

The key element here is to create a handle data reference and to set it as the data reference for the movie (or track). Any media data written to the movie (or track) will be written into memory at the location specified by the data reference.

Creating Movies in Memory

In Volume One, Chapter 9, we saw how to create a movie whose associated media data is contained entirely in RAM. There, we took advantage of the fact that `FlattenMovieData` can flatten a movie into a location specified by a data reference instead of by a file system specification record. Listing 15.11 shows the core of our code for doing this. (This should remind you of Listing 15.7.)

Listing 15.11 Flattening a movie into memory.

```
Movie                   myNewMovie = NULL;
Handle                  myDataRef = NULL;
Handle                  myHandle = NULL;
DataReferenceRecord     myDataRefRecord;

myHandle = NewHandleClear(0);
if (myHandle == NULL)
  goto bail;

myDataRef = QTDR_MakeHandleDataRef(myHandle);
if (myDataRef == NULL)
  goto bail;

myDataRefRecord.dataRefType = HandleDataHandlerSubType;
myDataRefRecord.dataRef = myDataRef;
```

```
myNewMovie = FlattenMovieData(myMovie,
             flattenFSSpecPtrIsDataRefRecordPtr,
             (FSSpecPtr)&myDataRefRecord,
             sigMoviePlayer,
             smSystemScript,
             0L);
```

Using FlattenMovieData assumes that we already have a movie (myMovie)
and want to copy it entirely into RAM. It's sometimes also useful to create a
new movie in RAM, using the NewMovie function and our standard calls to
NewMovieTrack, NewTrackMedia, and so forth. The easiest way to do this is to
set the movie's *default data reference* to a handle data reference, using the
SetMovieDefaultDataRef function. We can call SetMovieDefaultDataRef like
this:

```
myErr = SetMovieDefaultDataRef(myMovie, myDataRef,
        HandleDataHandlerSubType);
```

Listing 15.12 defines a function, QTDR_CreateMovieInRAM, that creates a
new movie whose media data is stored in a block of memory.

Listing 15.12 Creating a movie in memory.

```
Movie QTDR_CreateMovieInRAM (void)
{
   Movie              myMovie = NULL;
   Track              myTrack = NULL;
   Media              myMedia = NULL;
   short              myResRefNum = 0;
   short              myResID = 0;
   Handle             myDataRef = NULL;
   Handle             myHandle = NULL;
   FSSpec             myFSSpec;
   OSErr              myErr = noErr;

   // create a new handle to hold the media data
   myHandle = NewHandleClear(0);
   if (myHandle == NULL)
      goto bail;

   // create a data reference to that handle
   myDataRef = QTDR_MakeHandleDataRef(myHandle);
   if (myDataRef == NULL)
      goto bail;
```

```
myMovie = NewMovie(newMovieActive);
if (myMovie == NULL)
  goto bail;

myErr = SetMovieDefaultDataRef(myMovie, myDataRef, HandleDataHandlerSubType);
if (myErr != noErr)
  goto bail;

// create the movie track and media
myTrack = NewMovieTrack(myMovie,
            FixRatio(kVideoTrackWidth, 1),
            FixRatio(kVideoTrackHeight, 1), kNoVolume);
myErr = GetMoviesError();
if (myErr != noErr)
  goto bail;

myMedia = NewTrackMedia(myTrack, VideoMediaType, kVideoTimeScale, NULL, 0);
myErr = GetMoviesError();
if (myErr != noErr)
  goto bail;

// create the media samples
myErr = BeginMediaEdits(myMedia);
if (myErr != noErr)
  goto bail;

myErr = QTDR_AddVideoSamplesToMedia(myMedia, kVideoTrackWidth, kVideoTrackHeight);
if (myErr != noErr)
  goto bail;

myErr = EndMediaEdits(myMedia);
if (myErr != noErr)
  goto bail;

// add the media to the track
myErr = InsertMediaIntoTrack(myTrack, 0, 0, GetMediaDuration(myMedia), fixed1);
if (myErr != noErr)
  goto bail;

// add the movie atom to the movie file
AddMovieResource(myMovie, myResRefNum, &myResID, NULL);

bail:
  if (myDataRef != NULL)
    DisposeHandle(myDataRef);
```

```
    return(myMovie);
}
```

This function is virtually identical to other movie-creating functions we've seen in previous chapters, except that it calls SetMovieDefaultDataRef to cause all media data to be written to a block of memory. Previously, we relied on the fact that a new movie's default data reference is the file opened by a call to CreateMovieFile or NewMovieFromFile. Here, we are calling New-Movie to create a new movie with no attachment to any existing file, so we need to explicitly set the movie's default data reference.

If we want just a particular track to have its media data in memory, then we can pass a handle data reference when calling NewTrackMedia, like this:

```
myMedia = NewTrackMedia(myTrack, VideoMediaType,
            myTimeScale, myDataRef, HandleDataHandlerSubType);
```

The specified data reference overrides the default movie data reference.

Saving Movies from Memory

In all these cases, we've ended up with a movie that has some or all of its media data stored directly in memory, accessed using a handle data reference. We can then play the movie, edit the movie, enable and disable tracks (and so forth), exactly as if the media data were contained in a file accessed via a file data reference or stored remotely and accessed via a URL data reference. But what happens if we want to save this movie into a file on disk? Well, it depends. If we created the movie entirely in memory (as in Listings 15.11 and 15.12), then our underlying application framework code will detect that no file is attached to the movie yet. In this case, it will elicit a filename from the user, create a new file (or delete and re-create an existing file), and then call FlattenMovieData to write the media data into the new file. FlattenMovieData strips out any unneeded media samples, resolves all remaining media sample references, and writes the media data into the movie file on disk. This movie file contains only file data references. It's a self-contained movie file that holds all of its media data. So far, so good.

Things start to get interesting, however, if we've already got a movie file attached to our movie. (This would happen, for instance, if we open an existing movie file and then add a track whose media data is accessed using a handle data reference.) In this case, when the user decides to save the movie, our application framework code calls UpdateMovieResource instead of FlattenMovieData. UpdateMovieResource does not write any media data into the movie file; rather, it simply updates the movie atom, which contains the data references for each media. The updated movie file now contains a handle data reference. The problem here is that, when the movie file is closed and then reopened, QuickTime won't be able to find the media data. The handle data reference, in all likelihood, no longer picks out any valid media data.

Certainly, one way to avoid this problem is to make sure that we call FlattenMovieData at least once before we close a movie file. But that might not be desirable in some instances. For example, our movie might contain references to other files in addition to the references to memory-based data. We might not want to force *all* data references to be resolved, just one or two of them.

As far as I know, QuickTime doesn't currently provide a way to flatten only selected tracks in a movie. But we can work around this limitation, to some degree, by employing a simple technique involving initialization extensions. The idea is to "smuggle" a track's media data into the movie atom by attaching that data to the media's data reference as an initialization extension. When we then call UpdateMovieResource, the media data will be written to the movie file, since it now forms part of the movie atom. The movie file once again contains a handle data reference, but it's harmless; when Quick-Time reopens the movie file, it will notice the data reference extension and load the media data from that extension. Sweet.

It's actually quite easy to implement this smuggling. We do it by passing a handle data reference to NewTrackMedia, just as we did at the end of the previous section. But this time, instead of passing a handle data reference for a handle to a 0-length block of data, we'll pass a handle data reference for a NULL handle, where the handle data reference has an initialization extension. Let's begin by creating a handle data reference:

```
myDataRef = NewHandleClear(sizeof(Handle) + sizeof(char));
```

Remember that a handle data reference is a handle to a handle. Here we've created a handle to a 5-byte block of memory, all of whose bytes are set to 0. This represents a NULL handle and a 0-length filenaming extension. At this point, we'll tack on the atom header for the initialization extension:

```
myAtomHeader[0] = EndianU32_NtoB(sizeof(myAtomHeader));
myAtomHeader[1] = EndianU32_NtoB(kDataRefExtensionInitializationData);
myErr = PtrAndHand(myAtomHeader, myDataRef, sizeof(myAtomHeader));
```

We haven't actually added any initialization data to the data reference extension yet, only the 8-byte atom header. But that's all we need at this point. We're ready to call NewTrackMedia:

```
myMedia = NewTrackMedia(myTrack, VideoMediaType, kVideoTimeScale,
            myDataRef, HandleDataHandlerSubType);
```

When QuickTime sees the initialization extension atom header in the handle data reference, it knows to keep the media data in the data reference itself, rather than in the memory block addressed by the handle that forms the first four bytes of the data reference's referring data. The handle data handler is going to allocate whatever memory is needed to hold the data we add to our media, so we can dispose of our data reference (myDataRef) immediately if we like.

Now we can edit the media and track as usual, for instance, by calling AddMediaSample and InsertMediaIntoTrack. When we subsequently call Update-MovieResource, the handle data handler will write out a handle data reference with a fully configured initialization extension.

Listing 15.13 shows most of this assembled into a single routine, QTDR_CreateTrackInRAM. It adds a new video track to a movie, with the track's media data stored in RAM. In addition, the media data will be attached to the data reference as an initialization extension when the movie atom is updated.

Listing 15.13 Creating a track in memory.

```
OSErr QTDR_CreateTrackInRAM (Movie theMovie)
{
  Track                myTrack = NULL;
  Media                myMedia = NULL;
  Handle               myDataRef = NULL;
  unsigned long        myAtomHeader[2];
  OSErr                myErr = noErr;

  if (theMovie == NULL)
    return(paramErr);

  myDataRef = NewHandleClear(sizeof(Handle) + sizeof(char));
  if (myDataRef == NULL)
    return(MemError());

  myAtomHeader[0] = EndianU32_NtoB(sizeof(myAtomHeader));
  myAtomHeader[1] = EndianU32_NtoB(kDataRefExtensionInitializationData);

  myErr = PtrAndHand(myAtomHeader, myDataRef, sizeof(myAtomHeader));
  if (myErr != noErr)
    goto bail;
```

```
// create the movie track and media
myTrack = NewMovieTrack(theMovie,
            FixRatio(kVideoTrackWidth, 1),
            FixRatio(kVideoTrackHeight, 1), kNoVolume);
myErr = GetMoviesError();
if (myErr != noErr)
  goto bail;

myMedia = NewTrackMedia(myTrack, VideoMediaType, kVideoTimeScale,
            myDataRef, HandleDataHandlerSubType);
myErr = GetMoviesError();
if (myErr != noErr)
  goto bail;

// create the media samples
myErr = BeginMediaEdits(myMedia);
if (myErr != noErr)
  goto bail;

myErr = QTDR_AddVideoSamplesToMedia(myMedia, kVideoTrackWidth, kVideoTrackHeight);
if (myErr != noErr)
  goto bail;

myErr = EndMediaEdits(myMedia);
if (myErr != noErr)
  goto bail;

// add the media to the track
myErr = InsertMediaIntoTrack(myTrack, 0, 0, GetMediaDuration(myMedia), fixed1);

bail:
  if (myDataRef != NULL)
    DisposeHandle(myDataRef);

  return(myErr);
}
```

This is a neat technique, but it's got a few limitations that you should know about. First of all, it works only with QuickTime versions 4.0 and later. Under earlier versions of QuickTime, data reference extensions are simply ignored. Also, and more important, because the initialization extension is stored inside the movie atom, you should avoid creating very large extensions. The extensions will remain in RAM for significant periods of time, so it's good to keep them small.

▶ Conclusion

Data. We've gotta have it, at least if we want to do anything very interesting in our QuickTime movies. In this chapter, we've taken a look at a couple of useful ways of managing a movie's media data. First, we saw how to construct a movie that picks out its media data using media sample references. These references can refer to existing data that lives outside the movie file (as in the case of our slideshow movie) or that is already contained in the movie file (as in the case of our effects movie). A sample reference is simply a way to make use of some existing data without having to copy it into a movie file or between tracks.

We've also seen, however, that it's sometimes useful to be able to go in the reverse direction, by forcing a movie's media data to be packed into an existing movie file. (At the very least, this makes it much easier to move the movie file around since we don't need to worry about moving any other files that the movie depends upon.) Our standard means of doing this is to call `FlattenMovieData`, but sometimes that either doesn't work at all (as in the case of child movies) or doesn't work selectively enough for our purposes (as in the case of a single memory-based track). To work around some of the limitations of `FlattenMovieData`, we can use initialization data data reference extensions to attach media data directly to a data reference.

16

Modern Times
Updating the QTShell Application Framework

▶ Introduction

We began this set of books by developing a simple C-based application called QTShell that runs on both Windows and Macintosh operating systems. QTShell can open and display QuickTime movies, and it supports the standard movie editing operations. We've gradually tinkered with QTShell to add various capabilities. For instance, in Volume One (Chapter 12), we upgraded the Macintosh portions of the code to use the Navigation Services APIs instead of the Standard File Package APIs we used originally (and still use in our Windows code). This was an important step on the road to full Carbonization, which allowed QTShell to run natively on Mac OS X as well as on Mac OS 8 and 9. And in this book (Chapter 9, "Event Horizon"), we saw how to switch to the Carbon event model of processing events.

In this chapter, I want to present several more enhancements to QTShell. The Navigation Services functions that it currently calls, NavGetFile and NavPutFile, are now deprecated; they still work just fine, but they are no longer recommended. By moving to the more modern APIs provided by Navigation Services 3.0, we can pave the way for support for Unicode filenames and for displaying the Save As dialog box as a sheet, as in Figure 16.1. This is a nicer interface than the dialog box displayed by NavPutFile, which is shown in Figure 16.2.

I also want to show how to convert QTShell to use the *movie storage* functions introduced in QuickTime 6. A movie storage container is simply any container that can be addressed using a data reference, for instance a file or a block of memory. Currently QTShell works only with files specified using file system specification records (of type FSSpec). In Volume One (Chapter 9),

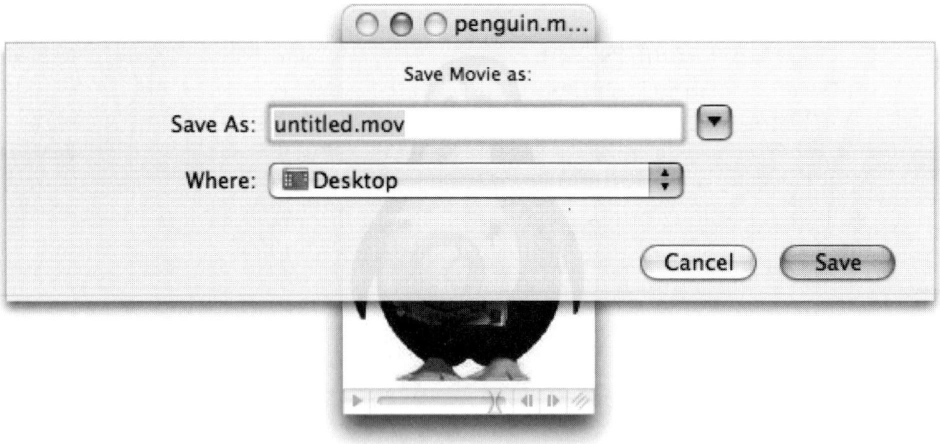

Figure 16.1 The Save As sheet.

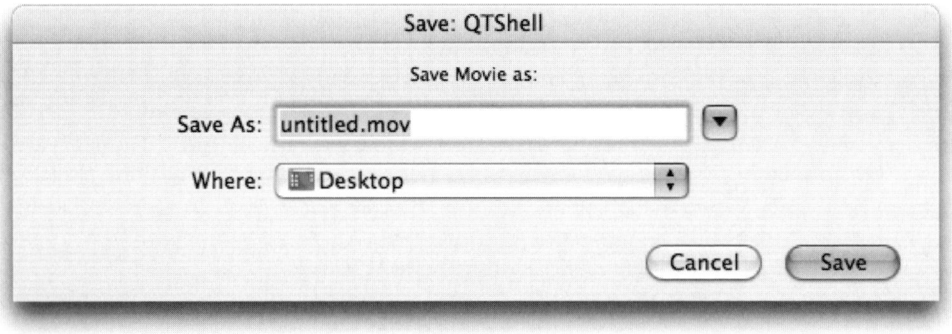

Figure 16.2 The Save As dialog box.

however, we saw how to open local and remote movie files using `NewMovie-FromDataRef` with file and URL data references. It would be nice to operate on all QuickTime movie data using a single set of APIs, and that's what the movie storage functions provide. Instead of calling `OpenMovieFile` and specifying a file using an `FSSpec`, we can call `OpenMovieStorage` and specify a storage container using a data reference. Then, when it's time to save changes to a movie, we can call `UpdateMovieInStorage` instead of `UpdateMovieResource`. And so on. To complement these storage APIs, QuickTime 6.4 introduced a large number of *data reference utilities* that can create data references from data of type `FSSpec`, `CFString`, `FSRef`, `CFURL`, and a handful of other types.

The ultimate goal in moving to the new Navigation Services APIs and the movie storage APIs is to be able to expunge all traces of file system specification records from QTShell. The main problem with FSSpecs is that they cannot represent files with non-ASCII Unicode names or names longer than 63 characters. These other data types—CFString, FSRef, and CFURL—can easily represent Unicode filenames and very long filenames.

Unfortunately, the complete removal of FSSpec data values from QTShell and all the associated utilities files that our applications depend upon, on both Macintosh and Windows, would require an overhaul that is beyond the scope of this chapter. But we'll do enough of the groundwork that finally making the jump to an FSSpec-free application will not be too difficult.

File Selection

Let's begin by getting rid of our calls to NavGetFile and NavPutFile. Navigation Services 3.0 and later versions replace these functions with a handful of functions that allow greater control over the file-selection process. They allow us to display the file-saving dialog box as a sheet (as in Figure 16.1) and they support retrieving information about selected files in the form of an FSRef, which supports Unicode and long filenames.

Choosing a File to Open

Currently QTShell calls the NavGetFile function to display the standard file-opening dialog box, shown in Figure 16.3. NavGetFile handles everything involved in displaying the dialog box and handling user actions in the box. When it exits, it fills out a record of type NavReplyRecord that contains information about the selected file, if any.

In Navigation Services 3.0, this scheme was changed significantly but not enough to cause major upheavals in our existing source code. We still need to get the default options for the dialog box, but now we need to call NavGetDefaultDialogCreationOptions, not NavGetDefaultDialogOptions:

```
NavGetDefaultDialogCreationOptions(&myOptions);
myOptions.optionFlags -= kNavNoTypePopup;
myOptions.optionFlags -= kNavAllowMultipleFiles;
myOptions.modality = kWindowModalityAppModal;
myOptions.clientName = CFStringCreateWithPascalString(NULL, gAppName,
  GetApplicationTextEncoding());
```

This departs from our existing code in several ways. First, the clientName field is a CFString, not a Pascal string. We can create that string from an existing Pascal string by calling CFStringCreateWithPascalString. Later we'll need to release the string like this:

```
CFRelease(myOptions.clientName);
```

Figure 16.3 The file-opening dialog box.

The other interesting option is the modality field, which can take these values:

```
enum {
  kWindowModalityNone          = 0,
  kWindowModalitySystemModal   = 1,
  kWindowModalityAppModal      = 2,
  kWindowModalityWindowModal   = 3
};
```

As you can see, we use the kWindowModalityAppModal constant, which causes the dialog box to prevent user interaction with all other windows in the application. A sheet would use the kWindowModalityWindowModal constant, which blocks user interaction with just one other window (the one the sheet is attached to).

Once we've set up the dialog box options, we create the dialog box by calling NavCreateGetFileDialog:

```
        myErr = NavCreateGetFileDialog(&myOptions, NULL, myEventUPP, NULL,
                (NavObjectFilterUPP)theFilterProc, (void*)myOpenList, &myDialogRef);
```

This call however does not display the dialog box to the user. This gives us an opportunity to further customize the appearance of the dialog box by calling NavCustomControl (as we'll do in a few moments). Once we've customized the box to our liking, we show it to the user by calling NavDialogRun.

When NavDialogRun returns, we can call NavDialogGetReply to retrieve a NavReplyRecord record that contains information about the selected file. We then proceed as before by getting an FSSpec for the selected file, which we return to the caller. Listing 16.1 shows the new definition of QTFrame_GetOneFileWithPreview.

Listing 16.1 Eliciting a movie file from the user.

```
OSErr QTFrame_GetOneFileWithPreview (short theNumTypes, QTFrameTypeListPtr theTypeList,
        FSSpecPtr theFSSpecPtr, void *theFilterProc)
{
#if TARGET_OS_WIN32
  StandardFileReply           myReply;
#endif
#if TARGET_OS_MAC
  NavDialogRef                myDialogRef = NULL;
  NavReplyRecord              myReply;
  NavTypeListHandle           myOpenList = NULL;
  NavEventUPP                 myEventUPP = NewNavEventUPP(QTFrame_HandleNavEvent);
  NavDialogCreationOptions    myOptions;
#endif
  OSErr                       myErr = noErr;

  if (theFSSpecPtr == NULL)
    return(paramErr);

  // deactivate any frontmost movie window
  QTFrame_ActivateController(QTFrame_GetFrontMovieWindow(), false);

#if TARGET_OS_WIN32
  // prompt the user for a file
  StandardGetFilePreview((FileFilterUPP)theFilterProc, theNumTypes,
    (ConstSFTypeListPtr)theTypeList, &myReply);
  if (!myReply.sfGood)
    return(userCanceledErr);
```

```
  // make an FSSpec record
  myErr = FSMakeFSSpec(myReply.sfFile.vRefNum, myReply.sfFile.parID, myReply.sfFile.name,
          theFSSpecPtr);
#endif

#if TARGET_OS_MAC
  // specify the options for the dialog box
  NavGetDefaultDialogCreationOptions(&myOptions);
  myOptions.optionFlags -= kNavNoTypePopup;
  myOptions.optionFlags -= kNavAllowMultipleFiles;
  myOptions.modality = kWindowModalityAppModal;
  myOptions.clientName = CFStringCreateWithPascalString (NULL, gAppName,
                         GetApplicationTextEncoding());

  // create a handle to an 'open' resource
  myOpenList = (NavTypeListHandle)QTFrame_CreateOpenHandle(kApplicationSignature,
                                   theNumTypes, theTypeList);
  if (myOpenList != NULL)
    HLock((Handle)myOpenList);

  // prompt the user for a file
  myErr = NavCreateGetFileDialog(&myOptions, NULL, myEventUPP,
          NULL, (NavObjectFilterUPP)theFilterProc, (void*)myOpenList, &myDialogRef);
  if ((myErr == noErr) && (myDialogRef != NULL)) {
    AEDesc              myLocation = {typeNull, NULL};

    // if no open-file location exists, use ~/Movies
    if (QTFrame_GetCurrentFileLocationDesc(&myLocation, kGetFileLoc) == noErr)
      NavCustomControl(myDialogRef, kNavCtlSetLocation, (void *)&myLocation);

    myErr = NavDialogRun(myDialogRef);
    if (myErr == noErr) {
      myErr = NavDialogGetReply(myDialogRef, &myReply);
      if ((myErr == noErr) && myReply.validRecord) {
        AEKeyword       myKeyword;
        DescType        myActualType;
        Size            myActualSize = 0;

        // get the FSSpec for the selected file
        if (theFSSpecPtr != NULL)
          myErr = AEGetNthPtr(&(myReply.selection), 1, typeFSS, &myKeyword,
                  &myActualType, theFSSpecPtr, sizeof(FSSpec), &myActualSize);
```

```
      NavDisposeReply(&myReply);
    }
  }

  NavDialogDispose(myDialogRef);
}

// clean up
if (myOpenList != NULL) {
  HUnlock((Handle)myOpenList);
  DisposeHandle((Handle)myOpenList);
}

if (myOptions.clientName != NULL)
  CFRelease(myOptions.clientName);

DisposeNavEventUPP(myEventUPP);
#endif

  return(myErr);
}
```

Choosing a Filename to Save

The changes required to upgrade our existing file-selection routine
QTFrame_PutFile are entirely analogous to those considered in the previous
section. We need to replace NavPutFile by the combination of NavCreatePut-
FileDialog, NavDialogRun, NavDialogGetReply, and NavDialogDispose. There is
only one "gotcha" here, and it's a big one: the FSSpec that we get when we
call AEGetNthPtr no longer specifies the file we want to save the movie into
(as it did with NavPutFile); rather, it specifies the *directory* that contains the
file. I'm guessing that this was changed to better support values of type
FSRef, which cannot specify non-existent files. The preferred way to respond
to NavDialogGetReply is apparently to ask for the parent directory of the
chosen filename in the form of an FSRef and then to create the file by calling
FSRefCreateFileUnicode, which takes the parent directory and a Unicode filename. Since we are retaining our dependence on FSSpec values, we need to
jump though a hoop or two.

What we need to do is find the directory ID of the parent directory
returned to us, so that we can create an FSSpec record for the chosen file
itself. Listing 16.2 shows some File Manager voodoo that accomplishes this.

Listing 16.2 Finding the directory ID of a file's parent directory.

```
myErr = AEGetNthPtr(&(myReply.selection), 1, typeFSS, &myKeyword, &myActualType,
        &myDirSpec, sizeof(FSSpec), &myActualSize);
if (myErr == noErr) {
  myFileName = NavDialogGetSaveFileName(myDialogRef);
  if (myFileName != NULL) {
    CInfoPBRec            myPB;

    myPB.dirInfo.ioVRefNum = myDirSpec.vRefNum;
    myPB.dirInfo.ioDrDirID = myDirSpec.parID;
    myPB.dirInfo.ioNamePtr = myDirSpec.name;
    myPB.dirInfo.ioFDirIndex = 0;
    myPB.dirInfo.ioCompletion = NULL;

    myErr = PBGetCatInfoSync(&myPB);
    if (myErr == noErr) {
      CFStringGetPascalString(myFileName, myString, sizeof(FSSpec),
        GetApplicationTextEncoding());
      myErr = FSMakeFSSpec(myPB.dirInfo.ioVRefNum,  myPB.dirInfo.ioDrDirID,
              myString, &myMovSpec);
      if (myErr == fnfErr)
        myErr = noErr;
    }

    if (myErr == noErr)
      *theFSSpecPtr = myMovSpec;
  }
}
```

The trick here is to know that on entry to the PBGetCatInfoSync call, the ioDrDirID field should be set to the directory ID of the parent directory of the directory containing the chosen file, which is what is contained in the FSSpec returned by AEGetNthPtr; on exit that field will contain the directory ID of the directory itself (not its parent). Once we've retrieved that directory ID, we can then call FSMakeFSSpec to create an FSSpec for the file itself.

Showing the Save Changes Dialog Box

QTShell uses one other Navigation Services function, NavAskSaveChanges, in the Macintosh version of the QTFrame_DestroyMovieWindow function. We need to replace this with the newer NavCreateAskSaveChangesDialog. Listing 16.3 shows the key changed portions of QTFrame_DestroyMovieWindow.

Listing 16.3 Closing a movie window.

```
if ((**myWindowObject).fIsDirty) {
  Str255                    myString;
  NavAskSaveChangesAction   myAction;
  NavDialogCreationOptions  myOptions;
  NavUserAction             myResult;
  NavEventUPP               myEventUPP = NewNavEventUPP(QTFrame_HandleNavEvent);
  NavDialogRef              myDialogRef = NULL;

  // get the title of the window
  GetWTitle(theWindow, myString);

  // install the application and document names
  NavGetDefaultDialogCreationOptions(&myOptions);
  myOptions.clientName = CFStringCreateWithPascalString(NULL, gAppName,
                         GetApplicationTextEncoding());
  myOptions.saveFileName = CFStringCreateWithPascalString(NULL, myString,
                           GetApplicationTextEncoding());

  // specify the action
  myAction = gShuttingDown ? kNavSaveChangesQuittingApplication :
             kNavSaveChangesClosingDocument;

  // display the "Save changes" dialog box
  myErr = NavCreateAskSaveChangesDialog(&myOptions, myAction, myEventUPP, NULL,
          &myDialogRef);
  if ((myErr == noErr) && (myDialogRef != NULL)) {
    myErr = NavDialogRun(myDialogRef);
    if (myErr == noErr) {
      myResult = NavDialogGetUserAction(myDialogRef);
      switch (myResult) {
        case kNavUserActionSaveChanges:
          // save the data in the window
          QTFrame_UpdateMovieFile(theWindow);
          break;

        case kNavUserActionCancel:
          // do not close the window, and do not quit the application
          gShuttingDown = false;
          return(false);

        case kNavUserActionDontSaveChanges:
          // discard any unsaved changes (that is, don't do anything)
          break;
      }
    }
```

```
    NavDialogDispose(myDialogRef);
  }

  if (myOptions.clientName != NULL)
    CFRelease(myOptions.clientName);

  if (myOptions.saveFileName != NULL)
    CFRelease(myOptions.saveFileName);

  DisposeNavEventUPP(myEventUPP);
}
```

Setting the Default Location

Let's end this discussion by making sure that the directory displayed in the file opening and saving dialog boxes is a reasonable default. The Navigation Services functions will always display the most recent directory selected by the user when choosing a file to open or save into. This information is saved on a per-application and per-user basis, in the application's preference file. So, if a user saves a movie file on the Desktop, the next time he or she opens the file-saving dialog box, the Desktop will be the directory shown—even if the user has quit the application and later relaunched it.

Our application doesn't need to create or read that preferences file explicitly because the Navigation Services functions take care of all that automatically. The only time that we might want to poke our noses into that file is when the user launches our application for the very first time. In that case, there will be no saved directory information. The default behavior of the Navigation Services APIs is to display the Documents folder in the user's home directory.

It's actually quite easy to change that default value to something more useful, perhaps the Movies folder in the user's home directory. To do this, we can use the Preferences APIs to read values out of the preferences file, which is called QTShell.plist and is stored in the Preferences folder that is inside of the Library folder in the user's home directory.

A preferences file is organized as a set of key-value pairs. The key is of type CFString, and the value can be any Core Foundation property list type. Navigation Services maintains at least two items in that file, addressed using these keys:

```
AppleNavServices:PutFile:0:Path
AppleNavServices:GetFile:0:Path
```

The values associated with these keys are the locations of the directories most recently displayed in the file-saving and file-opening dialog boxes.

For present purposes, we don't need to read the values associated with those keys. Rather, all we need to do is determine whether a specific key exists in the preferences file. If it does, we'll let Navigation Services handle the setting of the directory displayed in the corresponding dialog box. But if one or the other of these keys does not have a value in the preferences file, we'll step in and set the location shown in the dialog box to the better default location, the Movies folder in the user's home directory. Listing 16.4 shows our definition of QTFrame_GetCurrentFileLocationDesc, which does this. We'll pass in one of these application-defined constants:

```
#define kPutFileLoc            1
#define kGetFileLoc            2
```

QTFrame_GetCurrentFileLocationDesc then calls CFPreferencesCopyAppValue to find the appropriate preference item. If it exists, we return paramErr to the caller to indicate that a preference item already exists for the specified dialog box. Otherwise we'll construct an AEDesc value for the desired folder and pass that back to the caller.

Listing 16.4 Setting the default file location.

```
#if TARGET_OS_MAC
OSErr QTFrame_GetCurrentFileLocationDesc (AEDescPtr theLocation, short theFileType)
{
  CFStringRef             myLocKey;
  CFPropertyListRef       myLoc;
  FSRef                   myFSRef;
  FSSpec                  myFSSpec;
  OSErr                   myErr = noErr;

  if (theLocation == NULL)
    return(paramErr);

  if (theFileType == kPutFileLoc)
    myLocKey = CFSTR("AppleNavServices:PutFile:0:Path");
  else
    myLocKey = CFSTR("AppleNavServices:GetFile:0:Path");
```

```
// see whether our application's Preferences plist already contains a file location
myLoc = CFPreferencesCopyAppValue(myLocKey, kCFPreferencesCurrentApplication);
if (myLoc != NULL) {
  // there is an existing location
  CFRelease(myLoc);
  myErr = paramErr;
} else {
  // there is no existing location; return a descriptor for ~/Movies
  myErr = FSFindFolder(kUserDomain, kMovieDocumentsFolderType, kCreateFolder, &myFSRef);

  if (myErr == noErr)
    myErr = FSGetCatalogInfo(&myFSRef, kFSCatInfoNone, NULL, NULL, &myFSSpec, NULL);

  if (myErr == noErr)
      myErr = AECreateDesc(typeFSS, &myFSSpec, sizeof(FSSpec), theLocation);
}

  return(myErr);
}
#endif
```

All that remains is to call this function inside of QTFrame_GetOneFileWith-Preview and QTFrame_PutFile. If you look back at Listing 16.1, you'll see these lines of code immediately preceding the call to NavDialogRun:

```
if (QTFrame_GetCurrentFileLocationDesc(&myLocation, kGetFileLoc) == noErr)
  NavCustomControl(myDialogRef, kNavCtlSetLocation, (void *)&myLocation);
```

▶ Movie Storage Functions

QuickTime 6.0 introduced a set of functions called the *movie storage* APIs. The fundamental idea here is dead simple: instead of being restricted to opening, updating, creating, and deleting movie *files*, we should be able to perform these operations on any containers that hold movie data. As you know, the most general means of picking out movie data is by using a data reference. Accordingly, the movie storage APIs allow us to operate on movie data using data references and their associated data handlers.

Let's consider an example. Our application currently opens a movie specified by a file system specification record by calling OpenMovieFile, like this:

```
myErr = OpenMovieFile(&myFSSpec, &myRefNum, fsRdWrPerm);
```

If successful, OpenMovieFile returns a file reference number, which we use in all subsequent operations on the movie file. For instance, we can read the movie from that file using this code:

```
myErr = NewMovieFromFile(&myMovie, myRefNum, &myResID, NULL,
        newMovieActive, NULL);
```

When we later want to save the user's changes to a movie, we call Update-MovieResource, passing in the file reference number and the movie resource ID:

```
myErr = UpdateMovieResource(myMovie, (**myWindowObject).fFileRefNum,
        (**myWindowObject).fFileResID, NULL);
```

Using the new movie storage APIs, we can use OpenMovieStorage to open movie data specified by a data reference:

```
myErr = OpenMovieStorage(myDataRef, myDataRefType,
        kDataHCanRead + kDataHCanWrite, &myDataHandler);
```

If successful, OpenMovieStorage returns an instance of a data handler, which we use in all subsequent operations on the movie container. For instance, we can save the user's changes to a movie using this code:

```
myErr = UpdateMovieInStorage(myMovie, (**myWindowObject).fDataHandler);
```

Here's a list of the new movie storage APIs:

```
CreateMovieStorage          (replaces CreateMovieFile)
OpenMovieStorage            (replaces OpenMovieFile)
NewMovieFromStorageOffset   (replaces NewMovieFromFile)
CloseMovieStorage           (replaces CloseMovieFile)
DeleteMovieStorage          (replaces DeleteMovieFile)
AddMovieToStorage           (replaces AddMovieResource)
PutMovieIntoStorage         (replaces PutMovieIntoFile)
UpdateMovieInStorage        (replaces UpdateMovieResource)
FlattenMovieDataToDataRef   (replaces FlattenMovieData)
```

It's actually quite easy to upgrade QTShell to use these new functions. In this section, we'll see how to do this.

Maintaining Movie Storage Identifiers

First, as you probably have guessed from the snippet of code that calls UpdateMovieInStorage, we need to add a few fields to our window object record to keep track of the data reference, its type, and the data handler associated with the storage container.

```
typedef struct {
  WindowReference          fWindow;
  Movie                    fMovie;
  MovieController          fController;
  GraphicsImportComponent  fGraphicsImporter;
  FSSpec                   fFileFSSpec;
  short                    fFileResID;
  short                    fFileRefNum;
  Boolean                  fCanResizeWindow;
  Boolean                  fIsDirty;
  Boolean                  fIsQTVRMovie;
  QTVRInstance             fInstance;
  OSType                   fObjectType;
  Handle                   fAppData;
#if USE_DATA_REF_FUNCTIONS
  Handle                   fDataRef;
  OSType                   fDataRefType;
  DataHandler              fDataHandler;
#endif
} WindowObjectRecord, *WindowObjectPtr, **WindowObject;
```

Notice that we use the compiler flag USE_DATA_REF_FUNCTIONS to conditionalize our code. This allows us to switch back to using the file-based functions if the need arises.

Opening a Movie

Perhaps the trickiest part of migrating to the movie storage functions is deciding how to open a movie storage container. Our file-based code calls OpenMovieFile and then NewMovieFromFile. So we might expect to call OpenMovieStorage and then NewMovieFromStorageOffset. But that's not quite right. NewMovieFromStorageOffset requires us to specify an offset to the movie atom within the storage container. In most cases we don't know what that offset is. Further, if we simply pass an offset of 0, we won't be able to open any QuickTime movie files that are not Fast Start files (where the movie atom is the first atom in the file). So we need a different strategy.

What seems to work is to call `OpenMovieStorage` and then `NewMovieFrom-DataRef`. Listing 16.5 shows a section of our revised version of `QTFrame_Open-MovieInWindow`.

Listing 16.5 Opening a movie.

```
#if USE_DATA_REF_FUNCTIONS
myErr = QTNewDataReferenceFromFSSpec(&myFSSpec, 0, &myDataRef, &myDataRefType);
if (myErr != noErr)
  goto bail;

// ideally, we'd like read and write permission, but we'll settle for read-only permission
myErr = OpenMovieStorage(myDataRef, myDataRefType,
        kDataHCanRead + kDataHCanWrite, &myDataHandler);
if (myErr != noErr)
  myErr = OpenMovieStorage(myDataRef, myDataRefType, kDataHCanRead, &myDataHandler);

// if we couldn't open the file with even just read-only permission, bail....
if (myErr != noErr)
  goto bail;

// now fetch the first movie from the file
myErr = NewMovieFromDataRef(&myMovie, newMovieActive, &myResID, myDataRef, myDataRefType);
if (myErr != noErr)
  goto bail;
#else
// ideally, we'd like read and write permission, but we'll settle for read-only permission
myErr = OpenMovieFile(&myFSSpec, &myRefNum, fsRdWrPerm);
if (myErr != noErr)
  myErr = OpenMovieFile(&myFSSpec, &myRefNum, fsRdPerm);

// if we couldn't open the file with even just read-only permission, bail....
if (myErr != noErr)
  goto bail;

// now fetch the first movie from the file
myResID = 0;
myErr = NewMovieFromFile(&myMovie, myRefNum, &myResID, NULL, newMovieActive, NULL);
if (myErr != noErr)
  goto bail;
#endif
```

Then we need to save the movie storage identifiers in our window object record, like this:

```
#if USE_DATA_REF_FUNCTIONS
  (**myWindowObject).fDataRef = myDataRef;
  (**myWindowObject).fDataRefType = myDataRefType;
  (**myWindowObject).fDataHandler = myDataHandler;
#endif
```

Saving Changes to a Movie

To save a user's changes to a movie back into its storage container, we can call UpdateMovieInStorage. Listing 16.6 shows the lines we've altered in the function QTFrame_UpdateMovieFile.

Listing 16.6 Updating a movie's storage.

```
#if USE_DATA_REF_FUNCTIONS
if ((**myWindowObject).fDataHandler == NULL)
  myErr = QTFrame_SaveAsMovieFile(theWindow);
else
  myErr = UpdateMovieInStorage(myMovie, (**myWindowObject).fDataHandler);
#else
if ((**myWindowObject).fFileRefNum == kInvalidFileRefNum)
  myErr = QTFrame_SaveAsMovieFile(theWindow);
else
  myErr = UpdateMovieResource(myMovie, (**myWindowObject).fFileRefNum,
          (**myWindowObject).fFileResID, NULL);
#endif
```

Closing a Movie

When we're finished working with a movie, we can close it by calling Close-MovieStorage. We also need to dispose of the data reference and the data handler instance associated with the movie. Listing 16.7 shows the changed lines in the function QTFrame_CloseWindowObject.

Listing 16.7 Closing a movie.

```
#if USE_DATA_REF_FUNCTIONS
if ((**theWindowObject).fDataHandler != NULL) {
  CloseMovieStorage((**theWindowObject).fDataHandler);
  CloseComponent((**theWindowObject).fDataHandler);
  (**theWindowObject).fDataHandler = NULL;
}
```

```
if ((**theWindowObject).fDataRef != NULL) {
  DisposeHandle((**theWindowObject).fDataRef);
  (**theWindowObject).fDataRef = NULL;
}
#else
// close the movie file
if ((**theWindowObject).fFileRefNum != kInvalidFileRefNum) {
  CloseMovieFile((**theWindowObject).fFileRefNum);
  (**theWindowObject).fFileRefNum = kInvalidFileRefNum;
}
#endif
```

▶ Conclusion

Part of the price of delivering a modern QuickTime application is the inevitable need to continually upgrade its underpinnings as the operating system and user interface APIs evolve, or indeed as QuickTime itself evolves. In this chapter, we've seen how to use the currently recommended functions for selecting files and for opening and operating on movie data. The next step, which we have not taken here, would be to systematically replace all uses of the FSSpec data type by uses of the FSRef data type. This would give us a thoroughly modern application capable of opening movie files with Unicode or very long filenames.

In the meantime, let's reflect briefly on what we've learned in these books. We've principally been concerned with two topics: how to build an application that can open and play back QuickTime movies and how to create QuickTime movies. The playback side of the ledger is at once astonishingly simple and deceptively complex. It's simple in that we can obtain virtually all the expected movie playback and editing behaviors just by attaching a movie controller to an open QuickTime movie. The movie controller preprerolls and prerolls the movie, handles mouse and keyboard events directed at the movie, and tasks the movie often enough to keep it playing smoothly. But there are also many opportunities for a QuickTime-savvy application to support more complex behaviors than these. We've seen how to enhance a basic application to allow intermovie communication, full-screen movie playback, skinned movie display, and application message retrieval. We've also seen how to load movies asynchronously and how to display information about the state of a movie that's loading. The ultimate exercise for the reader of these books would be to coalesce all these playback enhancements into a single application. Since the CD contains all the source code from all these sample applications, you could probably throw together a QTKitchenSink application in a couple of hours.

We've also spent a considerable amount of time learning how to construct QuickTime movies. We have learned how to build movies with video data, timecodes, sprites, wired sprites, text, tweens, alternate tracks, video effects, skin data, and child movies. In almost all these instances, we've used the exact same sequence of operations to create a QuickTime movie and its associated media data. The only difference in each instance concerns the kind of media data that's written into the movie file. We've also seen how to use even higher-level APIs to capture sound and video data and to import or export movies. And we've learned how to modify existing Flash and Quick-Time VR movies to hold wired actions.

What other kinds of tools could we usefully add to our QuickTime toolkit? I can think of several important areas we haven't touched on in these two books. It would be nice to investigate some of the media types we haven't looked at yet, particularly sound-related media types and playback APIs, and to learn how to extend QuickTime by writing our own components. And it would be nice to see how to work with QuickTime using some other programming languages and development environments. For the moment, however, we are out of time.

Glossary

action list   A list of one or more action atoms. In Flash, a list of actions that are executed during the processing of a `stagShowFrame` tag or at other defined times.

ActionScript   A scripting language supported by Flash.

active source rectangle   The portion of a video digitizer's source rectangle that actually contains video data.

ActiveX control   A type of component object model (COM) object that can display a user interface and process events directed at that interface.

alternate data rate movie file   A movie file that references other movies, each tailored for downloading across a network connection of a certain speed.

alternate data rate record   A data structure (of type `QTAltDataRateRecord`) that specifies a data rate.

alternate language record   A data structure (of type `QTAltLanguageRecord`) that specifies a language.

alternate movie   Any one of a set of movies that contain media data appropriate for a specific characteristic or set of characteristics.

alternate reference movie file   A movie file that contains data references to all of the alternate movies as well as information about the criteria by which QuickTime should select one of those alternate movies when that movie file is opened.

alternate track   A track in an alternate track group.

alternate track group   A group of tracks in a QuickTime movie in which at most one track is enabled, according to the language of the track's media or the quality of the track's media.

atom   (1) A block of data preceded by an atom header. A QuickTime movie file is composed of a sequence of one or more atoms. (2) A block of data of type QTAtom that is contained in an atom container.

atom container   A block of memory that is structured in a hierarchical arrangement of container atoms (which contain other atoms) and leaf atoms (which contain data). An atom container is referenced by a handle of type QTAtomContainer.

atom container atom   See **atom (2)**.

atom header   An 8-byte structure that precedes the atom data in an atom. An atom header consists of a 4-byte length value and a 4-byte type.

audio parameters structure   A data structure (of type QTSAudioParams) that contains information about the audio media data being previewed locally.

auto-alternating   The process of enabling and disabling alternate tracks according to the current movie language or quality.

automation object   A kind of component object model (COM) object that provides some specific methods and properties.

broadcaster   An application that takes data from a source other than a hinted movie, compresses that data (if necessary), packetizes that data into streams, and then sends the streams out over a network.

button action   A Flash action that is executed on a button state transition. Compare to **frame action**.

button action condition   A piece of data that specifies one or more actions that are to be executed on a specific button state transition.

button record   A block of data that specifies the images to be used for each of the three button states.

button state transition   A change from one button state to another.

callback event   An event that causes a time base callback function to be executed.

Carbon   A set of programming interfaces and a runtime library that together define a subset of Macintosh Operating System and Toolbox APIs that are supported both on "classic" Mac operating systems (Mac OS 8 and 9) and on Mac OS X.

Carbon event   An event of a specified class and kind that is sent by the Carbon Event Manager to an event handler.

Carbon event loop timer   A timer that is associated with a specific Carbon event loop.

Carbon event loop timer callback function   A function that is called when an event loop timer fires.

Carbon Event Manager   The part of the Macintosh Operating System that manages Carbon events and Carbon timers. Compare to **Event Manager**.

Carbonize   To convert an application or other software module so that it conforms to the Carbon specification.

Carbon movie control   A custom control introduced in QuickTime 6 that can be used in Carbon applications on Mac OS X to display and control movies.

category   A feature of Objective-C that allows us to add instance methods to a class without subclassing it.

channel usage flags   A set of flags used to tell a sequence grabber channel component what operations it will perform.

child atom   An atom (2) that is contained in some other atom (2). Compare to **parent atom**.

child movie   A QuickTime movie that is contained in a parent movie, using the movie-in-movie capability introduced in QuickTime 4.1.

classic atom   See **atom (1)**.

classic Event Manager   See **Event Manager**.

client   See **receiver**.

CodeWarrior   An application development environment developed by Metrowerks.

CodeWarrior plug-in   A code module that extends the capabilities of the CodeWarrior IDE. Compare to **CodeWarrior settings panel plug-in**.

CodeWarrior settings panel plug-in   A code module that extends the capabilities of the CodeWarrior IDE by presenting a user interface in the Preference panels. Compare to **CodeWarrior plug-in**.

command ID   A value that is associated with a menu item and sent to a menu event callback function.

common dialog control   A control that can appear to the user as any one of the standard Windows dialog boxes for opening files, saving files, choosing colors, choosing fonts, and so forth.

COM object   See **Component Object Model object**.

Component Object Model object   An object that conforms to the Component Object Model, a specification defined by Microsoft that provides services for negotiating component interfaces, managing object life cycles, handling events, and so forth.

content region   The portion of a window in which an application displays the contents of a document. Compare to **drag region**.

content region mask   A 1-bit mask that determines the shape of a skinned window's content region.

current error value   The result code of the most recently executed Quick-Time function. Compare to **sticky error value**.

data handler   A QuickTime component (of type DataHandlerType) that is responsible for reading and writing a media's data. Data handlers also provide data input and output services for other parts of QuickTime.

data rate atom   An atom that specifies a data rate.

data reference   A handle to a block of memory that uniquely identifies the location of some media data for a QuickTime movie or other data that QuickTime can manage.

data reference atom   An atom that contains data reference data, in the form of a reference movie data reference record.

data reference extension   A block of additional data associated with a data reference to assist QuickTime in working with the data picked out by the data reference.

decompression status flags   A set of flags that contain information about a decompression operation.

default data reference   The data reference that is used for a media if no other data reference is explicitly specified.

displayable name   The name of an object in the file system in a form that can be displayed to the user.

display boundary rectangle   The rectangle in which previewed video data is to be displayed.

down state   The state of a Flash button when the mouse button is down and the cursor is within the bounds of the button image. Compare to **over state**, **up state**.

drag region   The portion of a window that a user can click on in order to move the window around on the screen. Compare to **content region.**

drag region mask   A 1-bit mask that determines the shape of a skinned window's drag region.

dynamic text box   In Flash, a text box whose text can change dynamically, without user intervention (perhaps because the value of an associated Flash variable has changed).

effect description   An atom container that indicates which effect to perform and which parameters, if any, to use when rendering the effect.

effects parameter   An atom that specifies additional information about an effect.

effects parameter file   A file that specifies an effect and zero or more of its parameters; it may also specify the poster picture that appears in the effects parameters dialog box.

effects parameters dialog box   A dialog box that usually includes a list of available effects and some controls allowing the user to modify the parameters associated with a selected effect.

effects source   See **effects source track**.

effects source track   A track in a movie that is used as the input source for an effect.

effects track   A video track (of type `VideoMediaType`) whose media data is an effect description.

error function   See **error notification function**.

error notification function   An application-defined function that is called whenever QuickTime encounters a nonzero result code during the execution of a Movie Toolbox function.

event callback function   A function that is executed when specific types of Carbon events occur.

event class   A category of events that relate to a specific event target (for instance, a window or a menu). See also **event kind**.

event-driven programming   A programming model in which an application is structured so that it is guided by events reporting the user's actions with the mouse and keyboard (and other occurrences in the computer).

event handler   See **event callback function**.

event kind   A specific type of event in an event class.

event loop   A block of code that retrieves events from the Event Manager and dispatches them to the appropriate event-handling routine.

event loop timer   See **Carbon event loop timer**.

event loop timer reference   A reference to an event loop timer.

Event Manager   The part of the Macintosh Operating System that applications can use to retrieve information about actions performed by the user or about events in the system. Compare to **Carbon Event Manager**.

event reference   An opaque data structure that contains information about an event, such as its class, its kind, and any additional parameters for the event.

event target   An opaque object that corresponds to an object in the application that can receive events, such as a control, a window, or the application itself.

event type specification   A data structure (of type EventTypeSpec) that specifies an event class and kind.

Extensible Markup Language   See **XML**.

Fast Start movie file   A QuickTime movie file in which the movie atom is stored as one of the first atoms in a single-fork movie file.

filter   A video effect that operates on one source image or video track. Compare to **generator**, **transition**.

Flash   A file format and playback engine developed by Macromedia, Inc. for displaying vector-based graphics and animations.

Flash application message   A message sent by a Flash track to the playback application requesting that it perform specific actions such as quitting or launching some other application. Compare to **QuickTime application message**.

Flash media handler   A media handler that provides support for displaying and managing Flash content inside of QuickTime movies.

Flash track   A track (of type FlashMediaType) that contains Flash data.

Flash variable   A variable associated with a Flash file.

flattened movie file   See **self-contained movie file**.

frame action   A Flash action that is executed immediately after a specified frame is rendered. Compare to **button action**.

FSCommand   See **Flash application message**.

generator   A video effect that operates on no source images or video tracks. Compare to **filter**, **transition**.

header block   The part of a Flash file that contains general information about the Flash file, such as its size, the dimensions of the Flash movie, and the number of frames in the movie.

help tag   A message that can appear when the cursor is left motionless over some interface element (typically a window, a control, or a menu item) for a preset amount of time.

hint track   A track that contains information that tells server software how to packetize the corresponding streamed track.

hot spot   A clickable area in a QuickTime VR movie.

hot spot atom   An atom in a QuickTime VR file that contains information about a hot spot.

hot spot image track   A track in a QuickTime VR movie that holds the image data for hot spots.

hot spot parent atom   An atom in a QuickTime VR file that contains one or more hot spot atoms.

HTTP streaming   A method of streaming movies that uses the HTTP protocol. Compare to **real-time streaming**.

ICM   See **Image Compression Manager**.

ICM frame time record   A data structure (of type `ICMFrameTimeRecord`) that specifies a time value for a decompression sequence. See also **Image Compression Manager**.

idle state   See **up state**.

idling   See **tasking**.

Image Compression Manager (ICM)   The part of QuickTime that provides services for compressing and decompressing images and sequences of images.

image decompressor component   A component (of type `decompressorComponentType`) that provides image decompression services.

image description   A data structure that contains information about an image.

image description extension   A block of data that is appended to an image description structure.

importing in place   The process of importing a movie file without having to make a copy of the file data.

initialization data data reference extension   A data reference extension that contains initialization data.

initialization extension   See **initialization data data reference extension**.

intercept procedure   An application-defined procedure that is called before certain QuickTime VR functions.

intercept record   A structure (of type QTVRInterceptRecord) that is passed to an intercept procedure and that contains information about the function call being intercepted.

language atom   An atom in a reference movie descriptor atom that indicates that an alternate movie should be selected based in part on the operating system's language.

low-resolution image track   In a QuickTime VR movie, a video track that (typically) shows the same location as the full resolution track but occupies a small fraction of the space of the full resolution track.

low-resolution preview track   See **low-resolution image track**.

Macromedia Flash   See **Flash**.

media characteristic   A feature that can be shared by two or more track types, such as the ability to draw data or create sound.

media parameters structure   A data structure (of type QTSMediaParams) that contains a video parameters structure and an audio parameters structure.

media sample   A single element of media data. (For instance, a video frame is usually a single sample.)

media sample reference   A reference to an existing media sample.

menu button   In Flash, a button in that—if you click it, hold the mouse button down, and then drag outside of the button—returns to its up state. Compare to **push button**.

modification state   See **window modification state**.

motion tweening A positional tweening operation supported by Flash. Compare to **shape tweening**.

movie A set of data (of type Movie) that is managed by the Movie Toolbox. A movie contains one or more tracks, each of which represents data of a specific type (for instance, video, sound, text, animation, and the like).

movie clip In Flash, an object with a timeline that is independent of the main timeline.

movie controller action Any one of a large number of actions that can be performed by a movie controller.

movie controller action filter function An application-defined function that receives notification of pending movie controller actions; the filter function can handle those actions or pass them on to the movie controller.

movie controller bar A visible set of controls for manipulating a movie, usually attached to the bottom of a movie.

movie drawing-complete procedure An application-defined function that is executed whenever QuickTime has finished drawing a new frame of a movie.

movie load state An indication of the state of the loading process and hence what operations can be safely performed on the movie.

movie tasking interval The time between two movie taskings.

multicast To broadcast a stream to more than one client machine. Compare to **unicast**.

new presentation parameters structure A data structure (of type QTSNewPresentationParams) that contains information about a new presentation.

node A position in a scene at which the user can view a panorama or object.

node information atom container An atom container that holds information about a particular node in a scene.

node header atom An atom that contains information about a single node, such as the node's type, ID, and name.

object See **object movie**, **object node**.

object image track A track in a QuickTime VR movie that holds the image data for an object.

object movie A QuickTime VR movie that contains a single object node.

object node   A type of node in a QuickTime VR movie that provides a view of a single object or group of objects. Compare to **panoramic node**.

object track   A track in a QuickTime VR movie that holds information about an object node.

over state   The state of a Flash button when the cursor is within the bounds of the button image. Compare to **down state**, **up state**.

packet   A discrete chunk of data sent across a network.

panorama   See **panorama movie**, **panoramic node**.

panorama image track   A track in a QuickTime VR movie that holds the image data for a panorama.

panorama movie   A QuickTime VR movie that contains a single panoramic node.

panorama track   A track in a QuickTime VR movie that holds information about a panoramic node.

panoramic node   A type of node in a QuickTime VR movie that provides a panoramic view of a location. Compare to **object node**.

parameter dialog box preview record   A data structure (of type `QTParamPreviewRecord`) that specifies the preview image in an effects parameters dialog box.

preference panel plug-in   See **CodeWarrior settings panel plug-in**.

preload   To load a track entirely into memory when a movie is opened.

prescreen buffer   An image buffer maintained by QuickTime VR that contains the image that is about to be copied to the screen.

prescreen buffer imaging completion procedure   An application-defined procedure that is called by the QuickTime VR Manager each time the prescreen buffer is about to be copied to the screen.

present   To display a movie at a certain size against a solid black background.

presentation   A collection of one or more streams of data, which can consist of packets of audio, video, text, or other data.

presentation notification procedure   A procedure that is called on specific events involving a presentation, such as when the presentation is first created and when a connection to the client machine occurs.

preview   To display captured data in a window on the screen (if it's visual data) or to play back captured data through the sound output hardware (if it's audio data). Compare to **record**.

preview track   See **low-resolution image track**.

progressive downloading   See **HTTP streaming**.

public media information   Any data associated with a media that does not need to be pegged to a specific time in a track.

push button   In Flash, a button that—if you click the mouse button, hold it down, and move the cursor outside of the button image—remains in its down state. Compare to **menu button**.

QTML   See **QuickTime Media Layer**.

QTVR   See **QuickTime VR**.

QTVR instance   An identifier (of type QTVRInstance) that specifies a Quick-Time VR movie.

QTVR track   A track in a QuickTime VR movie that maintains general information about the movie, such as the default imaging properties.

QuickTime   A software architecture developed by Apple Computer, Inc. for creating and playing back multimedia content.

QuickTime application message   A message sent from a QuickTime movie to the playback application. Compare to **Flash application message**.

QuickTime Media Layer (QTML)   A library for Windows operating systems that supports the QuickTime application programming interfaces; the Quick-Time Media Layer also provides an implementation of a number of the parts of the Macintosh Operating System (including the Memory Manager and the File Manager) and the Macintosh User Interface Toolbox (including the Dialog Manager, the Control Manager, and the Menu Manager).

QuickTime video effects architecture   An extensible system for applying video effects to single images or video tracks and to pairs of images or video tracks.

QuickTime VR   The part of QuickTime that allows users to interactively explore and examine photorealistic, three-dimensional virtual worlds and objects. See also **object**, **panorama**.

QuickTime VR flattener   A movie export component that prepares a Quick-Time VR movie for Fast Start downloading and provides the option of including a low-resolution image track.

QuickTime VR Manager   The programming interface to QuickTime VR.

QuickTime VR movie controller   A movie controller component that knows how to interpret user actions in a QuickTime VR movie.

QuickTime XML importer   A movie importer that knows how to parse certain kinds of XML files.

real-time streaming   A method of streaming movies that uses the RTP protocol. Compare to **HTTP streaming**.

receiver   A computer that receives streamed data. Compare to **transmitter**.

record   To write captured data into one or more files on disk. Compare to **preview**.

reference movie   See **alternate reference movie file**.

reference movie data reference record   A data structure (of type `Reference-MovieDataRefRecord`) that specifies a data reference; this record is the leaf data for a data reference atom.

reference movie descriptor atom   An atom (1) that describes a single alternate movie.

reference movie record atom   An atom (1) (of type `ReferenceMovieRecord-AID`) that contains one reference movie descriptor atom for each alternate movie described by the alternate reference movie.

region code   A value that specifies a version of a written language of a particular region in the world.

retain count   See **reference count**.

RezWack   A tool written by Apple that adds Macintosh resources to a Windows application or library.

RezWack tag data   Some data placed at the end of a file processed by the RezWack utility.

sample reference   See **media sample reference**.

scene   In a QuickTime VR movie, a collection of one or more nodes.

SDP   See **session description protocol**.

SDP file   A file that conforms to the session description protocol.

SDP importer   A component that converts SDP data into a movie.

self-contained movie file   A movie file that contains a movie's metadata and media data and therefore does not depend on any other files.

sequence A series of images.

sequence grabber See **sequence grabber component**.

sequence grabber channel component A component that controls a sequence grabber channel.

sequence grabber component A component that provides a set of high-level APIs for capturing video and sound data.

sequence grabber output An identifier for the location in which captured data is recorded.

sequence grabber panel component A component that communicates with a channel component or digitizer component to get and set the capture settings, usually by displaying a dialog box.

sequence identifier An identifier (of type ImageSequence) for a decompression sequence.

session description protocol A standard format for information about some of the network settings to be used by a presentation, such as the destination IP address for the broadcast and the ports to use for the data streams.

shape tweening In Flash, a tweening operation that morphs one shape into another. Compare to **motion tweening**.

skin The custom shape of a skinned movie window.

skinned movie window A movie window that has a custom shape.

skin track A track that contains data that specifies the content region and the drag region of a skinned movie window.

slideshow mode A way of playing a movie in which the movie advances to another frame only when the user presses the Right Arrow or Left Arrow key (which moves the movie forward one frame or backward one frame, respectively).

sound input device driver A device driver that manages communications between applications and the sound input hardware.

source name The name of a source track of an effects track.

source name atom An atom that links a source track to an effects track.

sourcer See **sourcer component**.

sourcer component A component that can read data from a specific kind of source.

sprite   A graphical object that has a number of properties, including its current image index, location, size, layer, graphics mode, and visibility state. In Flash, a movie clip.

stacked effect   An effect that uses as input the output of another effect.

standard parameters dialog box   See **effects parameters dialog box**.

sticky error   See **sticky error value**.

sticky error value   The first nonzero result code of a Movie Toolbox function that was generated since the last time the sticky error was cleared. Compare to **current error value**.

stream   A series of packets.

streaming   The process whereby one computer segments a file or a sequence of bytes into discrete chunks and sends them across a network to another computer.

structure region   The entire screen area occupied by the window, including the window's content region and its window frame.

tag   An identifier in a tagged data block that indicates the kind of block it is.

tagged data block   A part of a Flash file that defines the items that appear in the Flash movie (that is, the buttons, shapes, and sounds) or indicates where and when those items are to be drawn or played and possibly also animated.

tag header   A part of a tagged data block that includes the tag and the length of the block.

tasking   The process of explicitly allocating some processor time to Quick-Time (often by calling the `MoviesTask` function) so that it can do whatever is required to keep a movie playing or downloading.

task-sooner callback function   A function that is called when an application needs to task one of its movies before a specified event loop timer is scheduled to fire.

text digitizer   See **text digitizer component**.

text digitizer component   A component that captures text data from external sources, such as the closed-captioned data embedded in some television broadcasts.

time base callback event   An identifier (of type `QTCallBack`) for a callback event.

time base callback function   A function that is executed when a specific time in a movie is reached or when some other event related to the movie's time base occurs.

tip   See **help tag**.

tool tip   See **help tag**.

transition   A video effect that operates on two source images or video tracks. Compare to **generator**, **filter**.

transmitter   A computer that sends out streamed data. Compare to **receiver**.

tweening   The process of generating values that lie between two given values or that are in some other way algorithmically derived from some given data.

twip   A unit of measurement equal to 1/20th of a pixel.

unicast   To broadcast a stream to a single client machine. Compare to **multicast**.

up state   The state of a Flash button when the cursor is not within the bounds of the button image. Compare to **down state**, **over state**.

video digitizer   See **video digitizer component**.

video digitizer component   A component that digitizes a video data stream, if necessary, and often provides additional services such as resizing the video, clipping out portions of the video, and converting colors in the video.

video parameters structure   A data structure (of type QTSVideoParams) that contains information about the video media data being previewed locally.

video source boundary rectangle   The rectangle that defines the size of the source video image being captured by a video channel.

VR   See **QuickTime VR**.

VR world atom container   An atom container in a QuickTime VR file that holds general information about the scene contained in the QuickTime VR movie, including the name of the entire scene, the default node ID, and the default imaging properties.

VR world header atom   An atom in a VR world atom container that contains the name of the scene and the default node ID.

wacked file   A file that has been processed by the RezWack utility.

window class   The type of a window (for example, document window, dialog window, and so forth).

window definition message   Any one of several messages sent to a window definition procedure that indicates which task the procedure is to perform.

window definition procedure   A procedure that defines the general appearance and behavior of a window.

window definition specification   A data structure (of type `WindowDefSpec`) that specifies a custom window definition procedure.

window modification state   A property of a window that indicates whether the data in the window has been modified.

XML   Extensible Markup Language: a textual description of a document that contains structured information.

Index

A

About box, 268–270
  dialog pointer, 269
  displaying, 268
  handling events for, 268–270
  help tags, 270, 271
  illustrated, 268
action list, 173
actions
  application-specific, 152
  button, 173, 195
  button, conditions, 203, 206, 207
  finding, by event type, 202–203
  finding, for button state transitions, 201–203
  frame, 195
  inserting, 196
  uses, 174
  wired, 152
  See also Flash
ActionScript, 154
active source rectangle
  change of, 114
  size, 102
AddMediaDataRef function, 422–423
AddMediaSample function, 436
AddMediaSampleReference function, 421–422
  data location specification, 423
  declaration, 422
  defined, 421–422
AddMediaSampleReferences function, 421–422
AddMovieResource function, 427

AddVRAct_AddWiredActionsToQTVRMovie function, 306–310
  defined, 306
  definition (code), 307–310
AddVRAct_SetWiredActionsToHotSpot function, 302–303
AddVRAct_SetWiredActionsToNode function, 303–304
AddVRAct_WriteMediaPropertyAtom function, 305–306
allowscale command, 181
alternate data rate record, 331–332
alternate reference movie files, 325–339
  adding contained movies to, 336–339
  with contained movies, 329
  creating, 325, 328–329
  defined, 314
  quality, 333
  selection criteria specification, 331–333
  specifying, 329–331
  specifying, with XML, 327
  structure, 328
alternate track groups
  creating, 319–320
  defined, 313
  rescanning, 324
alternate tracks, 314–325
  changing, 324–325
  defined, 313
  English, 314
  French, 315
  media language, getting/setting, 316–318

alternate tracks *(continued)*
>	movie language, getting/setting, 320–323
>	quality, getting/setting, 318–319
>	selection, enabling/disabling, 323–324
>	selection process, 315
application framework, modifying, 359–362
application windows, 270–274
>	determination, 271
>	finding, 272
>	reference constant, 272
`ApplicationDataRecord` structure, 45, 77, 221
aspect ratio, full-screen movie, 219
asynchronous movie loading, 353–385
>	allowing, 356–357
>	application framework modification, 359–362
>	introduction, 353–355
>	load state change handling, 363–366
>	menu item adjustment, 366–367
>	movie load state check, 357–358
atom containers
>	inserting, 208
>	media property, 301
>	VR world, 296
audio channels
>	closing down, 105
>	configuring, 103–105
>	sample rates, 103–105
>	usage, setting, 103
>	volume, 103
audio parameters structure, 136
auto-alternating, 314, 324
autoplay, 176

B

`BeginFullScreen` function, 215
>	calling, 218, 219, 220, 239
>	parameters, 215
>	screen resolution, 216–220
>	window size, 216
broadcasters, 128
broadcasting, 125–149
>	APIs, 125, 128, 129
>	client, 135
>	controlling, 142–143

initializing for, 129, 130–131
>	pausing, 130, 142
>	setting up, 129–132
>	settings, 143–146
>	shutting down, 131–132
>	starting, 130, 140–142
>	stopping, 143
bugs, 341
>	fixing, 348–351
>	framework, 348–352
>	*See also* errors
button action conditions, 203, 206, 207
>	16-bit offset, 207
>	defined, 203
>	existing list of, 206
>	moving, 207
>	offset to list, 208
>	splicing, 208
button actions
>	defined, 195
>	list, attached to, 173
buttons, 159–163
>	data, reading, 203–208
>	data block, 206
>	defined, 159
>	down state, 159, 160
>	images, 160
>	menu, 161
>	over state, 159, 160
>	path, 192
>	push, 161
>	records, 203
>	state transitions, 161–162
>	up state, 159–160
>	*See also* Flash

C

callback events, 242–243
Carbon event loop timer callback function, 250
Carbon Event Manager, 252
>	advantages, 254
>	calls to, 250
>	event parameters, 258
>	function of, 252
>	handler arrangement, 258

menu handling and, 262
null events and, 274
support implementation, 255
Carbon events, 249–281
defined, 254
dispatching, 253
enclosing code handling, 250
event classes, 254
event kind, 254
event loop timers, 274–276
introduction, 249–250
menus, 261–267
overview, 251–255
retrieving, 253
tasking interval management, 276–279
See also events
Carbon movie control, 250, 279–280
creating, 279
defined, 279
support, 280
using, 280
CarbonLib, 249
CDSequenceNewDataSource function, 48–49
CFString data type, 452, 453
CFURL data type, 452, 453
channel components, 99–100
display boundary rectangle size, 102
sequence grabber, 99
channel output files, 119–121
eliciting, 120
setting, 119–121
channel settings, 109–116
settings dialog boxes display, 113–116
update event handling, 109–113
channel usage flags, 101
character ID, 192
child movies, 430
data, appending to data reference atom, 431
data, loading into memory, 432–433
flattened media sample, 434–435
flattening, into parent, 437–441
opening, 432
ClearMoviesStickyError function, 344–346
clicks
coordinates, 87
drag region (finding), 94–95
drag region (handling), 93–94

drag region (looking for), 92–93
hotspot, 292–293
on custom controller bar button, 321–322
passing, to effects component, 58–61
ripples from, 58, 59
cloud effect, 3, 4
CodeWarrior, 397
IDE, 389–390
plug-ins, 405–417
post-linker plug-in, 405, 406–411
settings panel plug-in, 405, 413–417
command IDs
assigning, 263
defined, 262
defining, 262–264
embedding, 264
framework, defining, 263
CompressImage function, 18, 20, 21, 42
constants
application window reference, 272
SMPTE effects, 25
source name, 10–11
contained movies
adding, 334–339
alternate reference movie file with, 329
defined, 326
flattened data, 335
with XML, 327
content region, 88
defined, 68
drag regions and, 92
mask, 68–69
reading, 76–77
storing, 76
ConvertCWFileSpecToFSSpec function, 409
ConvertEventRefToEventRecord function, 259
CopyTrackSettings function, 38
CreateCustomWindow function, 84
CreateMovieControl function, 279–280
CreateRezWackedFileFromBinary function, 409–410
cross-fade transitions, 2, 6
current media sample, 431–432
cursors
current location, passing, 58
full-screen mode, hiding, 216
hotspots, 93

custom window definition procedures, 76
  listing, 89–91
  return value, 86
  writing, 85–91
custom window shape
  opening, 84
  specifying, 83–85
  See also skinned movie windows
CWPlugin_GetDropInFlags function, 407–408
CWReportMessage function, 413
CWRezWack.c, 406, 407
CWRezWack_Linker, 406
CWRezWackUtils.h, 406

D

dangling pointers, 350
data rate atoms, 331
data reference atoms
  atom data for, 329
  creating, 330–331
  defined, 329
  reconfiguring, 431
  replacing by "flattened" atom, 435
data reference extensions, 431, 434, 446–448
data references
  adding to movie file, 425, 429
  and alternate movies, 314, 330–331
  of channel output files, 119
  creating, from data types, 452
  default, 443, 445
  handle, 442, 445, 446
  and memory-based movies, 442–443,
    445–447
  and movie storage functions, 451–452,
    462–464, 466
  and movie tracks, 430–435
  using, 419
  utilities, 452
data sources, 98
data types
  creating data references from, 452
  of function return value, 347
  See also specific data types
DecompressImage function, 43
decompression
  data, storing, 45–47

image, 41–43
image sequence, 43–45
operation control, 43
rectangle, 43
status flags, 54
decompression sequence
  setting up, 49–51
  tasking, 52
DecompressSequenceBeginS function, 44, 47–48
DecompressSequenceFrameWhen function, 44,
    51–52
default data references, 443
degrees, 289–290
DeleteTrackSegment function, 436
display boundary rectangle
  resetting, 115, 118
  size, 102
dissolve transitions, 2
document windows, 255–261
  event handler installation, 256–257
  event handling, 258–261
  event specification, 255–256
documentation effects, 28
down state, 159, 160
  defined, 160
  illustrated, 161
  See also buttons
drag region mask
  defined, 69
  illustrated, 69
  reading, 76–77
  storing, 76
drag regions, 88, 92–93
  clicks (finding), 94–95
  clicks (handling), 93–94
  clicks (looking for), 92–93
  content regions and, 92
dragging, handling, 91–95
droplets
  dragging file onto, 396–397
  DropPix, 423–424
  setting up, 396–399
dropped files
  handling, 424–425
  tracking, 424, 425
DropPix, 423–424
DropPix_MakeSlideShow function, 425
  definition (code), 427–429

for loop, 425
duration, movie, 18
dynamic text boxes, 193
    defined, 193
    Text Options panel for, 194

E

effect descriptions
    creating, 9–11
    defined, 5
    fire effect, 24
    getting from effects parameter files, 34–35
    as media sample, 13
    ripple effect, 58
    source name atoms, 10
    source name specification, 16
    See also video effects
effect parameters, 24–33
    defined, 24
    fire effect, 24
    values, 24
effects. *See* video effects
effects components
    input data, 48
    passing clicks to, 58–61
effects parameters dialog box
    buttons, 33
    cleaning up, 31
    customizing, 28
    defined, 25
    displaying, 25
    event handling, 28–31
    illustrated, 26, 61
    items embedded in custom dialog box, 63–64
    looking for events in, 31
    messages, handling, 33
    record, 27–28
    for single effect, 62–63
    standard, 61
    on Windows, 31–33
effects parameters files, 33–35
    atoms, 33–34
    defined, 33
    effect descriptions from, 34–35
    organization, 33
    reading/writing and, 34

effects tracks
    building, 8
    creating, 12
    defined, 5
    dimensions, setting, 12
    input map, 16
    layer, setting, 40
    offset, 37
    overlapping, 6
    source, 5–6
    See also video effects; video tracks
EffectsUtils_AddTrackReferenceToInputMap function, 16–18
    defined, 17–18
    uses, 16
EffectsUtils_AddVideoTrackFromGWorld function, 18–19, 20–24
EffectsUtils_CreateEffectDescription function, 9–11
    calling, 11
    defined, 9–10
    using, 13
EffectsUtils_GetPictResourceAsGWorld function, 18–20
    defined, 19–20
    function, 18
EffectsUtils_GetTypeFromEffectDescription function, 11–12
    defined, 21–23
    function, 13
emboss effect, 41
EndFullScreen function, 215–216
    calling, 232
    parameters, 216
    QTBig_HandleMessages and, 232
EnterMovies function, 342
error notification functions, 346–347
    in application development, 347
    declaration, 346
    defined, 346
error-reporting functions, 342–346
    GetMoviesError, 343
    GetMoviesStickyError, 343–345
errors
    handling theory/practice, 341
    movie load, handling, 363
    mysterious, 347–348
    post-link, 411–413

errors *(continued)*
  retrieving, 341–352
  sticky, 343–346
event atoms, 201
event callback function, 250
event classes
  defined, 254
  examples, 254
  See also Carbon events
event handlers
  application, installing, 267
  arrangement, 258
  idle, 304
  installing, 254–255, 256–257
  passing to, 258
  See also event callback function
event handling
  About box, 268–270
  in effects parameters dialog box, 28–33
  for full-screen window, 229–232
event loop timers, 274–276
  application-wide, 276
  callback function, 275
  callbacks, handling, 275, 350
  installing, 274, 276
  interval adjustment, 277–278
  references, 275
  resetting, 279
  for tasking open movies, 276
event loops, 251
Event Manager, 258
event reference, 258
event targets, 255
event type specifications, creating, 255
event-driven programming, 251
events
  callback, 242
  Carbon, 249–281
  "classic," 348
  dispatching, 251, 253
  effects parameters dialog box determination, 29
  handling, 252
  handling, in monitor window, 149
  idle, 374
  keyDown, 254

looking for, in effects parameters dialog box, 31
null, 274
refinement, 253
retrieving, 251, 253
sending, to effects parameters dialog box, 31–33
specifying, 255–256
type, finding actions by, 202–203
update, handling, 109–113
updateEvt, 254
EventTypeSpec data type, 255
exec command, 182
explode effect, 2
Export Settings dialog box, 384
Extensible Markup Language. *See* XML

F

FDecompressImage function, 43
field of view, 286, 290
file-opening dialog box, 454
files
  channel output, 119–121
  default location, setting, 460–462
  directory ID, finding, 458
  dragging onto droplets, 396–397
  dropped, 424–425
  effects parameters, 33–35
  Flash project, 154
  Flash (SWF), 163–180
  header, 239
  output, 119–124
  preference, 460
  resource, 393–394
  selection, 453
film noise effect, 52
  defined, 2
  illustrated, 3
  See also filters; video effects
filters, 15–18
  adding, 15
  applied to video track, 7
  defined, 1
  film noise, 2, 3
  implementation, 4
  See also video effects

fire effect, 3, 4
    duration, 15
    effect description, 24
    effect parameters, 24
    image override, 56
    See also video effects
Flash, 151–188
    authoring/playback architecture, 156
    buttons, 159–163
    content, importing, 152
    data, including in QuickTime file, 158–159
    defined, 151
    document window, 155
    movieclips, 156
    multimedia development environment, 153
    MX version, 157
    overview, 153–156
    playback mechanism, 154
    QuickTime vs., 154
    rendering text support, 156–157
    tweening support, 154
    video and, 156–159
Flash application messages, 234–235. *See also*
    FSCommands
Flash files (SWF), 163–180
    autoplay, 176
    byte stream, reading, 164–167
    data, 155
    defined, 154, 163
    format illustration, 164
    header block, 163–164
    importing, 175–180
    objects, 193
    opening, 155, 175
    rectangle data, reading, 169–170
    tagged data blocks, 163–164
    twips, 170
Flash media handler
    defined, 151
    FSCommands and, 182
    functions, 184–188
    pointing-hand cursor, 151
    updated, 192
Flash movies
    author, 175
    as Flash tracks, 189
    text boxes, 193

Flash Player, 155, 157
    contextual menu, 182
    defined, 155
Flash project files, 154
Flash sprites, 156. *See also* movieclips
Flash tracks
    attaching wired actions in, 152–153, 159
    control and, 159
    controlling QTVR movies, 190, 285
    controlling video/sound tracks, 152
    defined, 151
    Flash movies as, 189
    Flash variable, 193
    media sample, 203
    panning inside, 191
    playing, 159
    wired actions in, 195–211
    wired actions targeted at, 190–195
    zooming in, 191
Flash variables, 193
`FlashMediaGetDisplayedFrameNumber` function,
    185
`FlashMediaGetSupportedSwfVersion` function, 184
`FlashMediaSetFlashVariable` function, 185
`FlashMediaSetPan` function, 185
`FlashMediaSetZoom` function, 184–185, 192
    defined, 184
    definition (code), 185
    parameter, 184
`FlashParserStruct` data type, 165, 167
`FlattenMovieData` function
    calling, 445, 446
    defined, 334
    definition (code), 335
    location specification, 442
    use assumption, 443
Flix
    defined, 157
    video settings panel, 158
frame actions, 195
FSCommands, 181–184
    `allowscale`, 181
    defined, 181
    `exec`, 182
    Flash media handler and, 182
    `fullscreen`, 181, 183
    handling, targeted at applications, 183

FSCommands *(continued)*
   mechanism, 181
   quit, 182
   range extension, 181
   showmenu, 181–182
   See also Flash application messages
FSRef data type, 452, 453
FSSpec data type, 452
fullscreen command, 181, 183, 234–235, 248
full-screen mode
   cursor, hiding, 216
   entering, 215, 223–229
   exiting, 214, 215–216, 232–234
   screen resolution, 216–219
full-screen movies, 213–248
   aspect ratio, 219
   defined, 213
   events passed to, 221
   hidden elements, 213
   illustrated, 214
   introduction, 213–214
   playback, 221
   practice, 220–234
   rectangle, adjusting, 220
   restoring, 221
   scaling, 218–220
   theory, 215–219
   See also movies
full-screen window
   attaching movie to, 229
   attaching window object to, 223
   background color, 241
   centered, 220
   closing, 222
   data, destroying, 223
   data, initializing, 221–223
   event handling, 229–232
   messages, handling, 230–231
   size, 216
   state information, 221
   tracking, 226
   window type, 224
functions
   AddMediaDataRef, 422–423
   AddMediaSample, 436
   AddMediaSampleReference, 421–422
   AddMediaSampleReferences, 421–422
   AddMovieResource, 427

AddVRAct_SetWiredActionsToHotSpot, 302
AddVRAct_SetWiredActionsToNode, 303–304
AddVRAct_WriteMediaPropertyAtom, 305–306
AddWiredActionsToQTVRMovie, 306–310
BeginFullScreen, 215
CDSequenceNewDataSource, 48–49
ClearMoviesStickyError, 344–346
CompressImage, 18, 20, 21, 42
ConvertCWFileSpecToFSSpec, 409
ConvertEventRefToEventRecord, 259
CopyTrackSettings, 38
CreateCustomWindow, 84
CreateMovieControl, 279–280
CreateRezWackedFileFromBinary, 409–410
CWPlugin_GetDropInFlags, 407–408
CWReportMessage, 413
DecompressImage, 43
DecompressSequenceBeginS, 44, 47–48
DecompressSequenceFrameWhen, 44, 51–52
DeleteTrackSegment, 436
DropPix_MakeSlideShow, 425, 427–429
EffectsUtils_AddTrackReferenceToInputMap,
   16–18
EffectsUtils_AddVideoTrackFromGWorld,
   18–19, 20–24
EffectsUtils_CreateEffectDescription, 9–11,
   13
EffectsUtils_GetPictResourceAsGWorld, 18–20
EffectsUtils_GetTypeFromEffectDescription,
   11–12, 13
EndFullScreen, 215–216
EnterMovies, 342
error notification, 346–347
error-reporting, 342–346
FDecompressImage, 43
Flash media handler, 184–188
FlashMediaGetDisplayedFrameNumber, 185
FlashMediaGetSupportedSwfVersion, 184
FlashMediaSetFlashVariable, 185
FlashMediaSetPan, 185
FlashMediaSetZoom, 184–185, 192
FlattenMovieData, 334–335, 442–443
GetAString, 166–167
GetBits, 167–168
GetByte, 166
GetData, 416–417
GetDWord, 166
GetEventTypeCount, 256

GetMaxCompressionSize, 18, 20, 21, 42
GetMaxLoadedTimeInMovie, 354, 368
GetMediaLanguage, 316
GetMediaPublicInfo, 77
GetMediaQuality, 319
GetMediaSample, 196, 301, 431, 432
GetMediaSampleReference, 423
GetMediaSampleReferences, 423
GetMovieActive, 343
GetMovieIndTrackType, 70, 196
GetMovieLoadState, 358, 363
GetMovieNaturalBoundsRect, 218–219
GetMoviesError, 343
GetMoviesStickyError, 343–345
GetMovieTimeBase, 242
GetMovieTrackCount, 358
GetOffsetForButton, 204–205
GetPortNativeWindow, 224
GetRect, 169
GetSBits, 168
GetTrackAlternate, 320
GetTrackMedia, 196
GetTrackNextInterestingTime, 345–346, 436
GetWindowEventTarget, 256
GetWord, 166
GlobalToLocal, 87
gotoAndStop, 159
GraphicsExportSetDepth, 347
ICM, 18
ImageCodecCreateStandardParameterDialog,
    62, 63
ImageCodecStandardParameterDialogDoAction,
    63
ImageDescriptionForEffect, 8, 9
InitBits, 168
InitializeQTVR, 288
InsertMediaIntoTrack, 427
InsertTrackSegment, 38, 421
InstallEventLoopTimer, 348–349
InstallStandardEventHandler, 256–257
Link, 408–409
LocateFirstButton, 196–197
MakeImageDescriptionPixMap, 49
MCIsPlayerEvent, 274
MediaSetPublicInfo, 72–73
movie storage, 451, 461–467
MRM_MakeReferenceMovie, 336–339
NavAskSaveChanges, 458
NavCreateGetFileDialog, 454–455

NavGetDefaultDialogCreationOptions, 453
NavGetFile, 451, 453
NavPutFile, 451, 453
NewCWindow, 84
NewMovieFromDataRef, 353, 426
NewMovieFromFile, 353, 356
NewMovieFromStorageOffset, 464
NewMovieTrack, 426
NewTrackMedia, 446–447
OpenMovieFile, 356, 462–463
OpenMovieStorage, 463, 465
ParseTags, 197–198
PtInRgn, 87
PutData, 415–416
QTAL_AddLoaderBarPICTToKeyFrameSample,
    376–377
QTAL_AddSpriteLoaderSamplesToMedia, 376,
    378–380
QTAL_MovieDrawingCompleteProc, 370
QTAL_SetTrackToPreload, 375
QTAlt_AddMovieLanguagesToMenu, 323
QTAlt_GetMenuItemIndexForLanguageCode,
    317–318
QTAlt_HandleCustomButtonClick, 321–322
QTAlt_UpdateMovieLanguageMask, 317
QTApp_AdjustMenus, 108
QTApp_CheckMovieLoadState, 372–373
QTApp_HandleEvent, 92–93, 230
QTApp_HandleKeyPress, 229
QTApp_HandleMenu, 116–117
QTApp_Idle, 52, 105–106
QTApp_SetupWindowObject, 79, 80, 289
QTBC_CreateMonitorWindow, 147
QTBC_HandleMonitorWindowEvents, 148–149
QTBC_Init, 130–131
QTBC_PauseBroadcasting, 142–143
QTBC_SetupPresentation, 137–139
QTBC_StartBroadcasting, 140, 143
QTBC_Stop, 131–132
QTBC_StopBroadcasting, 132, 143
QTBC_UserItemProcedure, 147–148
QTBig_AddPTVItemToMovie, 240–241
QTBig_DumpWindowData, 222–223
QTBig_FullscreenCallBack, 246–247
QTBig_HandleMessages, 230–231
QTBig_InitWindowData, 222
QTBig_InstallCallBack, 243, 245–246
QTBig_MovieIsStoppable, 243–244

functions *(continued)*

QTBig_StartFullscreen, 225
QTBig_StopFullscreen, 229, 230–231
QTCap_GetChannelSettings, 110, 111, 114
QTCap_GetSoundSettings, 113–114
QTCap_GetVideoSettings, 115–116
QTCap_Init, 102
QTCap_Record, 122–124
QTCap_ResizeMonitorWindow, 117
QTCap_SetTrackFile, 120–121
QTCap_SGModalFilterProc, 112–113
QTCap_Stop, 108–109
QTCreateStandardParameterDialog, 25–27
QTDR_AddInitDataDataRefExtension, 434
QTDR_CreateMovieInRAM, 443–445
QTDR_CreateTrackInRAM, 447–448
QTDR_GetMovieFromURL, 357
QTEffects_AddEffectToMoveSegment, 41
QTEffects_AddFilmNoiseToImage, 46–47
QTEffects_AddPenguinMovieSamplesToMedia, 59–60
QTEffects_AddRippleEffectAsSpriteImage, 57
QTEffects_DumpWindowData, 54–55
QTEffects_HandleEffectsDialogEvents, 31–32
QTEffects_InitWindowData, 46
QTEffects_MakeSpriteEffectMovie, 56–57
QTEffects_RespondToDialogSelection, 30–31
QTEffects_RunEffect, 52–54
QTEffects_SetUpEffectSequence, 49–51
QTFlash_AddWiredActionsToFlashMovie, 196, 198–201
QTFlash_CreateButtonActionContainer, 201
QTFlash_CreateVarAction, 194–195
QTFlash_DoFSCommand, 183, 234
QTFlash_ExtractFlashMovieFromTrack, 185–188
QTFlash_GetFileCharacteristic, 176–180
QTFlash_InitWindowData, 175–176
QTFlash_IsAutoPlayMovie, 176
QTFlash_SetWiredActionsToButton, 196, 198, 201, 202–203
QTFrame_AdjustMenus, 264–265, 367
QTFrame_CarbonEventModelWindowHandler, 269–270
QTFrame_CarbonEventWindowHandler, 258
QTFrame_CarbonEventWindowTimer, 275, 351–352
QTFrame_CheckMovieControllers, 361–362

QTFrame_CheckMovieLoadState, 362, 363–366
QTFrame_CloseWindowObject, 237, 238, 466–467
QTFrame_CreateMovieWindow, 257, 348–349
QTFrame_DestroyMovieWindow, 237, 458–460
QTFrame_GetCurrentFileLocationDesc, 461–462
QTFrame_GetOneFileWithPreview, 455–457, 462
QTFrame_HandleEvent, 251–252, 351, 352
QTFrame_HandleMenuCommand, 262, 265–267
QTFrame_IsAppWindow, 271–273
QTFrame_MainEventLoop, 252–253, 276–277
QTFrame_OpenCommandLineMovies, 424
QTFrame_OpenMovieInWindow, 84, 241–242, 359–360, 465
QTFrame_PutFile, 457
QTFrame_SetWindowVisState, 224–225
QTFrame_ShowAboutBox, 270
QTFrame_ShowWindowAtPoint, 360
QTFrame_SizeWindowToMovie, 232
QTFrame_UpdateMovieFile, 466
QTGetEffectsList, 26
QTGetTimeUntilNextTask, 276
QTInstallNextTaskNeededSoonerCallback, 278–279
QTIsStandardParameterDialogEvent, 28–30
QTMIM_FlattenChildIntoParent, 437–441
QTRW_CreateRezWackedFileFromBinary, 399–400
QTRW_RezWackWinBinaryAndMacResFile, 399, 400, 402–405, 410, 411
QTSInitializeMediaParams, 136
QTSkin_AddSkinTrack, 74–76
QTSkin_ConvertPictureToRegion, 77–78
QTSkin_DumpWindowData, 95
QTSkin_GetPicHandleFromFile, 73–74
QTSkin_Init, 85
QTSkin_InitWindowData, 79, 80, 81–83
QTSkin_IsDragClick, 94–95
QTSkin_IsSkinnedMovie, 70
QTSMediaParams, 136
QTSNewPresentation, 132, 137, 139
QTSPresIdle, 139
QTSPresPreroll, 140
QTSPresSettingsDialog, 145
QTSPresStart, 140, 141
QTStandardParameterDialogDoAction, 27, 30
QTUtils_GetFrameCount, 345–346
QTUtils_GetMovieLanguge, 320–321

QTUtils_GetScreenResolution, 217
QTVRGetNodeInfo, 295
QTVRGetPanAngle, 289, 290
QTVRGetQTVRInstance, 288–289, 290
QTVRGetVRWorld, 296–297
QTVRInstallInterceptProc, 293–294
QTVRSetAngularUnits, 289
QTVRSetPrescreenImagingCompleteProc, 291
QTVRTriggerHotSpot, 293
QTVRUpdate, 291
QTVRUtils_FlattenMovieForStreaming,
    382–383
QTVRUtils_GetNodeHeaderAtomData, 295
QTVRUtils_GetNodeType, 296
QTVRUtils_IsQTVRMgrInstalled, 287–288
QuitAppModalLoopForWindow, 268, 270
RunAppModalLoopForWindow, 267
SetAutoTrackAlternatesEnabled, 324
SetMediaLanguage, 316
SetMediaQuality, 319
SetMenuItemCommandID, 264
SetModelessDialogCallbackProc, 31–32
SetMovieDefaultDataRef, 443
SetMovieDrawingCompleteProc, 371
SetMovieLanguage, 320
SetMoviesErrorProc, 347
SetNewHeaderAndTagLength, 208–211
SetTrackAlternate, 319–320
SetWindowRgn, 95
SGGetSrcVideoBounds, 102
SGIdle, 122
SGInitialize, 101
SGNewOutput, 119–120
SGPause, 114
SGSetAdditionalSoundRates, 103
SGSetDataOutput, 118–119
SGSetGWorld, 101
SGSettingsDialog, 109
SGStartPreview, 124
SGStartRecord, 118, 121–122
SGStop, 118, 122
SGUpdate, 109–110
ShowHideTaskBar, 218
SpriteUtils_AddCompressedImageToKey-
    FrameSample, 58
SpriteUtils_AddPICTImageToKeyFrameSample,
    57
StartMovie, 343

time base callback, 242–248
TrackTimeToMediaTime, 431–432
UpdateMovieInStorage, 452, 464
UpdateMovieResource, 445–446
VRObject_ImportVideoTrack, 344–345
WiredUtils_AddMovieSetLanguage, 324–325

G

generators, 12–15
    defined, 3
    implementation, 4
GetAString function, 166–167
GetBits function, 167–168
GetByte function, 166
GetData function, 416–417
GetDWord function, 166
GetEventTypeCount function, 256
GetMaxCompressionSize function, 18, 20, 21, 42
GetMaxLoadedTimeInMovie function, 354, 368
GetMediaLanguage function, 316
GetMediaPublicInfo function, 77
GetMediaQuality function, 319
GetMediaSample function, 196, 301, 431, 432
    calling, 431
    return, 432
    time passed to, 432
GetMediaSampleReference function, 423
GetMediaSampleReferences function, 423
GetMovieActive function, 343
GetMovieIndTrackType function, 70, 196
GetMovieLoadState function, 358, 363
GetMovieNaturalBoundsRect function, 218–219
GetMoviesError function, 343
GetMoviesStickyError function, 343–345
    calling, 343, 344
    defined, 343
    return, 345
GetMovieTimeBase function, 242
GetMovieTrackCount function, 358
GetOffsetForButton function, 204–205
    definition (code), 205
    parsing code, 204
GetPortNativeWindow function, 224
GetRect function, 169
GetSBits function, 168
GetTrackAlternate function, 320

GetTrackMedia function, 196

GetTrackNextInterestingTime function, 345–346, 436
   calling, 436
   defined, 345
   error value, 346
   return, 346

GetWindowEventTarget function, 256

GetWord function, 166

gFlashParserData structure, 171

GlobalToLocal function, 87

gotoAndStop function, 159

graphics world
   allocating, 48
   creating, from 'PICT' resource, 19
   creating video tracks from, 21–23
   size, saving, 225

GraphicsExportSetDepth function, 347

H

handle data references, 442, 445, 446

header block
   defined, 163
   illustrated, 170
   parsing, 170–171
   reading, 170–171
   skipping over, 171
   See also Flash files (SWF)

header files, 239

help tags
   adding, 271
   defined, 270
   illustrated, 271
   in Open File dialog box, 274
   problem, 271

hint tracks, 128

hit testing, 87

holodeck pattern, 381

horizontal barn zigzag effect, 1

hotspots
   adding wired actions to, 301–303
   atoms, 302
   image tracks, 294
   managing, 286
   parent atom, 294
   rollovers, setting Flash text with, 194–195
   triggering intercept procedure, 292–293

HTTP streaming, 127, 128

I–K

Image Compression Manager (ICM) functions, 18, 42

image decompressor components, 4

image description extension, 8

image overrides
   effects as, 55–58
   fire effect as, 56
   illustrated, 56
   ripple effect as, 55–56

image sequences
   converting QuickTime video into, 157–158
   decompression, 43–45

image windows
   data, initializing, 46
   opening, 45, 46

ImageCodecCreateStandardParameterDialog function, 62, 63

ImageCodecStandardParameterDialogDoAction function, 63

ImageDescriptionForEffect function, 8, 9

images
   button, 160
   decompressing, 41–43
   with emboss effect, 41
   JPEG, 157
   loader sprite, adding, 376–377
   preview, 137
   video effects and, 41–55
   with X-ray color tint effect, 42

importing in place, 420

InitBits function, 168

initialization data data reference extension, 434

InitializeQTVR function, 288

input maps
   adding track references to, 17–18
   as atom container, 16
   configuring, 16
   for effects track, 16
   setting, 16
   structure, 16, 17

InsertMediaIntoTrack function, 427

InsertTrackSegment function, 38, 421
   calling, 421
   for copying media data, 38

Inside Macintosh: Memory, 350
`InstallEventLoopTimer` function, 348–349
`InstallStandardEventHandler` function, 256–257
intercept procedures, 292–294
    defined, 292
    execution, 293
    installing, 292, 293
intercept records, 293
Internet Engineering Task Force (IETF), 125
    RTP, 127
    SDP, 133

L

language atoms, 332–333
languages
    adding, to pop-up menu, 323
    codes, 316
    current, finding, 321
    finding, 316
    media, getting/setting, 316–318
    menu item index, 318
`Link` function, 408–409
loader sprites
    sprite image for, 374
    wiring, 377–380
loader tracks, 373–380
    creating, 374–376
    images, adding, 376–377
    preload, 375
    wiring, 377–380
loading movies, 353–385
    application, progress bar, 354
    QuickTime VR, 381–384
    sprite, progress bar, 355
    synchronous, 353
    See also asynchronous movie loading
`LocateFirstButton` function, 196–197
low-resolution image tracks, 382
low-resolution preview tracks, 382

M

Macintosh
    development on, 395–405
    droplet setup, 396–399
    dropped file tracking, 424

Movie Track Properties panel, 389, 390
    Open URL dialog box, 388
Macintosh resources
    opening, 400–401
    use advantages, 388
    wacking, 399–405
    for Windows applications, 387–418
Macromedia Flash. *See* Flash
`MakeImageDescriptionPixMap` function, 49
MakeRefMovie
    defined, 325
    main window, 326
    movie pane, 327
`MCIsPlayerEvent` function, 274
media
    language, 316–318
    parameters structure, 136
    public, 72
    quality, 318–319
media characteristics
    defined, 70
    searching, 70–71
    skin, 70
    supported, 70
media property atoms
    adding atoms to, 305–306
    container, 301
    updating, 305–306
media sample references, 420–423
    adding, 426–427
    creating directly, 421–423
    creating indirectly, 421
    defined, 419, 420
    getting, 423
    slideshow movies example, 423–430
media samples
    deleting track reference for, 435–436
    replacing, 435–441
`MediaSetPublicInfo` function, 72–73
    declaration, 72
    parameters, 73
    use benefits, 76
memory
    creating movies in, 442–445
    creating tracks in, 447–448
    flattening movies into, 442–443
    loading child movies into, 432–433
    saving movies from, 445–449

memory-based movies, 442–448
    creating, 442–445
    saving, 445–448
menu buttons
    defined, 161
    state transitions, 161, 162
    See also buttons
menu items
    adjusting, 366–367
    assigning command IDs to, 263
    custom identifiers, 263
    handling, 196–201
    index, 262, 318
    selecting, 196
    specification, 262
menus, 261–267
    adjusting, 264–265
    Carbon Event Manager and, 262
    command IDs, 262–264
    handling functions, 262
    ID, 261
    selections, handling, 265–267
messages
    looking for, 93
    sending, to movie controller, 91
    window definition, 85–86, 89–91
metadata, reading from Flash data stream,
    176–180
modal dialog filter function, 109
    defined, 111–112
    illustrated, 112–113
modal windows, 267–274
    About box, 268–270
    handling, 270–274
monitor window
    closing, 108
    creating, 147
    defined, 98
    displaying, 105
    drawing user item in, 148
    handling events in, 149
    illustrated, 99
    initial size, setting, 102
    on application launch, 132
    QTBroadcast, 126
    QTCapture, 98, 99, 101, 102, 105, 106, 108
    redrawing, 111
    resizing, 117–118

size, 116–118
size, adjusting, 114–115
tracking, 130
motion tweening, 154
movie controllers
    application messages and, 236
    attaching, to full-screen window, 229
    checking, 361–362
    disposing of, 238
    functions, calling, 280
    no-interface, 367
    QuickTime VR, 283, 287, 367
    sending Windows messages to, 91–92
movie drawing-complete procedures, 354,
    367–373
    activating, 371
    calling, 371
    declaration, 369
    installing, 371–373
movie load state
    changes, handling, 363–366
    checking, 357–358, 363–366
    current, 358
    defined, 353
    threshold, 353
movie segments
    copy, creating, 39
    video effects and, 37–41
movie storage APIs, 451, 462–467
    defined, 462
    list, 463
    use example, 462–463
movie storage identifiers, 464
movie tasking interval functions, 250
Movie Toolbox
    alternate group functions, 315
    auto-alternating, 314, 324
    initializing, 342
Movie Track Properties panel, 389, 390
    Macintosh, 389, 390
    resource description, 391–392
    Windows, 389
movie tracks, 430–441
    child movie data in memory, 432–433
    current media sample, 431–432
    defined, 430
    media sample replacement, 435–441
    using, 430

movie windows
    attaching timers to, 348–349
    creating, 348–349
    hiding, 224–225
    new, opening in, 359–360
    normal mode, returning to, 232–234, 247
    open, cycling through, 238
    showing, 224–225
    visible, 360
    See also full-screen window
movieclips
    defined, 156
    embedding, 193
movies
    adding play-fullscreen item to, 240–241
    alternate, 325–339
    alternate data rate, 314
    broadcasting, 125–149
    child, 430, 431, 432, 433, 434–435
    closing, 466–467
    contained, 326, 327, 334–339
    current language, finding, 321
    duration, 18
    full-screen, 213–248
    language, getting/setting, 320–323
    load state, 353, 357–358
    loading, 353–385
    memory-based, 442–448
    one-source effect, 1, 15–18
    opening, 464–466
    opening, by URL, 357
    opening, in new window, 359–360
    parent, 430
    presented, 238–242
    reference, 314
    saving, from memory, 445–448
    saving changes to, 466
    skinned, 69–96, 79–80
    slideshow, 423–430
    starting/stopping, 65
    stop determination, 244
    two-source effect, 6
    video effects in, 1–35
    zero-source effect, 6, 12–15
MRM_MakeReferenceMovie function, 336–339
mysterious errors, 347–348

N

NavAskSaveChanges function, 458
NavCreateGetFileDialog function, 454–455
NavGetDefaultDialogCreationOptions function, 453
NavGetFile function, 451, 453
Navigation Services functions, 451, 452, 453, 460
NavPutFile function, 451, 453
NewCWindow function, 84
NewMovieFromDataRef function, 353, 426, 432, 465
NewMovieFromFile function, 353, 356
    calling, 356, 465
    defined, 353
NewMovieFromStorageOffset function, 464
NewMovieTrack function, 426
NewTrackMedia function, 446–447
nodes
    adding wired actions to, 303–304
    default, finding, 298
    entering procedures, 286
    header atom data, 295
    information, working with, 294–296
    information atom container, 294
    leaving procedures, 286
    object, 283
    panoramic, 283, 291–292
    spinning, 290
    view angles, controlling, 290–291
    See also QTVR movies
no-interface movie controller, 367
nondocument windows, 270–274
notification messages, handling, 141

O

object image tracks, 294
object movies
    defined, 283
    illustrated, 284
    tracks, 294
object nodes, 283. *See also* QTVR movies
object tracks, 294
one-source effect movie, 1, 15–18

Open File dialog box, 273–274
    help tag, 274
    with truncated filename, 273
Open URL dialog box, 388
OpenMovieFile function, 356, 462–463
    calling, 462
    return, 463
OpenMovieStorage function, 463, 465
Options dialog box, 384
output files
    channel, 119–121
    eliciting, 118
    recording to, 121–124
    setting, 118–121
over state, 159, 160. *See also* buttons

P

Packetizer dialog box, 146
pan angle, 286, 290–291
panning, 191, 192
panorama image tracks
    defined, 294
    tiles, 381
panorama tracks, 294
panoramic movies
    defined, 283
    illustrated, 284
    tracks, 294
panoramic nodes
    defined, 283
    drawing on, 291–292
    prescreen buffer, 291
    See also QTVR movies
parameter atoms, 25
parent movies, 430
ParseTags function, 197–198
parsing
    header block, 170–171
    tagged data blocks, 172–175
pointers
    About box dialog, 269
    dangling, 350
poster images, setting, 27–28
post-link errors
    handling, 411–413
    messages, 412

reporting, 413
    See also errors
post-link step
    adding, 394–395
    setting up, 395
post-linker plug-in, 405, 406–411
    capabilities specification, 407
    as dispatcher, 408
    Link function, 408–409
    link request, 408–409
    main function, 408
    target specification, 408
    See also CodeWarrior
preference files, 460
preference panel plug-in. *See* settings panel
        plug-in
prescreen buffer
    defined, 287
    imaging completion procedure, 291, 292
Present Movie dialog box, 240
presentation notification procedure, 130
presentations
    active, 129
    creating, 132–139
    defined, 129
    parameters structure, 132–133
    prerolled, 140, 141
    setting up, 137–139
    status messages, 134–135
    tracking, 130
    See also broadcasting
presented movies, 238–242
    defined, 238–239
    forcing, 239
preview images, 137
    index, 28
    setting, 27–28
preview track, 382
previewing
    data sources, 98
    QTCapture operation, 100
    video, 136
progress bars
    application, 354
    on QuickTime movie, 368
    rectangle calculation, 368
    size, 368
    sprite, 355

progressive downloading, 127
PtInRgn function, 87
'ptv ' atom, 238–242, 248
'ptvc' atom, 241
public media information, 72
push buttons
  defined, 161
  state transitions, 161, 162
  See also buttons
push effect, 2
PutData function, 415–416

Q

QTAL_AddLoaderBarPICTToKeyFrameSample
  function, 376–377
QTAL_AddSpriteLoaderSamplesToMedia function,
  376, 378–380
  definition (code), 378–380
  tasks, 376
QTAL_MovieDrawingCompleteProc function, 370
QTAL_SetTrackToPreload function, 375
QTAlt_AddMovieLanguagesToMenu function, 323
QTAlt_GetMenuItemIndexForLanguageCode func-
  tion, 317–318
QTAlt_HandleCustomButtonClick function,
  321–322
QTAlt_UpdateMovieLanguageMask function, 317
QTApp_AdjustMenus function, 108
QTApp_CheckMovieLoadState function, 372–373
QTApp_HandleEvent function, 92–93, 230
  calling, 230
  definition (code), 92–93
QTApp_HandleKeyPress function, 229, 230
QTApp_HandleMenu function, 116–117
QTApp_Idle function, 52, 105–106
QTApp_SetupWindowObject function, 79, 80, 289
  definition (code), 289
  skinned movie code, 79–80
QTAsynchLoad, 355
QTBC_CreateMonitorWindow function, 147
QTBC_HandleMonitorWindowEvents function,
  148–149
QTBC_Init function, 130–131
QTBC_PauseBroadcasting function, 142–143
QTBC_SetupPresentation function, 137–139
QTBC_StartBroadcasting function, 140, 143

QTBC_Stop function, 131–132
QTBC_StopBroadcasting function, 132, 143
QTBC_UserItemProcedure function, 147–148
QTBig_AddPTVItemToMovie function, 240–241
QTBig_DumpWindowData function, 222–223
QTBig_FullscreenCallBack function, 246–247
QTBig_HandleMessages function, 230–231
  definition (code), 230–231
  EndFullScreen and, 232
QTBig_InitWindowData function, 222
QTBig_InstallCallBack function, 243, 245–246
QTBig_MovieIsStoppable, 243–244
QTBigScreen
  callback tracking, 245
  defined, 214
  screen resolution, 218
  Test menu, 214
QTBig_StartFullscreen function, 225
  calling, 241
  defined, 225
  definition (code), 226–229
QTBig_StopFullscreen function, 229
  calling, 229
  definition (code), 232–234
QTBroadcast
  active presentations, 129
  audio settings, 136
  monitor window, 126
  Test menu, 126
  Transmission Settings dialog box, 144–145
QTCap_GetChannelSettings function, 110, 111,
  114
QTCap_GetSoundSettings function, 113–114
QTCap_GetVideoSettings function, 115–116
QTCap_Init function, 102
  calling, 108
  definition (code), 106–108
QTCap_Record function, 122–124
QTCap_ResizeMonitorWindow function, 117
QTCap_SetTrackFile function, 120–121
QTCap_SGModalFilterProc function, 112–113
QTCap_Stop function, 108–109
QTCapture
  defined, 98
  monitor window, 98, 99
  preview/record operations, 100
  Test menu, 98, 99

QTCreateStandardParameterDialog function, 25–27
  atom container, 26
  calling, 27
  defined, 25
  effectList parameter, 26
  flags specification, 27
QTDoScriptRecord structure, 182
QTDR_AddInitDataDataRefExtension function, 434
QTDR_CreateMovieInRAM function, 443–445
  calls, 445
  defined, 443
  definition (code), 443–444
QTDR_CreateTrackInRAM function, 447–448
QTDR_GetMovieFromURL function, 357
QTEffects, 37
  ApplicationDataRecord structure, 45
  defined, 5
  image windows opened by, 45
  shell application, 45
  Test menu, 5, 38
QTEffects_AddEffectToMoveSegment function, 41
QTEffects_AddFilmNoiseToImage function, 46–47
QTEffects_AddPenguinMovieSamplesToMedia function, 59–60
QTEffects_AddRippleEffectAsSpriteImage function, 57
QTEffects_DumpWindowData function, 54–55
QTEffects_HandleEffectsDialogEvents function, 31–32
QTEffects_InitWindowData function, 46
QTEffects_MakePenguinMovie function, 24
QTEffects_MakeSpriteEffectMovie function, 56–57
QTEffects_RespondToDialogSelection function, 30–31
QTEffects_RunEffect function, 52–54
  contents, 52
  defined, 52
  definition (code), 53
QTEffects_SetUpEffectSequence function, 49–51
QTFlash
  defined, 153, 190
  Test menu, 153, 191
QTFlash_AddWiredActionsToFlashMovie function, 196, 198–201
  calling, 196
  definition (code), 198–201

QTFlash_CreateButtonActionContainer function, 201
QTFlash_CreateVarAction function, 194–195
QTFlash_DoFSCommand function, 183, 234
QTFlash_ExtractFlashMovieFromTrack function, 185–188
  calling, 185
  definition (code), 186–188
QTFlash_GetFileCharacteristic function, 176–180
  calling, 176
  definition (code), 176–180
  while loop, 176
QTFlash_InitWindowData function, 175–176
QTFlash_IsAutoPlayMovie function, 176
QTFlash_SetWiredActionsToButton function, 196, 198, 201, 202–203
  calling, 203
  definition (code), 202–203
  functions, 203
  information passed by, 203
QTFrame_AdjustMenus function, 264–265, 367
QTFrame_CarbonEventModelWindowHandler function, 269–270
QTFrame_CarbonEventWindowHandler function, 258
  calling, 258
  definition (code), 260–261
QTFrame_CarbonEventWindowTimer function, 275, 351–352
  definition (code), 351–352
  with tasking management code, 277–278
QTFrame_CheckMovieControllers function, 361–362
QTFrame_CheckMovieLoadState function, 362, 363–366
  calling, 362
  definition (code), 363–366
QTFrame_CloseWindowObject function, 237, 238, 466–467
  calling, 237
  definition (code), 466–467
QTFrame_CreateMovieWindow function, 257, 348–349
  definition (code), 348–349
  revised definition (code), 257
QTFrame_DestroyMovieWindow function, 237, 458–460
  calls, 237
  definition (code), 458–460

QTFrame_GetCurrentFileLocationDesc function, 461–462

QTFrame_GetOneFileWithPreview function, 455–457, 462

QTFrame_HandleEvent function, 251–252, 351, 352

QTFrame_HandleMenuCommand function, 262, 265–267
  calling, 265
  definition (code), 266

QTFrame_IsAppWindow function, 271–273
  calling, 271
  definition (code), 272
  revised definition (code), 272–273

QTFrame_MainEventLoop function
  definition (code), 276–277
  revised definition (code), 252–253

QTFrame_OpenCommandLineMovies function, 424

QTFrame_OpenMovieInWindow function, 84, 241–242, 359–360
  adding code to, 241–242
  definition (code), 465

QTFrame_PutFile function, 457

QTFrame_SetWindowVisState function, 224–225

QTFrame_ShowAboutBox function, 270

QTFrame_ShowWindowAtPoint function, 360

QTFrame_SizeWindowToMovie function, 232

QTFrame_UpdateMovieFile function, 466

QTGetEffectsList function, 26

QTGetTimeUntilNextTask function, 276
  event loop timer period adjustment, 277
  interval adjustment, 276
  returns, 276, 277, 278

QTInstallNextTaskNeededSoonerCallback function, 278–279

QTIsStandardParameterDialogEvent function, 28–30
  defined, 29
  definition (code), 29–30
  result codes, 29

QTMIM_FlattenChildIntoParent function, 437–441
  defined, 441
  definition (code), 437–441

QTPFSDataRec structure, 239

.qtr extension, 393

QTRW_CreateRezWackedFileFromBinary function, 399–400

QTRW_RezWackWinBinaryAndMacResFile function, 399, 400
  calling, 410
  defined, 400
  definition (code), 402–405
  error code return, 411
  function, 400

QTShell, 214, 281
  About box, 268–270
  application framework, modifying, 359–362
  applications built on top of, 264
  default location settings, 460–462
  defined, 249
  event handler call reference and, 259
  file opening selection, 453–457
  file selection, 453
  filename save selection, 457–458
  limitation of problem, 249
  loose ends, 281
  movie storage functions, 451
  opening Flash movies, 155
  opening QTVR movies, 287
  receiving streamed data, 125
  Save Changes dialog box, 458–460
  updating, 359–362, 451–467

QTSInitializeMediaParams function, 136

QTSkin_AddSkinTrack function, 74–76

QTSkin_ConvertPictureToRegion function
  calling, 77–78
  defined, 78
  definition (code), 78–79
  key step, 78

QTSkin_DumpWindowData function, 95

QTSkin_GetPicHandleFromFile function, 73–74

QTSkin_Init function, 85

QTSkin_InitWindowData function, 79, 80, 81–83
  defined, 79
  definition (code), 81–83

QTSkin_IsDragClick function, 94–95

QTSkin_IsSkinnedMovie function, 70

QTSkins, 67

QTSMediaParams function, 136

QTSNewPresentation function, 132, 137, 139

QTSPresIdle function, 139

QTSPresPreroll function, 140

QTSPresSettingsDialog function, 145

QTSPresStart function, 140, 141

QTStandardParameterDialogDoAction function, 27, 30

QTUtils_GetFrameCount function, 345–346

QTUtils_GetMovieLanguge function, 320–321

QTUtils_GetScreenResolution function, 217

QTVR instances
  defined, 288
  getting, 288–290
  tracking, 289

QTVR movies
  adding wired actions to, 301, 306–310
  defined, 283
  Flash track controlling, 190, 285
  loading, 381–384
  management, 283
  object node, 283
  panning, during idle events, 299–300
  panoramic node, 283
  playback, 287–294
  progress bar on, 368
  scenes, 286
  sending wired actions to, 298–301
  See also QuickTime VR

QTVR tracks
  defined, 294
  media property atom container, 301
  nodes list, 294
  samples, 296

QTVRGetNodeInfo function, 295

QTVRGetPanAngle function, 289, 290

QTVRGetQTVRInstance function, 288–289
  calling, 288, 290
  reference, obtaining, 288–289

QTVRGetVRWorld function, 296–297

QTVRInstallInterceptProc function, 293–294

QTVRSetAngularUnits function, 289

QTVRSetPrescreenImagingCompleteProc function, 291

QTVRTriggerHotSpot function, 293

QTVRUpdate function, 291

QTVRUtils_FlattenMovieForStreaming function, 382–383

QTVRUtils_GetNodeHeaderAtomData function, 295

QTVRUtils_GetNodeType function, 296

QTVRUtils_IsQTVRMgrInstalled function, 287–288

QTVRWorldHeaderAtom structure, 297

QuickTime
  broadcasting, 128–139

Flash vs., 154
Flash with, 151–188
streaming, 126, 127–128
video effects architecture, 1

QuickTime application messages, 235–238
  close-window, 237–238
  defined, 235
  full-screen, 237
  handling, 237, 238
  kQTAppMessageDisplayChannels, 235
  kQTAppMessageEnterFullScreenRequested, 236, 237
  kQTAppMessageExitFullScreenRequested, 236, 237
  kQTAppMessageSoftwareChanged, 235
  kQTAppMessageWindowCloseRequested, 236, 237, 238
  movie controller and, 236
  public, 235
  sending, 235

QuickTime Media Layer (QTML), 32, 79, 388

QuickTime Player, 125, 240

QuickTime SDK for Windows, 393

QuickTime Streaming Server (QTSS), 128

QuickTime VR, 283–311
  default behavior, 4
  defined, 283
  file format, 294–298
  flattener, 382
  node transitions, 4
  programming with, 283–311
  tracks, 189
  wired actions and, 298–310
  See also QTVR movies

QuickTime VR Manager, 286–287
  availability determination, 287–288
  capabilities, 286–287
  closing connection to, 288
  for controlling view angles, 290–291
  defined, 283
  function interception, 286–287
  hotspot handling, 286
  information gathering, 286
  initializing, 287–288
  node-entering/node-leaving behaviors, 286
  positioning, 286
  prescreen buffer access, 287

QuickTime VR movie controller, 367
  defined, 283
  progress bar and, 367
quit command, 182
QuitAppModalLoopForWindow function, 268, 270

R

radians, 289–290
real-time streaming, 125
  as client-side technology, 125
  defined, 127
Realtime Streaming Protocol (RTSP), 127
Realtime Transport Protocol (RTP), 127
recording, 118–124
  captured data, 121–124
  channel output files, 119–121
  output file, 118–119
  stopping/starting, 122
  See also sequence grabber
rectangle, in Flash data stream, 167–170
reference movie data reference record, 329–330
reference movie descriptor, 328
reference movie descriptor atoms, 331, 332
  atom data, 332
  connection speed, 332
  quality, 333
reference movie record atoms, 328
  copying, 335
  space for, 334
  structure, 334
reference movies. *See* alternate reference movie
    files
regions
  content, 68–69, 76–77
  drag, 92–93
  drag mask, 69, 76–77
  movie, indicating, 86–87
  storage, 87
  structure, 77, 78–79
resource scripts, 387
Rez, 394
RezWack, 390
  function, 393, 395
  path to, 394
  settings panel, 406
  settings panel in Constructor, 415
  settings panel project window, 414

tag data, 395
tag data, appending, 401
using, 394
RezWack post-linker, 405, 406
  menu, 411
  project window, 407
RezWack PPC, 405
  defined, 396
  handling files dropped onto, 397–398
ripple effect
  concentric ripples, 61
  defined, 55
  effect description, 58
  image data storage, 57
  as image override, 55–56
  sample description, 58
  See also video effects
ripple sprites, 58
RunAppModalLoopForWindow function, 267

S

sample descriptions, 72, 76, 423, 426
  creating, 8–9
  ripple effect, 58
  video effects sample, 45, 48
sample references. *See* media sample references
scenes
  default node, finding, 298
  defined, 286
  See also QTVR movies
screen resolution, 216–220
  change, undoing, 218
  changing, 216–220
  current, retrieving, 218
  determining, 216–217
  See also full-screen mode
SDP importer, 142
sequence grabber, 97–98
  channel component instances, 109
  channel components, 99
  components, opening, 100–101
  defined, 97
  initializing, 106–108
  modal dialog filter function, 111, 112–113
  output, 119
  overview, 98–105
  panel component, 100

sequence grabber *(continued)*
  for recording, 118–124
  services, 98
  shutting down, 108–109
  starting, 106–108
  uses, 98
session description protocol (SDP), 126
  defined, 133
  file sample, 133
  file selection, 134
  files, 126, 133
  QuickTime support, 134
SetAutoTrackAlternatesEnabled function, 324
SetMediaLanguage function, 316
SetMediaQuality function, 319
SetMenuItemCommandID function, 264
SetModelessDialogCallbackProc function, 31–32
SetMovieDefaultDataRef function, 443
SetMovieDrawingCompleteProc function, 371
SetMovieLanguage function, 320
SetMoviesErrorProc function, 347
SetNewHeaderAndTagLength function, 208–211
  calling, 208
  complication, 209
  definition (code), 209–211
settings dialog boxes
  displaying, 111, 113–116
  sound, 113
  video, 100, 109, 110, 115–116
settings panel plug-in
  in Constructor, 415
  copying settings data into, 415–416
  copying settings data out of, 416–417
  project window, 414
  writing, 413–417
SetTrackAlternate function, 319–320
SetWindowRgn function, 95
SGGetSrcVideoBounds function, 102
SGIdle function, 122
SGInitialize function, 101
SGNewOutput function, 119–120
SGPause function, 114
SGSetAdditionalSoundRates function, 103
SGSetDataOutput function, 118–119
  calling, 118, 121
  flags, 118–119
  parameters, 118–119
SGSetGWorld function, 101

SGSettingsDialog function, 109, 110
SGStartPreview function, 124
SGStartRecord function, 118, 121–122
SGStop function, 118, 122
SGUpdate function, 109–110
shape tweening, 154
ShowHideTaskBar function, 218
showmenu command, 181–182
skin data, 70, 71
  determination, 70
  retrieving, 77
skin tracks
  adding, 69
  creating, programmatically, 72–76
  defined, 69
  skin data, 70
skinned movie windows
  cleanup, 95
  content region, 68–69
  defined, 65
  illustrated, 66, 67
  initialization code, 81–83
  messages, handling, 89–91
  moving, 69
  shutting down, 95–96
  structure region, 77
  visible region, 80
skinned movies, 69–96
  application data initialization, 81–83
  creating, 69–76
  data, 68
  defined, 67
  determination, 70
  illustrated, 66, 67
  ingredients, 69
  playback, 76–96
  self-contained, 72
  user interaction with, 67–68
slideshow mode, 240
slideshow movies, 423–430
  creating, 425
  dropped files, 424–425
  picture information retrieval, 425–426
  sample references, 426–430
  video track size, 430
Society of Motion Picture and Television Engineers (SMPTE), 1, 25
Sorenson 2 encoding, 157

sound input device drivers, 97
sound settings dialog box, 105
    adding sample rates to, 105
    displaying, 113
sound tracks, slideshow mode and, 240
source name atoms, 10
    data, 10
    inspecting, 11
source tracks, 5–6
    defined, 5
    media handler, 37
    two-source movie, 6
    zero-source movie, 6, 12–15
Sourcer Settings dialog box, 146
sourcers, 129
sprite tracks
    adding samples to, 59–60
    creating, 374–376
    disabling, 377
    key frame samples, 57
    matrix, adjusting, 374
    override samples, 57
    preload setting, 375
sprites
    adding effects as, 57–58
    adding window-close request to, 236
    defined, 156
    image data storage, 57
    image override, 55–58
    loader, 374
    loader image, adding, 376–377
    ripple, 58
    video effects and, 55–61
    See also Flash sprites
SpriteUtils_AddCompressedImageToKeyFrame-
        Sample function, 58
SpriteUtils_AddPICTImageToKeyFrameSample func-
        tion, 57
sputter rate, 24. See also fire effect
standard parameters dialog box. See effects
        parameters dialog box
StartMovie function, 343
state transitions, 161–162
    defined, 161
    finding actions for, 201–203
    menu buttons, 161, 162

    number of, 161
    push button, 161, 162
    See also buttons
status flag decompression, 54
status messages
    client, 142
    presentation, 134–135
sticky errors, 343–346
    clearing, 343–344
    getting, 343–344
    value, 343, 344
    See also errors
streaming, 127–128
    capabilities, 126
    defined, 127
    HTTP, 127, 128
    real-time, 125, 127
    RTP, 127, 128
streams
    reading bits from, 167–169
    reading bytes from, 164–167
    reading metadata from, 176–180
    See also Flash files (SWF)
structure region, 88
    converting picture to, 78–79
    defined, 77

T

tagged data blocks
    defined, 163
    length, 209
    long tag header, 173
    parsing, 172–175
    short tag header, 173
    tag header, 172
    tag ID, 172, 173
    tags, counting, 174–175
    tags, reading, 172
    See also Flash files (SWF)
task sooner notifications, 278–279
tasking interval management, 276–279
text digitizer components, 98–99
time base
    automatic creation, 242
    parameter, 244

time base callback functions, 242–248
    activating, 244–245
    calling, 243
    defined, 242
    installing, 244–246
    short, 246
time base callbacks
    activating, 244–245
    creating, 244
    handling, 246–248
tips. *See* help tags
tracks
    alternate, 314–325
    effect, 5–6, 8, 12, 16, 40
    Flash, 151–153, 159, 190–211, 285
    loader, 373–380
    low-resolution image, 382
    low-resolution preview, 382
    movie, 430–441
    segments, deleting, 436
    sound, 240
    source, 5–6, 12–15, 37
    sprite, 374–376
    video, 18, 19, 21–23, 39, 40
TrackTimeToMediaTime function, 431–432
transitions, 18–24
    adding, 18
    applied to video tracks, 39
    cross-fade, 2, 6
    defined, 1
    dissolve, 2
    effect source tracks, 5
    explode, 2
    horizontal barn zigzag, 1
    implementation, 4
    push, 2
    See also video effects
Transmission Settings dialog box, 144–145
traveling matte effect, 7
tweening, 154
twips, 170
two-source movies, 6

U

unicasting, 128
up state, 159–160. *See also* buttons

update events, handling, 109–113
UpdateMovieInStorage function, 452, 464
UpdateMovieResource function, 445–446
    calling, 446, 447, 463
    movie atom update, 446

V

vertical field of view. *See* field of view
video
    Flash and, 156–159
    parameters structure, 136
    previewing, 136
    QuickTime, converting into image sequence,
        157–158
    source boundary rectangle, 114
video channels
    closing down, 103
    configuring, 101–103
    display boundary rectangle, resetting, 118
    flags, enabling, 102
video digitizers
    active source rectangle, 102, 114
    defined, 97
video effects
    applying, 1, 38, 41
    applying to tracks, 7
    architecture, 7
    cloud, 3
    cross-fade, 2
    dissolve, 2
    emboss, 41
    explode, 2
    film noise, 2, 3, 52
    fire, 3, 4, 15
    generators, 3
    horizontal barn zigzag, 1
    as image overrides, 55–58
    in images, 41–55
    low-level functions, 61–64
    movie segments and, 37–41
    in movies, 1–35
    one-source, 1, 15–18
    parameters, displaying, 62
    parameters, modifying, 5
    push, 2
    referencing, 4

ripple, 55–56
running, 51–54
sample descriptions, 8–9
setting up, 47–55
sources, 7, 48
sprites and, 55–61
stacking, 6
three-source, 7
traveling matte, 7
two-source, 6
types, getting, 11–12
using, 4
utilities, 8–12
X-ray color tint, 42
zero-source, 6, 12–15
video settings dialog box, 100, 109
displaying, 115–116
illustrated, 110
See also settings dialog boxes
video tracks
creating, from graphics world, 21–23
creating, from 'PICT' resources, 18, 19
filter application to part of, 420
filters applied to, 7
hidden, 40
importing, from one movie to another, 344
overlapping, 39
segments, creating copy of, 421
slideshow, 430
See also effects tracks
view center, 286
VR world
atom container, 296
atom data, finding, 297
header atom, 297
working with, 296–298
VRObject_ImportVideoTrack function, 344–345

W

wacked files
creating, 402–405
setting up names for, 399–400
wacking
process, 396
resources, 399–405

window classes, 272–273
inspecting, 272
retrieving, 273
window definition messages
common, 85–86
defined, 85
handling, 89–91
receiving, 86
window definition procedures
custom, 76, 89–91
custom, writing, 85–91
defined, 76
listing, 89–91
window definition specification
pointer to, 84–85
setting up, 85
window events, handling, 258–261
windows
application, 272
content region, 68
controls, 80
custom shape assignment to, 76
document, 255–261
modal, 267–274
monitor, 98, 99, 105
nondocument, 270–274
objects, locking/unlocking, 350
opening, with custom shape, 84
skinned movie, 65, 66, 67, 68–69
structure region, 77
Windows, Microsoft
development on, 391–395
dropped file handling, 425
executable files, 395
Movie Track Properties panel, 389
Open URL dialog box, 388
Windows applications
distributing, 393–394
embedding resource files in, 393–394
Macintosh resources for, 387–418
post-link step, 394–395
Windows resources
defined, 387
description, 391–392
embedding in applications, 393–394
file creation, 391–393
opening, 393

wired actions, 152
    adding, to hotspots, 301–303
    adding, to nodes, 303–304
    adding, to QTVR movies, 301, 306–310
    attaching, in Flash track, 153, 159
    changing alternate tracks with, 324–325
    child atoms for, 303
    in Flash tracks, 195–211
    operands, 300–301
    QuickTime supported, 298
    QuickTime VR and, 298–310
    sending, to QTVR movies, 298–301
    set-language, adding, 324–325
    targeted at Flash tracks, 190–195
wired atom containers, 201
    event atoms, 201
    extracting from, 202
WiredUtils_AddMovieSetLanguage function,
    324–325

X–Z

XML
    alternate movie file specification with, 327
    contained movie with, 327
    defined, 71
    HTML vs., 71
    skinned movie specification, 71
XML importer, 71–72
XMLtoRefMovie utility, 327
X-ray color tint effect, 42
zero-source effects movies, 6
    creating, 13–15
    structure, 6
    See also video effects
zoom angle. *See* field of view
zooming, 191–192

About the CD-ROM

The accompanying CD-ROM contains the source code and project files for the applications described in the books *QuickTime Toolkit, Volume One: Basic Movie Playback and Media Types* and *QuickTime Toolkit, Volume Two: Advanced Movie Playback and Media Types.* Look in the folders Volume One or Volume Two for the materials appropriate for the book you are reading. Inside each of these folders, the materials are grouped by chapter. Note that a few chapters do not have associated sample applications.

On Windows, you can open the .mak project files using Microsoft Visual Studio. On Macintosh, you can use Metrowerks CodeWarrior IDE to open the .mcp project files. The Extras folder for each book also contains an Xcode project for the Carbon version of QTShell, which forms the basis of all the other applications.

You may need to adjust the access paths specified in the project files. Here is the folder arrangement assumed in all the projects supplied:

QuickTimeSDK
    MacSampleCode
        qtshell
        qtcontrollerfun
        (etc.)

    QTDevMac
        CIncludes
        Libraries
        RIncludes

    QTDevWin
        CIncludes
        Libraries
        RIncludes
        Tools

You can download the latest QuickTime software development kit from *http://developer.apple.com/quicktime/*.

The use of the source code is governed by the following license agreement.

License Agreement

© 2004, Apple Computer, Inc. All rights reserved.

This Apple software is supplied to you by Apple Computer, Inc. ("Apple") in consideration of your agreement to the following terms, and your use, installation, modification or redistribution of this Apple software constitutes acceptance of these terms. If you do not agree with these terms, please do not use, install, modify or redistribute this Apple software.

In consideration of your agreement to abide by the following terms, and subject to these terms, Apple grants you a personal, non-exclusive license, under Apple's copyrights in this original Apple software (the "Apple Software"), to use, reproduce, modify and redistribute the Apple Software, with or without modifications, in source and/or binary forms, provided that if you redistribute the Apple Software in its entirety and without modifications, you must retain this notice and the following text and disclaimers in all such redistributions of the Apple Software. Neither the name, trademarks, service marks or logos of Apple Computer, Inc. may be used to endorse or promote products derived from the Apple Software without specific prior written permission from Apple. Except as expressly stated in this notice, no other rights or licenses, express or implied, are granted by Apple herein, including but not limited to any patent rights that may be infringed by your derivative works or by other works in which the Apple Software may be incorporated.

The Apple Software is provided by Apple on an "AS IS" basis. APPLE MAKES NO WARRANTIES, EXPRESS OR IMPLIED, INCLUDING WITHOUT LIMITATION THE IMPLIED WARRANTIES OF NON-INFRINGEMENT, MERCHANTABILITY AND FITNESS FOR A PARTICULAR PURPOSE, REGARDING THE APPLE SOFTWARE OR ITS USE AND OPERATION ALONE OR IN COMBINATION WITH YOUR PRODUCTS.

IN NO EVENT SHALL APPLE BE LIABLE FOR ANY SPECIAL, INDIRECT, INCIDENTAL OR CONSEQUENTIAL DAMAGES (INCLUDING, BUT NOT LIMITED TO, PROCUREMENT OF SUBSTITUTE GOODS OR SERVICES; LOSS OF USE, DATA, OR PROFITS; OR BUSINESS INTERRUPTION) ARISING IN ANY WAY OUT OF THE USE, REPRODUCTION, MODIFICATION AND/OR DISTRIBUTION OF THE APPLE SOFTWARE, HOWEVER CAUSED AND WHETHER UNDER THEORY OF CONTRACT, TORT (INCLUDING NEGLIGENCE), STRICT LIABILITY OR OTHERWISE, EVEN IF APPLE HAS BEEN ADVISED OF THE POSSIBILITY OF SUCH DAMAGE.

Publisher's Limited Warranty

The Publisher warrants the media on which the software is furnished to be free from defects in materials and workmanship under normal use for 30 days from the date that you obtain the Product. The warranty set forth above is the exclusive warranty pertaining to the Product, and the Publisher and MacTech disclaim all other warranties, express or implied, including, but not limited to, implied warranties of merchantability and fitness for a particular purpose, even if advised of the possibility of such purpose. Some jurisdictions do not allow limitations on an implied warranty's duration, therefore the above limitations may not apply to you.

Publisher's Limitation of Liability

Your exclusive remedy for breach of this warranty will be the repair or replacement of the Product at no charge to you or the refund of the applicable purchase price paid upon the return of the Product, as determined by the Publisher in its discretion. In no event will the Publisher or MacTech or their directors, officers, employees, or agents, or anyone else who has been involved in the creation, production, or delivery of this software be liable for indirect, special, consequential, or exemplary damages, including, without limitation, for lost profits, business interruption, lost or damaged data, or loss of goodwill, even if the Publisher, or an authorized dealer or distributor or supplier has been advised of the possibility of such damages. Some jurisdictions do not allow the exclusion or limitation of indirect, special, consequential, or exemplary damages or the limitation of liability to specified amounts, therefore the above limitations or exclusions may not apply to you.